Lecture Notes in Computer Science

Commenced Publication in 1973
Founding and Former Series Editors:
Gerhard Goos, Juris Hartmanis, and Jan van Leeuwen

Tomasz Janowski Hrushikesha Mohanty (Eds.)

Distributed Computing and Internet Technology

4th International Conference, ICDCIT 2007
Bangalore, India, December 17-20
Proceedings

 Springer

Volume Editors

Tomasz Janowski
United Nations University
Center for Electronic Governance
International Institute for Software Technology, Center for Electronic Governance
P.O. Box 3058, Macau
E-mail: tj@iist.unu.edu

Hrushikesha Mohanty
University of Hyderabad
Central University PO, AP
Department of Computer and Information Science
India 500 046
E-mail: Mohanty.hcu@gmail.com

Library of Congress Control Number: 2007940906

CR Subject Classification (1998): D.1.3, C.2.4, D.2, F.2, H.3, H.4, D.4.6, K.6.5

LNCS Sublibrary: SL 3 – Information Systems and Application, incl. Internet/Web
and HCI

ISSN   0302-9743
ISBN-10   3-540-77112-3 Springer Berlin Heidelberg New York
ISBN-13   978-3-540-77112-8 Springer Berlin Heidelberg New York

Springer is a part of Springer Science+Business Media

springer.com

© Springer-Verlag Berlin Heidelberg 2007
Printed in Germany

Typesetting: Camera-ready by author, data conversion by Scientific Publishing Services, Chennai, India
Printed on acid-free paper   SPIN: 12200078   06/3180   5 4 3 2 1 0

Preface

This volume contains the papers presented at the 4th International Conference on Distributed Computing and Internet Technology (ICDCIT 2007) held during December 17–20, 2007 in Bangalore, India. The conference was organized by Kalinga Institute of Industrial Technology (KIIT), Bhubaneshwar, India, www.kiit.org, and co-organized by the Center for Electronic Governance at United Nations University – International Institute for Software Technology (UNU-IIST-EGOV), Macao, www.egov.iist.unu.edu.

In the tradition of the ICDCIT conference series, ICDCIT 2007 welcomed presentations of research ideas and results in theory, methodology and applications of distributed computing and internet technology. In addition, the conference emphasized that research in this area can play an important role in building a foundation for the development of e-Society Applications (e-Applications) and at the same time, that e-Applications can provide relevance and context for such research. Establishing a connection between foundational and applied research in distributed systems and internet technology with software and services that enable e-Applications was a key feature of ICDCIT 2007.

A total of 177 papers from 20 countries were submitted for ICDCIT 2007. Each paper was reviewed by at least two members of the Program Committee or additional referees. As a result, 13 papers were accepted as long (12 page) and 20 as short (6 page) contributions. The papers were classified into seven categories covering a range of issues from basic technology, through services and engineering, to applications. In addition, three invited papers were received from Wojciech Cellary, Maurice Herlihy and David Peleg.

The program was arranged into the corresponding seven sessions. In "Session 1 - Network Protocols", sensor, mobile and wireless networks were the focus, with a range of issues covered such as: efficient scheduling, energy-efficient clustering, mobility-aware access control, self-stabilizing routing, overlay networks for P2P applications, and self-organized clustering. In his invited talk, David Peleg presented a review of the literature on time-efficient broadcasting for radio networks. With the ubiquity of wireless and mobile networks, security and privacy concerns must be addressed. Consequently, "Session 2 - Security and Privacy" included papers on: key management, information leakage, distributed certification authorities, trust management in P2P networks, declarative access control to XML documents, and security in resource-constrained sensor networks. Building upon network protocols and their properties, "Section 3 - Network Management" included papers on: congestion-based pricing, distributed resource management, energy-efficient routing and scheduling grid applications, while "Session 4 - Network Services" presented value-added services such as: content delivery, distributed storage management, fault-tolerance and selective querying.

The remaining three sessions were devoted to applications, from development issues, through middleware support, to actual delivery of e-Society services. In his invited paper, Maurice Herlihy showed how to resolve the efficiency versus ease-of-use dichotomy in software transactional memory systems. Other contributions to "Session 5 - e-Application Engineering" included formal semantics for a Web-based business process language, a dependable P2P network for distributed collaborative applications, and rapid development of Web form applications. "Session 6 - e-Application Services" comprised papers on middleware services for e-Applications, such as: managing and analyzing data streams, recommending services to users through modeling their interests, aggregating Web services to support grid applications, and semantic description of service interfaces. "Session 7 - e-Applications" demonstrated a number of concrete e-Society applications. The session featured an invited paper from Wojciech Cellary on territorial versus content communities, and the emergence of the information society. Other contributions to this session included: a P2P file system based on virtual folders, a Tsunami warning system based on distributed sensor networks, automatic discovery of relationships between ontological concepts, privacy-preserving e-commerce protocol for digital transactions, forward secrecy for secure e-mail exchanges, and secure business-to-business collaborations over a grid. This session completed the conference program.

Many people and organizations contributed to the success of the conference. We wish to thank Achuyta Samanta, Chancellor, KIIT University, and Mike Reed, Director, UNU-IIST for their supporting of the conference. We also wish to thank the General Chair as well as the Steering and Organizing Committees for their support and help at various stages of the conference. Our most sincere thanks go to the ICDCIT 2007 Program Committee whose full cooperation in carrying out quality reviews was critical for establishing a strong conference program. Particular thanks go to Elsa Estevez and Adegboyega Ojo for taking up an especially heavy load of review work. We also wish to sincerely thank additional reviewers who helped us maintain the timeline for the review process. We express our sincere thanks to the invited speakers – Fran Allen, Wojciech Cellary, Maurice Herily and David Peleg – for their contributions to the conference program. We are particularly grateful for financial and logistics support extended by KIIT and UNU-IIST for hosting the conference. We also acknowledge UNU-IIST, University of Hyderabad and IIT Kanpur for providing infrastructural support to carry out this editorial work. We remember, with gratitude, the assistance at various stages of this conference provided by our students: Sumagna Patnaik, Jitesh, Satya, Prasad and Krishna. Lastly, we would like to thank Springer for publishing this proceedings volume in its prestigious *Lecture Notes in Computer Science* series.

December 2007   Tomasz Janowski
                                                     Hrushikesha Mohanty

Organization

ICDCIT 2007 was organized by Kalinga Institute of Industrial Technology (KIIT), Bhubaneshwar, India, www.kiit.org, and co-organized by the Center for Electronic Governance at United Nations University – International Institute for Software Technology (UNU-IIST-EGOV), Macao, www.egov.iist.unu.edu.

Patrons

Mike Reed	UNU-IIST, Macao
Achuyta Samanta	KIIT, India

Steering Committee

R.K. Ghosh (Chair)	IIT Kanpur, India
P.K. Mishra	KIIT, India
Hrushikesha Mohanty	University of Hyderabad, India
R.K. Shyamsundar	IBM Research Lab, India
S.C. De Sarkar	KIIT, India

Conference Committee

Gerard Huet	INRIA, France	General Chair
Tomasz Janowski	UNU-IIST-EGOV, Macao	Program Co-chair
Hrushikesha Mohanty	University of Hyderabad, India	Program Co-chair
D.N. Dwivedy	KIIT, India	Organization Chair
Samaresh Mishra	KIIT, India	Publicity Co-chair
Dillip Das	KIIT, India	Publicity Co-chair

Program Committee

Hamideh Afsarmanesh	University of Amsterdam, Netherlands
Rahul Banerjee	BITS-Pilani, India
Shalabh Bhatnagar	IISC, India
Chiranjib Bhattacharyya	IISC, India
Luis Camarinha-Matos	UNINOVA, Portugal
Alejandra Cechich	UNComa, Argentina
Goutam Chakraborty	Iwate Pref. University, Japan
Mainak Chaudhuri	IIT, Kanpur, India

David Cheung	HKU, Hong Kong
Jim Davies	Oxford University, UK
Gillan Dobbie	University of Auckland, New Zealand
Jin Song Dong	NUS, Singapore
Elsa Estevez	UNU-IIST-EGOV, Macao and UNS, Argentina
Mariagrazia Fugini	Polytechnic of Milan, Italy
Manoj Gore	NIT Allahabad, India
Janusz Gorski	Gdansk University of Technology, Poland
Veena Goswamy	KIIT, India
Manish Gupta	IBM, India
Yanbo Han	ICT Institute, CAS, China
D. Janakiram	IIT, Chennai, India
Tomasz Janowski	UNU-IIST-EGOV, Macao
Kanchana Kanchanasut	AIT, Thailand
Kamal Karlapalem	IIIT, Hyderabad, India
Arzad Alam Kherani	IIT, Delhi, India
Jimmy Lee	CUHK, Hong Kong
Sanjay Madria	UMR, USA
Rajib Mall	IIT, Kharagpur, India
Hrushikesha Mohanty	University of Hyderabad, India
Atul Negi	University of Hyderabad, India
Adegboyega Ojo	UNU-IIST-EGOV, Macao and Unilag, Nigeria
Adenike Osofisan	University of Ibadan, Nigeria
Vassilios Peristeras	DERI, Ireland
R. Ramanujam	IMSC, Chennai, India
Srini Ramaswamy	University of Arkansas, USA
Abhik Roychoudhury	NUS, Singapore
G. Sajith	IIT, Guwahati, India
Vivek Sarkar	IBM T.J. Watson Center, USA
V.N. Sastry	IDRBT, Hyderabad, India
Jochen Scholl	University of Washington, USA
Indranil Sengupta	IIT, Kharagpur, India
G. Shivakumar	IIT, Bombay, India
Rajiv Wankar	University of Hyderabad, India

Additional Referees

Karm Veer Arya	Madhumita Chatterjee
Rilwan Basanya	Vinu V. Das
A. Baskar	Ekaterina Ermilova
Wilson Naik Bhukya	R.K. Ghosh
Agustina Buccella	Simon S. Msanjila
Adnane Cabani	Anupama Potluri
Saswat Chakrabarti	O.B.V. Ramanaiah

Teerapat Sanguankotchakorn
Surasak Sanguanpong
Subir Sarkar
M.P. Singh
Sudarsan Sithu
Shamik Sural
Aruna Tripathy

Somnath Tripathy
Siba Udgata
A. Vadivel
Aurora Vizcano
Kenji Yoshigoe
Chuanlei Zhang

Table of Contents

Section 1 - Network Protocols

Time-Efficient Broadcasting in Radio Networks: A Review 1
    David Peleg

An Efficient and Optimized Bluetooth Scheduling Algorithm for
Piconets 19
    Vijay Prakash Chaturvedi, V. Rakesh, and Shalabh Bhatnagar

EETO: An Energy-Efficient Target-Oriented Clustering Protocol in
Wireless Sensor Networks 31
    Weifang Cheng, Xiangke Liao, Changxiang Shen, and Dezun Dong

On the Design of Mobility-Tolerant TDMA-Based Media Access
Control (MAC) Protocol for Mobile Sensor Networks 42
    Arshad Jhumka and Sandeep Kulkarni

Self-stabilizing Routing Algorithms for Wireless Ad-Hoc Networks 54
    Rohit Khot, Ravikant Poola, Kishore Kothapalli, and
    Kannan Srinathan

A Structured Mesh Overlay Network for P2P Applications on Mobile
Ad Hoc Networks 67
    Thirapon Wongsaardsakul and Kanchana Kanchanasut

A Scalable and Adaptive Clustering Scheme for MANETs 73
    Nevadita Chatterjee, Anupama Potluri, and Atul Negi

Section 2 - Security and Privacy

A Key Establishment Scheme for Large-Scale Mobile Wireless Sensor
Networks 79
    Ashok Kumar Das and Indranil Sengupta

Monitoring Information Leakage During Query Aggregation 89
    Sastry Konduri, Brajendra Panda, and Wing-Ning Li

An Efficient Certificate Authority for Ad Hoc Networks 97
    Jaydip Sen and Harihara Subramanyam

Design and Analysis of a Game Theoretic Model for P2P Trust
Management 110
    M. Harish, N. Anandavelu, N. Anbalagan, G.S. Mahalakshmi, and
    T.V. Geetha

Hasslefree: Simplified Access Control Management for XML
Documents   116
    Ashish Tripathi and M.M. Gore

LISA: LIghtweight Security Algorithm for Wireless Sensor Networks   129
    Somanath Tripathy

Section 3 - Network Management

An Optimal Weighted-Average Congestion Based Pricing Scheme for
Enhanced QoS   135
    Koteswara Rao Vemu, Shalabh Bhatnagar, and N. Hemachandra

Distributed Resource Adaptation for Virtual Network Operators   146
    Con Tran, Jahangir Sarker, and Zbigniew Dziong

Maximum Lifetime Tree Construction for Wireless Sensor Networks   158
    G.S. Badrinath, Phalguni Gupta, and Sajal K. Das

Overlay Network Management for Scheduling Tasks on the Grid   166
    Kovendhan Ponnavaikko and D. Janakiram

Section 4 - Network Services

An End-Systems Supported Highly Distributed Content Delivery
Network   172
    Jaison Paul Mulerikkal and Ibrahim Khalil

An Analytical Estimation of Durability in DHTs   184
    Fabio Picconi, Bruno Baynat, and Pierre Sens

A Multiple Tree Approach for Fault Tolerance in MPLS Networks   197
    Sahel Alouneh, Anjali Agarwal, and Abdeslam En-Nouaary

Selective Querying and Other Proposals for a Less Congested Gnutella
Network   203
    *K.G. Srinivasa, Anuj Bhatt, Sagnik Dhar, K.R. Venugopal, and
    L.M. Patnaik*

Section 5 - e-Application Engineering

Language Support and Compiler Optimizations for STM and
Transactional Boosting   209
    Guy Eddon and Maurice Herlihy

Unifying Denotational Semantics with Operational Semantics for Web
Services   225
    Huibiao Zhu, Jifeng He, and Jing Li

PHAC: An Environment for Distributed Collaborative Applications on
P2P Networks   240
    *Adnane Cabani, Srinivasan Ramaswamy, Mhamed Itmi, and
    Jean-Pierre Pécuchet*

Webformer: A Rapid Application Development Toolkit for Writing
Ajax Web Form Applications   248
    David W.L. Cheung, Thomas Y.T. Lee, and Patrick K.C. Yee

Section 6 - e-Application Services

Continuous Adaptive Mining the Thin Skylines over Evolving Data
Stream   254
    Guangmin Liang and Liang Su

Service Recommendation with Adaptive User Interests Modeling   265
    Cheng Zhang and Yanbo Han

An Approach to Aggregating Web Services for End-User-Doable
Construction of GridDoc Application   271
    Binge Cui

An Adaptive Metadata Model for Domain-Specific Service Registry   277
    Kun Chen, Yanbo Han, Dongju Yang, Yongshan Wei, and Wubin Li

Section 7 - e-Applications

Globalization from the Information and Communication Perspective   283
    Wojciech Cellary

WAND: A Robust P2P File System Tree Interface   293
    Saikat Mukherjee, Srinath Srinivasa, and Saugat Mitra

A Tsunami Warning System Employing Level Controlled Gossiping in
Wireless Sensor Networks   306
    Santosh Bhima, Anil Gogada, and Rammurthy Garimella

Relation Extraction and Validation Algorithm   314
    Lobna Karoui and Nabil El Kadhi

A Fair-Exchange and Customer-Anonymity Electronic Commerce
Protocol for Digital Content Transactions   321
    Shi-Jen Lin and Ding-Chyu Liu

A Practical Way to Provide Perfect Forward Secrecy for Secure E-Mail
Protocols   327
    Sangjin Kim, Changyong Lee, Daeyoung Kim, and Heekuck Oh

Augmentation to GT4 Framework for B2B Collaboration over Grid   336
    Jitendra Kumar Singh, K.N. Praveen, and R.K. Ghosh

Author Index   345

Time-Efficient Broadcasting in Radio Networks:
A Review

David Peleg*

Department of Computer Science and Applied Mathematics,
The Weizmann Institute of Science, Rehovot 76100, Israel
`david.peleg@weizmann.ac.il`

Abstract. Broadcasting is a basic network communication task, where a message initially held by a source node has to be disseminated to all other nodes in the network. Fast algorithms for broadcasting in radio networks have been studied in a wide variety of different models and under different requirements. Some of the main parameters giving rise to the different variants of the problem are the accessibility of knowledge about the network topology, the availability of collision detection mechanisms, the wake-up mode, the topology classes considered, and the use of randomness. The paper reviews the literature on time-efficient broadcasting algorithms for radio networks under a variety of models and assumptions.

1 Introduction

1.1 The Problem

A *radio network* consists of nodes, each equipped with a device enabling it to transmit and receive messages. At any given time, each node decides whether to act as a *transmitter* or as a *receiver*. Reception conditions are modeled by a network connecting the nodes, where the existence of a (directed) edge from a node v to a node u indicates that transmissions of v can reach u directly.

A node acting as a transmitter in a given time step transmits a message that reaches all of its outgoing neighbors in the network in the same time step. However, being within range of a transmitting node does not necessarily ensure that its transmitted message is received successfully. A node acting as a receiver in a given step successfully *hears* a message if and only if exactly one of its incoming neighbors transmits in this step. If two or more incoming neighbors v and v' of u transmit simultaneously in a given step, then none of their messages is heard by u. In this case we say that a *collision* occurred at u.

This paper considers *broadcasting* in radio networks, which is the following basic communication task. Initially, one distinguished node s, called the *source*, has a message M that has to be delivered to all other nodes in the network.

---

* Supported in part by grants from the Minerva Foundation and the Israel Ministry of Science and Technology.

T. Janowski and H. Mohanty (Eds.): ICDCIT 2007, LNCS 4882, pp. 1–18, 2007.

Remote nodes, which cannot receive the transmissions of s directly, have to get M via intermediate nodes.

The model considered in most of the literature on broadcasting algorithms in radio networks is synchronous. All nodes have individual clocks that tick at the same rate, measuring time steps, also referred to as *rounds*. Any execution of a broadcasting operation can be described as a sequence $\langle T_1, \ldots, T_t \rangle$, hereafter referred to as a *broadcasting sequence*, where each T_i is a *transmission set* consisting of the nodes that acted as transmitters in time step i. The execution time of a broadcasting algorithm in a given radio network is the number of rounds it takes since the first transmission until all nodes of the network hear the source message, or in other words, the length of the corresponding broadcast sequence.

The current paper reviews the literature on time-efficient broadcasting algorithms for radio networks under a variety of models and assumptions.

The question of time-efficient broadcasting has been examined from two related but distinct viewpoints. The first, more mathematical, viewpoint concerns investigating the absolute optimum time required for broadcasting. For a radio network G, let $b(G)$ denote the length of the shortest possible execution of the broadcasting operation for G. The study of broadcasting time from this viewpoint concentrated on the abstract question of identifying or tightly bounding the function b, and thus focused on establishing the existence or non-existence of short broadcasting sequences for a given network, using a variety of algorithmic, probabilistic and non-constructive methods.

Towards bounding the function $b(G)$, it was necessary to identify the graph theoretic parameters governing its behavior. Clearly, the *radius* of a network G from the source s, denoted $R(G, s)$ (i.e., the largest distance between s and any other node in G) serves as a lower bound for the length of any broadcasting sequence on G. For uniformity over the different sources, we use the network diameter D (i.e., the largest distance between any two nodes in G) instead. (Note that $D/2 \leq R(G, s) \leq D$ for every node s in G.) It also stands to reason that n, the number of nodes in the network, plays a role in the cost of broadcasting. Consequently, let us define $\hat{b}(n, D) = \max b(G)$, where the maximum is taken over all radio networks G of n nodes and diameter D. The mathematical problem stated above now becomes identifying the function $\hat{b}(n, D)$.

The second viewpoint deals with the more algorithmic question of developing protocols for time-efficient broadcasting in realistic settings. This question can be studied in a variety of models. To begin with, one may consider a centralized setting. In this setting, we assume that the graph topology is known in advance, and the goal is to design, in an offline pre-processing stage, an optimal (time minimal) or near-optimal solution for the broadcasting problem. Such a solution can sometimes be represented in the form of a fixed *schedule*, which essentially describes the optimal execution, i.e., specifies a broadcasting sequence $\langle T_1, \ldots, T_t \rangle$. The schedule can be applied as a broadcast procedure in the natural way: In step i, every node $v \in T_i$ which already holds a copy of the source message M transmits it. A node $v \in T_i$ that does not have a copy yet, remains silent.

The schedule S is a *broadcast schedule* for the source s in G if after applying it, every node in the network has a copy of M.

While the question of determining the minimum length of broadcasting schedules for radio networks is very basic and of considerable theoretical interest, in reality such schedules are hardly ever used, for a variety of practical considerations. For instance, such centrally computed fixed schedules are only useful when the network is relatively stable; in dynamic environments, where the network topology constantly changes, such schedules are hard to construct, maintain and update.

The common practice is therefore to employ distributed broadcasting protocols, which generate the broadcasting sequence "on the fly", while performing the broadcasting operation itself. This approach has obvious advantages in terms of simplicity and flexibility. On the down side, the typical situation in the distributed context is that nodes are unaware of the topology of the network and have limited or no knowledge of other parameters of the network, such as its diameter or size. They may not even be aware of their immediate neighborhood, namely, the identity of their neighbors. Networks in which the nodes have such limited knowledge are often called *ad hoc* networks. This lack of centralized knowledge rules out the efficient design of optimal or even near-optimal execution sequences. In fact, distributed broadcasting algorithms that rely on partial knowledge of the topology must usually involve trial-and-error, possibly incurring wasteful (but unavoidable) collisions, and are generally expected to generate significantly slower broadcasting sequences. Hence the focus in this area is on developing efficient algorithms that quickly adapt to the network at hand, possibly through learning its topology or some of its properties, and manage to tailor a relatively short execution sequence for it. Let $\hat{b}_{DD}(n, D)$ (respectively, $\hat{b}_{DR}(n, D)$) denote the time required for broadcasting on an n-node radio network of diameter D by a distributed deterministic (resp., randomized) algorithm. (Clearly, this function depends on the precise model and class of networks under consideration.)

Interestingly, despite the obvious advantages of adaptivity, which advocate the use of fully distributed, local, online and dynamically adapting solutions, in some cases the best algorithms currently known are essentially *oblivious*, in the sense that the actions taken by each node depend only on its identity and the current time step, but not on the history of the execution. Such algorithms can be thought of as requiring the nodes to follow fixed pre-computed schedules, designed by a central authority. Note, though, that there is an inherent difference between these oblivious schedules and the ones mentioned earlier. Our previous discussion concerned individualized schedules, specially tailored for every given radio network separately, relying on a complete knowledge of its topology. In contrast, the approach of using oblivious schedules provides a *general* distributed solution, applicable in situations where no knowledge of the network topology is available. In particular, this implies that the oblivious schedules provided by the construction algorithm must be *universal*, i.e., efficiently applicable for broadcasting on *every* network, regardless of its topology.

A well-studied technique developed for constructing such universal schedules is based on the combinatorial notion of *selection sequences* and *selective families* of transmission sequences for broadcasting. Subsequently, selective families, and the related structures of strongly selective families, cover-free families, superimposed codes and selectors, were used for broadcasting as well as for other communication tasks in radio networks, such as wakeup and synchronization.

1.2   Model Parameters

The complexity of broadcasting in radio networks critically depends on the particular setting and model parameters, and may change significantly depending on whether or not the nodes know the network, how their actions are coordinated, what mechanisms are available to the network nodes, and so on. Let us briefly overview the main parameters affecting the performance of broadcasting algorithms in radio networks.

Collision detection: In the event of a collision of two transmissions or more, one of a number of possibilities might happen at each of the receiving nodes. Three main alternatives are the following.

(C1) The receiving node hears nothing, and cannot tell if a collision occurred or none of its neighbors transmitted, i.e., it cannot distinguish a collision from silence.

(C2) The receiving node detects the fact that a collision has occurred.

(C3) The signal of exactly one of the transmitted messages prevails, and that message is received correctly by the receiving node.

The most commonly studied model in the literature on broadcasting algorithms in radio networks is the "collision-as-silence" model, which assumes that possibility (C1) always occurs, namely, the effect of a collision is the same as that of a step in which no transmissions took place. Certain papers consider the alternative *collision detection* model, which assumes that possibility (C2) always occurs, namely, the receiving nodes always recognize collisions. A third model, which is just as reasonable but has received even less attention, is the *flaky collision* model, in which at any receiver, the result of a collision may be either of possibilities (C1) or (C3), i.e., some collisions result in one message getting through, while some other result in the effect of silence. One may envision an even weaker variant of the flaky model, again rather reasonable, where the outcome of a collision could be any of three possibilities. In practice, more elaborate models can be considered, such as different interference and transmission ranges, or models allowing for the availability of carrier sensing mechanisms.

Wakeup model: The way the nodes join the broadcasting process can be modeled in two different ways. Most of the existing literature on broadcasting algorithms in radio networks considers the *conditional wakeup* model, where the nodes other than the source are initially idle and cannot transmit until they receive the source message for the first time and subsequently wake up. Namely, the clock of a node starts in the round when the node first receives the source message (the clock of the source starts at the beginning of the execution). One may assume without loss of generality that the number of rounds that have passed since the beginning of the execution is appended to every message, so that all nodes can emulate the source's clock.

Alternatively, one may consider the *spontaneous wakeup* model, where all nodes are assumed to be awake when the source transmits for the first time, and may contribute to the broadcasting process by transmitting control messages even before they received the source message. In other words, the clocks of all nodes start simultaneously, in the round when the source transmits for the first time. In this model, nodes far away from the source can utilize their waiting time to perform some pre-processing stage during which they can gather necessary information and possibly construct some auxiliary structures in the network (a sparse spanner, for example), facilitating faster message propagation at a later stage.

The task of broadcasting in the conditional wakeup model can in fact be interpreted as activating the network from a single source, and is related to the task of waking up the network. In this latter task, some nodes spontaneously wake up and have to wake up other nodes by sending messages. Thus broadcasting in the conditional wakeup model, i.e., activating the network from a single source, is equivalent to waking up the network when exactly one node (the source) wakes up spontaneously. The broadcasting models with spontaneous wakeup and conditional wakeup have also been called broadcasting with and without spontaneous transmissions, respectively.

Directionality: Most papers in the area assume that the radio network at hand is undirected, i.e., for every two nodes u and v, if v is within range of u's transmissions then u is within range of v as well. However, some papers consider also a model for radio networks based on a *directed* graph, allowing us to model asymmetric situations. (Such asymmetry can result from topographic conditions or from differences in the strength of the transmission equipment at different nodes.) Throughout most of what follows we will consider undirected graphs, except where mentioned otherwise.

Graph classes: In addition to the study of general (arbitrary topology) radio networks, some recent interest arose concerning a special subclass, referred to as *UDG radio networks*, where the network is modeled as a *unit disk graph* (UDG) whose nodes are the nodes. These nodes are represented as points in the Euclidean plane. Two nodes are joined by an edge if their distance is at most 1. The node transmitters have power enabling them to transmit to distance 1.

Randomness: Both deterministic and randomized broadcasting algorithms were considered in the literature. Randomized algorithms can also be oblivious, in which case the actions of the nodes depend on their identity and the time as well as on the outcomes of their random choices, but not on the execution history.

The harsh model: In most of the literature on algorithms for radio networks, the effects of transmission collisions are modeled by the collision-as-silence model, and the wakeup pattern of the network nodes is assumed to follow the conditional wakeup model. Consequently, in this paper we will focus on a model assuming both conditional wakeup and collision-as-silence, except where mentioned otherwise. We hereafter refer to this model as the *harsh* model for radio networks. Note that it is typically easier to establish lower bounds on broadcasting time in this model, although the resulting bounds will not apply to the other models. On the other hand, algorithms working in the harsh model will clearly apply also in models supporting collision detection or allowing spontaneous wakeup.

2   Efficient Schedules and Bounds on $b(G)$ and $\hat{b}(n, D)$

The literature concerning algorithmic aspects of radio broadcasting can be divided into two subareas, one dealing with centralized communication, in which it is assumed that nodes have complete knowledge of the network topology, and hence can simulate a central transmission scheduler (cf. [1,23,24,25,49,58,61,79]), and the other assuming only limited, usually local, knowledge of topology and studying distributed communication in such networks.

The first papers to formulate the abstract model of radio networks and address the question of broadcasting in radio networks were [23,24]. These papers described methods for the centralized design of a broadcasting schedule in radio networks, assuming complete knowledge of the network topology. In [23], it was also shown that the problem of finding a shortest broadcasting schedule (or alternatively, computing the minimum broadcasting time $b(G)$) for an arbitrary input graph G is NP-hard. As often happens, this hardness result has led to the development of two research directions, concerning *global bounds* and *approximations*.

The study of global bounds on broadcasting time was initiated in [25], which established an upper bound of $\hat{b}(n, D) = O(D \log^2(n/D))$ on broadcasting time. This upper bound was proved by presenting a deterministic algorithm for generating a broadcasting schedule of length $O(D \log^2 n)$ for every n-node network of diameter D. Shortly afterwards, a randomized algorithm completing broadcasting in time $O(D \log n + \log^2 n)$ with high probability was presented in [10]. This, in turn, implied that $\hat{b}(n, D) = O(D \log n + \log^2 n)$. Note, however, that this proof of the upper bound on $\hat{b}(n, D)$ is probabilistic, or non-constructive. A deterministic construction for such schedules of length $O(D \log n + \log^2 n)$ was later presented in [75].

On the other hand, it was proven in [1] that there exists a family of n-node networks of radius 2, for which any broadcasting schedule requires $\Omega(\log^2 n)$ communication rounds. This lower bound holds even assuming that the nodes have complete knowledge of the network and there are no restrictions on the coordination mechanism. Given that the diameter D is also a lower bound on broadcasting time, as mentioned earlier, it followed that $\hat{b}(n, D) \geq D + \Omega(\log^2 n)$.

Note, though, that there is a fine distinction between these two lower bounds. The diameter D is a *global* or *universal* lower bound, in the sense that $b(G) \geq D$ for every graph G of diameter D. In contrast, the $\Omega(\log^2 n)$ lower bound of [1] is *specific* or *existential*, in the sense that it only implies that $b(G) \geq \log^2 n$ for *some* low diameter graphs; clearly, there are also low diameter graphs G for which $b(G) \ll \log^2 n$, and in fact, there are $O(1)$ diameter graphs G for which $b(G) = O(1)$.

This gap between the upper and lower bounds established in [10] and [1] raised the intriguing question, formulated in [1,81], of whether further pipelining may be possible, leading to a separation of the D and $\log n$ terms in the upper bound. This has motivated a succession of improvements of the upper bound on $\hat{b}(n, D)$. The separation was first achieved in [58], which established a bound of $\hat{b}(n, D) = D + O(\log^5 n)$. This was again done via a non-constructive proof, by presenting a randomized algorithm for constructing short broadcasting schedules (of length $D + O(\log^5 n)$) with high probability. This algorithm is based on partitioning the underlying graph into low-diameter clusters and coloring them with $O(\log n)$ colors, and subsequently constructing a broadcasting schedule in each cluster separately, by applying the construction algorithm of [10] as a subprocedure. (Using the algorithm of [25] as the subprocedure instead, the resulting construction algorithm is deterministic but the broadcasting schedule it constructs is of length $D + O(\log^6 n)$.) The clustering method from [58] has next been improved in [49], which reduced the upper bound on $\hat{b}(n, D)$ to $D + O(\log^4 n)$, again using a randomized algorithm and hence yielding a non-constructive proof. (Using the algorithm of [25] as the subprocedure instead, the resulting algorithm is deterministic but the constructed broadcasting schedules are of length $D + O(\log^5 n)$.)

Finally, the optimal bound of $D + O(\log^2 n)$, yielding the sought $\hat{b}(n, D) = D + \Theta(\log^2 n)$, was established in [61]. This bound was once again established via a probabilistic (non-constructive) proof, although based on a different construction method (whose deterministic version yielded only broadcasting schedules of length $D + O(\log^3 n)$). That paper still left open the question of constructing broadcasting schedules of length $D + O(\log^2 n)$ *deterministically*. While this question has not been completely answered yet, explicit constructions of broadcasting schedules of length $O(D + \log^2 n)$ and $D + O(\frac{\log^3 n}{\log \log n})$ were recently presented in [79] and [34] respectively.

The study of approximations for optimal broadcasting time has so far led mostly to negative results. It has been proved in [47] that approximating the broadcasting time $b(G)$ for arbitrary n-node network G by a multiplicative factor of $o(\log n)$ is impossible, under the assumption that $NP \subseteq BPTIME(n^{O(\log \log n)})$. Under the same assumption, it was also proved in [48] that there exists a constant c such that there is no polynomial time algorithm which produces, for every n-node graph G, a broadcasting schedule of length at most $b(G) + c \log^2 n$. (Naturally, since D is a global lower bound on $b(G)$, the algorithm of [25] can be thought of also as an approximation algorithm for $b(G)$, with ratio $O(\log^2(n/D))$.)

3 Distributed Broadcasting Algorithms

3.1 Deterministic Distributed Algorithms

The study of distributed broadcasting in radio networks was initiated in [10]. The model studied therein assumed that nodes have limited knowledge of the topology, and specifically, that they know only their own identity and that of their neighbors. Under these assumptions, even in the harsh model, broadcasting can be achieved deterministically by a simple linear time algorithm based on depth-first search [4], establishing that $\hat{b}_{DD}(n, D) = O(n)$. Obtaining a matching lower bound on $\hat{b}_{DD}(n, D)$ proved to be more elusive than previously anticipated. The highest lower bound to date is $\hat{b}_{DD}(n, D) = \Omega(n^{1/4})$, due to [76], where a class of graphs of diameter 4 is constructed, such that every broadcasting algorithm requires time $\Omega(n^{1/4})$ on at least one of these graphs. A linear lower bound, $\hat{b}_{DD}(n, D) = \Omega(n)$, was proved in [10] on a class of radio networks of diameter 3, however, it turns out that the proof applies only to the flaky collisions model. In the collision detection model, the question of establishing matching upper and lower bounds for distributed deterministic broadcasting was posed as an open problem in [10], and its status remains practically unchanged to date. (The best upper bound currently known in this model is still $O(n)$; in addition, the problem has been resolved for some specific graph classes, as discussed later in Section 4.2).

A number of subsequent papers [1,18,26,28,33,37,45,78] studied deterministic distributed broadcasting in ad-hoc radio networks, i.e., under the more strict assumption that nodes know only their own identities but not those of their neighbors, and that the topology of the network is unknown. A lower bound of $\hat{b}_{DD}(n, D) = \Omega(D \log n)$ on broadcasting time in the harsh model was proved in [18], and this lower bound was subsequently sharpened to $\hat{b}_{DD}(n, D) = \Omega(n \frac{\log n}{\log(n/D)})$ in [77]. The two fastest distributed deterministic algorithms to date in this model, presented in [42] and [77], achieve broadcasting in time $O(n \log^2 D)$ and $O(n \log n)$ respectively. The algorithm of [77] was constructed by first defining an algorithm in a model allowing collision detection, and then applying a technique for simulating collision detection in the collision-as-silence model, developed in [76]. In contrast, the algorithm of [42] is oblivious and makes use of efficient deterministic selection sequences. Combining these two algorithms thus yields $\hat{b}_{DD}(n, D) = O(n \min\{\log^2 D, \log n\})$, leaving a small gap between the best upper and lower bounds currently known.

The problem was considered also in the spontaneous wakeup model. A deterministic algorithm completing broadcast in time $O(n)$ for arbitrary n-node networks is presented in [26]. For this model, a matching lower bound of $\hat{b}_{DD}(n, D) = \Omega(n)$ on deterministic broadcasting time, even for the class of networks of constant radius, was proved in [78], by an adaptation of the proof of [10].

Again, it is not clear whether allowing a collision detection mechanism can be used to improve broadcasting time. In particular, it is not known whether allowing both spontaneous wakeup and collision detection may lead to sub-linear time broadcasting algorithms.

3.2 Randomized Distributed Algorithms

The first paper to study randomized distributed broadcasting algorithms in radio networks was [10]. The model does not assume knowledge of the network topology or availability of distinct identities. The paper presents a randomized broadcasting algorithm with expected time $O(D \log n + \log^2 n)$.

Hence in view of the lower bounds of [10,76], there is an exponential gap between determinism and randomization in the time of radio broadcasting, in the collision-as-silence and flaky collisions models, for low diameter networks.

Lower bounds for randomized distributed broadcasting were given in [81,1]. In [81] it was shown that for any (deterministic or randomized) broadcasting algorithm and parameters $D \leq n$, there exists an n-node network of diameter D requiring expected time $\Omega(D \log(n/D))$ to execute this algorithm, yielding a lower bound of $\hat{b}_{DR}(n, D) = \Omega(D \log(n/D))$ in the harsh model. The $\Omega(\log^2 n)$ lower bound of [1], for some networks of radius 2, rules out the existence of schedules shorter than $c \log^2 n$ for some constant $c > 0$, hence it implies also that for randomized algorithms, $\hat{b}_{DR}(n, D) = \Omega(\log^2 n)$. Let us remark that this lower bound holds also in models with collision detection or spontaneous wakeup. Subsequently, randomized algorithms working in expected time $O(D \log(n/D) + \log^2 n)$, and thus matching the above lower bounds, were obtained independently in [42,77], establishing a tight bound of $\hat{b}_{DR}(n, D) = O(D \log(n/D) + \log^2 n)$. These algorithms are oblivious, using techniques based on universal selection sequences, and subsequently they operate in the harsh model.

It is currently unclear what happens if the model is not harsh, and specifically, whether the upper bound can be improved in a model allowing collision detection, spontaneous wakeup or both. The left part of the lower bound may possibly still hold even assuming collision detection or spontaneous wakeup. Conversely, the right part of the lower bound holds for schedule length, hence it certainly holds in any distributed model, including non-harsh ones, but it might potentially be strengthened in the harsh model.

4 Other Variants

4.1 Directed Graphs

A model based on *directed* graphs was used in [12,18,21,22,37,26,28,33,42,45,74]. The aim of these papers was to construct broadcasting algorithms working as fast as possible in arbitrary directed radio networks without knowing their topology. It turned out that in the directed setting, the complexity of broadcasting may depend also on an additional parameter, namely, the maximum node degree Δ.

The randomized algorithms of [10,42] apply also to directed networks, hence broadcasting can be performed on directed networks in the harsh model by a randomized algorithm in time $O(D \log(n/D) + \log^2 n)$, just as on undirected networks [42].

Deterministic broadcasting protocols in ad-hoc radio networks were dealt with in [21,13,22,12,37,46]. A scheme based on polynomials over finite fields was presented in [21]. This scheme achieves broadcast in time $O(D\frac{\Delta^2}{\log^2\Delta}\log^2 n)$, for arbitrary n-node networks with diameter D and maximum degree Δ. (The result was stated for undirected graphs, but it holds also for arbitrary directed graphs, defining D as the source radius, namely, the maximum distance from the source to any other node.) This direction was studied further in [13,22]. A protocol completing broadcast in time $O(D\Delta\log^{\log\Delta} n)$ was constructed in [12]. Finally, an $O(D\Delta\log^\alpha n)$ time protocol, for any $\alpha > 2$, was described in [37]. The protocol works for arbitrary directed graphs, and the exponent α can be decreased to 2 if the nodes are assumed to know n, and to 1 if the nodes know n and Δ. The above algorithms are efficient for networks with low diameter and node degrees. However, if D and Δ are large (say, linear in n), then the broadcasting time becomes $\Omega(n^2)$.

The first deterministic algorithm relying on universal selective families of sequences and avoiding the dependency on Δ, presented in [26], required $O(n^{11/6})$ time. Successively faster algorithms were then developed in [45,28,33]. The fastest deterministic broadcasting algorithm currently available for directed networks in the harsh model has time $O(n\log^2 D)$ [42]. The algorithm is oblivious and makes use of efficient deterministic selection sequences. On the other hand, a lower bound of $\Omega(n\log D)$ on deterministic broadcasting time was proved in [37] for directed networks. This lower bound holds also in a model allowing spontaneous wakeup (but still assuming collision-as-silence).

The $\Omega(n\frac{\log n}{\log(n/D)})$ time lower bound proved in [77] for undirected networks in the harsh model clearly holds also for directed networks. In fact, for directed networks, the $\Omega(D\log n)$ time lower bound of [18] was extended in [26] to a model allowing spontaneous wakeup (but no collision detection).

It is worth noting that following the introduction of selective families in [26], a variety of probabilistic, combinatorial and coding-based techniques were developed for constructing selective families and related structures such as strongly selective families, cover-free families, superimposed codes and selectors, and these structures were used for broadcasting and other communication tasks in radio networks, such as wakeup and synchronization [37,38,39,28,29,30,42,60,68]. For a recent review of selection sequences and their uses, see [30].

4.2   Unit Disk Graphs

A more specific model of radio networks that has recently received considerable attention is based on assuming that the network nodes are placed in the 2-dimensional plane and representing these nodes by their geometric positions in the plane. The underlying graph is thus no longer arbitrary. Rather, the transmission range of each node v is characterized as some region $R(v)$ around its location, and a node u can receive the transmissions of v if it belongs to $R(v)$. The regions are often assumed to be unit disks, implying that the transmission range of each node includes all nodes at distance at most 1 from it. In this case, the resulting network is a *unit disk graph* (UDG), where two nodes are joined by an edge if and only if their Euclidean distance is at most 1. Another common alternative is to allow a generalized representation as a (directed) disk graph, where radii of disks representing reachability regions may differ from node to node [43]. Reachability areas of arbitrary shapes were considered, e.g., in [46,80].

Broadcasting in such geometric radio networks and some of their variations was considered, e.g., in [43,46,80,86,88].

Broadcasting schedules and bounds on $\hat{b}(n, D)$: In [88] it is proved that computing an optimal broadcasting schedule is NP-hard even when restricted to such graphs. That paper also gives an $O(n \log n)$ algorithm for constructing an optimal broadcast schedule when the nodes are situated on a straight line. In [86] broadcasting was considered in networks with nodes randomly placed on a straight line. Fault-tolerant broadcasting in radio networks arising from regular locations of nodes on the line and in the plane, with reachability regions being squares and hexagons, rather than circles, is discussed in [80]. Broadcasting with restricted knowledge was considered in [46] but only the special case of nodes situated on the line was analyzed.

The problem of bounding $\hat{b}(n, D)$ becomes easier in the setting of UDG networks, and admits tight bounds of $\hat{b}(n, D) = \Theta(D)$. The lower bound is trivial, and the upper bound follows, e.g., from [63,73], but can also be derived directly in a straightforward manner.

Distributed broadcasting algorithms in unknown topology: The first paper to study deterministic distributed broadcasting in arbitrary geometric radio networks with restricted knowledge of topology was [43]. Several models were studied assuming a positive knowledge radius, i.e., assuming that the knowledge available to a node concerns other nodes inside some disk around it. In the case of knowledge radius 0, an $O(n)$ time broadcasting algorithm is shown for the spontaneous wakeup model, assuming that nodes are labeled by consecutive integers.

In the distributed context, where nodes are unaware of the network topology (including their immediate neighborhood), the efficiency of broadcasting turns out to depend not only on the diameter but also on one additional parameter, namely, the *spacing* among nodes [50]. Let d be a lower bound on the Euclidean distance between any two nodes of the network. Then broadcasting time depends inversely on d, or in other words, it depends on the network *granularity*, $g = 1/d$. Assume each node of the network initially knows only its own coordinates in the Euclidean plane and the parameter d. Considering only deterministic broadcasting algorithms, the decisions made by a node at every round are based entirely on its coordinates and on the messages it received so far. An algorithm for broadcasting in the harsh model is presented in [50], completing broadcast in time $O(Dg)$ in any UDG radio network of diameter D and granularity g. A matching lower bound is presented in [51]. It should be noted that in a network of diameter D and granularity g, n may be as large as $O(D^2 g^2)$, hence $O(Dg)$ is generally an improvement over the $O(n)$ bound that follows from the algorithm of [43].

The problem was studied also for the spontaneous wakeup model (still assuming collision-as-silence). Two different broadcasting algorithms are given in [50], one working in time $O(D + g^2)$ and the other in time $O(D \log g)$. Depending on parameter values, one or the other of these algorithms may be more efficient. The combined algorithm obtained by interleaving these two algorithms completes broadcast in time $O(\min\{D + g^2, D \log g\})$. A matching lower bound of $\Omega(\min\{D + g^2, D \log g\})$ on broadcasting time for this model is established as well. These results give a provable separation between the conditional and the spontaneous wakeup models for broadcasting in UDG radio networks; for networks of small diameter (e.g., D bounded or polylogarithmic in g) the lower bound for the conditional wakeup model is significantly larger than the upper bound for the spontaneous wakeup model.

One may consider also a variant of the model based on restricted network configurations, where the nodes must be deployed on the points of a *d-spaced grid* in the plane. This variant has also been examined in [50,51] within the harsh model. A lower bound of $\Omega(D\sqrt{g})$ on the time required by any broadcasting algorithm is established in [50], and an algorithm achieving broadcast in time $O(Dg^{5/6} \log g)$ is presented in [51]. This implies a separation between the arbitrary deployment setting and the grid deployment setting in the harsh model, showing that broadcasting in the former setting is strictly harder.

The problem is studied in [73] in the spontaneous wakeup model with a more elaborate reception model (with different interference and transmission ranges, and a carrier sensing mechanism allowing some form of collision detection). The broadcast algorithm described therein is based on initially constructing a connected dominating set and subsequently a constant density spanner for the network (in expected time $O(\Delta \log \Delta \log n + \log^4 n)$), and then using this spanner to disseminate the broadcast message with high probability in overall time $O(D + \log n)$.

4.3   Related Work

This concluding section briefly reviews some of the results appearing in the literature on variations of the problem, the model or the type of solution, that do not fall under the categories discussed so far.

As mentioned earlier, one may distinguish a special class of algorithms, referred to as *oblivious* distributed algorithms, where the actions taken by each node depend only on its identity and the time but not on the history of the execution. Oblivious algorithms for broadcasting are studied in [78], where it is shown that obliviousness degrades the time efficiency of broadcast. In particular, it is shown that there are oblivious randomized algorithms completing broadcast in $O(n \min\{D, \log n\})$ time, and every such algorithm requires $\Omega(n)$ expected time for broadcasting. Matching bounds of $\Theta(n \min\{D, \sqrt{n}\})$ are given for on broadcasting time by oblivious deterministic algorithms.

Much of the literature on broadcasting algorithms concerns the *static* case, where the network topology is fixed through time. In practice, there are applications where the network nodes are *mobile*, and their movements affect also the topology of the network, since a moving node exits the transmission range of some of its previous neighbors and enters the transmission range of some new nodes. For discussions of broadcasting techniques and protocols for mobile wireless ad hoc networks, see [90,91].

The broadcast operation has been studied extensively in other (wired) types of communication networks, e.g., message passing networks (cf. [6,7,15,55,66,85,87]) and telephone networks (cf. [53,54] and the surveys [57,65]).

The literature reviewed herein considers broadcast as a single operation. In many cases, there is a need to perform a long sequence of message broadcasts repeatedly. Such settings were studied in [23], and later in [11], which presents a pre-processing stage such that subsequently, repeated broadcast operations can be performed at an average throughput of a broadcast operation every $O(\log \Delta \log n)$ time slots, where Δ is the maximum degree of the network. Using a pre-constructed spanner to speed up broadcasting was proposed in [5].

A related communication task that has been thoroughly studied in all types of communication networks is *gossiping*, where each of the nodes of the network (in parallel) must broadcast its local information to all the other nodes [20,33,41,61,64,65,83]. Also related is the task of *repetitious communication*, where each node repeatedly exchanges information with its neighbors [2,56].

Yet another related type of distributed operation is the *wakeup* problem. In the context of radio networks, this problem was first studied in [60] for single-hop networks (modeled by complete graphs), and then in [32,29,27] for arbitrary networks. Randomized wakeup algorithms for radio networks were studied in [69]. In all these papers it was assumed that a subset of all nodes wake up spontaneously, possibly at different times, and have to wake up the other (initially dormant) nodes.

The model as defined herein assumes synchronous communication. The broadcasting problem has been studied also in the *asynchronous* model. In particular, upper and lower bounds for broadcasting time in asynchronous radio networks are established in [31] under a variety of possible adversarial models.

A number of papers study other complexity measures for broadcasting, such as the total number of transmissions [63] or the total energy requirements [3,19,35,36,52,89]. These measures are sometimes studied in combination with time complexity [14,44,62].

In certain variants of broadcast, the problem definition includes some element of termination detection, e.g., they may require the source node to receive an acknowledgement informing it that the broadcasting process has completed. Issues of termination detection and acknowledgement delivery in radio networks are studied in [26,59].

Fault tolerant broadcasting in radio networks was considered in a number of papers [8,9,16,17,40,71,72,80,82,84]; see [83] for a survey of this area.

References

1. Alon, N., Bar-Noy, A., Linial, N., Peleg, D.: A lower bound for radio broadcast. J. Computer and System Sciences 43, 290–298 (1991)
2. Alon, N., Bar-Noy, A., Linial, N., Peleg, D.: Single Round Simulation on Radio Networks. J. Algorithms 13, 188–210 (1992)

3. Ambuhl, C., Clementi, A., Di Ianni, M., Lev-Tov, N., Monti, A., Peleg, D., Rossi, G., Silvestri, R.: Efficient Algorithms for Low-Energy Bounded-Hop Broadcast in Ad-Hoc Wireless Networks. In: Proc. 21st Symp. on Theoretical Aspects of Computer Science, pp. 418–427 (2004)
4. Awerbuch, B.: A new distributed depth-first-search algorithm. Inform. Process. Lett. 20, 147–150 (1985)
5. Awerbuch, B., Baratz, A., Peleg, D.: Efficient broadcast and light-weight spanners. Technical Report CS92-22, The Weizmann Institute, Rehovot, Israel (1992)
6. Awerbuch, B., Cidon, I., Kutten, S., Mansour, Y., Peleg, D.: Optimal Broadcast with Partial Knowledge. SIAM J. Computing 28, 511–524 (1998)
7. Awerbuch, B., Goldreich, O., Peleg, D., Vainish, R.: A tradeoff between information and communication in broadcast protocols. J. ACM 37, 238–256 (1990)
8. Awerbuch, B., Even, S.: Reliable Broadcast Protocols in Unreliable Networks. Networks 16, 381–396 (1986)
9. Awerbuch, B., Segall, A.: A Reliable Broadcast Protocol. IEEE Trans. Communications 31, 896–901 (1983)
10. Bar-Yehuda, R., Goldreich, O., Itai, A.: On the time complexity of broadcast in radio networks: an exponential gap between determinism and randomization. J. Computer and System Sciences 45, 104–126 (1992)
11. Bar-Yehuda, R., Israeli, A., Itai, A.: Multiple communication in multihop radio networks. SIAM J. Computing 22, 875–887 (1993)
12. Basagni, S., Bruschi, D., Chlamtac, I.: A mobility-transparent deterministic broadcast mechanism for ad hoc networks. IEEE/ACM Trans. Networking 7, 799–807 (1999)
13. Basagni, S., Myers, A.D., Syrotiuk, V.R.: Mobility-independent flooding for real-time multimedia applications in ad hoc networks. In: Proc. IEEE Emerging Technologies Symp. on Wireless Communications & Systems (1999)
14. Berenbrink, P., Cooper, C., Hu, Z.: Energy efficient randomized communication in unknown ad hoc networks. In: Proc. 19th Symp. on Parallelism Algorithms and Architectures (2007)
15. Bertsekas, D., Gallager, R.: Data Networks. Prantice Hall, New Jersey (1987)
16. Bhandari, V., Vaidya, N.H.: On reliable broadcast in a radio network. In: Proc. 24th Symp. on Principles of Distributed Computing, pp. 138–147 (2005)
17. Bhandari, V., Vaidya, N.H.: Reliable Broadcast in Wireless Networks with Probabilistic Failures. In: Proc. 26th Joint Conf. of IEEE Computer and Communication Societies (INFOCOM), pp. 715–723 (2007)
18. Bruschi, D., Del Pinto, M.: Lower bounds for the broadcast problem in mobile radio networks. Distributed Computing 10, 129–135 (1997)
19. Călinescu, G., Li, X.Y., Frieder, O., Wan, P.J.: Minimum-Energy Broadcast Routing in Static Ad Hoc Wireless Networks. In: Proc. 20th Joint Conf. of IEEE Computer and Communications Societies (INFOCOM), pp. 1162–1171 (2001)
20. Chandra, R., Ramasubramanian, V., Birman, K.P.: Anonymous Gossip: Improving Multicast Reliability in Mobile Ad-Hoc Networks. In: Proc. 21st Conf. on Distributed Computing Systems, pp. 275–283 (2001)
21. Chlamtac, I., Faragó, A.: Making transmission schedule immune to topology changes in multi-hop packet radio networks. IEEE/ACM Trans. Networking 2, 23–29 (1994)
22. Chlamtac, I., Faragó, A., Zhang, H.: Time-spread multiple access (TSMA) protocols for multihop mobile radio networks. IEEE/ACM Trans. Networking 5, 804–812 (1997)

23. Chlamtac, I., Kutten, S.: On broadcasting in radio networks – problem analysis and protocol design. IEEE Trans. Communications 33, 1240–1246 (1985)
24. Chlamtac, I., Kutten, S.: Tree-based broadcasting in multihop radio networks. IEEE Trans. Computers 36, 1209–1223 (1987)
25. Chlamtac, I., Weinstein, O.: The wave expansion approach to broadcasting in multihop radio networks. IEEE Trans. Communications 39, 426–433 (1991)
26. Chlebus, B.S., Gąsieniec, L., Gibbons, A., Pelc, A., Rytter, W.: Deterministic broadcasting in unknown radio networks. Distributed Computing 15, 27–38 (2002)
27. Chlebus, B.S., Gasieniec, L., Kowalski, D.R., Radzik, T.: On the Wake-Up Problem in Radio Networks. In: Proc. 32nd Int. Colloq. on Automata, Languages and Programming, pp. 347–359 (2005)
28. Chlebus, B.S., Gąsieniec, L., Ostlin, A., Robson, J.M.: Deterministic radio broadcasting. In: Welzl, E., Montanari, U., Rolim, J.D.P. (eds.) ICALP 2000. LNCS, vol. 1853, pp. 717–728. Springer, Heidelberg (2000)
29. Chlebus, B.S., Kowalski, D.R.: A better wake-up in radio networks. In: Proc. 23rd Symp. on Principles of Distributed Computing, pp. 266–274 (2004)
30. Chlebus, B.S., Kowalski, D.R.: Almost Optimal Explicit Selectors. In: Liśkiewicz, M., Reischuk, R. (eds.) FCT 2005. LNCS, vol. 3623, pp. 270–280. Springer, Heidelberg (2005)
31. Chlebus, B.S., Rokicki, M.: Asynchronous broadcast in radio networks. In: Kralovic, R., Sýkora, O. (eds.) SIROCCO 2004. LNCS, vol. 3104, pp. 57–68. Springer, Heidelberg (2004)
32. Chrobak, M., Gąsieniec, L., Kowalski, D.R.: The wake-up problem in multi-hop radio networks. In: Proc. 15th ACM-SIAM Symp. on Discrete Algorithms, pp. 985–993 (2004)
33. Chrobak, M., Gąsieniec, L., Rytter, W.: Fast broadcasting and gossiping in radio networks. In: Proc. 41st Symp. on Foundations of Computer Science, pp. 575–581 (2000)
34. Cicalese, F., Manne, F., Xin, Q.: Faster centralized communication in radio networks. In: Proc. 17th Symp. on Algorithms and Computation, pp. 339–348 (2006)
35. Clementi, A.E.F., Huiban, G., Penna, P., Rossi, G., Verhoeven, Y.C.: Some recent theoretical advances and open questions on energy consumption in ad-hoc wireless networks. In: Proc. 3rd Workshop on Approximation and Randomization Algorithms in Communication Networks, pp. 23–38 (2002)
36. Clementi, A.E.F., Crescenzi, P., Penna, P., Rossi, G., Vocca, P.: On the Complexity of Computing Minimum Energy Consumption Broadcast Subgraphs. In: Proc. 18th Symp. on Theoretical Aspects of Computer Science, pp. 121–131 (2001)
37. Clementi, A.E.F., Monti, A., Silvestri, R.: Selective families, superimposed codes, and broadcasting on unknown radio networks. In: Proc. 12th Ann. ACM-SIAM Symp. on Discrete Algorithms, pp. 709–718 (2001)
38. Clementi, A.E.F., Crescenzi, P., Monti, A., Penna, P., Silvestri, R.: On Computing Ad-hoc Selective Families. In: Goemans, M.X., Jansen, K., Rolim, J.D.P., Trevisan, L. (eds.) RANDOM 2001 and APPROX 2001. LNCS, vol. 2129, pp. 211–222. Springer, Heidelberg (2001)
39. Clementi, A.E.F., Monti, A., Silvestri, R.: Distributed broadcast in radio networks of unknown topology. Theoretical Computer Science 302, 337–364 (2003)
40. Clementi, A.E.F., Monti, A., Silvestri, R.: Round Robin is optimal for fault-tolerant broadcasting on wireless networks. J. Parallel and Distributed Computing 64, 89–96 (2004)
41. Czumaj, A., Gąsieniec, L., Pelc, A.: Time and Cost Trade-Offs in Gossiping. SIAM J. Discrete Mathematics 11, 400–413 (1998)

42. Czumaj, A., Rytter, W.: Broadcasting algorithms in radio networks with unknown topology. J. Algorithms 60, 115–143 (2006)
43. Dessmark, A., Pelc, A.: Broadcasting in geometric radio networks. J. Discrete Algorithms 5, 187–201 (2007)
44. Dessmark, A., Pelc, A.: Deterministic radio broadcasting at low cost. Networks 39, 88–97 (2002)
45. De Marco, G., Pelc, A.: Faster broadcasting in unknown radio networks. Information Processing Letters 79, 53–56 (2001)
46. Diks, K., Kranakis, E., Krizanc, D., Pelc, A.: The impact of knowledge on broadcasting time in linear radio networks. Theoretical Computer Science 287, 449–471 (2002)
47. Elkin, M., Kortsarz, G.: Logarithmic inapproximability of the radio broadcast problem. J. Algorithms 52(1), 8–25 (2004)
48. Elkin, M., Kortsarz, G.: Polylogarithmic inapproximability of the radio broadcast problem. In: Jansen, K., Khanna, S., Rolim, J.D.P., Ron, D. (eds.) APPROX 2004. LNCS, vol. 3122, pp. 105–116. Springer, Heidelberg (2004)
49. Elkin, M., Kortsarz, G.: Improved schedule for radio broadcast. In: Proc. 16th ACM-SIAM Symp. on Discrete Algorithms, pp. 222–231 (2005)
50. Emek, Y., Gąsieniec, L., Kantor, E., Pelc, A., Peleg, D., Su, C.: Broadcasting in UDG radio networks with unknown topology. In: Proc. ACM Symp. on Principles of Distributed Computing (2007)
51. Emek, Y., Kantor, E., Peleg, D.: On the Effect of the Deployment Setting on Broadcasting in Euclidean Radio Networks (unpublished manuscript, 2007)
52. Ephremides, A., Nguyen, G.D., Wieselthier, J.E.: On the Construction of Energy-Efficient Broadcast and Multicast Trees in Wireless Networks. In: Proc. 19th Joint Conf. of IEEE Computer and Communications Societies (INFOCOM), pp. 585–594 (2000)
53. Farley, A.M.: Minimal Broadcast Networks. Networks 9, 313–332 (1979)
54. Farley, A.M., Hedetniemi, S.T., Mitchell, S., Proskurowski, A.: Minimum Broadcast Graphs. Discrete Math. 25, 189–193 (1979)
55. Feige, U., Peleg, D., Raghavan, P., Upfal, E.: The Complexity of Randomized Broadcast. J. on Random Structures & Algorithms 1, 447–460 (1990)
56. Fernandez, A., Mosteiro, M.A., Thraves, C.: Deterministic Communication in the Weak Sensor Model. In: Proc. 11th Conf. On Principles Of Distributed Systems (2007)
57. Fraigniaud, P., Lazard, E.: Methods and problems of communication in usual networks. Discrete Applied Math. 53, 79–133 (1994)
58. Gaber, I., Mansour, Y.: Centralized broadcast in multihop radio networks. J. Algorithms 46, 1–20 (2003)
59. Gargano, L., Pelc, A., Pérennes, S., Vaccaro, U.: Efficient communication in unknown networks. Networks 38, 39–49 (2001)
60. Gąsieniec, L., Pelc, A., Peleg, D.: The wakeup problem in synchronous broadcast systems. SIAM J. Discrete Mathematics 14, 207–222 (2001)
61. Gąsieniec, L., Peleg, D., Xin, Q.: Faster communication in known topology radio networks. In: Proc. 24th ACM Symp. on Principles Of Distributed Computing, pp. 129–137 (2005)
62. Gąsieniec, L., Kantor, E., Kowalski, D.R., Peleg, D., Su, C.: Energy and Time Efficient Broadcasting in Known Topology Radio Networks. In: Proc. 21st Symp. on Distributed Computing. LNCS, vol. 4731, pp. 253–267. Springer, Heidelberg (2007)

63. Gandhi, R., Parthasarathy, S., Mishra, A.: Minimizing broadcast latency and redundancy in ad hoc networks. In: Proc. 4th ACM Symp. on Mobile ad hoc networking and computing, pp. 222–232 (2003)
64. Haas, Z.J., Halpern, J.Y., Li, L.: Gossip-based ad hoc routing. IEEE/ACM Trans. Networking 14, 479–491 (2006)
65. Hedetniemi, S., Hedetniemi, S., Liestman, A.: A Survey of Gossiping and Broadcasting in Communication Networks. Networks 18, 319–349 (1988)
66. Humblet, P.A., Soloway, S.R.: Topology Broadcast Algorithms. Computer Networks 16, 179–186 (1989)
67. Hwang, F.K.: The time complexity of deterministic broadcast radio networks. Discrete Applied Mathematics 60, 219–222 (1995)
68. Indyk, P.: Explicit constructions of selectors and related combinatorial structures, with applications. In: Proc. 13th ACM-SIAM Symp. on Discrete Algorithms, pp. 697–704 (2002)
69. Jurdzinski, T., Stachowiak, G.: Probabilistic algorithms for the wakeup problem in single-hop radio networks. In: Bose, P., Morin, P. (eds.) ISAAC 2002. LNCS, vol. 2518, pp. 535–549. Springer, Heidelberg (2002)
70. Kesselman, A., Kowalski, D.R.: Fast Distributed Algorithm for Convergecast in Ad Hoc Geometric Radio Networks. In: Proc. 2nd Conf. on Wireless on Demand Network Systems and Service, pp. 119–124 (2005)
71. Koo, C.-Y.: Broadcast in radio networks tolerating byzantine adversarial behavior. In: Proc. 23rd Symp. on Principles of Distributed Computing, pp. 275–282 (2004)
72. Koo, C.-Y., Bhandari, V., Katz, J., Vaidya, N.H.: Reliable broadcast in radio networks: the bounded collision case. In: Proc. 25th Symp. on Principles of Distributed Computing, pp. 258–264 (2006)
73. Kothapalli, K., Onus, M., Richa, A., Scheideler, C.: Efficient Broadcasting and Gathering in Wireless Ad Hoc Networks. In: Proc. IEEE Symp. on Parallel Architectures, Algorithms and Networks, pp. 346–351 (2005)
74. Kowalski, D.R., Pelc, A.: Faster deterministic broadcasting in ad hoc radio networks. SIAM J. Discrete Mathematics 18, 332–346 (2004)
75. Kowalski, D.R., Pelc, A.: Centralized deterministic broadcasting in undirected multi-hop radio networks. In: Jansen, K., Khanna, S., Rolim, J.D.P., Ron, D. (eds.) APPROX 2004. LNCS, vol. 3122, pp. 171–182. Springer, Heidelberg (2004)
76. Kowalski, D.R., Pelc, A.: Time of deterministic broadcasting in radio networks with local knowledge. SIAM J. Computing 33, 870–891 (2004)
77. Kowalski, D.R., Pelc, A.: Broadcasting in undirected ad hoc radio networks. Distributed Computing 18, 43–57 (2005)
78. Kowalski, D.R., Pelc, A.: Time complexity of radio broadcasting: adaptiveness vs. obliviousness and randomization vs. determinism. Theoretical Computer Science 333, 355–371 (2005)
79. Kowalski, D.R., Pelc, A.: Optimal deterministic broadcasting in known topology radio networks. Distributed Computing 19, 185–195 (2007)
80. Kranakis, E., Krizanc, D., Pelc, A.: Fault-tolerant broadcasting in radio networks. J. Algorithms 39, 47–67 (2001)
81. Kushilevitz, E., Mansour, Y.: An $\Omega(D \log(N/D))$ lower bound for broadcast in radio networks. SIAM J. Computing 27, 702–712 (1998)
82. Pagani, E., Rossi, G.P.: Reliable broadcast in mobile multihop radio networks. In: Proc. 3rd ACM/IEEE Conf. on Mobile Computing and Networking (MOBICOM), pp. 34–42 (1997)
83. Pelc, A.: Fault-tolerant broadcasting and gossiping in communication networks. Networks 28, 143–156 (1996)

84. Pelc, A., Peleg, D.: Broadcasting with locally bounded Byzantine faults. Information Processing Letters 93, 109–115 (2005)
85. Peleg, D.: Distributed Computing: A Locality-Sensitive Approach. SIAM (2000)
86. Ravishankar, K., Singh, S.: Broadcasting on $[0, L]$. Discrete Applied Mathematics 53, 299–319 (1994)
87. Segall, A.: Distributed Network Protocols. IEEE Trans. Inf. Th. 29, 23–35 (1983)
88. Sen, A., Huson, M.L.: A new model for scheduling packet radio networks. In: Proc. 15th Joint Conf. of IEEE Computer and Communication Societies (INFOCOM), pp. 1116–1124 (1996)
89. Song, W.-Z., Li, X.-Y., Frieder, O., Wang, W.: Localized Topology Control for Unicast and Broadcast in Wireless Ad Hoc Networks. IEEE Trans. Parallel Distrib. Syst. 17, 321–334 (2006)
90. Toh, C.K.: Ad Hoc Mobile Wireless Networks. Prentice Hall, Englewood Cliffs (2002)
91. Williams, B., Camp, T.: Comparison of broadcasting techniques for mobile ad hoc networks. In: Proc. 3rd ACM Symp. on Mobile Ad Hoc Networking and Computing, pp. 194–205 (2002)

An Efficient and Optimized Bluetooth Scheduling Algorithm for Piconets

Vijay Prakash Chaturvedi, V. Rakesh, and Shalabh Bhatnagar

Department of Computer Science and Automation,
Indian Institute of Science, Bangalore - 560012, India
vijayp@csa.iisc.ernet.in, rakesh.vugranam@gmail.com,
shalabh@csa.iisc.ernet.in

Abstract. Bluetooth is an emerging standard in short range, low cost and low power wireless networks. MAC is a generic polling based protocol, where a central Bluetooth unit (master) determines channel access to all other nodes (slaves) in the network (piconet). An important problem in Bluetooth is the design of efficient scheduling protocols. This paper proposes a polling policy that aims to achieve increased system throughput and reduced packet delays while providing reasonably good fairness among all traffic flows in a Bluetooth Piconet. We present an extensive set of simulation results and performance comparisons with two important existing algorithms. Our results indicate that our proposed scheduling algorithm outperforms the Round Robin scheduling algorithm by more than 40% in all cases tried. Our study also confirms that our proposed policy achieves higher throughput and lower packet delays with reasonable fairness among all the connections.

1 Introduction

Bluetooth (BT) is a wireless technology that has been developed with the original aim to eliminate cables between devices. BT is built on a fast frequency hopping (1600 hops/sec) physical layer operating in the 2.4 GHz frequency ISM band. The immense potential in this technology opened a wide range of applications; the three most popular usage scenarios being replacement for cables that are used to connect devices, universal bridging to connect data networks, and ad-hoc networking to provide a mechanism to form small personal area networks (PANs).

The smallest network unit formed among BT devices is called a *piconet*, which comprises of a master node and one or more slave nodes. During the process of *piconet* establishment, the device that initiates a link connection with another device within its range takes the role of the master while the latter takes the role of a slave. Eventually, other slave devices may join the master and thus increase the size of the *piconet*. Exchange of information takes place only between the master and a slave (i.e., there is no direct slave-slave communication).

The limitation of the BT polling scheme is that once a master polls a slave, the next slot is reserved for the slave irrespective of whether it has data to transmit or not, resulting in a pairwise scheduling of slots between the master

T. Janowski and H. Mohanty (Eds.): ICDCIT 2007, LNCS 4882, pp. 19–30, 2007.

and the individual slave nodes. For such a system, the default Round Robin scheduler, suggested in the BT specification, is not suitable for the BT Piconet as it does not perform well in the presence of asymmetric and heterogeneous traffic conditions.

Thus one requires a scheme that employs an efficient scheduling mechanism which can predict the availability of data at the master and slaves, thereby preventing wastage of slots, and an adaptive packet selection scheme that can adapt (by not allocating slots to slaves that are predicted not to have data packets for transmission) the data transmission according to channel conditions, by choosing the correct packet types. We focus here on scheduling Asynchronous Connection-Less (ACL) data traffic in the presence of asymmetric and heterogeneous traffic.

The rest of the paper is organized as follows: Section 2 gives an overview of the BT technology and polling mechanism. Section 3 introduces our proposed *piconet* scheduling scheme and its features. Section 4 describes the simulation model and results. Finally, Section 5 concludes the paper.

2   Bluetooth Overview

[1] describes BT architecture and its working in detail. A BT system consists of a radio unit, a link control unit and a support unit for link management and host terminal interface functions. It provides both a point-to-point or point-to-multi-point connection. In the latter case, the channel is shared among several bluetooth units. Two or more peer units sharing the same channel form a *piconet*. One of the units in the *piconet* forms the master node (or simply the master), while the remaining units act as slave nodes (or simply the slaves). All the units in a *piconet* follow an identical frequency-hopping scheme as determined by the master. Upto a maximum of seven slaves and a master can be active in a *piconet*. Multiple piconets with overlapping coverage areas form a *scatternet*. A master in a *piconet* can be a slave in another *piconet*. The bridging units which are connected to two piconets use a time division multiplex system for switching between the hopping schemes of the two piconets at regular intervals.

A Time Division Duplex (TDD) scheme is used for transmission of packets where each slot is of $625\mu s$. The master transmits packets in even numbered slots and the slave being polled may transmit in the following odd slot. The packets transmitted by master or slave may cover 1, 3 or 5 time slots.

indent Two types of links may be established between master and slave(s): Synchronous Connection Oriented (SCO), and Asynchronous Connection-Less (ACL), respectively. The SCO link is a point-to-point link between the master and the specific slave. The SCO link reserves slots and can be viewed as a circuit-switched connection. The ACL link, on the other hand, provides a packet switched connection between the master and slave(s). Data packets are of two types, DM and DH. DM1 (Data Medium rate) may cover upto 1 time slot, DM3 upto 3 time slots, and DM5 upto 5 time slots respectively. DH (Data High rate) packets are similar to DM packets except for the encoding techniques they use. Hence a DH packet contains more data.

2.1   Bluetooth Scheduling

According to BT core specifications, the master schedules transmission based on traffic demands to and from the different slaves. Slaves are allowed to transmit after having been polled by the master, i.e., after they have received a POLL packet. During the POLL period, the master can send either data packet or the POLL packet (empty packet). Slaves have an uplink queue for transmission to the master and the master has a downlink queue for transmission to each of the slaves. The slaves start transmission by sending their data or respond with the NULL packet. When in the active mode slaves listen in the master-to-slave slots for packets. In the active mode, these devices are known as active slaves. When active slaves have no data to send, allocating time slots for them leads to a wastage of BT radio resources. The same thing is true when the master polls slaves with the POLL packet instead of data packet.

The BT polling methods are responsible for controlling access to the BT channel and slot utilization. However, the BT specification has left open the method for accessing the radio channel. Most of the current implementations use the Round Robin (RR) policy for scheduling transmissions in BT piconets as it is easy to implement and does not require a lot of complexity. However, RR does not perform well when the traffic arriving at the different slaves is not uniform.

2.2   Conventional Algorithms

Most of the work in literature deals with the problem of designing efficient MAC scheduling and SAR policies in BT. This is motivated by the need to achieve maximum slot usage, minimum average packet delays, fairness among all the scheduled connections and adaptive usage of different packet types that are available as per the BT standard.

The Pure Round Robin (RR)[2] scheme was suggested as the default scheduling algorithm for BT MAC. This scheme (RR) defines a fixed cyclic order in which every slave gets a chance to transmit one data packet, irrespective of whether they have data to transmit or not. The limitation of this algorithm is that all the master-slave pairs are polled at the same rate, wasting slots in the case when slaves do not have any data to transmit.

The Deficit Round Robin (DRR) algorithm [3] behaves almost like RR, but gives higher priority to active slaves with backlogged data and thus improves the behavior of the RR algorithm. For example, with only upstream traffic, the DRR algorithm polls each slave until it has no more data, which corresponds to reception of a NULL packet from the slave. However, the behavior of the DRR algorithm reveals certain weaknesses. For example, if there are many packets waiting in a slave's queue, DRR becomes unfair on a short time scale since it polls this slave until its queue becomes empty, while the other slaves of the *piconet* wait with their data, which increases the delays of packets in their queues.

3   Proposed Work

3.1   Issues with Scheduling Algorithms

When comparing different polling algorithms, the main criteria to take into account as required by BT are efficiency, fairness, and low complexity.

- Efficiency implies transmission of the maximum amount of data. In particular, time slots should not be wasted by using too many POLL and NULL packets, which prevents the transmission of data packets waiting in queues.
- Fairness implies a fair distribution of both bandwidth and delays among the different slaves, independent of the flow characteristics.
- Further, the algorithm should not be complex, as increase in complexity increases the manufacturing costs and the power consumption.

Moreover, polling algorithms have to be as independent as possible of other layers in order to easily fit into the BT stack. With these issues in mind, we propose a polling algorithm which is fair and efficient and has low complexity. We first describe and discuss the ideas and principles of this new polling scheme. Then, we analyze in detail its features and other related issues. We also support our idea with the help of experimental results.

3.2   Principle

We start by noting that RR scheme is a very *fair* scheduling mechanism and if all slaves have uniform amount of data, it performs the best. The most important drawback with the RR algorithm, however, is the round-robin scheme adopted for polling and also there is no QoS support for traffic in this scheme. We aim at polling the slaves in a dynamic order depending on a few factors described later in detail. The new polling scheme which we refer to as the optimal parameterized scheduling (OPS) algorithm, dynamically assigns slots to active slaves in a *piconet* depending on queue length at each of these slaves and QoS parameters defined for the *piconet*. We propose here

- An SPSA algorithm to find the optimal threshold queue length values for allocating timeslots to each of the polled slaves.
- A modified round robin (MRR) heuristic for polling slaves, that is seen to improve performance considerably.

In this model a queue for each active slave is maintained at master. $Q_{s,i}$ represents the queue of slave i for master and $Q_{m,i}$, the queue of the master for slave i. The QoS requests (FR and MD) and Traffic for each slave is fed to a slave analyzer. Using ITP from QoS requests, the state of $Q_{m,i}$ and the characteristics of the traffic through baseband layer, the slave analyzer computes the following:

1. An instantaneous probability of data being ready in $Q_{s,i}$ ($P_{data_{s,i}}$)
2. An instantaneous probability of data being ready in $Q_{m,i}$ ($P_{data_{m,i}}$).

3. Number of Slots since Last Poll (NSLP) for slave to master in the upstream traffic ($N_{s,i}$).
4. NSLP for master to slave in the downstream traffic ($N_{m,i}$).

Then, each slave analyzer provides to the Selection algorithm two parameters P_{data_i} and N_i, defined as follows:

$$P_{data_i} = P_{data_{s,i}} + P_{data_{m,i}} \qquad (1)$$

$$N_i = N_{s,i} + N_{m,i} \qquad (2)$$

Selecting the slave with the highest P_{data_i} increases the chance of having data packets transmitted; thus, P_{data_i} is directly linked to efficiency. The parameter N_i is used to limit the delays for each slave, and is linked to fairness. Using all P_{data_i} and N_i values, the selection algorithm decides which slave has the highest priority.

Since $0 \leq P_{data_i} \leq 1$ and $N_i \geq 1$, the algorithm calculates first $\sum_i P_{data_i}$ (which is greater than zero as long as there is more than one active flow) and $\sum_i N_i$, in order to obtain the following.

$$p_{data_i} = \frac{P_{data_i}}{\sum_i P_{data_i}} \quad \text{and} \quad n_i = \frac{N_i}{\sum_i N_i} \qquad (3)$$

Thus n_i represents an estimate of fraction of the number of slots received by slave i upto the current instant. Also, p_{data_i} is an estimate of the total amount of data exchanged between slave i and master out of the total data exchanged upto that instant.

As it is clear that P_{data_i} represents efficiency and N_i represents the fairness factor, we can define a parameter α, which can be used to control efficiency and fairness.

$$P_{r_i} = \alpha * p_{data_i} + (1 - \alpha) * n_i \qquad (4)$$

To be efficient, α must be close to 1. In case one does not require much efficiency but wants to have more fairness, then the value of α should be close to 0. This parameter α should be ideally set by HCI layer and passed on to MAC layer. Through simulations the ideal value of α was determined to be between 0.7 and 0.8.

However, BT packet, after its segmentation by the L2CAP, may require several Baseband packets to be fully transmitted. If the master of the *piconet* started but has not finished receiving all Baseband packets for a BT packet from slave i, that means that Baseband packets of this BT packet are waiting in $Q_{s,i}$. Consequently, the master is sure that the next time it polls slave i, it will receive a Baseband packet with data. In that case, as the presence of data in $Q_{s,i}$ is certain, the probability must be $P_{data_{s,i}} = 1$.

The poller must now determine when it has received the first segments of a BT packet but not the whole BT packet. A simple way is to compare the length of the Baseband packet and its maximum possible length. If they are different, the end of the transmission of the BT packet is then reached, otherwise the transmission of the BT packet will require at least another Baseband packet.

3.3   Optimal Parameterized Scheduling

In a typical situation, each slave in the *piconet* has varying data input rates. Consequently, numerous baseband slots are wasted by polling sources with low input rate, thereby decreasing link utilization, increasing queuing delay and leading to unfair sharing of bandwidth. To address these issues, we propose a scheduling algorithm that assigns time slots to slave and master queues according to the amount of payload in each queue. Further, priorities are set based on flow bits. [4] describes the simultaneous perturbation stochastic approximation (SPSA) algorithm, which we use to find optimal values for queue length thresholds at each slave. The main idea here is to estimate the gradient using simulation output performance measures at only two settings of the N-dimensional parameter vector being optimized rather than $N + 1$ or $2N$ settings required by the usual symmetric difference estimates.

The idea in the following is that we divide each queue at the slave nodes into three regions based on two queue length thresholds N_1 and N_2 that are tuned according to the algorithm below. If queue length at a slave node is less than N_1 when the slave is polled, one time slot is allotted; if it is between N_1 and N_2, three time slots are allotted and if it exceeds N_2, five time slots are allotted to the polled slave. Our algorithm computes online the optimal values of N_1 and N_2. Let $N_1(n)$ and $N_2(n)$ respectively denote the threshold updates at the nth iteration of the algorithm. Then we have the following algorithm.

Suppose $\Gamma : R \rightarrow [a_{min}, a_{max}]$ denote the projection operator defined as

$$\Gamma(x) = max(a_{min}, min(x, a_{max})). \tag{5}$$

Let $\delta > 0$ be a small constant. Let $\Delta_i(n)$, $i = 1, 2$ and $n \geq 0$ be independent and identically distributed (i.i.d) random variables having the symmetric Bernoulli distribution $\Delta_i(n) = \pm 1$ w.p.1/2. Let $\{a(n)\}$ and $\{b(n)\}$ be two step-size sequences that satisfy the following condition.

$$\sum_n a(n) = \sum_n b(n) = \infty; \quad \sum_n a(n)^2, \sum_n b(n)^2 < \infty; \quad a(n) = o(b(n)). \tag{6}$$

The above are standard requirements on step-size sequences. In particular, the last condition above implies that $a(n)$ converges to 0 faster than $b(n)$. Let $L \geq 1$ be a given integer. Also, let

$$\hat{\theta}(n) = (N_1(n) + \delta.\Delta_1(n), N_2(n) + \delta.\Delta_2(n))^T \tag{7}$$

denote a perturbed parameter vector at the nth epoch. We assume that simulations are run according to the parameter, $\hat{\theta}(n)$, $n \geq 0$. Then we have,

$$N_1(n + 1) = \Gamma\left(N_1(n) - a(n)\frac{Z(nL)}{\delta\Delta_1(n)}\right) \tag{8}$$

$$N_2(n + 1) = \Gamma\left(N_2(n) - a(n)\frac{Z(nL)}{\delta\Delta_2(n)}\right) \tag{9}$$

$$Z(nL+m+1) \;=\; (1-b(n))Z(nL+m) + b(n)h(q(nL+m)), \; \forall m = 0,1,2,...,L-1 \tag{10}$$

Here $h(.)$ denotes a cost function, which we take to be the queue length itself. Note that iteration (10) is run over L epochs in between two successive updates of (8) - (9). This results in good algorithmic behavior. We set $L = 100$ in our experiments. Using a standard Ordinary Differential Equation(O.D.E) based analysis, it can be seen that (10) converges as $n \to \infty$ with

$$\|Z(nL) \;-\; J(\theta(n) + \delta\Delta(n))\| \;\longrightarrow\; 0 \tag{11}$$

Here $J(\theta(n) + \delta\Delta(n)) \triangleq J(\hat{\theta}(n))$ is defined as

$$J(\hat{\theta}(n)) \;=\; \lim_{p \to \infty} \frac{1}{p} \sum_{i=0}^{p-1} h(q(i)) \tag{12}$$

where for all $i \geq 0$, $q(i)$ is governed according to $\hat{\theta}(n)$. From the above, we can rewrite (8) and (9) as

$$N_i(n+1) \;=\; \Gamma\left(N_i(n) \;-\; a(n)\frac{J(\theta(n) + \delta\Delta(n))}{\delta\Delta_i(n)} \right), \; \forall i = 1,2 \tag{13}$$

One can write the Taylor series expansion of $J(\theta(n) + \delta\Delta(n))$ as

$$J(\theta(n) + \delta\Delta(n)) \;=\; J(\theta(n)) \;+\; \delta\Delta(n)^T\nabla J(\theta(n)) \;+\; o(\delta). \tag{14}$$

Thus for $i = 1,2,...,n$, we have

$$\frac{J(\theta(n) + \delta\Delta(n))}{\delta\Delta_i(n)} \;=\; \frac{J(\theta(n))}{\delta\Delta_i(n)} + \nabla_i J(\theta(n)) + \sum_{j=1,j\neq i}^{n} \frac{\Delta_j(n)}{\Delta_i(n)} \nabla_j J(\theta(n)) + O(\delta) \tag{15}$$

Now we note that

$$\mathbb{E}\left[\frac{J(\theta(n))}{\delta\Delta_i(n)} | \theta(n) \right] \;=\; 0 \tag{16}$$

$$\mathbb{E}\left[\sum_{j=1,j\neq i}^{n} \frac{\Delta_j(n)}{\Delta_i(n)} \nabla_j J(\theta(n)) | \theta(n) \right] \;=\; 0 \tag{17}$$

Thus,

$$\mathbb{E}\left[\frac{J(\theta(n) + \delta\Delta(n))}{\delta\Delta_i(n)} | \theta(n) \right] \;=\; \nabla_i J(\theta(n)) \;+\; O(\delta). \tag{18}$$

Hence (8), (9) and (10) can be used to asymptotically track the trajectories of the O.D.E.

$$\dot{N}_i = \hat{\Gamma}(-\nabla_i J(\theta(t))), \quad i = 1,2 \tag{19}$$

where for any bounded and continuous $v(.)$, $\hat{\Gamma}(v(.))$ is defined as

$$\hat{\Gamma}(v(y)) = \lim_{\eta \to 0} \left(\frac{\Gamma(y + \eta v(y)) - \Gamma(y)}{\eta} \right). \tag{20}$$

The fixed points of the above O.D.E correspond to the set $K = \{\theta | \hat{\Gamma}(\nabla_i J(\theta)) = 0, \text{ where } i = 1, 2\}$. We have the following main result.(for a proof, see [4])

Theorem 1. *In the limit as $\delta \to 0$ and $n \to \infty$, we have $\theta(n) = (N_1(n), N_2(n))$ asymptotically converges to set K, where $N_1(n)$ and $N_2(n)$ are given by (8)-(9).*

Note that K is the set of all Kuhn-Tucker points and not just local minima. In principle, the algorithm may converge to any Kuhn-Tucker point, however, because of the gradient descent nature of the algorithm, the scheme actually converges to a local minimum.

For conduct of our simulations, the following parameters were chosen:

$$a(0) = b(0) = 1, \delta = 0.1, a(n) = \frac{100}{n}, b(n) = \frac{1}{n^{0.7}}, Z(0) = 0, a_{min} = 0, a_{max} = 50$$

The slot assignment policy can be given as follows:

- Count the *payload*
- Let $q(n)$ denote the queue length for a given slave at nth decision epoch; assign a certain number of time slots at nth epoch as below.
- If $q(n) \geq N_2$, assign 5 time slots to that slave
- Else if $N_1 \leq q(n) < N_2$, assign 3 time slots to that slave
- Else if $N_1 > q(n) > 0$, assign 1 time slot to that slave
- Else switch to the next slave

It was found that the SPSA based algorithm converges to $N_1 = 15$ and $N_2 = 30$, respectively, for which we get a stable and optimized performance in terms of queue lengths of slaves.

Next, for scheduling between slaves, we propose and use a modified round robin (MRR) policy whereby if after a slave is polled, it is observed that it has no data to send, then that slave is not polled for another K_0 cycles. From our simulations, we observed that a choice of $K_0 = 8$ works well. Hence we use $K_0 = 8$ in our simulations (below).

4   Description of Simulation

The simulator used is the same as that used in the implementation of BT stack by IBM called Bluehoc 2.0 [8]. Bluehoc simulator is the BT extension of Network Simulator (ns-version 2.1b7a) [9]. The Bluehoc simulation program implements basic features of BT radio, BT baseband, L2CAP and LMP specifications along with Round Robin scheduling algorithm. The Bluehoc implementation only provides for one way traffic from master to slaves. We have made changes to the Bluehoc code to make it into a two way traffic as happens in real networks. In addition we have implemented the RR and DRR algorithms in addition to implementation of our own algorithm. All simulations were performed on a *piconet* consisting of four slaves and a master. For all the measurement points, enough simulations have been run to claim a 90% confidence that the average results shown have less than 10% error.

4.1   Data Traffic Model

Data traffic was generated for each master-slave pair independently. The length of the data packets was also assumed to be i.i.d exponentially distributed with an average packet size of 1500 bytes. The load in the *piconet* was varied by varying the inter-arrival times (ITP) for the packets. For instance, for low-load scenario, inter-arrival time was increased and for high-load scenario inter-arrival time was decreased. We implemented and compared three algorithms namely Round Robin (RR) Scheduling or RR Service polling, Deficit Round-Robin (DRR) and our own implementation, which we refer to as Optimized Parameter Scheduling (OPS) algorithm.

We have used three important performance metrics for evaluating our algorithm and comparing it with the existing algorithm. These are throughput, end-to-end delay and fairness.

- *Throughput* gives an indication of how much data a connection can receive per second.
- *End-to-end delay* of a packet is defined as delay incurred from the time the packet is enqueued in the transport layer buffer to the time it is dequeued. The total channel capacity in our case was $1Mbps$.
- *Fairness* has been calculated separately in terms of both throughput and delay as explained below using means given in [5].

Assuming that there are n individual connections (these include master-to-slave and slave-to-master connections, each considered separately), and T_i is the throughput for the i_{th} connection, the *Fairness in throughput* is calculated using (21). If the connections share the bandwidth equally then fairness $f = 1$, else it will be less than 1.

$$Fairness, f(T_1, T_2, ..., T_n) = \frac{(\sum_{i=1}^n T_i)^2}{n \sum_{i=1}^n (T_i)^2} \qquad (21)$$

Fairness in delay is calculated similarly using (22), where D_i represents the average packet delay on every connection between the master and the slaves.

$$Fairness, f(D_1, D_2, ..., D_n) = \frac{(\sum_{i=1}^n D_i)^2}{n \sum_{i=1}^n (D_i)^2} \qquad (22)$$

4.2   Simulation Results

Figure 1(a) shows a comparison of all three algorithms in terms of throughput achieved by the four slaves. It can be easily seen that our algorithm performs the best again among all the three algorithms, and enhances the throughput by $10 - 40\%$ vis-a-vis the RR polling algorithm. The second best algorithm here is the DRR algorithm. We see that our OPS algorithm gives a throughput in the range of 0.45 to $0.8Mbps$. This is due to the reason that SPSA based gradient approximation is used for finding the optimal number of slots for transmission by each slave.

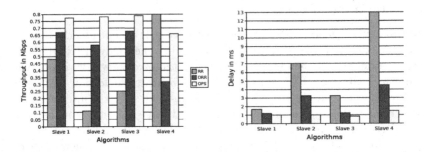

Fig. 1. (a) Comparison of Throughput   (b) Comparison of End-to-End delay

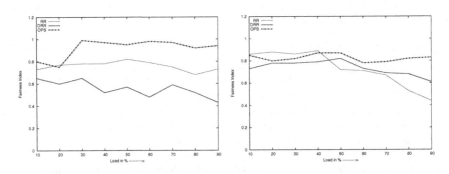

Fig. 2. (a) Fairness in Throughput Vs Load   (b) Fairness in Delay Vs Load

Figure 1(b) shows a comparison of all the three algorithms in terms of End-to-End delay incurred by the various slaves during data transmission. It can be easily seen that the behavior of our OPS algorithm is again much better than that of RR and DRR algorithms. It can be seen from the simulation results that end-to-end delays for slaves 1,2 and 3 are in the range of $1ms$, whereas for slave 4 the same is in the range of 2-4ms, respectively. The reason for the relatively better performance is that we are using MD and $(N_{s,i})$ as restricting parameters for the delays.

Figure 2(a) shows the comparison of *Fairness in Throughput* vs load. It can be seen that the proposed OPS algorithm performs reasonably well and performs much better than DRR. The algorithm RR comes second in this case, as RR algorithm polls all slaves in a strict cyclic order.

Figure 2(b) shows a comparison of fairness in end-to-end packet delays versus load. It can be seen that the proposed OPS scheme performs the best for loads above 40% in terms of end-to-end packet delays for all four slaves. It can be observed as before that the RR algorithm performs better in case of low loads as it is definitely very fair, giving equal opportunity for transmission to all active slaves. Our algorithm also ensures that there is no starvation of resources to slaves, by polling all slaves within the MD request time as in the case of RR algorithm. It is also worth noting that our OPS scheme gives better results at higher number of slaves.

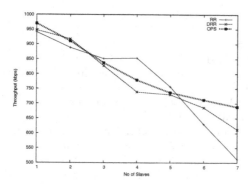

Fig. 3. Comparison of Throughput Vs Number of Slaves

Figure 3 gives the variation in total average throughput as a function of the number of slaves for all the three algorithms under study. It can be seen that the throughput of algorithms using the *RR* scheme drops very fast with increase in number of slaves, where as the OPS algorithm shows a more consistent performance, even when all seven slaves in a piconet are active. It can be seen here that the average throughput achieved by OPS algorithm is between 0.7 to $0.9Mbps$, which shows the least variation in throughput performance amongst all algorithms.

We see that our algorithm performs efficiently in most of the scenarios. The improvement in terms of throughput varies from $10 - 40\%$ vis-a-vis the Round-Robin algorithm. However more important is the fact that the algorithm is efficient and fair.

5   Conclusion and Future Work

In this paper we have suggested an Optimized MAC scheduling scheme which works efficiently in terms of throughput and end-to-end delays, while maintaining fairness among all active slaves in a *piconet*. Our proposed algorithm employs SPSA based gradient estimates to find the optimal number of slots to allocate to each polled slave. Our proposed algorithm also takes into consideration the QoS requests and data rates for various slaves. Our simulation results highlight the significant improvement in the performance of the *piconet*.

There is obviously room for further exploration of the idea presented in this paper. Some of the possible future directions are listed below.

- In the current work, we have considered only ACL traffic consisting of a mix of DHx/DMx packets, however this can be extended for SCO traffic.
- In the present scenario we have used fixed values of α, however, in future the value of α can be varied dynamically depending upon QoS requests and traffic conditions.
- Also, we have shown implementations using our algorithm in a *piconet*, the same can be extended for *scatternets*.

References

1. http://www.bluetooth.com
2. Das, A., Ghose, A., Razdan, A., Saran, H., Shorey, R.: Enhancing performance of asynchronous data traffic over the Bluetooth wireless ad-hoc network. In: INFO-COM, pp. 591–600 (2001)
3. Shreedhar, M., Varghese, G.: Efficient Fair Queueing Using Deficit Round Robin. In: SIGCOMM, pp. 231–242 (1995)
4. Bhatnagar, S., Fu, M.C., Marcus, S.I., Wang, I.-J.: Two-timescale simultaneous perturbation stochastic approximation using deterministic perturbation sequences. ACM Trans. Model. Comput. Simul. 13(2), 180–209 (2003)
5. Daniele, M., Andrea, Z., Gianfranco, L.: Performance Evaluation of Bluetooth Polling Schemes: An Analytical Approach. MONET 9(1), 63–72 (2004)
6. Johansson, N., Korner, U., Johansson, P.: Performance Evaluation of Scheduling Algorithms for Bluetooth. In: IFIP Conference Proceedings, vol. 159, pp. 139–150 (1999)
7. Chatschik, B.: An Overview of the Bluetooth Wireless Technology. In IBM Research Report (2001)
8. http://sourceforge.net/projects/bluehoc
9. http://www.isi.edu/nsnam/ns

EETO: An Energy-Efficient Target-Oriented Clustering Protocol in Wireless Sensor Networks

Weifang Cheng, Xiangke Liao, Changxiang Shen, and Dezun Dong

School of Computer, National University of Defense Technology, China
{wfangch,xliao,shen,dong}@nudt.edu.cn

Abstract. A large number of sensors are usually deployed around some discrete targets in wireless sensor networks for target surveillance purpose. In such networks, clustering is beneficial not only to network management and data aggregation, but also to the target coverage issues. This paper builds a target coverage relation model for target surveillance networks. Based on this model, we abstract the clustering as finding the minimum K-hop dominating set which is proved to be NP complete. Then, we propose a distributed energy-efficient target-oriented clustering protocol (EETO). EETO partitions the network into multiple connected sub-branches based on the corresponding target-oriented relation graph. Each sub-branch is a cluster, where the cluster members are all the K-hop coverage neighbors of the cluster head. EETO groups the sensors which cover the same target set into one cluster. Therefore, related data can be aggregated timely and completely at the cluster head. The message overhead of EETO is only $O(1)$, which is scalable. Detailed simulation results show that EETO reduces energy consumption, improves load balancing and prolongs the coverage lifetime of the network.

1 Introduction

In recent years, wireless sensor networks have received a lot of attention due to their wide applications in military and civilian operations, such as environmental monitoring, battlefield surveillance, and health care [1], [2]. In wireless sensor networks, sensing coverage is a fundamental problem and has been studied by many researchers [3]. A large number of sensors are usually deployed around some discrete targets in the military applications. In such target surveillance networks, the goal of target coverage is to cover the discrete targets efficiently.

There are many NP complete problems about target coverage, such as the maximum coverage with minimum sensors (MCMS) [5] and the maximum set covers problem (MSC) [6], [7]. It is almost impossible to find the optimal solution of such problems in the large sensor networks [3]. Therefore, the distributed solutions are needed, but distributed approaches are only based on the localized information so that they cannot get the optimal solution. In this paper, we borrow the clustering idea to decrease the scale of coverage problems, which partitions the large scale problem into multiple small intra-cluster sub-problems. Clustering is beneficial to large networks since it can adapt quickly to system

T. Janowski and H. Mohanty (Eds.): ICDCIT 2007, LNCS 4882, pp. 31–41, 2007.

changes and scale well. Current clustering algorithms mainly consider reducing data transmissions to save energy and prolong the network lifetime. They generally have the following concerns: (1) the remaining energy of sensors; (2) the distance of cluster heads and sink; (3) the position distribution of cluster heads; (4) the intra-cluster communication cost. However, few of these algorithms consider the requirements of targets surveillance networks. In these algorithms, sensors monitoring the common target may belong to different clusters, so that we cannot solve the coverage sub-problems within the cluster. Moreover, the related data derived from the same target cannot be aggregated timely and completely at the cluster head. Therefore, it is necessary to design new clustering approaches for targets surveillance networks.

As is shown in above analysis, we observe that the sensors monitoring the same target set naturally cluster together. The targets covered by different clusters do not overlap, so the optimal solutions of the clusters can combine to the global optimal solution of the network. Therefore, the scale of the coverage issues can be degraded. Furthermore, since the related data of the same targets are derived from sensors in the same cluster, they can be aggregated timely and completely at the cluster head. Thus we can argue that clustering like this meets the requirements of target surveillance networks.Based on the observation, we build a target coverage relation model for the target surveillance networks. Then we abstract the clustering as finding the minimum K-hop dominating set which is proved to be NP complete. Finally we propose a distributed energy-efficient target-oriented clustering protocol (EETO). The message overhead of EETO is only .

The rest of this paper is organized as follows. Section 2 discusses related work. Section 3 defines the notions of the target coverage model, describes the clustering problem and proves it to be NP complete. Section 4 presents the EETO protocol in detail. Section 5 illustrates an example and proves the correctness and completeness of EETO. Section 6 shows the effectiveness of EETO via simulations. Finally, Section 7 gives concluding remarks and directions for future work.

2   Related Work

LEACH [9] is the first clustering routing protocol in wireless sensor networks. LEACH is executed periodically. The process of every round is as follows. In the cluster set-up phase, each node chooses a random number between 0 and 1. If the number is less than a threshold, the node becomes a cluster head. The non-cluster-head node decides the cluster to which it will belong based on the received signal strength of the cluster heads. In the data transmission phase, each cluster member transmits its data to its own cluster head in its TDMA slot. Finally the cluster head aggregates all the data and transmits it to the sink. Aiming at the deficiency of threshold computing, DCHS [10] does some improvement.

LEACH-C [11] and LEACH-F [11] make some changes based on LEACH. They both let the base station choose cluster heads. However in LEACH-F, for each cluster the base station creates a cluster head list to indicate the order with which the cluster members take the head.

PEGASIS [12] forms all the nodes as a chain which is the only cluster. The data aggregation is done on the chain one by one, so it saves energy but increases the delay. Lindsey etc. propose binary and three-hierarchy data aggregation approaches [13].

HEED [14] selects cluster heads according to a hybrid of their residual energy and a secondary parameter, such as node proximity to its neighbors or node degree. The clustering process terminates in iterations. Compared to LEACH, its clustering speed is faster and the cluster head distribution is more uniform.

As we can see, the above existing clustering approaches do not consider the targets deployment, so they can not adapt to the requirements of the target surveillance networks. LSCP [15] focuses on the applications where the targets are discovered and tracked through the signal it produced, but they only focus on such special targets. Our approach EETO, however, is especially designed for the target surveillance networks.

3   Target Coverage Relation Model

Given a randomly deployed sensor network, sensors set $S = s_1, s_2, ...s_{N_0}$,and randomly deployed M targets,targets set $A = a_1, a_2, ...a_M$.Then each sensor s_i gets its tentative covered target set $G(s_i) \subseteq A$.A series of definitions of target coverage relation model are given as follows.

Definition 1. *Target Coverage Relation Graph: An undirected weighted graph* $G = (V, E)$, *weight function* $w : E \longrightarrow N$. *Herein,* $V = S$; $\forall i, j = 1...N_0, (s_i, s_j)$ $\in E$. *if and only if* $G(s_i) \bigcap G(s_j) \neq \emptyset$, *i.e., any two nodes have a edge if and only if the intersection of their covered target sets is not empty. The weight of the edge is the cardinality of the intersection, i.e.,* $w(s_i, s_j) = |G(s_i) \bigcap G(s_j)|$.

In the rest of this paper, all the terms, such as "shortest path" and "connected" and "dominating set", are based on the target coverage relation graph, but not the traditional communication graph.

Definition 2. *Relation Degree: In the target coverage graph, the weight of the edge is called the relation degree of the two nodes connected by the edge.*

Definition 3. *Cooperation Degree: In the target coverage graph, for node* s_i, *the sum of the weight of its connected edges is called its cooperation degree, which is denoted by*

$$c(s_i), \forall i = 1...N_0, c(s_i) = \sum_{(s_i, s_j) \in E} w(s_i, s_j) \tag{1}$$

Definition 4. *Coverage Neighbor: In the target coverage graph, the nodes connected by an edge is a coverage neighbor of each other.*

Definition 5. *K-hop Coverage Neighbor: In the target coverage graph, all the nodes which have a shortest path not greater than K with s_i are called as K-hop Coverage Neighbors of s_i.*

Definition 6. *Dominating Set: A subset of the target coverage relation graph $G = (V, E)$, for $\forall s_i \in V$, we get $s_i \in Z$, or $(\exists s_i \in Z)(s_i, s_j) \in E$.*

Definition 7. *Minimum Dominating Set: The dominating set which has the minimum cardinality.*

Definition 8. *K-hop Dominating Set: A subset Z of the target coverage relation graph $G = (V, E)$, for $\forall s_i \in V$, we get $s_i \in Z$, or $(\exists s_i \in Z)$, the shortest path length between s_i and s_j is not greater than K .*

Definition 9. *Minimum K-hop Dominating Set: The K-hop dominating set which has the minimum cardinality.*

Based on the target coverage relation model, wireless sensor network can be modeled as a target coverage relation graph, which consists of several connected sub-graphs. We should note that the term "connected" does not mean the traditional communication but the target coverage relation. Therefore, the nodes in a subgraph group into a cluster naturally.

If occasionally some deployment makes some connected sub-graphs too large, some clusters may be too large. As a result, the load of the cluster heads is unbalanced. In this case, we need partition the large connected sub-graph into multiple small connected sub-branches. In order to control the size of the cluster, we obey the following rule: the shortest path length between any cluster member and its cluster head is not greater than , i.e., all cluster members are the -hop coverage neighbors of its cluster head. Supposing that the maximum node degree is D , if the cluster size is limited to N_{max}, then $1 + D + D^2 + ... + D^k \leq N_{max}$ holds, so we get $K \leq \log_D (N_{max} \times (D - 1) + 1) - 1$.

Thus the clustering of the network is to find the K-hop dominating set Z of its corresponding target coverage relation graph $G = (V, E)$. The nodes in Z are taken as cluster heads which partition G into $|Z|$ connected subbranches. In order to group coverage neighbors in the same cluster, it is better if $|Z|$ is less. Therefore, the optimal clustering issue is to find the minimum K-hop dominating set. When $K = 1$, we get a special case of minimum dominating set problem which has been proved NP complete [4]. Thus the clustering problem of minimum K-hop dominating set is also NP complete.

4   EETO Protocol

Based on the above clustering theory of target coverage relation model, we propose a distributed energy-efficient target-oriented clustering protocol (EETO) in this section. EETO is executed periodically like traditional clustering approaches. Every round includes cluster heads election, cluster formation and data transmission. Firstly we introduce the EETO clustering parameters. Then we explain the key idea of EETO and present the EETO algorithm.

4.1   EETO Clustering Parameter

Analyzing the target coverage relation model, we observe that if one node's co-operation degree is higher, it may have more tentative covered targets. Further-more, its relation degree with coverage neighbors may be higher. If these nodes are elected as cluster heads, there are three disadvantages: firstly, the number of clusters is smaller, which results in an approximate solution of the minimum K-hop dominating set; secondly, the large number of raw data derived from the cluster heads needn't be transmitted and can be directly aggregated, so that the data transmissions are reduced; thirdly, sensors monitoring the common targets and having high relation degree are in the same cluster, which meets our orig-inal intention of clustering. Therefore, the cooperation degree is a natural rule for cluster heads election. Similar to other clustering protocols, prolonging the network lifetime is an important goal of EETO. Since the cluster heads consume energy faster, the remaining energy is one rule of cluster heads election. Thereby, we define the metric function

$$metric(s_i) = \alpha \times e(s_i) + \beta \times c(s_i) \qquad (2)$$

Herein, and is respectively the remaining energy and cooperation degree of , and are the weighted factors. Concerning both energy and cooperation degrees, EETO pre-elects the nodes which have the maximal value among the -hop cov-erage neighbors as the cluster heads.$e(s_i)$ and $c(s_i)$ is respectively the remaining energy and cooperation degree of s_i, α and β Concerning both energy and co-operation degrees, EETO pre-elects the nodes which have the maximal metric value among the K-hop coverage neighbors as the cluster heads.

In general, different nodes may monitor different targets. Even if two nodes monitor the same targets, their view is different. As a result, their energy con-suming is widely divergent. Therefore, it is necessary to exchange metric at every clustering round. The iteration approach of HEED [14] has a little more message overhead. In order to reduce the message overhead, EETO broadcasts among the K-hop coverage neighbors.

In order to ensure that the cluster head can communicate with its cluster members, we suppose that K-hop coverage neighbors can communicate reliably with each other. The first step to find the K-hop coverage neighbors is to find the direct coverage neighbors. All nodes broadcast their tentative covered targets. Each node maintains a direct coverage neighbor table NE, consisting of neighbor ID and corresponding relation degree. If the covered targets of another node intersect with its own, it put this node ID into NE. The NE tables from all the nodes form the global view of the target coverage relation graph.

After finding direct coverage neighbors, nodes discover their K-hop coverage neighbors by flooding beacon messages with ttl not greater than K throughout the network. ttl is the hops of the coverage neighbors passed by the beacon. Besides NE, each node maintains a K-hop coverage neighbor list NK, consisting of neighbor ID and which represents the shortest path length between the neigh-bor and the node. Since the cluster size is limited to N_{max}, the size of NK is not greater than N_{max}. Since the network topology is relatively static, coverage neighbor discovery needn't be executed every clustering round.

4.2 EETO Clustering Algorithm

To simplify the description, we define the following denotations in table 1.

Table 1. EETO denotation and meaning

Denotation	Meaning
NE	Coverage neighbor set
NK	K-hop coverage neighbor set
length(s_i, s_j)	Shortest path length between s_i and s_j
Winner	Pre-elected cluster head
MEMBER	Cluster member set
COMPETE	Competing cluster head set
Head	Final cluster head
M-METRIC	Message including
M-SELECTED	Message to inform some node of being elected as the cluster head
M-HEAD	Message to declare that it is a cluster head
M-CHOICE	Message to declare its own elected cluster head
M-JOIN	Message to declare that it join in some cluster head
M-EXIT	Message to declare that it exit some cluster head

The key idea of EETO is described as follows.

1. Each node broadcasts M-METRIC to NK.

2. Choose the node which has the maximum metric as pre-elected cluster head Winner. At the same time, send M-SELECTED to Winner. All the nodes that received M-SELECTED will finally be the cluster heads.

3. To ensure that the nodes in one cluster consist of a connected subgraph, all the Winners broadcast M-HEAD to NK, so that they can gain nearby nodes to join them.

4. If one node has received multiple M-HEAD, then place the source ID into COMPETE.

5. If one competing cluster head is the direct coverage neighbor, it elects the competing node as Head. If more competing nodes are the direct coverage neighbors, it elects the competing node which has the highest relation degree as Head.

6. Otherwise, in order to balance load, it elects the node which has the minimum length in COMPETE as Head.

7. If multiple competing cluster heads have the same minimum length, the arbitration is needed. We let all the nodes on the shortest path to the cluster head choose the same cluster head. Therefore, the arbitrating node backs off,

waiting for a period proportional to length and letting the closer arbitrating nodes make decision first.

8. In the course of waiting, after receiving M-CHOICE from a coverage neighbor, the node chooses the same Head. If there is no M-CHOICE, after the waiting timer expires, the node randomly elects one node which has the minimum length in COMPET as Head.

9. After arbitrating, if $length < K$, there maybe other nodes waiting for its decision; therefore, it broadcasts M-CHOICE to NE.

10. If the final cluster head is not the pre-elected node, send M-JOIN and M-EXIT to Head and Winner respectively.

Each cluster formed by EETO can be regarded as a sub-network, where sensors are the cluster head and members, and surveillance targets are all the targets covered by all the sensors. When solving coverage problems, the cluster head can perform centralized coverage algorithms, or activate cluster members to do distributed algorithms. The algorithms are performed in the much smaller cluster, so that the efficiency is higher and scales well.

The data transmission phase is similar to LEACH: the cluster members transmit their data to corresponding cluster heads according to their TDMA slots; then cluster heads aggregate data from their members and transmit it to the sink. It is obvious that the relative data derived from the same targets can be timely and completely aggregated at the cluster head, so we need not build multi hierarchies aggregation structure [8]. Moreover, different clusters monitor almost totally different targets, thus the data between different clusters have little redundancy. As a result, the data aggregated by cluster heads can be directly reported to sink, so that the communication delay can be highly reduced.

5 Performance Evaluations

This section evaluates the performance through detailed experiments. All experiments are implemented in MATLAB 7.0 and run on the PC computer with 1.6GHz CPU and 512M memory. We simulated 10000 sensors and 500 targets distributed randomly in an area of $1000m \times 1000m$, with the default sensing range $R_0 = 30m$. The experiments compare EETO with HEED from five aspects as follows:

(1) The percentage of cluster heads;

(2) The distribution of the cluster size;

(3) The percentage of targets covered by different clusters. For briefness, we call such targets as cracked targets.

(4) The percentage of covered targets. A target can not be covered again by the network, if all nodes which can cover the target have died.

(5) Network coverage lifetime. We consider the network lifetime when the first target, half targets or all targets can not be covered. For briefness, we call the three types of network coverage lifetime as FNCL, HNCL and LNCL respectively.

Figure 1 shows that the percentage of cluster heads. It is easy to see that the percentage of cluster heads decreases almost linearly with the increasing of K.

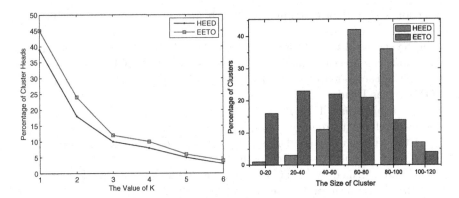

Fig. 1. K vs. percentage of cluster heads

Fig. 2. K=3, distribution of the cluster size

Furthermore, the number of cluster heads in EETO is a little more than that in HEED. This is because that some nodes which are communication neighbors but not coverage neighbors are classified as one cluster in HEED, but in EETO they are in different clusters. More cluster heads mean more clusters, but more clusters do not always affect the network lifetime. Because even the nodes which cover different targets are sorted into the same cluster, they have no relative data. Therefore, their data can not be aggregated at the cluster head. This means that the data transmissions are not reduced, so the consuming energy is not reduced.

The distribution of the cluster size is shown in figure 2. In HEED, the cluster size is well-proportioned, and the size of most clusters is from 60 to 80 or from 80 to 100. This is because HEED protocol balances load by limiting the cluster communication radius. However in EETO, the cluster size is quite disproportioned, and the small clusters with less than 20 nodes have respectable proportion. This is because the targets have imbalanced distribution. In fact, the cluster size is not the standard of load balancing. Even for two clusters with the same size, they cover different targets, and the data redundancy is not identical, so the load is identical neither. However how to balance load among the clusters is our future work.

Figure 3 gives the effect on the percentage of targets covered by different clusters (cracked targets). It is obvious that the greater K results in the lower percentage of cracked targets, because the number of clusters is decreased. As we expect, in EETO the cracked targets are less than about 8% than that in HEED. When , the cracked targets approximate to zero in EETO, but 4.5% in HEED. EETO lets coverage neighbors in the same cluster, thus the performance of EETO is much better than HEED.

Figure 4 shows the percentage of covered targets when time elapses. We can see that the covered percentage in EETO is higher than that in HEED. Moreover, in the first 300 rounds, the EETO curve drops very slowly and slower than HEED. This is because EETO let coverage neighbors in the same cluster, so relative data are aggregated timely and consuming energy is reduced. Therefore the covered time for some targets is prolonged.

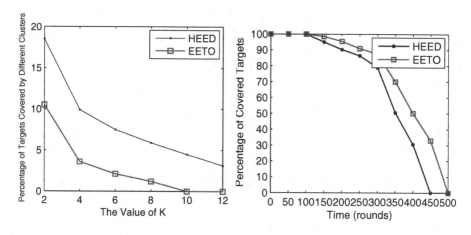

Fig. 3. Targets covered by different clusters   **Fig. 4.** Percentage of covered targets

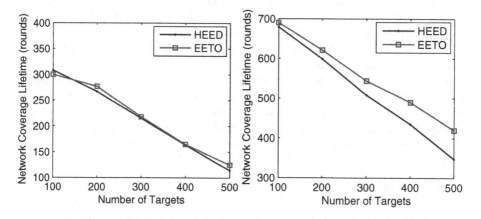

Fig. 5. Coverage lifetime (FNCL)   **Fig. 6.** Coverage lifetime (HNCL)

The relation of the network coverage lifetime and the number of targets is shown in figure 5-7. Obviously the network coverage lifetime decreases with the increasing number of targets. The FNCL curves of HEED and EETO are very close, as shown in figure 5. Because after deployment the target covered by the least nodes will become the first one which can not be covered again, FNCL mainly depends on the energy consuming speed of nodes that cover the target. Therefore clustering algorithms have little improvement on FNCL. However, for HNCL and LNCL, EETO performs much better than HEED, as shown in figure 6 and 7. Especially when the number of targets increases, the performance improvement is remarkable. Since EETO focuses on target surveillance networks, more targets benefit the performance of EETO. As the number of targets increases to 500, the network coverage lifetime improves 17% (HNCL) and 14% (LNCL).

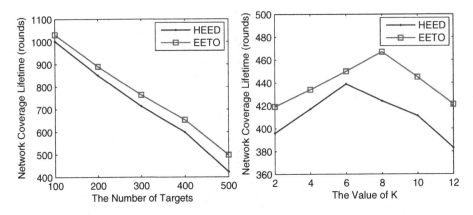

Fig. 7. Coverage lifetime (LNCL)   **Fig. 8.** K vs. coverage lifetime (HNCL)

It is obvious that the value of K has effect on the network load balancing: when K is too small, the benefit of clustering will be very tiny; when K is too great, the cluster size will be very large, which will result in the energy consuming speed of the cluster heads is too rapid. The network coverage lifetime when half targets can not be covered can reflect the performance of load balancing. The higher HNCL means that load is more balanced. Figure 8 shows the relationship of K and HNCL. We can see that EETO performs better than HEED whatever value K has. In practice, K has an optimal value. However the value can not be required by simulations, because it is affected by the distribution of targets and sensors. The issue will be considered in our future work.

6   Conclusions

There are a large number of existing clustering approaches in wireless sensor networks. However, almost all the traditional work study clustering as viewed from routing. Therefore their aims are reducing data transmissions to prolong the network lifetime, but they do not combine the real applications of wireless sensor network. This paper studies the clustering protocols from a fire-new view. In target surveillance networks, clustering is beneficial not only to network management and data aggregation, but also to the solution of target coverage issues. This paper builds a target coverage relation model for target surveillance networks. Based on the model, we abstract the clustering as finding the minimum K-hop dominating set which is proved to be NP complete. Then, we propose a distributed energy efficient target-oriented clustering protocol (EETO). EETO partitions the network into multiple connected sub-branches based on the target-oriented relation graph. Each sub-branch is a cluster, where the cluster members are the K-hop coverage neighbors of the cluster head. EETO groups the sensors which cover the common targets as one cluster. Therefore, the target coverage issues can be decomposed into sub-problems within the cluster. Moreover, related data can be aggregated timely and completely at the cluster head. The message overhead of EETO is $O(1)$, so it is scalable. Detailed simulation results show that EETO not only reduces energy consuming, but also improves load balancing and prolongs the coverage lifetime of the network. In the future work we will study the target coverage issues based on the EETO clustering.

References

1. Akyildiz, I.F., Su, W., Sankarasubramaniam, Y., Cayirci, E.: A survey on sensor networks. ACM Trans. on Multimedia Computing, Communications and Applications, 102–114 (August 2002)
2. Szewczyk, R., Mainwaring, A., Polastre, J., Anderson, J., Culler, D.: An analysis of a large scale habitat monitoring application. In: ACM Conference on Embedded Networked Sensor Systems(SenSys), pp. 214–226 (2004)
3. Cardei, M., Wu, J.: Energy-Efficient Coverage Problems in Wireless Ad Hoc Sensor Networks. Journal of Computer Communications, Special Issue on Sensor Networks (2005)
4. Garey, M.R., Johnson, D.S.: Computers and Intractability: A Guide to the Theory of NP-Completeness. W.H.Freeman and Company, NY (1978)
5. Ai, J., Abouzeid, A.A.: Coverage by directional sensors in randomly deployed wireless sensor networks. Journal of Combinatorial Optimization 11(1), 21–41 (2006)
6. Cardei, M., Du, D.-Z.: Improving Wireless Sensor Network Lifetime through Power Aware Organization. ACM Wireless Networks 11(3), 333–340 (2005)
7. Cardei, M., Thai, M.T., Li, Y., Wu, W.: Energy-Efficient Target Coverage in Wireless Sensor Networks. In: Proceedings of IEEE INFOCOM 2005, Miami, FL (2005)
8. Fan, K.-W., Liu, S., Sinha, P.: Scalable Data Aggregation for Dynamic Events in Sensor Networks. In: Proc. of ACM SENSYS, Boulder, Colorado (2006)
9. Heinzelman, W., Chandrakasan, A., Balakrishnan, H.: Energy-Efficient communication protocol for wireless microsensor networks. In: Proc. of the 33rd Annual Hawaii Int'l. Conf. on System Sciences, pp. 3005–3014. IEEE Computer Society, Maui (2000)
10. Handy, M.J., Haase, M., Timmermann, D.: Low energy adaptive clustering hierarchy with deterministic cluster-head selection. In: Proc. of the 4th IEEE Conf. on Mobile and Wireless Communications Networks, pp. 368–372. IEEE Communications Society, Stockholm (2002)
11. Heinzelman, W.: Application-Specific protocol architectures for wireless networks [Ph.D. Thesis]. Massachusetts Institute of Technology, Boston (2000)
12. Lindsey, S., Raghavendra, C.S.: PEGASIS: Power-Efficient gathering in sensor information systems. In: Proc. of the IEEE Aerospace Conf., pp. 1125–1130. IEEE Aerospace and Electronic Systems Society, Montana (2002)
13. Lindsey, S., Raghavendra, C.S., Sivalingam, K.: Data gathering in sensor networks using the energy*delay metric. In: Proc. of the IPDPS Workshop on Issues in Wireless Networks and Mobile Computing (2001)
14. Younis, O., Fahmy, S.: Heed: A hybrid, energy-efficient, distributed clustering approach for ad-hoc sensor networks. IEEE Trans. on Mobile Computing 3(4), 660–669 (2004)
15. Fang, Q., Zhao, F., Guibas, L.J.: Lightweight sensing and communication protocols for target enumeration and aggregation. In: Proc. of the 4th ACM MobiHoc, pp. 165–176. ACM Press, New York (2003)

On the Design of Mobility-Tolerant TDMA-Based Media Access Control (MAC) Protocol for Mobile Sensor Networks

Arshad Jhumka[1] and Sandeep Kulkarni[2]

[1] Department of Computer Science, University of Warwick, UK
[2] Department of Computer Science and Engineering, Michigan State University, USA
arshad@dcs.warwick.ac.uk, sandeep@cse.msu.edu

Abstract. Several media access control (MAC) protocols proposed for wireless sensor networks assume nodes to be stationary. This can lead to poor network performance, as well as fast depletion of energy in systems where nodes are mobile. This paper presents several results for TDMA-based MAC protocol for mobile sensor networks, and also introduces a novel mobility-aware TDMA-based MAC protocol for mobile sensor networks. The protocol works by first splitting a given round into a control part, and a data part. The control part is used to manage mobility, whereas nodes transmit messages in the data part. In the data part, some slots are reserved for mobile nodes. We show that the protocol ensures collision-freedom in the data part of a schedule.

1 Introduction

Sensor networks are becoming increasingly popular due to the variety of applications that they allow. For example, sensor networks can be deployed in regions for disaster recovery, or in a battlefield where they can be used to collect and relay information. A sensor network consists of a set of sensor nodes that communicate with each other via radio communication. To prevent message collisions, a media access control (MAC) protocol is needed. Different approaches are adopted for designing such protocols. For example, a Time Division Multiple Access (TDMA) protocol can be used to divide time into a sequence of slots. Each node is then assigned a set of time slots in which it can transmit messages. Two nodes can transmit messages in the same slot if and only if their messages will not collide. This guarantees absence of collisions. Another technique that is widely used is CSMA/CA approach, where nodes adopt a handshaking approach before sending messages. Such an approach is adopted in IEEE 802.11. This type of approach is known as collision avoidance.

In this paper, we focus on the problem of providing a TDMA-based MAC protocol for sensor networks in which nodes are mobile. Such networks can be found in several situations, e.g., disaster recovery with workers equipped with sensor devices, or on a battlefield. Most MAC protocols proposed for wireless sensor networks assume that nodes are stationary. These may not work well in mobile sensor

T. Janowski and H. Mohanty (Eds.): ICDCIT 2007, LNCS 4882, pp. 42–53, 2007.

networks, leading to poor network performance. Moreover, because of the scarcity of energy in sensor networks, MAC protocols tend to optimize battery lifetime. Battery lifetime is optimized when the protocols at the datalink layer put the sensors in sleep mode, only to wake up periodically for communication. One event that drains energy from sensor nodes is message transmissions. To minimize this, MAC protocols need to ensure that collisions are avoided. However, MAC protocols optimized for energy use in static networks may lead to a fast depletion of energy in mobile sensor networks because of unexpected collisions. Hence, MAC protocols for mobile networks need to handle mobility in an efficient way.

1.1 Contributions

We make the following contributions for TDMA-based MAC protocols:

- We introduce two novel mobility models, namely *intra-cluster* and *inter-cluster* mobility that are general enough to capture various existing mobility models such as random movement, going in specific direction, going at a maximum speed etc.
- We show that it is impossible to guarantee collision-freedom under an arbitrary slot assignment in presence of both intra-, and inter-cluster mobility.
- We identify underlying causes for the impossibility results, and develop a static TDMA-based algorithm that tolerates both intra-, and inter-cluster mobility.
- We provide a novel TDMA-based mobility-tolerant protocol, M_TDMA (mobile TDMA), that guarantees collision-freedom in the data part of a schedule in the presence of both intra-, and inter-cluster mobility. The algorithm is fully distributed.

1.2 Paper Structure

In Sect 2, we present related work. We present the different models we use in the paper in Sect 3, and in Sect 4, we formalize the problem of collision-free communication in TDMA-based system. In Sect 5, we develop static TDMA-based algorithms that are mobility-tolerant. In Sect 6, we develop an adaptive mobility-tolerant MAC protocol that is based on TDMA. For reasons of space, proofs have been omitted and can be found in [7].

2 Related Work

We here survey related work on MAC protocols, and mobility.

MAC protocols for static networks: Collision-avoidance protocols [19] are based on the premise that nodes sense the medium before transmitting, whereby collisions are avoided. If the medium is busy, then the nodes wait for increasingly longer period of time before retransmitting, using the exponential backoff technique. Another collision-avoidance protocol, S-MAC [20], is based on IEEE

802.11. It introduces coordinated sleep/wakeup cycles to extend the battery life of the sensors to minimize the amount of energy used.

On the other hand, there are protocols that guarantee collision-freedom. For example, techniques such as frequency division multiple access (FDMA) [15] and code division multiple access (CDMA) [17] and TDMA [2] ensure that collisions do not occur during communications. FDMA works by asssigning different frequencies to nodes, making it unsuitable for sensor networks. CDMA works by requiring that codes used used to encode messages are orthogonal to each other. The encoding/decoding processes are too expensive to run on sensor nodes. On the other hand, TDMA works by splitting the time line into slots, which are then allocated to nodes. The problem with the approaches above is that they are not suitable to sensor networks where nodes are mobile.

MAC protocols for mobile sensor networks: One mobility-aware MAC protocol is MS-MAC [11], which builds on top of S-MAC. It incorporates a mobility-handling mechanism that passes mobility information on messages. An active zone is created around a mobile node such that all nodes that are within the active zone run the synchronization period of S-MAC more often, resulting in lower connection time. This work differs from ours in that their stated goal is lower connection time. In contrast, our goal is collision-freedom. Another work that addresses topology changes is by Herman and Tixueil [6]. The TDMA protocol that they proposed is self-stabilizing, and resilient to topology changes. However, the topology changes are brought about by nodes leaving the network. In contrast, our approach tolerate topology changes when nodes can both join and leave the network. The mobility-aware protocol (MMAC) by Ali et.al [1] is based on TRAMA [12], a scheduling-based protocol for static networks. MMAC works by introducing a mobility-adaptive frame time, enabling the protocol to adapt to mobility patterns. The protocol uses a localization service to be able to predict the future position of nodes. The sensitivity of their protocol to wrong prediction is not known. In contrast, our approach does not rely on a localization service, and also does not depend on computing the 2-hop neighbourhood. Another strand of work focuses on tolerating bit errors that resulting from Doppler shifts, as a result of mobility [13]. This bit errors cause frame corruptions, and hence retransmissions that in turn deplete the energy resources of the system. Some variations of this protocol by the same authors appear in [14].

Mobility models: In our paper, we introduce two novel mobility models, namely the intra-, and inter-cluster mobility. A comprehensive survey on mobility models can be found in [3]. The most widely used model is perhaps the random walk mobility model (also known as Brownian movement [5]). A slight enhancement of this is the Random Waypoint model [8], in which pauses are introduced between changes of directions and speed. It is argued that these models do not faithfully reflect reality. A recent work on mobility models [10] sought to address this problem, and develop a mobility model based on social theory. The model comprises one aspect with the establishment of the model, and another part that deals with the evolution and dynamics of the model. The authors argue that, in MANETs, individuals with similar incentives will tend to aggregate. Mobility models for MANETs may not be suitable for sensor networks as applications for sensor networks are likely to be for tracking, monitoring, which is not the case for MANETs. However, the models we introduce is general enough to permit modeling of more sophisticated models.

3   Models and Assumptions

Sensor node. A sensor node (for short, node) is a device that is equipped with a sensor component for environment sensing and a radio component for communication. A node is battery-powered. We assume that nodes do not have access to devices such as GPS. Every node has a unique id. We also assume each node to have a clock, and that all nodes are synchronized in time, using an appropriate clock synchronization protocol [16].

Communication. Sensor nodes communicate via radio signals. We assume that each sensor has a communication range C and an interference range I. The communication range of a sensor is the maximum distance up to which its radio signal is strong enough for communication with a high probability. When a node k is in the communication range of another node l, we say that k is in the *i-band* (read as inner band) of l. On the other hand, the interference range is the maximum distance over which the strength of the signal is non-negligible, where communication can occur with low probability. When a node k is in the interference range of another node l, but is outside l's communication range, we say that k is in the *o-band* (read as outer-band) of l.

We denote the set of nodes with which a node n can communicate as $Comm(n)$, and the set of nodes at which node n can interfere as $Int(n)$. In general, $Comm(n) \subseteq Int(n)$, for each n. Given two nodes i, and j, if there exists a node $k \in Comm(i) \cap Int(j)$, then we say that i and j can collide at k. We can also say that j and i can interfere at k.

Topology. We consider the network as an undirected graph $S = (V, E)$. However, with nodes being mobile, the graph changes into $S' = (V', E')$, where $V' \subseteq V$, because some nodes may fail too.

Collisions. Message collisions can occur either when a sensor is receiving messages originating from different sensors or when it is sending a message while receiving another.

Clusters. A cluster is a set of nodes, with a designated clusterhead. We denote a cluster i by C_i, and its head by h_i. In this paper, whenever the identity of the head is important, we will denote cluster C_i by $cluster(h_i)$. In our work, we use the clustering algorithm by Demirbas et.al [4] at startup.

Mobility model. In this paper, we introduce two new mobility models:

- Intra-cluster mobility, and
- inter-cluster mobility

To be able to define these notions of mobility, we define the *state of a cluster* C_i *at instant* $n \geq 0$ to be (C_i^n, T_i^n), where C_i^n is the set of nodes in cluster C_i at instant n (this could be time period n, n^{th} snapshot or slot n), and T_i^n is the topology of cluster C_i at instant n. Whenever the topology and instant is not important, we will refer to a cluster only by C_i.

intra-cluster mobility: When nodes are mobile, if they remain within their assigned cluster, the set of nodes within that cluster remains unchanged, though the topology may change. Given two consecutive states of a cluster C_i, i.e., given (C_i^n, T_i^n) and (C_i^{n+1}, T_i^{n+1}), we say there is *intra-cluster mobility in cluster* C_i at instant $(n+1)$ if $C_i^n = C_i^{n+1}$ and $T_i^n \neq T_i^{n+1}$.

inter-cluster mobility: When a node leaves its cluster, it has either crashed or has joined a new one due to mobility, causing the set of nodes in its original cluster to change. Similarly, when a clusterhead h_i crashes or joins a new cluster C_j, causing its previous cluster C_i to cease to exist, using our notation for cluster states, we denote the remaining set of nodes by $(\emptyset_i^{n+1}, \emptyset_i^{n+1})$ - note that this set of nodes is not a cluster since it does not have a head.

Given cluster C_i with states (C_i^n, T_i^n) and (C_i^{n+1}, T_i^{n+1}), we say that *node p has left cluster C_i at instant* $(n+1)$ if $p \in C_i^n \wedge p \notin C_i^{n+1}$. We also say that *node p has joined cluster C_i at instant* $(n+1)$ if $p \notin C_i^n \wedge p \in C_i^{n+1}$. We say that there is there is *inter-cluster mobility from cluster C_i to cluster C_j* if there exists instants t_1 and t_2, and a node p such that p has left C_i at t_1, and joined C_j at t_2. Note that there need not be any relationship between t_1 and t_2 since a clusterhead may detect the presence of a new node n before the previous head detects n's absence.

TDMA Service

TDMA is a technique whereby the timeline is split into a series of time periods (or periods), and each period is divided into a series of time slots. Each node is then assigned a slot in which it transmit its message in every period. Slots have to be assigned carefully to avoid message collisions. Because slot assignment in TDMA is closely linked with the network topology, any topology change is likely to invalidate the assignment, causing collisions. To address this problem, we develop several results for TDMA in mobile sensor networks.

4   Problem Formulation, and Some Issues

We express the problem of collision-free MAC protocol for mobile sensor networks as follows: Given a sensor network $S = (V, E)$, develop a slot assignment protocol that ensures collision-free communication both in the absence and presence of (i) intra-cluster mobility, and (ii) inter-cluster mobility.

Since the protocol is based on TDMA, we first provide a formalization for slot assignment in a TDMA protocol, which generalizes that developed by Kulkarni and Arumugam [9]. Assume the timeline is broken down into a sequence of rounds $p_1, p_2, \ldots$, and each round p_i is divided into n equal slots. When a node joins a system, it needs to know about three parameters, namely (i) in which round it can *start* transmitting, (ii) at what *frequency*, and (iii) in which *slot* $(1 \ldots n)$. Thus, a node i will be given the information $(start\_round_i, frequency_i, slot_i)$ to determine when to transmit a message. Using this information, the node can compute the set of slots in which it can transmit as follows:

$$slots\_set_i = \{n * (start\_round_i - 1) + slot_i\} \cup$$
$$\{s | \forall k : 1 \ldots, s = (n * (start\_round_i - 1) + slot_i) + (k * frequency_i * n)\}$$

Two nodes j and k have overlapping slots if $(slots\_set_j \cap slots\_set_k \neq \emptyset)$. We then formalize the problem as follows:

> Assign $(start\_round_i, frequency_i, slot_i)$ information to each node i such that *two nodes j and k have overlapping slots if and only if they are not in the collision group of each other.*

The collision group (CG) of a sensor node n is defined as follows:

$$CG(n) = \{m | m \in Comm(n) \text{ or } \exists k \text{ such that } m \text{ and } n \text{ can interfere at } k\}$$

We now present two different approaches to solve the problem. In the first approach, we develop a slot assignment that is inherently resilient to mobility. However, the approach has a worst-case latency. To address this worst-case latency, we develop a scalable slot assignment protocol that is adaptive to mobility.

We denote the set of slots assigned to node n under a given assignment A as $slots\_set_n^A$. Whenever assignment A is trivial, we will denote the slot assigned as $slots\_set_n$. From the formalization of TDMA, we define collision-freedom:

Definition 1 (Collision freedom). *Given a network $S = (V, E)$, we say that S is collision-free under a time-slot assignment $A : V \to 2^N$ if $\forall k, l \in V, k \neq l : slots\_set_k^A \cap slots\_set_l^A \neq \emptyset \Rightarrow k \notin CG(l) \land l \notin CG(k)$.*

Whenever the assignment is obvious from the context, we will say that network S is collision-free instead of S is collision-free under assignment A.

Proposition 1. *Given a network S that is collision-free under an assignment A. Any subnetwork $S' = (V', E')$, where $V' \subseteq V$ and $E' = \{(v, v') | v, v' \in V' \land (v, v') \in E\}$ is also collision-free under A.*

Theorem 1 (Collision-freedom and intra-cluster mobility).
Given a cluster C_i that is collision-free under assignment A such that $\exists m, n \in C_i \cdot slots\_set_m \cap slots\_set_n \neq \emptyset$. Then, it is impossible to guarantee collision-freedom in presence of arbitrary intra-cluster mobility.

Theorem 2 (Collision-freedom and inter-cluster mobility).
Given cluster C_i, and C_k that are both collision-free under assignment A such that $\exists m \in C_i, n \in C_k \cdot (slot\_set_m \cap slots\_set_n \neq \emptyset)$. Then, it is impossible to guarantee collision-freedom in presence of arbitrary inter-cluster mobility.

Because mobility can now bring a node that was formerly outside the collision group of another node within its collision group, we look at the impact of assigning to every node a unique time slot in which to transmit.

5   Static TDMA-Based MAC Protocol

We now state the following two lemmas.

Lemma 1 (Collision-freedom in presence of inter-cluster mobility).
Define the set of slots used by a cluster C_i^n at instant n by $\bigcup_{i \in C_i^n}$ slots_set$_i$, and denote it by slots(C_i^n). Given two collision-free clusters C_k^n and C_l^n at instant n. If slots(C_k^n) $\cap$ slots(C_l^n) $= \emptyset$, then (i) $\forall i \in C_k^n$, the cluster $C_l^{n+1} = C_l^n \cup \{i\}$ is collision-free, and (ii) the cluster $C_k^{n+1} = C_k^n \setminus \{i\}$ is also collision-free.

Lemma 1 states that whenever slots asssigned to clusters do not overlap, there can be free movement of nodes between clusters.

Lemma 2 (Collision-freedom in presence of intra-cluster mobility)
Given a collision-free cluster (C_k^n, T_k^n) at instant n, such that $\forall m, n \in C_k^n \cdot$ slots _set$_m$ $\cap$ slots_set$_n$ $= \emptyset$. Assume there is intra-cluster mobility in C_k at instant $(n + 1)$. Then, cluster (C_k^{n+1}, T_k^{n+1}) remains collision-free in presence of intra-cluster mobility at instant $(n + 1)$.

From the two lemmas, it is clear that assigning each node a distinct set of slots guarantee collision-freedom in presence of both intra-, and inter-cluster mobility. We present a trivial algorithm that implements it:

```
Given sensor network S = (V,E)
algorithm
      round int init 0;sensor_num int init 1;
      for each node i ∈ S do{
          assign (1, 1,sensor_num) to i;
          sensor_num := sensor_num++;}od
```

Fig. 1. Algorithm ensuring each node has a distinct slots set

However, each round will be n slots long, leading to a latency of $O(n)$, where n is the network size. So, this algorithm is unsuitable for applications with real-time properties. To address this, we present a scalable and fully distributed TDMA-based protocol that ensures collisions occur only at specific times.

6   An Adaptive TDMA-Based MAC Protocol

Given that when nodes have distinct slots lead to worst-case latency, we focus on developing a protocol for the case where nodes do not have distinct slots.

The protocol works as follows: Initially, at start-up, the network is partitioned into clusters using the FLOC algorithm [4], with each cluster having its own head. Then, a MAC schedule is generated, where each sensor node in the network is assigned a time slot in a given period. Within a cluster, every node is assigned a unique slots set, using a variant of the algorithm in Fig. 1. However, these slots may be shared across clusters. The head is responsible for managing the slots within its cluster.

In analogy to fault tolerance, where redundancy is needed to tolerate faults, we introduce *redundant slots* at the cluster level in the MAC schedule to tolerate mobility. In Fig. 2, the schedule consists of control, and data slots. In the control slots, only control information is transmitted, whereas sensor nodes transmit data in their assigned data slots. The idea is to ensure collision-freedom in the data slots, whereas managing any potential collisions that occur in the control slots. At start-up, every node is assigned a slots set, and, in each cluster, some data slots are kept free for future allocation.

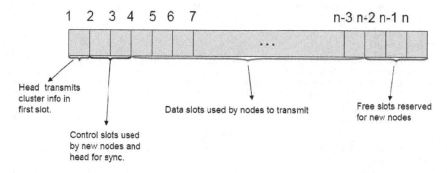

Fig. 2. The schedule is broken down into (i) a control part, and (ii) data part. The first three slots are control slots. The head transmits cluster info. in the first slot. In the second slot, the new node(s) inform the head of their presence in the cluster. In the 3rd slot, the head broadcasts a new node's slot info. The data slots are either assigned or unassigned.

Once the system is setup, i.e., the system is partitioned into a set of clusters [4] and each node within a cluster have distinct slots sets(using pre-programming, or techniques from [2]), mobility needs to be managed and tolerated. To this end, we develop a fully distributed algorithm that manages intra-, and inter-cluster mobility. A detailed description of the mobility-tolerant MAC protocol is presented in Fig 3. Note that from using the FLOC algorithm [4], we have the following property at system start-up: The network has been partitioned into a set of non-overlapping clusters. We now make the following assumptions:

- Any node remains within a cluster for a least one round, unless it crashes.
- If in a given round r, a node is in the i-band of its chead, then in round $r+1$, it will at most be in the o-band of the head, unless the head crashes.
- No more than 1 round elapses for a node to not hear from a head i.e., a node may not go for more than 1 period without hearing from a head.
- Heads may not collide on $k \geq 2$ consecutive rounds. This is justifiable as, in the kind of applications our work is targeting, coverage [18] is important. Hence, it means that heads, thus clusters, will rarely be close to each other.

```
on every sensor
variables:
% Node information
node_id, node_slot: int; head:{0,1, ⊥};
cluster_id: int; band:{i,o}; status:{⊥, waiting, ⊤, ?} init ⊤;
node_access: int X int X int X int; %(node_id,node_slot, start,period)
% timing information
current_slot, next_slot init 0;  round init 1;
%cluster information
max_slots: int; new_slot: int init ⊥;
schedule[1...max_slots]: array of node_access sequences
algorithm M_TDMA:
    do forever{
    case ⟨event⟩ of
    1. ⟨tick()⟩
         current_slot:=current_slot + 1;
         if (current_slot mod max_slots = 1) then
             round := round + 1;fi
    2. ⟨current_slot = (max_slots * (round - 1) + 1)⟩
         if (head) then
             bcast(⟨node_id, head, schedule[],round⟩); fi
    3. ⟨rcv(⟨hd_id, hd, sched[], rnd⟩)⟩
         if (head ∧ status = ?) then
             status := ⊤;
         if (head != 1 ∧ cluster_id = hd_id) then
             head, schedule,cluster_id, band, round, status := 0, sched, hd_id, i|o, rnd, ⊤; fi
         if (head != 1 ∧ cluster_id ≠ hd_id) then
             head, schedule,cluster_id, band, round, status := 0, sched, hd_id, i|o, rnd, ⊥; fi
         if (status = ⊤) then
             node_access := look_up(schedule,node_id); fi
    4. ⟨current_slot = (max_slots * (round - 1) + 2)⟩
         if (head ∧ not rcv(⟨cluster_id,1,sched[], current_round⟩)) then
             status := ?; fi
         if (status = ⊤∧ not rcv(⟨cluster_id,1,sched[], current_round⟩) ∧ band=o)
             head,cluster_id,node_access, band, status:= ⊥, ⊥, ⊥, ⊥, ⊥; fi;
         if (status = ⊤∧ not rcv(⟨cluster_id,1,sched[], current_round⟩) ∧ band=i)
             status:= ?; fi;
         if (status =? ∧ not rcv(⟨cluster_id,1,sched[], current_round⟩) ∧ band=i)
             status:= ⊥; cluster_id, head := run_cluster [4];fi
         if (status = ⊥) then
             bcast(⟨node_id⟩);
             status := waiting; fi
```

Fig. 3. Algorithm M_TDMA that guarantees inter-cluster collision-freedom in data part of schedule in presence of mobility

```
 5. ⟨rcv⟨(new_id)⟩⟩
      if (head ∧| {k:4..max_slots| schedule[k] = ⟨⟩}| ≥ 2) then
          new_slot:=choose{k:4..max_slots| schedule[k] = ⟨⟩}
          period:=1;
          schedule[new_slot]:= ⟨(new_id, new_slot, round, period)⟩; fi

      if (head ∧| {k:4..max_slots| schedule[k] = ⟨⟩}| = 1) then
          new_slot:=choose{k:4..max_slots| schedule[k] = ⟨⟩}
          period:=2;
          schedule[new_slot]:= ⟨(new_id, new_slot, round, period), ⊥⟩; fi

      if (head ∧| {k:4..max_slots| schedule[k] = ⟨⟩}| = 0) then
          new_slot:=choose{k:4..max_slots| |schedule[k]| > 1};
          schedule:=update_schedule(schedule,new_id,new_slot);
 6. ⟨current_slot = (max_slots * (round - 1) + 3)⟩
      if (head ∧ new_slot ≠ ⊥) then
          bcast(⟨new_id,new_slot,round,period⟩);
          new_slot:= ⊥; fi
 7. ⟨rcv⟨(id,slot,start,period)⟩⟩
      if (node_id = id) then
          node_access:= (id,slot,start,period);
          next_slot:= (start - 1)*max_slots + slot;
          status:= ⊤; fi
 8. ⟨current_slot = (max_slots * (round - 1) + 4)⟩
      if (not rcv(⟨(id,slot,start,period)⟩) ∧ status = waiting) then
          exponential_backoff();
 9. ⟨current_slot = next_slot⟩
      if (status ≠ ?) then
          bcast(⟨node_id, cluster_id, payload⟩); fi
      next_slot:= current_slot + (max_slots * period);
10. ⟨(max_slots * (round - 1) + 4) ≤ current_slot ≤ (max_slots * round)⟩
      if (head) ∧ not (rcv⟨(id, cluster, payload)⟩) ∧ status ≠ ? then
          schedule:= reclaim_slots(schedule); fi
```

Fig. 3.(*continued*)

At each time click, the algorithm M_TDMA determines if one or more events
have occurred, and takes the corresponding actions. We explain the algorithm.

Event 1 is a timing event, updating the slot and round number.

Event 2 is triggered when the first slot of a round is reached. The head
broadcasts cluster information: (id, head, cluster schedule, round number).

Event 3 is triggered when a node receives the cluster info. If the head hears
its own message, it knows that it did not collide. "Status = ?" ("undecided")
shows that previously there was some problem. As it hears its own message, it
knows the problem has cleared, updating its status to ⊤ ("OK").

Any other node previously in the cluster, upon receiving the message, will
update their state, and keep their status as ⊤. A node that is new to the cluster, on the other hand, will update its state, but its status will be set to ⊥

("unassigned"). If a non-head node hears a message, and its status is "?", then it updates according to the message sender. If it's its head, it sets its status to ⊤ again, and keep all its previous information. On the other hand, if it hears from a new head, it knows it is in a new cluster, and sets its status to ⊥, and updates its relevant state.

Event 4. In the 2nd slot, if a head does not hear its own message, then it knows there is probably a collision. It sets it status to "?". Any node which was previously in the o-band of the head, and which did not hear the message believes that they are no longer member of the cluster and resets their status to "⊥". Other nodes that were in the i-band of the head set their status to "?" since the message loss could be due to a collision, a crash or o-band.

Also, any node new to the cluster will broadcast its id, so it can assigned a slot by the head. This new node then starts "waiting".

Event 5. Upon receiving a new node id, the head checks if there are any unassigned slots. If there are, it assigns one to the new node, and updates the cluster schedule. Fhe function *choose* randomly picks a value from a set.

If a single slot is free, then the following occurs: The head cannot allocate the slot fully to the new node, as it will not be able to tolerate any new nodes. So, the head halves the bandwidth (half allocated to the new node, and the other half kept for further nodes) by doubling the period at which the new node transmits. Hence, the head updates the schedule by keeping a sequence of ids, with the last element being a place holder ⊥. If there is no full slot left, the head knows that there is some bandwidth left. It checks the place holder, further halves the bandwidth. In fact, as new nodes come, the head allocates only half of the remaining bandwidth. When a node leaves a cluster, its bandwidth is reclaimed and reassigned later.

Event 6. In the 3rd slot, the head broadcasts the following access pattern for the new node: (id, slot, start round, period).

Event 7. Once a node receives its access right, it updates its media access, and calculates the next transmission slot. It also updates its status to ⊤.

Event 8. If a new node is "waiting", and does not receive a message by the 4th slot of the period, it knows that either the clusterhead is not present or it has collided in the second slot. Thus, it executes exponential backoff before retransmitting in the second slot of some later period.

Event 9. If a node is not in the "?" state, then it can broadcast its payload in the slot it is supposed to transmit. Once it finishes transmission, it calculates the next slot it is to transmit.

Event 10. The head checks whether any gap in the schedule is unassigned or "vacated". If it a "vacated" one, then it is reclaimed for later usage.

Theorem 3. *Given a network S, partitioned into a set of k clusters, $C_1 \ldots C_k$. Given each cluster C_i is initially collision-free, with each node $n \in C_i$ having a unique slot. Then M_TDMA guarantees collision-freedom in S in data part of schedule in presence of intra-, and inter-cluster mobility.*

References

1. Ali, M., Suleman, T., Uzmi, Z.: Mmac: A mobility-adaptive, collision-free mac protocol for wireless sensor networks. In: Proc. 24th IEEE IPCCC (2005)
2. Arisha, K., Youssef, M., Younis, M.: Energy-aware tdma-based mac for sensor networks. In: Proc. IEEE Workshop on Integrated Management of Power-Aware Communications, Computing and Networking (2002)
3. Camp, T., Boleng, J., Davies, V.: A survey of mobility models for ad hoc network research. Wireless Communication and Mobile Computing Special Issue on Mobile Ad Hoc Networking: Research, Trends and Applications 2(5), 483–502 (2002)
4. Demirbas, M., Arora, A., Mittal, V., Kulathumani, V.: A fault-local self-stabilizing clustering service for wireless ad hoc networks. IEEE Trans. Parallel Distrib. Systems 17(9), 912–922 (2006)
5. Einstein, A.: Investigations on the Theory of the Brownian Movement. Dover Publications, Mineola, NY (1956)
6. Herman, T., Tixueil, S.: A distributed tdma slot assignment for wireless sensor networks
7. Jhumka, A., Kulkarni, S.: On the design of mobility-tolerant tdma-based media access control (mac) protocol for mobile sensor networks. Technical report, Dept. of Computer Science, University of Warwick (2007)
8. Johnson, D.B., Maltz, D.A.: Dynamic Source Routing in ad hoc Wireless Network, ch. 5, pp. 153–181. Kluwer Academic Publishers, Dordrecht (1996)
9. Kulkarni, S., Arumugam, M.: SS-TDMA: A self-stabilizing MAC for sensor networks. IEEE Press, Los Alamitos (2006)
10. Musolesi, M., Mascolo, C.: Designing mobility models based on social networks theory. Mobile Computing and Communications Review 1(2) (2007)
11. Pham, H., Jha, S.: An adaptive mobility-aware mac protocol for sensor networks (ms-mac)
12. Rajendran, V., Obrazcka, K., Garcia-Luna-Aceves, J.J.: Energy-efficient collision-free medium access protocol for wireless sensor networks. In: Proc. ACM Sensys (2003)
13. Raviraj, P., Sharif, H., Hempel, M., Song, C., Ali, H., Youn, J.: A mobility based link layer approach for mobile wireless sensor networks. In: IEEE International Conference on Electro Information Technology (2005)
14. Raviraj, P., Sharif, H., Hempel, M., Song, C.: An energy efficient mac approach for mobile wireless sensor networks. In: IEEE International Conference on Computer Systems and Applications, pp. 565–570 (2006)
15. Rom, R., Sidi, M.: Multiple Access Protocols: Performance and Analysis. Springer, Heidelberg (1989)
16. Sundararaman, B., Buy, U., Kshemkalyani, A.: Clock synchronization in wireless sensor networks: A survey. Ad-Hoc Networks 3, 281–323 (2005)
17. Viterbi, A.J.: CDMA: Principles of Spread Spectrum Communicatoin. Addison Wesley Longman Publishing Co. Inc., Reading (1995)
18. Wang, L., Kulkarni, S.: Sacrificing a little coverage can substantially increase network lifetime. In: Proc. IEEE SECON (2006)
19. Woo, A., Culler, D.: A transmission control scheme for media access in sensor networks. In: Proc. International Conference on Mobile Computing and Networks, pp. 221–235 (2001)
20. Ye, W., Heidemann, J., Estrin, D.: An energy-efficient mac for wireless sensor networks. In: Proc. Int. Joint Annual Conference of IEEE Computer and Communication Societies (INFOCOM), pp. 1567–1576 (2002)

Self-stabilizing Routing Algorithms for Wireless Ad-Hoc Networks

Rohit Khot, Ravikant Poola, Kishore Kothapalli, and Kannan Srinathan

Center for Security, Theory, and Algorithmic Research,
International Institute of Information Technology
Gachibowli Hyderabad 500 032, India
{rohit_a,ravikantp}@research.iiit.ac.in, {kkishore,srinathan}@iiit.ac.in

Abstract. This paper considers the problem of unicasting in wireless ad hoc networks. Unicasting is the problem of finding a route between a source and a destination and forwarding the message from the source to the destination. In theory, models that have been used oversimplify the problem of route discovery in ad hoc networks. The achievement of this paper is threefold. First we use a more general model in which nodes can have different transmission and interference ranges and we present a new routing algorithm for wireless ad hoc networks that has several nice features. We then combine our algorithm with that of known greedy algorithms to arrive at an average case efficient routing algorithm in the situation that GPS information is available. Finally we show how to schedule unicast traffic between a set of source-destination pairs by providing a proper vertex coloring of the nodes in the wireless ad hoc network. Our coloring algorithm achieves a $O(\Delta)$–coloring that is locally distinct within the 2-hop neighborhood of any node.

1 Introduction

In this paper we consider the problem of delivering unicast messages in wireless ad-hoc networks. Unicasting is an important communication mechanism for wireless networks, and it has therefore attracted a lot of attention both in the systems and in the theory community. Unicasting can be achieved inefficiently simply by broadcasting. While unicasting in wired networks has been well understood, in wireless networks it is not an easy task. Mobile ad-hoc networks have many features that are hard to model in a clean way. Major challenges are how to model wireless communication and how to model mobility. So far, people in the theory area have mostly looked at static wireless systems (i.e. the mobile units are always available and do not move). Wireless communication is usually modeled using the packet radio network model or the even simpler unit disk graph model. In this model, the wireless units, or nodes, are represented by a graph, and two nodes are connected by an edge if they are within transmission range of each other. Transmissions of messages *interfere* at a node if at least two of its neighbors transmit a message at the same time. A node can only receive a message if it does not interfere with any other message.

T. Janowski and H. Mohanty (Eds.): ICDCIT 2007, LNCS 4882, pp. 54–66, 2007.

The packet radio network model is a simple and clean model that allows to design and analyze algorithms with a reasonable amount of effort. It assumes that the transmission range, r_t, of a node is the same as its interference range, r_i. In reality, the interference range of a node can be at least twice as large as its transmission range. Ignoring this fact results in inefficient algorithms that are not suitable in all situations. For example, in routing, when $r_i > r_t$, due to interference, it can take $o(n)$ steps to find the next hop in a path. Also, when physical carrier sensing is not available if the nodes do not know any estimate of the size of the network, $\Omega(n)$ time steps are required to successfully transmit even a single message in an n node wireless network [1].

We will use a much more general model that recently appeared in [2] for designing self-stabilizing algorithms for wireless overlay networks. In this work, we show how to design efficient algorithms for routing in wireless ad hoc networks. Our algorithms work without knowledge of size or a linear estimate of size of the network and also can handle interference problems in wireless networks. Our algorithms even work under the condition that the node labels are only locally distinct.

1.1   Model and Assumptions

We review our model for wireless networks and our model for routing in this section.

Wireless Communication Model. In our model, we do not just model transmission and interference range but we also model physical carrier sensing. Physical carrier sensing is used by the Medium Access Control (MAC) layer to check whether the wireless medium is currently busy. To give a short introduction, the physical carrier sensing is realized by a Clear Channel Assessment (CCA) circuit. This circuit monitors the environment to determine when it is clear to transmit. It can be programmed to be a function of the Receive Signal Strength Indication (RSSI) and other parameters. The RSSI measurement is derived from the state of the Automatic Gain Control (AGC) circuit. Whenever the RSSI exceeds a certain threshold, a special Energy Detection (ED) bit is switched to 1, and otherwise it is set to 0. By manipulating a certain configuration register, this threshold may be set to an absolute power value of t dB, or it may be set to be t dB above the measured noise floor, where t can be set to any value in the range 0-127. The ability to manipulate the CCA rule allows the MAC layer to optimize the physical carrier sensing to its needs.

We assume that we are given a set V of mobile stations, or *nodes*, that are distributed in an arbitrary way in a 2-dimensional Euclidean space. For any two nodes $v, w \in V$ let $d(v, w)$ be the Euclidean distance between v and w. Furthermore, consider any cost function c with the property that there is a fixed constant $\delta \in [0, 1)$ so that for all $v, w \in V$,

- $c(v, w) \in [(1 - \delta) \cdot d(v, w), (1 + \delta) \cdot d(v, w)]$ and
- $c(v, w) = c(w, v)$, i.e. c is symmetric.

c determines the transmission and interference behavior of nodes and δ bounds the non-uniformity of the environment. Notice that we do not require c to be monotonic in the distance or to satisfy the triangle inequality. This makes sure that our model even applies to highly irregular environments.

We assume that the nodes use some fixed-rate power-controlled communication mechanism over a single frequency band. When using a transmission power of P, there is a transmission range $r_t(P)$ and an interference range $r_i(P) > r_t(P)$ that grow monotonically with P. The interference range has the property that every node $v \in V$ can only cause interference at nodes w with $c(v, w) \leq r_i(P)$, and the transmission range has the property that for every two nodes $v, w \in V$ with $c(v, w) \leq r_t(P)$, v is guaranteed to receive a message from w sent out with a power of P (with high probability) as long as there is no other node $v' \in V$ with $c(v, v') \leq r_i(P')$ that transmits a message at the same time with a power of P'.

For simplicity, we assume that the ratio $\rho = r_i(P)/r_t(P)$ is a fixed constant greater than 1 for all relevant values of P. This is not a restriction because we do not assume anything about what happens if a message is sent from a node v to a node w within v's transmission range but another node u is transmitting a message at the same time with w in its interference range. In this case, w may or may not be able to receive the message from v, so any worst case may be assumed in the analysis. The only restriction we need, which is important for any overlay network algorithm to eventually stabilize is that transmission range should have strong threshold,that is beyond the transmission range a message cannot be received any more (with high probability). This is justified by the fact that when using modern forward error correction techniques, the difference between the signal strength that allows to receive the message (with high probability) and the signal strength that does not allow any more to receive the message (with high probability) can be very small (less than 1 dB).

Nodes can not only send and receive messages but also perform physical carrier sensing. Given some sensing threshold T (that can be flexibly set by a node) and a transmission power P, there is a *carrier sense transmission (CST) range* $r_{st}(T, P)$ and a *carrier sense interference (CSI) range* $r_{si}(T, P)$ that grow monotonically with T and P. The range $r_{st}(T, P)$ has the property that if a node v transmits a message with power P and a node w with $c(v, w) \leq r_{st}(T, P)$ is currently sensing the carrier with threshold T, then w senses a message transmission (with high probability). The range $r_{si}(T, P)$ has the property that if a node v senses a message transmission with threshold T, then there was at least one node w with $c(v, w) \leq r_{si}(T, P)$ that transmitted a message with power P (with high probability). More precisely, we assume that the monotonicity property holds. That is, if transmissions from a set U of nodes within the $r_{si}(T, P)$ range cause v to sense a transmission, then any superset of U will also do so.

Routing Model. In our model for routing, we only assume that the node labels for the source and the destination are distinct. The other nodes need labels that are only locally distinct. Our algorithms do not also require that nodes know their co-ordinate position via GPS. The routing algorithm ideally should not impose heavy storage requirement at any node. For example, space to store a constant amount of information can be assumed. Each message sent during the algorithm should also be limited to contain a constant amount of information, where the label of any node is taken as an unit of information.

1.2   Related Work

Routing algorithms for wireless ad hoc networks has been the subject of several papers, [3,4,5,6] to cite a few. Routing algorithms fall into broadly two categories namely *pro-active* and *reactive*. The pro-active algorithms maintain routing information that can be used to find a path between s and t quickly via lookup operations. Algorithms such as [7] fall under this category. The main drawback of such strategies is that they impose heavy storage overhead at the wireless nodes. Also, as the ad hoc network undergoes changes in topology, heavy recomputations may need to be performed. Reactive algorithms such as AODV[5], DSR[6], TORA[8], in contrast, rely on caching and occasional update. While the average performance of these strategies may be good, they may perform particularly bad in the worst case. For an experimental evaluation of some of these protocols see [9].

Geometric routing algorithms are also studied heavily in recent years [3,4,10,11,12]. Here, firstly it is assumed that the nodes know their actual geometric position. Secondly, a planar overlay network is also assumed to be available. The underlying geometry is used to route from s to t is done as follows. Assume that a path till node u in a path $s \rightsquigarrow u \rightsquigarrow t$ is found. From node u, to find the next hop in the path, a greedy approach can be taken. That is, node v that is closer to t than u is selected as the next hop. This can fail in certain scenarios. In such cases, the planar overlay network is used. Here the next hop node is the node lying that is closer to t than s on the straight line connecting s and t. This is also called as *face routing* and one needs a planar overlay network to be able to do face routing. The work and time bounds when using this strategy are shown to be optimal in [4]. A combination of greedy algorithms and the face routing algorithms is also studied [4,13]. Most of these papers mentioned assume a Unit Disk Graph model of wireless networks. Routing algorithms based on topology control strategies such as Yao graphs [14] are also known [15]. While the topology control algorithms show the existence of energy-efficient paths, converting such existential mechanisms to constructive mechanisms for wireless networks is not easy.

Vertex coloring of wireless networks is a problem that has been studied in many papers, e.g., [16,17,18,19], especially in the context of using such a coloring in a TDMA scheme. Packet scheduling in wireless networks has been studied in [18]. The results of [18] show how to use distance-2 vertex coloring to arrive at good scheduling strategies.

1.3   Our Results

As we saw in section 1.2, most of the algorithms proposed use the Unit Disk graph model which is a very weak model. We instead use a much more general and realistic model that was proposed recently in [2]. We present routing algorithm for mobile wireless ad hoc networks. That is, given a source node s and destination node t, we present algorithms to find a path between s and t. Our algorithms do not require that the spanner be a planar overlay network which is assumed in several papers on wireless routing algorithms. Further, the path returned by our algorithm is only a constant times bigger than the shortest path between s and t in the original network.

We also present scheme to schedule unicast traffic in the wireless network. That is, given a set of source-destination pairs of the form $\{(s_i, t_i)\}_{i \geq 1}$, once a path between s_i and t_i is found, then we propose simple scheme to schedule the packet transfers in the network so that no packet is lost due to wireless interference. Our scheme relies on an $O(\Delta)$ coloring of the nodes in the network where Δ is maximum number of nodes within transmission range of a node. This coloring also has the properties that it is local and $r_t \oplus r_i$-distinct. The $r_t \oplus r_i$-distinctness ensures that the transmissions of nodes remain interference free. For definition of $r_t \oplus r_i$, please see Section 2.

Our algorithms are also self-stabilizing [20] which is an important property for distributed systems. Thus our algorithms can start in an arbitrary state and therefore adapt to changes in the wireless ad hoc network. We only require that the source node s and t have unique labels and the other nodes have labels that are locally distinct. The nodes should also synchronize up to some reasonably small time difference, which can be easily accomplished using GPS signals or any form of beacons. Another important feature of our algorithms is that a constant amount of storage at any node suffices. The above properties make our algorithms applicable to sensor networks without any modifications.

1.4 Structure of the Paper

The remainder of this paper is organized as follows. In Section 2, we present some preliminary definitions and assumptions which will be used by the algorithms in this paper. In Section 3, we present and analyze the wireless routing algorithm and in section 4 we propose our scheme to schedule concurrent unicast requests.

2 Preliminaries

In this section we present the notation used in the rest of the paper and then provide a review of the constant density spanner construction algorithm which we make use of in this paper.

Let V be the set of nodes in the network. For any transmission range r, let the graph $G_r = (V, E)$ denote the graph containing all edges $\{v, w\}$ with $c(v, w) \leq r$. Throughout this paper, r_t denotes the transmission range and δ_{uv} denotes the shortest distance between u and v in G_{r_t}.

Our results build on top of a distributed algorithm recently proposed for organizing the wireless nodes into a constant density spanner [2]. A constant density spanner is defined as follows: Given an undirected graph $G = (V, E)$, a subset $U \subseteq V$ is called a *dominating set* if all nodes $v \in V$ are either in U or have an edge to a node in U. A dominating set U is called *connected* if U forms a connected component in G. The *density* of a dominating set is the maximum over all nodes $v \in U$ of the number of neighbors that v has in U. In our context, *constant density spanner* is a connected dominating set U of constant density with the property that for any two nodes $v, w \in V$ there are two nodes $v', w' \in U$ with $\{v, v'\} \in E$, $\{w, w'\} \in E$, and a path p from v' to w' along nodes in U so that the length of p is at most a constant factor larger than the distance between v and w in G.

Our spanner protocol for G_{r_t} consists of the following 3 phases that are continuously repeated.

- Phase I: The goal of this phase is to construct a constant density dominating set in G_{r_t}. This is achieved by extending Luby's algorithm [21] to the more complex model outlined in Section 1.1. We denote by U the set of nodes in the dominating set and these nodes are also called *active* nodes. Since the dominating set resulting from phase I may not be connected, further phases are needed to obtain a constant density spanner.
- Phase II: The goal of this phase is to organize the nodes of the dominating set of phase I into color classes that keep nodes with the same color sufficiently far apart from each other. Only a constant number of different colors is needed for this, where the constant depends on δ. Every node organizes its rounds into time frames consisting of as many rounds as there are colors, and a node in the dominating set only becomes active in phase III in the round corresponding to its color.
- Phase III: The goal of this phase is to interconnect every pair of nodes in the dominating set that is within a hop distance of at most 3 in G_{r_t} with the help of at most 2 gateway nodes, using the coloring determined in phase II to minimize interference problems. We denote by $\mathcal{G}$ the set of *gateway* nodes.

Each phase has a constant number of time slots associated with it, where each time slot represents a communication step. Phase I consists of 3 time slots, phase II consists of 4 time slots, and phase III consists of 4 time slots. These 11 time slots together form a *round* of the spanner protocol. We assume that all the nodes are synchronized in rounds, that is, every node starts a new round at the same time step. As mentioned earlier, this may be achieved via GPS or beacons.

The spanner protocol establishes a constant density spanner by running sufficiently many rounds of the three phases. All of the phases are self-stabilizing. More precisely, once phase I has self-stabilized, phase II will self-stabilize, and once phase II has self-stabilized, phase III will self-stabilize. In this way, the entire algorithm can self-stabilize from an arbitrary initial configuration.

For an illustration of the spanner construction, see Figure 1. It is not difficult to see that the spanner protocol results in a 5-spanner of constant density. The following result is shown in [2]:

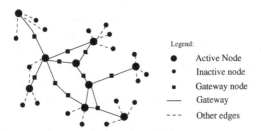

Fig. 1. Figure illustrates a constant density spanner

Theorem 1. *For any desired transmission range, the spanner protocol generates a constant density spanner in $O(\Delta \log n \log \Delta + \log^4 n)$ communication rounds, with high probability, where Δ is the maximum number of nodes that are within the transmission range of a node.*

3   Unicasting Between s and t

In this section, we propose a new algorithm for route discovery in ad hoc networks. The algorithm works on top of the constant density spanner described in Section 2.

In the following let s be a source node that intends to send a message to a target node t. We assume that s has a way to refer to node t by either the label of t or some other unique identifier. Our algorithm does not require the common assumption that a planar embedding of the original network is available. In our algorithm nodes exchange four types of messages namely RREQ, RREP, REPORT and REPLY. The RREQ, standing for Route Request, message is of the form $\langle$RREQ, $s, t, d\rangle$ where s and t is the source and target nodes and d is the distance over which the RREQ message is to be forwarded. Here distance is measured as distance between active nodes, thus $d = 1$ indicates that the RREQ message has to be forwarded to all the active nodes that are reachable from the current node by using at most 2 gateway nodes. The RREP message is of the form $\langle$RREP, s, t, flag$\rangle$ where flag $= 1$ if the current active node has t as direct neighbor and is 0 otherwise. The REPORT message is of the form $\langle$REPORT, $t\rangle$, to find node t from inactive nodes. If t is found at u , u replies with The REPLY message $\langle$REPLY, $\ell, u\rangle$ denotes u is the required node asked to find in REPORT message. We now describe the algorithm by first assuming that s knows the distance in hops to t, which is denoted by δ_{st}, where δ_{st} is the shortest distance between s and t. We call our algorithm WaveRouting algorithm and is described below.

Following Section 2, each active node has 4 reserved slots for this phase. In the first slot, an RREQ are sent and in the second an RREP message may be sent. Using techniques similar to that of Phase II in Section 2, it is possible to also organize the gateway nodes into color classes so that gateway nodes that are not $r_t \oplus r_i$ apart belong to different color classes. This results in the situation that the gateway nodes also can own time slots with the property that messages sent by a gateway node during the time slot owned by it is free of interference problems. For this phase, the gateway nodes have 2 slots to send an RREQ in the first slot and an RREP in the second slot.

Without loss of generality, we assume that the source node s is an active node. Otherwise, s would send an RREQ request to an active node in the transmission range of s. Each item below is a communication step.

Algorithm WaveRouting(s, t, δ_{st})

1. If ℓ is the source node s, then ℓ initiates an RREQ message of the form $\langle RREQ, \ell, t, \delta_{\ell t} \rangle$ and sends the message in the first time slot.
2. If g is a gateway node that receives an RREQ message then g forwards the RREQ message to gateway nodes and active nodes that are within the r_t range from g. Node g however does not decrement the counter δ_{st}.
3. If ℓ is active and receives an RREQ message, and $\ell \neq t$, then ℓ issues a REPORT message of the form $\langle REPORT, t \rangle$. If $\ell = t$ then ℓ prepares an RREP message and sends it in the third slot. The RREP message has the form $\langle RREP, s, t, 1 \rangle$.
4. If u is inactive and receives a REPORT message from ℓ, and $u = t$ then u responds with a REPLY message of the form $\langle REPLY, \ell, u \rangle$.
5. If ℓ is active and sent a REPORT message in the previous slot and did not receive any REPLY message, then ℓ decrements the present value of δ_{st} and forwards the RREQ message. If δ_{st} is 0 after decrementing, no RREQ is sent and instead an RREP message of the form $\langle RREP, s, t, 0 \rangle$ is sent signifying that ℓ could not find a path to t.
6. If ℓ is active and receives an RREP message and $\ell \neq s$ then ℓ forwards the RREP message. If $\ell = s$ and receives an RREP message with flag $= 1$, then a path from ℓ to t is found. If $\ell = s$ and receives an RREP message with flag $= 0$ then this indicates a failure.

The path between s and t would simply be the reverse of the path along which successful RREP messages, that is RREP with flag $= 1$, arrive. This path can be located easily.

The above protocol achieves the following time and work bounds. Recall that δ_{st} refers to the length of the shortest path between s and t.

Lemma 1. *Given a stable constant density spanner as in [2] and a source s and destination t, a path between s and t can be found in $O(\delta_{st})$ time steps if such a path exists. If no st–path exists, then the absence of such a path can also be reported in $O(\delta_{st})$ time steps. Further, the path returned has length at most $5\delta_{st}$.*

Proof. The proof follows easily from the observation that in 3 time steps, δ_{st} is decremented by 1 until δ_{st} goes to 1. It thus holds that for the entire set of RREQ and RREP messages to reach s, it takes $6\delta_{st}$ time steps. No message is lost due to interference problems as the messages are sent by respective nodes during their own time slots.   □

Lemma 2. *Given a stable constant density spanner as in [2] and a source s and destination t, the work required to find a path between s and t is $O(\delta_{st}^2)$ using the above protocol.*

Proof. The WaveRouting protocol requires active and gateway nodes in an area of radius δ_{st} to send and receive RREP/RREQ messages. The inactive nodes respond only to a REPORT message from an active node. Since the spanner construction of [2] has constant density, it holds that in an area $A = \pi\delta_{st}^2$ rounds s, there are only $O(A)$ active and gateway nodes. Hence the stated work bound holds.   □

It is not natural to assume that the source node s knows the length of the shortest path to t. However, this assumption can be easily removed. The modified algorithm is called AdaptiveWaveRouting and is described below.

Algorithm AdaptiveWaveRouting(s, t)

1. $\hat{\delta}_{st} = 1$
2. Call WaveRouting($s, t, \hat{\delta}_{st}$). If an RREP with flag $= 1$ is received, stop.
3. If no path between s and t is found, then set $\hat{\delta}_{st} := 2 \cdot \hat{\delta}_{st}$ and go to step 2.

We now show that using the Adaptive WaveRouting algorithm, if a path between s and t exists, then such a path can be found in $O(\delta_{st})$ time steps.

Lemma 3. *Given a stable constant density spanner as in [2] and a source s and destination t, a path between s and t can be found in $O(\delta_{st})$ time steps. Further, the path found between s and t has length at most $5\delta_{st}$.*

Proof. The AdaptiveWaveRouting protocol increases the value of $\hat{\delta}_{st}$ by a factor of 2 until a path between s and t is found. For each value of $\hat{\delta}_{st}$), the time required is $O(\hat{\delta}_{st})$ by Lemma 1. Hence the total time to find a path between s and t is bounded by $c(1 + 2 + 4 + \ldots + \delta_{st}) \leq 2c\delta_{st}$ for some constant c. Hence the lemma holds.   □

Lemma 4. *Given a stable constant density spanner as in [2] and a source s and destination t, the work required to find a path between s and t is $O(\delta_{st}^2)$ using the above protocol.*

Proof. Using arguments similar to that of Lemma 3, for each value of $\hat{\delta}_{st}$, the work performed using the WaveRouting protocol is $O(\hat{\delta}_{st}^2)$ by Lemma 1. Hence the total work performed is $O(\delta_{st}^2)$.   □

Self-stabilization

Notice that in the AdaptiveWaveRouting algorithm, no assumption is made with respect to the initial situation of the nodes in the wireless network. Since the spanner construction of [2] is known to be self-stabilizing even under adversarial behavior, we arrive at the following corollary.

Lemma 5. *Algorithm AdaptiveWaveRouting can be made to self-stabilize even under adversarial behavior.*

3.1   Extensions

Due to the lower bound shown in [13], our result is optimal in the worst case. However, our result in the current form is not comparable to the greedy or geometric routing algorithms in the average case. The advantage these algorithms have is the position information of individual nodes in the network. The position information allows the greedy algorithms to proceed in the direction of the destination with geometric algorithms coming to the rescue in the case that no intermediate node is closer to the destination than the source node.

We have till now assumed that nodes do not have any information about the actual position of itself or of the destination, i.e., no GPS information was needed. But if such information is available a-priori, then we show how to combine our AdaptiveWaveRouting algorithm with that of greedy algorithms. By greedy algorithms, we mean the class of routing algorithms that forward the packet along a next hop that is geometrically closest to the destination. The idea is that as long as greedy routing is possible, we use greedy routing. Once the greedy routing scheme reaches a local minima, then we switch to AdaptiveWaveRouting. This should result in also average case optimal time-and work-efficient routing algorithm. The details are omitted in this version.

4   Scheduling Unicasting Requests

Given a set of source-destination pairs $\{(s_i, t_i)\}_{i \geq 1}$, using the AdaptiveWaveRouting algorithm, a path connecting s_i to t_i can be found if such path exists. However, it still remains to show how to schedule the packet transmissions so that the schedule is free of wireless interference. For this, we require that a node transmitting a packet should have no other node that is within the $r_t \oplus r_i$ range also transmitting simultaneously. This problem has been studied under the assumption that the routes are available in [18]. In general, the problem can be posed as finding a valid coloring of the nodes in network such that the color of any node is unique in a $r_t \oplus r_i$ neighborhood. (In the unit disk model, this is referred to as distance-2 coloring [16]). Coloring ad hoc networks is also studied in [17] where the nodes need to know an estimate of the size of the network and the coloring achieved is not unique in $r_t \oplus r_i$ range. In this section we show that a $O(\Delta)$, distance $r_t \oplus r_i$ coloring can be achieved very easily using the spanner construction. In the context of routing, then only nodes that are in the chosen path between s_i and t_i for some i participate in requesting a color. Thus, only nodes that need to forward the packet obtain a color. Then the color value can be associated with time slots which gives $r_t \oplus r_i$ interference free transmission slots. In the following we show how to achieve the required coloring.

4.1   Distributed Coloring of Ad Hoc Networks

In this section, we present the protocol for phase IV which results in $O(\Delta)$ coloring. In this phase, the inactive nodes request the active nodes in their neighborhood to allocate a color. The active nodes always prefix their color to the chosen color with the effect that the palettes of active nodes are locally distinct. Thus our algorithm need not have any color verification phase. In this phase, active nodes use an aCST range of r_i and the inactive nodes use an aCST range of r_i.

Each active node maintains a counter k that is initialized to 0 and serves as an upper bound on the highest color that is allotted till now by the active node. Once all the colors till k are allotted, the active nodes updates k to $4k$ and colors are assigned from the range $[k+1, 4k]$ uniformly at random.

Below we present the protocol. In the following each item represents a communication step. Inactive nodes maintain a state among {awake, asleep}.

1. If v is awake, v sends a REQUEST message of the form $\langle$REQUEST$, v,$ color$(v)\rangle$ that contains the id of node v and the color of v with probability p to be determined later. color(v) is set to -1 if v is not assigned any color yet.

2. If ℓ is active and senses or receives a collision then ℓ sends a COLLIDE signal. If ℓ is active and receives a REQUEST message containing the id of node v with color$(v) = -1$, ℓ responds with a color message of the form $\langle$COLOR$, v,$ color$(v)\rangle$ that contains an allotment of color to node v. If ℓ senses a free channel, then ℓ sends a FREE message of the form $\langle \ell,$ FREE$\rangle$.

3. If v is awake and receives a COLLIDE signal and v did not send a REQUEST message in the previous time slot then v goes to asleep state. If v is asleep and receives a FREE message then v goes to awake state.

We now analyze the protocol and show bounds on the number of colors used, the time taken for the protocol, and also the locality property of the coloring achieved.

Theorem 2. *Given a stable set of active nodes that are colored in Phase II, Phase IV takes $O(\Delta \log \Delta \log n)$ time steps with high probability to achieve an $O(\Delta)$ coloring.*

Proof. We prove the convergence of phase IV to a valid $O(\Delta)$ coloring in $O(\Delta \log n \log \Delta)$ rounds after phase III has reached a stable state. Since, at that point the active nodes have reserved rounds that are distinct within the $r_i \oplus r_i$ range, we can treat the actions of active nodes independent of each other.

Let (v, ℓ) be an inactive node-active node pair such that v has to send a REQUEST message to ℓ. Node v has at most $O(\Delta)$ inactive nodes in its interference range sending a REQUEST message to some leader node. If more than one node in awake state, with respect to ℓ, decides to send a REQUEST message, then ℓ will send a collision message. Since the collision message will be received by the inactive nodes, within r_t range of ℓ, awake nodes that decided not to send a REQUEST message to ℓ in the previous slot will go to asleep state.

Consider time to be partitioned into groups of consecutive rounds such that each group ends with a round where the active node ℓ sends either an COLOR message or a FREE message. (A group ending with an COLOR message signifies a successful group and a group ending with a FREE message is a failed group).

Notice that at the end of every group, whether successful or not, all the inactive nodes within the r_t range of ℓ go to awake state (by step 3 of the protocol).

It is not difficult to show that the expected number of rounds in each group, successful or failed, is $O(\log \Delta)$ and any group is successful with constant probability. Due to symmetry reasons any inactive node is equally likely to be send a REQUEST message in a successful group. Thus, during any successful group, for a given pair (v, ℓ) , $\Pr[$ v sends a REQUEST message successfully to $\ell] \geq 1/c\Delta$, for some constant $c > 1$.

Using Chernoff bounds, for any given pair (v, ℓ) the probability that it takes more than Δk groups so that v sends a REQUEST message to ℓ successfully will be polynomially small for $k = O(\log n)$. It can also be shown that each group has $O(\log \Delta)$ rounds not only on expectation but also with high probability. Thus any node v requires at most $O(\Delta \log n \log \Delta)$ rounds to send a REQUEST message to ℓ successfully w.h.p.

Notice that number of colors used by the active nodes in Phase II is a constant cd_1. Also, the maximum color allotted by any active node is 4Δ. Thus the highest color any inactive node gets is $4cd_1\Delta = O(\Delta)$. □

Finally, notice that any inactive node gets a color that is constant times bigger than the neighborhood of some active node in its neighborhood. Thus, the coloring achieved maintains locality with respect to the 2-neighborhood of any node. Thus, areas that are sparsely populated use lesser number of colors. This property is useful when using the coloring to get a natural TDMA scheme. We can also modify the above scheme so that only those inactive nodes that lie on some st–path only request (and receive) a colour.

5   Conclusions

In this paper we discussed a better model for wireless ad-hoc networks and presented efficient algorithms to perform unicasting in ad-hoc networks. Further challenges include handling mobility of nodes and an empirical analysis of the proposed protocols.

References

1. Jurdzinski, T., Stachowiak, G.: Probabilistic algorithms for the wakeup problem in single-hop radio networks. In: Proc. 13th International Symposium on Algorithms and Computation, pp. 535–549 (2002)
2. Onus, M., Richa, A., Kothapalli, K., Scheideler, C.: Constant density spanners for wireless ad-hoc networks. In: ACM SPAA (2005)
3. Kuhn, F., Wattenhofer, R., Zollinger, A.: Asymptotically optimal geometric mobil ad-hoc routing. In: ACM DIALM (2002)
4. Kuhn, F., Wattenhofer, R., Zhang, Y., Zollinger, A.: Geometric ad-hoc routing: of theory and practice. In: Proc. of the 22nd IEEE Symp. on Principles of Distributed Computing (PODC) (2003)

5. Perkins, C.: Adhoc on demand distance vector (aodv) routing, Internet draft, draft–ietf–manet–aodv–04.txt (1999)
6. Johnson, D.B., Maltz, D.A.: Dynamic source routing in ad hoc wireless networks. In: Mobile Computing, vol. 353, Kluwer Academic Publishers, Dordrecht (1996)
7. Perkins, C., Bhagwat, P.: Highly dynamic destination-sequenced distance-vector routing (DSDV) for mobile computers. In: Proc. of ACM SIGCOMM, pp. 234–244 (1994)
8. Park, V., Corson, M.: A highly adaptive distributed routing algorithm for mobile wireless networks. In: Proceedings of IEEE Infocom, pp. 1405–1413 (1997)
9. Broch, J., Maltz, D., Johnson, D., Hu, Y., Jetcheva, J.: A performance comparison of multi-hop wireless ad hoc network routing protocols. In: Proceedings of the 4th annual ACM/IEEE International conference on Mobile computing and networking, pp. 85–97 (1998)
10. Gao, J., Guibas, L., Hershberger, J., Zhang, L., Zhu, A.: Geometric spanner for routing in mobile networks. In: MobiHoc 2001. Proc. of the 2nd ACM Symposium on Mobile Ad Hoc Networking and Computing, pp. 45–55 (2001)
11. Bose, P., Morin, P., Brodnik, A., Carlsson, S., Demaine, E., Fleischer, R., Munro, J., Lopez-Ortiz, A.: Online routing in convex subdivisions. In: International Symposium on Algorithms and Computation (ISSAC), pp. 47–59 (2000)
12. Bose, P., Morin, P., Stojmenovic, I., Urrutia, J.: Routing with guaranteed delivery in ad hoc wireless networks. ACM/Kluwer Wireless Networks 7(6), 609–616 (2001)
13. Kuhn, F., Wattenhofer, R., Zollinger, A.: Worst-case optimal and average-case efficient geometric ad-hoc routing. In: Proceedings of the 4th ACM international symposium on Mobile ad hoc networking & computing, pp. 267–278 (2003)
14. Yao, A.C.C.: On constructing minimum spanning trees in k-dimensional spaces and related problems. SIAM J. Comp. 11, 721–736 (1982)
15. Hassin, Y., Peleg, D.: Sparse communication networks and efficient routing in the plane. In: Proceedings of the ACM symposium on Principles of distributed computing, pp. 41–50 (2000)
16. Parthasarathy, S., Gandhi, R.: Distributed algorithms for coloring and domination in wireless ad hoc networks. In: Proc. of FSTTCS (2004)
17. Moscibroda, T., Wattenhofer, R.: Coloring unstructured radio networks. In: ACM SPAA, pp. 39–48 (2005)
18. Kumar, V.A., Marathe, M., Parthasarathy, S., Srinivasan, A.: End-to-end packet-scheduling in wireless ad-hoc networks. In: ACM SODA, pp. 1021–1030 (2004)
19. Krumke, S., Marathe, M., Ravi, S.: Models and approximation algorithms for channel assignment in radio networks. Wireless Networks 7(6), 575–584 (2001)
20. Dijkstra, E.W.: Self stabilization in spite of distributed control. Communications of the ACM 17, 643–644 (1974)
21. Luby, M.: A simple parallel algorithm for the maximal independent set problem. In: Proc. of the 17th ACM Symposium on Theory of Computing (STOC), pp. 1–10 (1985)

A Structured Mesh Overlay Network for P2P Applications on Mobile Ad Hoc Networks

Thirapon Wongsaardsakul and Kanchana Kanchanasut

Internet Education and Research Laboratory and
School of Engineering and Technology,
Asian Institute of Technology, Pathumthani 12120, Thailand
{Thirapon.Wongsaardsakul,kanchana}@ait.ac.th

Abstract. In this paper, we describe a Structured Mesh Overlay Network (SMON) based on a Distributed Hash Table (DHT) technique on top of a proactive routing protocol, Optimized Link State Routing (OLSR). SMON is a P2P cross-layer overlay network based on concept of CrossROAD. CrossROAD uses a pure flooding technique to form and maintain an overlay network. The broadcast mechanism has a negative effect on bandwidth usage of the network. On the other hand, we introduce a new algorithm for overlay formation and maintenance in order to reduce a number of overlay broadcast messages. The simulation results show that SMON reduces the number of overlay control overhead around 95% as compared to CrossROAD, while it maintains high query success ratio and low query delay.

1   Introduction

The fundamental problem of P2P systems is the lookup in the main operation of P2P systems; in other words, how a peer can efficiently locate other peers responsible for data items. Peers in P2P systems generally form a structured overlay network by basing on DHT techniques whose main advantage is to provide a certain bound on a number of hops for service lookups. MANET and P2P systems share various similarities such as decentralization, self-organization, and dynamic topology. Consequently, various approaches [1,2,3] try to improve service discovery performance by deploying the concept of DHT to MANET.

CrossROAD [4] is a structured overlay network on MANET, and an approach, which provides the service lookups without relying on a centralized index server. It is the cross-layer design that can directly collaborate with OLSR. The OLSR routing contains IP addresses of reachable nodes participating in the network. Knowing who are currently taking part in the network, a CrossROAD node can use the information to construct an overlay network locally and react to topology changes efficiently.

However, the first limitation of CrossROAD is that it uses the pure broadcast mechanism to form and maintain the overlay network. The flooding technique generates many redundant message transmissions resulting in large amount of

T. Janowski and H. Mohanty (Eds.): ICDCIT 2007, LNCS 4882, pp. 67–72, 2007.
© Springer-Verlag Berlin Heidelberg 2007

network bandwidth consumption and network congestion. Apart from the mentioned limitation, the OLSR routing message is modified for carrying the Cross-ROAD message. Consequently, this routing message modification does not offer backward compatibility with OLSR standard.

To address the limitations of CrossROAD, we propose SMON, a structured overlay network which provides service lookup facilities for P2P applications. Similarly, SMON is the application overlay network that directly interacts with OLSR routing layer. However, we introduce a new algorithm of overlay formation and maintenance in order to reduce a number of overlay broadcast messages. We take into account that our design should provide backward compatibility.

The paper is organized in the following order to discuss the topic. The next section describes related work on P2P service discovery protocols. The third section presents SMON and compare SMON with CrossROAD. In section 4, we present our performance evaluation of SMON by simulation. Finally, our conclusions and future work are given in the last section.

2   Related Work

Efficient service discovery is a vital operation for the usability of MANET. Service discovery allows MANET nodes to locate desired services and publish their available services. Ekta-RD [2] is a resource discovery application created on top of Ekta, P2P cross-layer routing design, by integrating Pastry and DSR. MAPNaS [3] is, on the other hand, built on top of MADPastry, another P2P cross-layer routing architecture, combining Pastry and AODV. Both resource discovery mechanisms in this category rely on the support of P2P cross-layer routing architectures, which mainly attempt to reduce number of control traffic. However, a resource discovery message is likely traversed by using an indirect path instead of a shortest path due to DHT properties. This detour route eventually has an effect on a call setup delay when a resource discovery is required for an application such as audio or video call.

3   SMON

Each peer is assigned unique ID, hash valued of its IP address. This ID represents overlay address. For peer discovery, only overlay peer with the smallest ID is allowed to periodically broadcast a list of all members of the overlay network. Hence, the new peer will receive the full list of overlay members in short time after it joins the overlay network. Moreover, because only the peer with smallest ID is allowed to broadcast the list of overlay peers, the number of broadcast messages is significantly reduced.

In order to make the proposal compatible with OLSR standard, we define new overlay control messages, consisting of JOIN and LIST OF OVERLAY MEMBERS as shown in Fig. 1 using message types outside the range of message types reserved by OLSR protocol. The overlay control messages can be treated just like the normal OLSR control messages where they can be packed inside OLSR packets just like other OLSR control messages. OLSR provides the backward compatibility that allows nodes, which do not recognize a new message, to operate properly. If an unknown message is received at a node, it will be forwarded via MPRs according to the OLSR forwarding algorithm.

The type field indicates whether this message is a JOIN or LIST OF OVERLAY MEMBERS ones. The former is sent by a joining peer, while the latter is only advertised by a peer with the smallest ID. The second and third field shows a number of overlay members and a list of IP addresses.

Fig. 1. Overlay Control Message Format

When the new peer wishes to join the overlay network, it broadcasts a JOIN message that contains its IP address specified in the list of IP addresses field. Then, it waits for a LIST OF OVERLAY MEMBERS message. After the reception, the new peer constructs the overlay network locally according to the list of IP addresses in the message. When a peer with the smallest ID broadcasts the LIST OF OVERLAY MEMBERS message, other peers can overhear this message. Therefore, each peer checks whether the list of IP addresses in the message contains its IP address. If not, it will resend a JOIN message in order to keep overlay consistency.

We next consider merge and split operations of two overlay networks. The set of all peers in the first overlay is denoted by $P=P_1,P_2,\ldots,P_n$, where n is the total number of peers of the first overlay and the set of all peers in the second overlay is denoted by $Q=Q_1,Q_2,\ldots,Q_m$, where m is the total number of peers in the second overlay. Assuming that P_1 and Q_1 are the peers with smallest node ID of the first and second overlay networks. When these two overlay networks are merging, P_1 receives the list of overlay members from Q_1. Similarly, Q_1 receives the list of overlay members from P_1. Therefore, a new set of overlay members of P_1 and Q_1 is a union set $PQ=P_1,P_2,\ldots,P_n,Q_1,Q_2,\ldots,Q_m$. After merging, either P_1 or Q_1 who has the smallest ID continues broadcasting the new list of overlay members PQ.

As for split operation, an overlay network is divided into two. Consider an overlay network with a set R containing all the peers in the network, we define set $R=R_1,R_2,\ldots,R_i$ where i is number of peers in the overlay. After split operation on overlay network, set R is partitioned into two smaller sets S and T, where $R=S \bigcup T$ and $S \bigcap T=\emptyset$. Next, S_1 and T_1, which are peers with the smallest ID, begin advertising the full list of overlay members R within their partitions. Even though the set R is advertised, each peer locally checks the availabilities of peers by using information from its OLSR routing table before performing service registering and lookups.

The differences between CrossROAD and SMON can be summarized as follows. First, in term of the number of overlay broadcast messages, a CrossROAD node periodically broadcasts the PublishService messages. If it has n services, it will advertise n times. Thus, a total number of PublishService messages increases according to a number of service. On the other hand, a total number of overlay messages in SMON is lower because only peer with smallest ID is allowed to advertise the list of overlay member messages.

In order to show the total number of broadcast messages for all nodes of CrossROAD and SMON, we consider at a stable stage from between t_0 and t_1. We assume that in this interval time there is no network partition, and every peer holds one service. Let n_t denotes the number of interval broadcast times between t_0 and t_1, n_s is the total number of services, and N is the number of nodes. Hence, the total number of P2P overlay control overhead of CrossROAD within the interval is $n_t \times N$, where $n_s = N$. In SMON, the total number of LIST OF OVERLAY MEMBERS messages is equal to 1 because there is one node with the smallest ID that advertises the message, and the total number of JOIN messages is N. Therefore, the overlay control overhead of SMON is $(n_t \times 1) + N$. In the simulation, N is 50, and n_t is 60. Hence, control overhead of SMON is reduced around 96.33% as compared to CrossROAD.

The next difference between SMON and CrossROAD is the OLSR compatibility. We use extended headers defined in OLSR standard to support the SMON overlay messages. The extended headers allow nodes that do not recognize the new messages to operate with SMON nodes seamlessly. The last difference is the number of nodes in performance evaluation. Eight nodes were used to evaluate the performance of CrossROAD in the static environment. In contrast, we simulate SMON by having used 50 nodes under mobility environments.

4   Performance Evaluation

We evaluate SMON by using Network Simulator NS2. The performance of our proposal is compared to the pull and push service discovery models under mobility scenarios. We are interested in the performance of SMON in heterogeneous MANET environments, divided into 2 types: one with mixture of different types of mobile nodes and the other one with gateway connectivity. The first heterogeneous scenario [5] simulates disaster area where rescuers carry PDAs (20 nodes with 2 Mpbs and 100 m) and laptops (30 nodes with 11 Mpbs and 250 m) in an area of square 1000 m x 1000 m. Random waypoint mobility is used with maximum speed of 2 m/s with pause time of 60 s. Next, the MANET with the gateway scenario shows how the SMON performance when the gateway is the only node sending the queries. We extend heterogeneous scenario to construct the gateway scenario. One gateway interface is connected to the wired node, and the other interface is a wireless interface that connects to mobile nodes. For all simulations, there are 25 CBR flows as background data traffic. The packet size and rate are

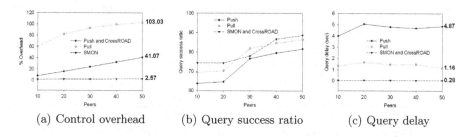

(a) Control overhead   (b) Query success ratio   (c) Query delay

Fig. 2. Control overhead, query success ratio, and delay in heterogeneous network

512 byte and 3 packets per second. Every peer has one unique service, and the query rate is 2 times per second. All simulations run for a duration of 900 s.

We use the following metrics to evaluate the SMON performance. The first metric is overlay control overhead that is the number of any messages from service discovery and the overlay over the number of routing messages. A query success ratio is another metric that is the percentage of success random lookups. The last metric is an average query delay that is a difference between the time a peer uses in searching and finding the service. We assume that CrossROAD nodes use push method to advertise theirs overlay presences. Therefore, overlay control overhead of CrossROAD is identical to overhead of push method. However, query success ratio and query delay of CrossROAD are the same with SMON because CrossROAD and SMON use the same service discovery mechanism.

In Fig. 2(a), the increase in number of services has an effect on the increase in number of overlay control overhead in push method, whereas the increase in service quires results in an increasing number of overlay control overhead in pull method. On the other hand, SMON overlay control overhead slightly increases and remains as constant value because the number of services and queries has no effect on the number of overlay control overhead. In the simulation results, we find that SMON reduces the number of overlay control overhead about 95% as compared to CrossROAD. Query success ratios of three protocols are similar. In Fig. 2(c), a peer in push model periodically advertises its service information every 10 s. Consequently, the average query delay is about 5 s. In pull model, most of the delay is accumulated from jitter, defined in OLSR RFC. Whenever a node has to forward an OLSR message, it should keep the message at least jitter time, a random value between 0 to $HELLO\_interval/4$. On the contrary, the query delay of SMON is the lowest because a service request is encapsulated in a unicast packet, which can be immediately forwarded by intermediate nodes without any delay. In gateway scenario, the wired node is the only one that asks for services via the gateway. Upon receiving the service requests, the gateway sends service quires to MANET on behalf of the wired node. The results from gateway scenario are shown in Fig. 3(a) and Fig. 3(b). The query success ratios of three models are similar, and SMON has the lowest query delay.

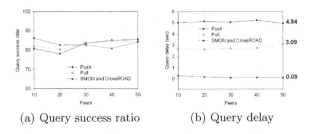

(a) Query success ratio   (b) Query delay

Fig. 3. Query success ration, and query delay in gateway scenario

5   Conclusion

We have presented the P2P overlay network cross-layer design on OLSR. SMON is the structured mesh overlay network that support efficient service lookups in P2P environments. We propose a new algorithm of creating and maintaining the overlay network on MANET to limit number of exchanging overlay messages. The simulation results has shown that SMON reduced number of overlay control overhead significantly, while it still maintains high query success ratio and low query delay, comparing to CrossROAD. As future work, we plan to investigate the performance of SMON under high mobility environments.

Acknowledgements

This work is based on a P2P multimedia communication system, EasyDC, developed for the Digital Ubiquitous Mobile Broadband OLSR Project by the Internet Education and Research Laboratory (intERLab).

References

1. Li, Z., Yin, X., Yao, P., Huang, J.: Implementation of P2P Computing in Design of MANET Routing Protocol. In: Proceedings of the First International Multi-Symposiums on Computer and Computational Sciences (April 2006)
2. Pucha, H., Das, S.M., Hu, Y.C.: Ekta: An Efficient DHT Substrate for Distributed Applications in Mobile Ad Hoc Networks. In: Proceedings of the Sixth IEEE Workshop on Mobile Computing Systems and Applications (December 2004)
3. Zahn, T., Schiller, J.: Performance Evaluation of a DHT-based Approach to Resource Discovery in Mobile Ad Hoc Networks. In: Proceedings of the Fourth Annual IEEE International Conference on Wireless on demand Network Systems and Services (January 2007)
4. Delmastro, F.: From Pastry to CrossROAD: CROSS-layer Ring Overlay for AD hoc Networks. In: Third IEEE International Conference on Pervasive Computing and Communications Workshops (March 2005)
5. Kanchanasut, K., Tunpan, A., Awal, M.A., Das, D.K., Wongsaardsakul, T., Tsuchimoto, Y.: A Multimedia Communication System for Collaborative Emergency Response Operation in Disaster-affected Areas, Technical Report No. TR_2007-1 January 2007, intERLab, Asian Institute of Technology (2007)

A Scalable and Adaptive Clustering Scheme for MANETs

Nevadita Chatterjee*, Anupama Potluri, and Atul Negi

Department of Computer and Information Sciences
University of Hyderabad, Gachibowli, 500046
chatterjee_nevadita@yahoo.co.in, {apcs,atulcs}@uohyd.ernet.in

Abstract. Clustering has evolved as an important research topic in MANETs as it improves the system performance of large MANETs. Most existing schemes have large overhead associated with cluster formation and cluster maintenance. They also trigger reclustering periodically. This renders these schemes non-scalable. In this paper, we present a clustering scheme that minimizes message overhead for cluster formation and maintenance. We do not require reclustering as clusters in our scheme do not degenerate into single node clusters over time. We simulated our clustering scheme in *ns-2*. The results show that the number of clusters formed are in proportion to the number of nodes in the MANET. We also show that our scheme is resilient to variations in mobility. This shows that our scheme is scalable as well as adaptable.

1 Introduction

Mobile Ad hoc Networks (MANETs) are infrastructureless and cooperative networks where every node participates in the multi-hop routing to reach all nodes in the network. In large MANETs, flooding due to routing severely degrades the efficient use of bandwidth and depletes battery-power of nodes. Hence, many clustering schemes have been proposed where the nodes in a network are divided into clusters. Hierarchical routing is adopted, where a standard proactive or reactive protocol can be used within the cluster but other protocols are used for inter-cluster routing. In the dominating set based clustering schemes [1], [2] routing is done based on a set of dominating nodes (DS). These schemes are quite expensive and not very scalable when the number of nodes in the MANET are large and are moving at high speeds. In MOBIC [4], the node with less relative mobility is elected as cluster head. Reclustering is triggered when two cluster heads are in transmission range of each other for a certain period of time or a node cannot access any cluster head. In Connectivity based K−Hop Clustering [3], a node declares itself a cluster head if it has the highest connectivity in its *k-hop* neighborhood or has a lower ID if more than one node in its neighborhood has the same connectivity. A node in the *k-hop* neighborhood of more than one

---

* Currently with Motorola India Pvt. Ltd.. This work was done while a graduate student in University of Hyderabad.

T. Janowski and H. Mohanty (Eds.): ICDCIT 2007, LNCS 4882, pp. 73–78, 2007.
© Springer-Verlag Berlin Heidelberg 2007

cluster head declares itself as a cluster gateway. Cluster maintenance is done by exchanging periodic messages to keep track of the *k-hop* neighbors of each node.

The effectiveness of a clustering scheme depends on the number of clusters formed. If the number of clusters formed are too many or too few, the advantages of clustering are lost. It is also important that the clustering scheme is scalable as the number of nodes in the MANET increase. The scheme must also be able to adapt itself to varying patterns of mobility. In this paper, we present our scheme which is an attempt to address the problems of scalability and adaptability in clustering of MANETs.

The rest of the paper is organized as follows: in Section 2, we present our scalable and adaptive clustering scheme. In Section 3 we discuss the simulation results. We conclude with Section 4.

2   Scalable and Adaptive Clustering Scheme

We propose a multi-hop clustering scheme [6] that has minimal communication overheads to form and maintain clusters. In our clustering scheme, each node in the cluster can be, atmost, a distance of K hops from its cluster head. However, we do not enforce this strictly. At any point of time, as long as the node is reachable from that cluster's members, it can maintain its membership in that cluster instead of triggering re-affiliation to a new cluster. Thus, we try to amortize the costs of maintaining the hop count from the cluster head.

2.1   Cluster Formation

The cluster formation starts as a node boots up in the network. When a node boots up, it broadcasts a cluster solicitation message to its immediate neighbors. If it does not get any reply within the specified time interval t, it declares itself as a cluster head. If it receives cluster advertisements in response to its solicitation message, the node examines the hop distance value field in the advertisements. If this is less than or equal to K, then, the node joins the cluster with the minimum hop count by sending a cluster acceptance message to the node(s) from which advertisements were received. However, if the hop count advertised is greater than K for all advertisements received, then, the node declares itself as a cluster head. Reception of multiple cluster advertisements by the new node indicates that it is within reachable distance of multiple clusters. Therefore, the node declares itself a cluster gateway and informs all the nodes which responded to its cluster solicitation. This is summarised in Algorithm 1.

2.2   Cluster Maintenance Scheme

The maintenance of the cluster structure is done by using any proactive routing protocol. In our scheme we have extended the DSDV [5] protocol to keep track of nodes in the cluster. The fields that are added in the control plane messages of DSDV are: *cluster head ID* to enable a node to recognise that the messages

---

Algorithm 1. *ClusterJoin( )*

1: send ClusterSolicitation( )
2: start Timer(time t)
3: **if** (Advertisements received) **then**
4:    **if** $getSmallestHopDistance(advtNode) \leq k$ **then**
5:       $clusterheadId \leftarrow advtNode.clusterheadId$
6:       $hopDistance \leftarrow advtNode.hopDistance$
7:       send ClusterAcceptance( )
8:    **end if**
9: **else**
10:    $clusterhead \leftarrow myaddress$
11:    $hopDistance \leftarrow 0$
12: **end if**

---

are from its cluster; *status* to indicate whether the originating node is a cluster gateway; *hop distance* to indicate the number of hops the node is away from the cluster head.

Cluster maintenance is triggered when a node does not receive DSDV messages from any of its cluster members. The node resets its cluster head and triggers the cluster join process. The other nodes in the cluster clear their routing tables when they no longer receive DSDV messages from this node. If the node leaving the cluster is the cluster head itself, then, all the nodes in the cluster reset their cluster head ID and elect the node with the lowest ID in their routing tables to be their new cluster head. If the node's movement has resulted in partitioning of the cluster, one partition contains the cluster head whereas the other partition has no cluster head. In the former, the nodes in the cluster simply clear their routing tables for all the nodes they have not heard from. In the second partition, the nodes elect the node with the lowest ID as the new cluster head. If the node has moved out of range of all nodes in the MANET, it waits for a certain period of time and triggers cluster join process. This is summarised in Algorithm 2.

Algorithm 2. *ClusterMaintenance( )*

1: **if** $ClusterheadUnreachable()$ **then**
2:    **if** $(clusterhead \leftarrow getLowestID(k))$ **then**
3:       $hopDistance \leftarrow dist(clusterhead)$
4:    **end if**
5: **else**
6:    ClusterJoin()
7: **end if**

---

3   Simulation and Discussion of Results

A MANET consisting of 50, 75, 100, 150 and 250 nodes with a simulation time of 2000 seconds was done using *ns-2* [7]. The mobile nodes were placed in a 2500

× 2500 m flat grid. The random waypoint mobility model was used with the mobility of the nodes in the range of 0-10m/s. Different pause times - 0, 2, 4 and 10 seconds - were used for determining the effect of mobility on clustering. Different K values - 2, 3 and 4 - are used to observe the effect of increasing hop distance of the cluster member from the cluster head. The parameters used to evaluate the performance of the clustering scheme are the following: *average number of cluster heads* and *number of cluster heads over time*. The first measures the effectiveness of cluster formation. The second parameter measures the effectiveness of maintenance by measuring how many clusters exist in the MANET over the duration of the simulation considering various factors such as mobility and density.

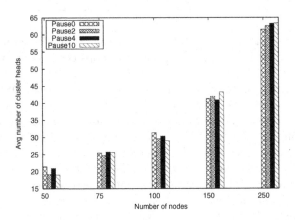

Fig. 1. Average Number of Cluster Heads with Different Density and Mobility

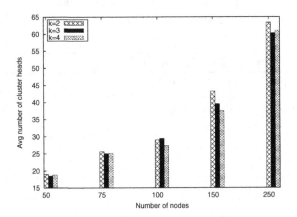

Fig. 2. Average Number of Cluster Heads with Varying K-values

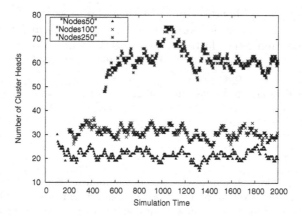

Fig. 3. Cluster Heads formed during Simulation with pause time 0

In Figure 1, we observe that the number of cluster members change from 2.5 on the average for 50 nodes to 4 members for 250 nodes. Thus, as density increases, we add more members into a cluster. However, the increase is less than linear. This can be explained by the fact that our algorithm forces a node to join the cluster whose cluster head is closest to the node. Therefore, the nodes in the cluster are normally at a distance less than k-$hops$ from the cluster head. This also leads to the result observed in Figure 2 where it is seen that varying k does not change the number of clusters formed too much. This is especially true for low density MANETs as the nodes are quite far from each other and so join the nearest cluster. On the other hand, when nodes are more close to each other, more of them will join the same cluster as they are within the k-hop distance. With increase in the value of k, the number of clusters will reduce as density increases. No reclustering or reaffiliation is triggered during the lifetime of the node unless it is out of range of all members of its cluster or its cluster head has disappeared from the cluster. This results in the membership of a cluster remaining constant over time irrespective of mobility of nodes. This can be readily observed in Figure 3. We have shown the results only for pause time 0 for lack of space but the same result is observed for all pause times.

4   Conclusions

In this paper, we have presented a novel multi-hop clustering scheme which is scalable and adaptable for various mobility and density conditions. The cluster formation phase involves very little control message overhead. Cluster mainte-nance is done by extending DSDV messages. Our simulation results show that the number of clusters formed is proportional to the number of nodes in the MANET. The increase is less than linear showing that as density of nodes in-creases in the MANET, the number of members in the cluster increases due to k-hop reachability criteria that is the basis of cluster formation in our scheme.

The clusters formed do not vary much with mobility as shown by the results for pause time zero. Our results also prove that our cluster maintenance is very effective in maintaining the cluster structure as the number of clusters does not vary much across the duration of simulation. This is achieved without resorting to a costly reclustering operation. Thus, our scheme helps reduce most of the control overhead associated with most of the other clustering schemes, making it scalable.

References

1. Wu, J., Li, H.: On Calculating-Connected Dominating Set for Efficient Routing in Ad Hoc Wireless Networks. In: Proc. 3rd International Workshop of Discrete Algorithms and Methods for Mobile Comp. and Commun., pp. 7–14 (1998)
2. Chen, Y.Z.P., Liestman, A.L.: Approximating Minimum Size Weakly-Connected Dominating Sets for Clustering Mobile Ad Hoc Networks. In: Proc. 3rd ACM International Symposium Mobile Mobile Ad Hoc Net. and Comp., pp. 165–172 (2002)
3. Chen, G., Nocetti, F., Gonzalez, J., Stojmenovic, I.: Connectivity-Based k-Hop Clustering in Wireless Networks. In: HICSS 2002. Proceedings of the 35th Annual Hawaii International Conference on System Sciences, vol. 7, pp. 188–198 (2002)
4. Basu, P., Khan, N., Little, T.D.C.: A Mobility Based Metric for Clustering in Mobile Ad Hoc Networks. In: ICDCSW 2001. Proceedings of the 21st International Conference on Distributed Computing Systems, p. 413 (2001)
5. Perkins, C., Bhagwat, P.: Highly Dynamic Destination-Sequenced Distance-Vector Routing (DSDV) for Mobile Computers. In: ACM SIGCOMM'94 Conference on Communications Architectures, Protocols and Applications, pp. 234–244 (1994)
6. Chatterjee, N., Potluri, A., Negi, A.: A Self-Organizing Approach to MANET Clustering. In: HiPC 2006. Poster Paper, International Conference on High Performance Computing, December 18-21, 2006, Bangalore, India (2006), http://www.hipc.org/hipc2006/posters/manet.pdf
7. The Network Simulator ns-2.29 (2005), http://www.isi.edu/nsnam/ns/2005

A Key Establishment Scheme for Large-Scale Mobile Wireless Sensor Networks

Ashok Kumar Das and Indranil Sengupta

Department of Computer Science and Engineering
Indian Institute of Technology, Kharagpur 721 302, India
{akdas,isg}@cse.iitkgp.ernet.in

Abstract. In this paper, we propose a key establishment scheme suitable for mobile sensor networks for establishing keys between sensor nodes in an environment where the sensor nodes are highly mobile. Our analysis and simulation results show that our scheme has high network connectivity as well as higher security against sensor node captures compared to those for the existing schemes. Moreover, our scheme supports efficiently addition of new nodes after initial deployment and also works for any deployment topology.

1 Introduction

A wireless sensor network consists of many tiny computing nodes, called sensors, are deployed for the purpose of sensing data and then transmitting the data to the nearby base stations. Public-key cryptosystems are not suited in such networks for secure communications because of resource limitations of the nodes and also due to the vulnerability of physical captures of the nodes by the enemy. Thus, the symmetric ciphers (for example, DES, AES, RC5) are the viable option for encrypting secret data. But, setting up symmetric keys among communicating nodes remains a challenging problem. The topology of the network is in general dynamic, because the connectivity among the sensor nodes may vary with time due to several factors such as node addition, node departures, and the possibility of having mobile nodes. In this paper, we assume that the nodes are highly mobile. Though several techniques [1,2,3] are proposed in the literature in order to establish secret pairwise keys among communicating sensor nodes, they are not much suitable for mobile sensor networks because the bootstrapping procedure involves considerable communication and computational overheads and can not be repeated quite often. In this paper, we propose a key pre-distribution mechanism suitable for mobile sensor networks.

2 Overview of the Dong and Liu's Scheme

The basic idea behind the Dong and Liu's scheme [4] is to deploy additional sensor nodes, called *assisting nodes*, which are only helpful for the pairwise key establishment between sensor nodes in a sensor network. The sensor nodes which

T. Janowski and H. Mohanty (Eds.): ICDCIT 2007, LNCS 4882, pp. 79–88, 2007.
© Springer-Verlag Berlin Heidelberg 2007

are not assisting nodes, called as the *regular sensor nodes*. Let n be the network size and m the number of assisting sensor nodes. In the *key pre-distribution phase*, before deployment, the key setup server generates a unique master key MK_u for every sensor node u which will be shared between u and the base station only. Every assisting node i will get preloaded with a hash value $H(MK_u||i)$ for every regular sensor node u, where H is a one-way hash function (for example, SHA-1) and "$||$" denotes the concatenation operation.

After deployment of nodes, in the *pairwise key establishment phase*, if a regular sensor node u wants to establish a pairwise key with its neighbor regular sensor node v, it will send a request to every neighbor assisting node i. The request message includes the IDs of u and v and will be protected by the key $H(MK_u||i)$, which is already preloaded to the assisting node i. After receiving such a request from u, the assisting node i generates a random key R, makes two copies of it, one is protected by $H(MK_u||i)$ (for node u) and the other is protected by $H(MK_v||i)$ (for node v) and finally sends these two protected copies of R to node u. Node u then gets R by decrypting the protected R using the key $H(MK_u||i)$ and forwards another protected copy of R to node v. Similarly, node v retrieves R by decrypting the protected R using the key $H(MK_v||i)$. Thus, u will receive a random key from every neighbor assisting neighbor node. If $\{R_1, R_2,\ldots, R_l\}$ be such a set of all these random keys, the final key between u and v is computed as $k_{u,v} = R_1 \oplus R_2 \oplus \cdots \oplus R_l$. If a regular sensor node could not find any assisting sensor node in its neighborhood, the *supplemental key establishment phase* will be performed, where a regular sensor node may discover the set of assisting nodes with a certain number of hops in order establish a pairwise key with its neighbor node.

3   Our Proposed Scheme

3.1   Motivation

In Dong and Liu's scheme [4], the assisting nodes are only used for pairwise key establishment purpose between regular sensor nodes and hence they do not help for secure node-to-node communication as well as authentication in a sensor network. Thus, in case of node compromising, they will not be helpful for secure communications.

Though their scheme provides high network connectivity and much better resilience against node captures than the EG scheme [1], the q-composite scheme [2], the random pairwise keys scheme [2] and the polynomial-pool based scheme [3], the main drawback of their scheme is that it does not support dynamic regular sensor node addition after initial deployment. Addition of new regular sensor nodes is extremely important for a sensor network, because sensor nodes may be compromised by an attacker or may be expired due to energy consumption, and as a result, we always expect to deploy some fresh nodes to join in the network in order to continue security services.

To overcome the above aforementioned problems, we propose a key establishment scheme suited for highly mobile sensor nodes. We make the assumption that a mobile node is aware of its physical movement.

3.2   Description of Our Approach

We consider a heterogeneous wireless sensor network consisting of two types of sensors: a small number m of High-end sensors (H-sensors) which will be static after deployment and a large number n of Low-end sensors (L-sensors) which will be randomly deployed and highly mobile. The H-sensors are equipped with high power batteries, large memory storages and data processing capacities, and large radio transmission range. On the other hand, the L-sensors are inexpensive and extremely resource constraints. For example, the H-sensors can be PDAs and the L-sensors are the MICA2-DOT motes [5]. We assume that an attacker can eavesdrop on all traffic, inject packets and reply old messages previously delivered. We further assume that if an attacker captures a node, all the keying information it holds will also be compromised. After deployment, we assume that H-sensors will be static, whereas L-sensors are highly mobile nodes in the network.

The main idea behind our scheme is to deploy a small number of additional H-sensor nodes along with a large number of L-sensor nodes in the network, so that H-sensors can help in pairwise key establishment procedure between sensor nodes. For convenience, we call the H-sensors as the *auxiliary nodes* because they will help for pairwise key establishment procedure and the L-sensors as the *regular sensor nodes*. Our protocol has the following phases.

Key pre-distribution phase: This phase is done in offline by a key setup server before deployment of the nodes in a target field. It consists of the following steps:

Step-1: For each auxiliary sensor node AS_i ($i = 1,2,\ldots,m$), the setup server assigns a unique identifier, say, id_{AS_i}. Similarly, for each regular sensor node u, the setup server also assigns a unique identifier, say, id_u.

Step-2: For each deployed auxiliary sensor node AS_i, the setup server assigns a unique randomly generated master key MK_{AS_i} which will be shared with the base station only. Similarly, for each deployed regular sensor node u, the setup server randomly generates a master key MK_u which will be shared with the base station only.

Step-3: The setup server then constructs a pool $\mathcal{N}$ of all identifiers of the regular sensor nodes to be deployed in a target field. We note that $\mathcal{N}$ consists of the identifiers of n regular sensor nodes.

Step-4: For each auxiliary sensor node AS_i, the setup server creates n key-plus-id combinations $\{(k_{AS_i,u_j}, id_{u_j}),\ j = 1, 2, \ldots, n\}$, where each key k_{AS_i,u_j} shared between AS_i and the regular sensor node u_j is computed as $k_{AS_i,u_j} = PRF_{MK_{u_j}}(id_{AS_i})$ using the master key MK_{u_j} of the regular sensor node u_j and the identifier id_{AS_i}. Here PRF is a pseudo random function proposed by Goldreich et al. [6].

Step-5: For all the deployed m auxiliary sensor nodes AS_i ($i = 1,2,\ldots,m$), the setup server randomly generates a t-degree bivariate polynomial $f(x,y) \in F_q[x,y]$ over a finite field F_q, with the property that $f(x,y) = f(y,x)$. Based on the security of the polynomial-based key distribution scheme [7], the value of t is chosen much larger (i.e., $t >> m$) so that even if an adversary compromises all the auxiliary nodes in the network, the polynomial $f(x,y)$ remains completely secure. The setup server then computes a polynomial share $f(id_{AS_i},y)$ for each deployed auxiliary node AS_i.

Step-6: For each deployed regular sensor node u, the setup server selects a set $S = \{id_{v_1}, id_{v_2}, \ldots, id_{v_l}\}$ of l node ids from the pool $\mathcal{N}$. For each pair (u, v_j), the setup server creates a key-plus-id combination (k_{u,v_j}, id_{v_j}) where k_{u,v_j} is computed as $k_{u,v_j} = PRF_{MK_{v_j}}(id_u)$.

Step-7: Finally, the setup server loads (i) the identifier id_{AS_i}, (ii) the master key MK_{AS_i}, (iii) n key-plus-id combinations computed in Step-4 and (iv) the polynomial share $f(id_{AS_i},y)$ to the memory of each auxiliary sensor node AS_i. Each regular sensor node u is loaded with the following information: (i) its own identifier id_u, (ii) its own master key MK_u and (iii) l key-plus-id combinations computed in Step-6.

Direct key establishment phase: After deployment, nodes will locate their physical neighbors within their communication ranges. Let AS_j be a neighbor auxiliary node of an auxiliary node AS_i. In order to establish a pairwise key between AS_i and AS_j, they first exchange their ids. After receiving the id of AS_j, AS_i computes a secret key shared with AS_j as $k_{AS_i,AS_j} = f(id_{AS_i}, id_{AS_j})$. Similarly, AS_j computes a secret key shared with AS_i as $k_{AS_i,AS_j} = f(id_{AS_j}, id_{AS_i})$. Since $f(x,y)$ is a symmetric polynomial, so the nodes AS_i and AS_j store the key k_{AS_i,AS_j} for their future secret communications.

In order to establish a secret key between an auxiliary sensor node, say, AS_i and a neighbor regular sensor node u, they will exchange their ids. We note that the auxiliary node AS_i has already the secret key-plus-id combination $(k_{AS_i,u}, id_u)$ during the key pre-distribution phase before deployment. After receiving the id of AS_i, u computes the key $k_{AS_i,u}$ shared with AS_i using its own master key MK_u as $k_{AS_i,u} = PRF_{MK_u}(id_{AS_i})$ and stores this key for future communication with AS_i.

Let u and v be two neighbor regular sensor nodes. In order to establish a key between them, they will exchange their ids. We note that if the key ring of one of them contains the id of other node, then they will be able to establish a secret key. Let the key ring of u contain the id id_v of v. Node u then sends a short notification to node v that it has a key $k_{u,v}$ shared with v. After receiving such a notification from node u, node v easily computes the key $k_{u,v}$ as $k_{u,v} = PRF_{MK_v}(id_u)$ using its own master key MK_v and the id id_u of the node u. Nodes u and v store this key $k_{u,v}$ for their future secret communications.

We now consider the case where two neighbor regular sensor nodes are not able to establish a secret key so far. In this case, if a regular sensor node u wants to establish a secret pairwise key with its neighbor regular sensor node v, node v will send a request to its auxiliary node. Let AS_i be an auxiliary node discovered by the node v within its neighborhood. Then the auxiliary node AS_i will generate a random key $k_{u,v}$, create two protected copies of it, one is for u and other is for v and send a reply containing these two protected copies of $k_{u,v}$ to node v. Upon receiving such a reply from AS_i, node v will retrieve $k_{u,v}$ and forward other copy to u. u will also retrieve $k_{u,v}$. Finally, u and v will store $k_{u,v}$ for their future secret communications. In this scenario, the protocol for establishing pairwise key between u and v is summarized below:

(1) Node u generates a random nonce RN_u and sends the following message to node v: $u \to v: (id_u || RN_u)$.

(2) Node v also generates a random nonce RN_v, computes a secret key $k_{AS_i,v} = PRF_{MK_v}(id_{AS_i})$ and sends the following message to its auxiliary node AS_i: $v \to AS_i: T = (id_u || id_v || RN_u || RN_v) || MAC_{k_{AS_i,v}}(T)$.

(3) The auxiliary node AS_i first computes $MAC_{k_{AS_i,v}}(T)$. If the computed MAC and the received MAC match, v is considered as a legitimate node. If the authentication is successful, then only the auxiliary node AS_i generates a random key $k_{u,v}$ shared between u and v and sends two copies of it, one is protected by $k_{AS_i,u}$ (for node u) and another is protected by $k_{AS_i,v}$ (for node v) to node v as follows: $AS_i \to v: E_{k_{AS_i,u}}(k_{u,v} \oplus id_u \oplus RN_u), E_{k_{AS_i,v}}(k_{u,v} \oplus id_v \oplus RN_v)$.

(4) Node v decrypts $E_{k_{AS_i,v}}(k_{u,v} \oplus id_v \oplus RN_v)$ using the previously computed key $k_{AS_i,v}$, retrieves $k_{u,v}$ using its own identifier and its own random nonce as $k_{u,v} = (k_{u,v} \oplus id_v \oplus RN_v) \oplus (id_v \oplus RN_v)$ and forwards other protected copy of $k_{u,v}$ along with the identifier id_{AS_i} of AS_i to node u: $v \to u: id_{AS_i} || (E_{k_{AS_i,u}}(k_{u,v} \oplus id_u \oplus RN_u))$.

Similarly, after receiving the last message from v, u retrieves $k_{u,v}$ using a computed key $k_{AS_i,u} = PRF_{MK_u}(id_{AS_i})$. The auxiliary sensor node AS_i discards the generated key $k_{u,v}$ from its memory. After key establishment, nodes u and v also discard their computed keys $k_{AS_i,u}$ and $k_{AS_i,v}$ from their memory. We note that each auxiliary node acts as a KDC (Key Distribution Center). We also observe that the transaction between two nodes is uniquely determined by attaching the random nonce of a node in the message by another node. After forming secure communication links by the nodes in the network, regular sensor nodes send their sensing data to their nearby auxiliary nodes. Data is routed back to the base station via auxiliary nodes.

Supplemental key establishment phase: Since the accurate deployment of the auxiliary nodes in their expected locations may not be guaranteed in some scenarios, it is still possible that a regular sensor node cannot find an auxiliary sensor node in its neighborhood. In this situation, we have the *supplemental key establishment phase*. In this phase, a regular sensor node discovers an auxiliary sensor node that is no more than h hops away from itself. This can be also easily achieved by having a regular sensor node u's neighbors to help collecting the id of an assisting node in their neighborhood. Once an auxiliary sensor node is discovered, the remaining steps are similar to the direct key establishment phase.

Dynamic node addition phase: In order to deploy a new regular sensor node u, the key setup server has to generate a unique identifier id_u and a unique random master key MK_u, and loads these in its key ring. The setup server then selects a set $S = \{id_{v_1}, id_{v_2}, \ldots, id_{v_l}\}$ of l node ids' from the pool $\mathcal{N}$. For each pair (u, v_j), the setup server creates a key-plus-id combination (k_{u,v_j}, id_{v_j}) where k_{u,v_j} is computed as $k_{u,v_j} = PRF_{MK_{v_j}}(id_u)$ and loads in its key ring. For each deployed auxiliary node AS_i, the key setup server also generates a key-plus-id combination $(k_{AS_i,u}, id_u)$ where $k_{AS_i,u} = PRF_{MK_u}(id_{AS_i})$ and the base station securely sends this to each deployed auxiliary node via auxiliary nodes only in the network.

In order to deploy a new auxiliary sensor node, say, AS_i, the key setup server assigns a unique identifier, say, id_{AS_i}. After that the setup server computes a polynomial share $f(id_{AS_i}, y)$ and n key-plus-id combinations $\{(k_{AS_i,u_j}, id_{u_j}), j = 1, 2, \ldots, n\}$, where n is the number of regular sensor nodes and each key k_{AS_i,u_j} is computed as $k_{AS_i,u_j} = PRF_{MK_{u_j}}(id_{AS_i})$ using the master key MK_{u_j} of the regular sensor node u_j and the identifier id_{AS_i}, and finally loads these informations in its key ring.

After deployment of such new nodes in the network, they establish pairwise keys with their neighbor nodes using our direct key establishment phase and if required, using the supplemental key establishment phase. Thus, we see that dynamic node addition in our protocol is done efficiently.

4   Analysis of Our Scheme

4.1   Network Connectivity

For simplicity, we assume that nodes are evenly distributed in the target field. Let m be the number of auxiliary sensor nodes and n the number of regular sensor nodes in the target field. Let d be the average number of neighbor nodes of each node. Let p denote the probability that two neighbor nodes can establish a pairwise key between them in the direct key establishment phase. Since the sensor network consists of m auxiliary nodes and n regular sensor nodes, total number of communication links is $(\sum_{i=1}^{m+n} d)/2 = \frac{(m+n)d}{2}$. Out of these links, we have $\frac{md}{2}$ secure links because of pairwise keys establishment between auxiliary nodes and their neighbor regular sensor nodes.

In order to establish a pairwise key between two neighbor regular sensor nodes u and v without help of any auxiliary sensor node, one of them should possess the id of other node along with the pre-calculated key. Let p' denote the probability that the id of a regular sensor node will be resident in another regular sensor node's key ring. We then have, $p' = 1 - \binom{n-1}{l} / \binom{n}{l} = \frac{l}{n}$. Let p_1 be the probability that two regular sensor nodes u and v can establish a key in such case. We then have, $p_1 = 1-$ (probability that none of u and v will establish a pairwise key). Hence, we have, $p_1 = 1 - (1 - p')^2$. Now, we have another $\frac{nd}{2} \times p_1$ secure links due to pairwise keys establishment between regular sensor nodes without help of any auxiliary sensor nodes. Thus, so far, we have $\frac{md}{2} + \frac{nd}{2} \times p_1$ secure links.

In order to establish a pairwise key between two neighbor regular sensor nodes u and v with help of an auxiliary sensor node, if u initiates a request to establish a pairwise key with v, v is required to communicate with an auxiliary sensor node in its communication range. The probability that an auxiliary node AS_i is not in the neighborhood of the regular sensor node v can be estimated by $1 - \frac{d}{m+n}$. Since there are m auxiliary nodes in the network, the probability that the regular sensor node v fails to discover any auxiliary node AS_i in its neighborhood can be estimated by $(1 - \frac{d}{m+n})^m$. As a result, in this case, the probability of establishing a pairwise key between u and v is given by $p_2 = 1 - (1 - \frac{d}{m+n})^m$. Hence, the overall network connectivity is given by $p = (\frac{md}{2} + \frac{nd}{2} \times p_1 + \frac{nd}{2} \times (1 - p_1) \times p_2)/(\frac{(m+n)d}{2}) = (m+n \times (p_1+p_2-p_1p_2))/(m+n)$. Figure 1 shows the relationship between the probability p of establishing keys between neighbor nodes vs. the fraction of auxiliary sensor nodes $\frac{m}{n}$. We assume that each regular sensor node has available storage of 200 cryptographic keys. From this Figure, we observe that p increases faster as d increases. Moreover, for a small fraction of auxiliary sensor nodes $\frac{m}{n}$, our scheme guarantees a high probability of establishing keys between neighbor sensor nodes.

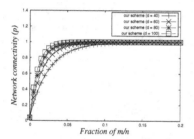
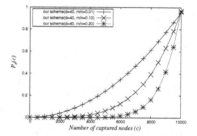

Fig. 1. Direct network connectivity p of our scheme vs. the fraction of auxiliary sensor nodes $\frac{m}{n}$, with $n = 10000$

Fig. 2. Resilience against node capture of our scheme vs. the number of compromised nodes, with $m = 500, 1000, 2000$ and $n = 10000$

4.2   Resilience Against Node Captures

The resilience against node capture attack of a scheme is measured by estimating the fraction of total secure communications that are compromised by a capture of c nodes *not including* the communication in which the compromised nodes are directly involved. We note that based on the security of PRF function [6], it is computationally difficult to compute the master key MK_u of a node u from the key $k_{u,v} = PRF_{MK_u}(id_v)$. Since there are m auxiliary nodes and n regular sensor nodes in the network, total number of links is $\frac{(m+n)d}{2}$. The total secure links in the network is $\frac{d}{2} \times (m+n(p_1+p_2-p_1p_2))$. Let us assume that an attacker will randomly compromise a fraction f_c of sensor nodes. The probability that all the keys are compromised when the nodes will establish the keys using auxiliary sensor node is estimated by $f_c^{(m\times d)/n}$. Hence, the required fraction of total secure communication compromised due to capture of a fraction f_c of sensor nodes is given by $P_e(c) = (1 - \frac{n}{m+n} \cdot \frac{p_1}{p}) \times f_c^{(m\times d)/n}$. The resilience against node capture of our scheme is shown in Figure 2. This Figure shows that our approach is highly resilient against node capture attack. It is also noted that the security of our scheme can be enhanced by deploying more auxiliary nodes in the network.

5   Simulation Results

We have implemented our proposed scheme for static networks as well as mobile networks. We have considered the following parameters for simulation of network connectivity of our scheme as follows: the number of regular sensor nodes is $n = 10000$, the number of auxiliary nodes is $m \leq 1000$, the average number of neighbor nodes for each node is $d = 80$, the communication range of each sensor node is $\rho = 30$ meters and the area A of the target field is taken so that the maximum network size becomes $n = \frac{(d+1)\times A}{\pi \rho^2}$.

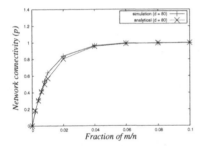
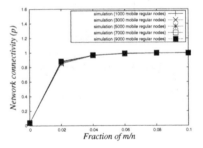

Fig. 3. Simulation vs. analytical results of direct network connectivity p of our scheme, with $n = 10000$, $m \leq 1000$ and $d = 80$, under static network

Fig. 4. Simulation results of direct network connectivity p of our scheme for mobile regular sensor nodes under different situations, with $n = 10000$, $m \leq 1000$ and $d = 80$

The regular sensor nodes are randomly deployed in the target field which is a flat region. For deployment of auxiliary sensor nodes, we logically divide the target field into $c \times c$ cells, where $c = \lceil \sqrt{m} \rceil$. For each cell, an auxiliary sensor node is to be deployed randomly in that cell. The simulation results vs. the analytical results of direct network connectivity p of our scheme are plotted in Figure 3. In this Figure, we assume that all the nodes are static. From this Figure we observe that our simulation results closely tally with the analytical results. We have also simulated the direct network connectivity p of our scheme under mobile environment. We assume that after deployment the auxiliary sensor nodes remain static, whereas the regular sensor nodes will be highly mobile. We have considered that any regular sensor node can move from its current location in the target field in the range of twice its communication range. The simulation results for mobile regular nodes are shown in Figure 4. From this Figure, we see that our scheme is much suitable for highly mobile sensor networks.

6   Comparison with Previous Schemes

Figure 5 shows the comparison of direct network connectivity p between our scheme and Dong and Liu's scheme, with different values of d ($d = 60, 80$), where d is the average number of neighbor nodes of each node. We see from this figure that our scheme has better network connectivity compared to that for the Dong and Liu's scheme.

Figure 6 shows the relationship between the fraction of compromised links between non-compromised nodes vs. the number of captured nodes. For the EG scheme [1], the q-composite scheme [2], the polynomial-pool based scheme [3] and our scheme, we assume that each node is capable of holding 200 cryptographic keys in its memory. The network connectivity probability p is taken as $p = 0.33$ with suitable values of the parameters for the different schemes. We clearly see that our scheme provides significantly much better security against node captures than the EG,the q-composite and the polynomial-pool based schemes. Moreover, our scheme has better security than the Dong and Liu's scheme.

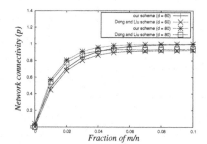

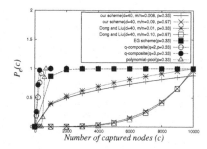

Fig. 5. Comparison of network connectivity (p) between our scheme and Dong & Liu's scheme

Fig. 6. Comparison of resilience against node captures between different schemes

7   Conclusion

We have proposed a key establishment scheme for mobile sensor networks with the help of additional auxiliary sensor nodes. Performance evaluation and security analysis show that our scheme provides very high network connectivity as well as high resilience against node capture attack than the existing schemes. Our simulation results demonstrate that our scheme is highly applicable for mobile sensor networks. Our scheme also supports dynamic node addition after initial deployment.

References

1. Eschenauer, L., Gligor, V.D.: A key management scheme for distributed sensor networks. In: 9th ACM Conference on Computer and Communication Security, pp. 41–47 (2002)
2. Chan, H., Perrig, A., Song, D.: Random key predistribution schemes for sensor networks. In: IEEE Symposium on Security and Privacy, Berkeley, California, pp. 197–213 (2003)
3. Liu, D., Ning, P.: Establishing pairwise keys in distributed sensor networks. In: Proceedings of 10th ACM Conference on Computer and Communications Security (CCS) (2003)
4. Dong, Q., Liu, D.: Using Auxiliary Sensors for Pairwise Key Establishment in WSN. In: Networking 2007. Proceedings of 2007 IFIP International Conferences on Networking (2007)
5. Crossbow Technology Inc.: Wireless sensor networks, `http://www.xbow.com`
6. Goldreich, O., Goldwasser, S., Micali, S.: How to construct random functions. Journal of the ACM 33, 792–807 (1986)
7. Blundo, C., Santis, A.D., Herzberg, A., Kutten, S., Vaccaro, U., Yung, M.: Perfectly-secure key distribution for dynamic conferences. In: Brickell, E.F. (ed.) CRYPTO 1992. LNCS, vol. 740, pp. 471–486. Springer, Heidelberg (1993)

Monitoring Information Leakage During Query Aggregation

Sastry Konduri, Brajendra Panda, and Wing-Ning Li

Computer Science and Computer Engineering Department
University of Arkansas
Fayetteville, AR 72701, USA
`bpanda@uark.edu, wingning@uark.edu`

Abstract. Data sharing and information exchange have grown exponentially with the information explosion in the last few years. More and more data are being shared among different types of users residing in different places, performing different kinds of tasks for different kinds of applications. Privacy control is a major issue for today's data managers. In this research, we presented two models to solve the information leakage problem occurring during query aggregation. The first model is the base model that uses a single inference dispersion value for each user where as the second model uses multiple inference dispersion values for each user with a view to provide more accessibility.

1 Introduction

In the past few years, with the unprecedented information explosion, data sharing and information exchange have grown tremendously. So, more and more data are being shared among different kinds of users doing different kinds of jobs, residing in different places, for different kinds of applications. As a result, privacy control has become a major issue for today's data managers. By implementing access control policies, one can ensure that users are able to access only the data they are authorized to access. But in almost all databases, dependencies among various data items exist. For example, in his report [1], Anderson stated that the combination of birth date and zip code along with some other data in a healthcare database is sufficient to identify 98% of the UK's population. If we assume that a user has the required access to obtain the birth date, zip code, and some other needed data in the above mentioned database, he may be able to correctly identify a person 98% of the time.

Database management systems are intended to provide the means for efficient storage and retrieval of information. If they are properly designed, they will not only be able to control access to the database, but will also be able to prevent inferences. So, a good database should always be designed with some means of controlling inference problems. The goal of any query based inference detection system is to detect if a user can indirectly access data using two or more queries.

In this paper, we have presented two models for controlling inference during query aggregation. A module called inference interpreter is the heart of each of

T. Janowski and H. Mohanty (Eds.): ICDCIT 2007, LNCS 4882, pp. 89–96, 2007.

these models. Whenever a user queries the database, the query is passed through the inference interpreter. Based on the data items already sent to the user and the data items currently requested the interpreter determines if there is a possibility of inference. The interpreter rejects the query if it finds that inference is possible; otherwise, the query is processed. The interpreter determines inference mathematically by using a mechanism called aggregation graphs and setting up a threshold called inference dispersion.

Both models presented in this paper are based on the following assumptions. The database D is composed of a set of data items $(d_1, d_2, d_3 \ldots d_n)$. We assume that the only way of inferring some data in the database is by using aggregation. Furthermore, we also assume that users do not work together to pool their collective knowledge to reach inferences, which they could not reach individually.

The rest of this paper is organized as follows. Sections 2 and 3 discuss the two models respectively. Some related research are presented in section 4 and section 5 offers the conclusions and future research plan.

2   The Base Model

As stated earlier, our model assumes a non-collaborative environment - that is, users do not share information. Users try to obtain data items from the database by querying it. Every query posed by a user is made to pass through the inference interpreter as mentioned in previous section.

2.1   Inference Interpreter

The inference interpreter maintains a table called the status table, which contains information about all users, each user's domain, the set of data items given to the user, the expiration date, and the inference dispersion. The user column of the status table identifies the user. The domain column represents the domain of the particular user. Whenever a user requests some data items from the database, the interpreter checks to see if the data item is in the domain of the user, and, if it is not in the domain, it generates an error message. The data items column represents the data items, which were already sent to the user. Before explaining the concept of Inference Dispersion, we first introduce the concept of *aggregation graphs*.

An aggregation graph is the graphical representation of the aggregation among data items. As stated earlier, our model is based on data classification using aggregation where the data items at a higher level can be obtained from the data items at the lower level. We call this *depends on* relationship. This means that a data item in the higher level depends on a set of data items in the next level below it. Such a relationship is represented by a set of directed edges from a node to its children nodes. Figure 1 depicts an example aggregation graph.

2.2 Inference Dispersion (Δ)

For each user, the inference interpreter maintains a parameter called *inference dispersion*, represented by Δ. Inference dispersion indicates how close the user is from inferring some data, which is not in his domain. By setting a threshold over the value of Δ, our model controls the inference. Initially the value of Δ is set to 0. For calculating the inference dispersion of a user, the inference interpreter first determines the aggregation graphs corresponding to all the data items in the user's domain. There may be more than one aggregation graph associated with a user. To demonstrate this, consider a user u with data items $(d_1, d_2, d_3, \ldots, d_n)$ in the domain. In these n data items, a given set of k data items ($k < n$) may be aggregated to infer a particular data item d_i, where as another set of p data items ($p < n$) may lead to a data item d_j as well.

As mentioned before, in our model, the aggregation is the only means of inference. That is the aggregation graphs associated with a user indicate the means of inference for that user. So, if by imposing some conditions on accessing the data items in the aggregation graphs the inference interpreter determines that no inference is possible in each of the graphs then it allows the user to access the requested data item. Let us assume that the aggregation graphs $(a_1, a_2, a_3, \ldots, a_k)$ are associated with a user u. Now, suppose the aggregation graph a_i ($1 \leq i \leq k$) looks as shown in Figure 1.

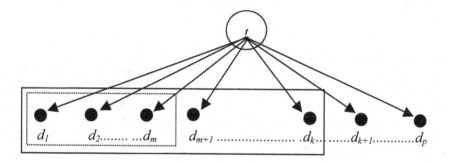

Fig. 1. An Example of an Aggregation Graph a_i

In Figure 1, the data items in the box with solid edges, that is, the data items d_1 to d_k are the data items in the domain of user u. An important point to note here is that there may be some data items (d_{k+1} to d_p) in the aggregation graph, which are not in the domain of the user. The data item t is called the target data item; it is the item, which may be inferred from the data items at the lower level. The data items in the dotted box are those, which the user u has already obtained. It is possible that a single data item may be present in more than one aggregation graph.

For each aggregation graph a_i, the inference interpreter calculates a value Δ_i that indicates how close a user is to obtaining the target data item using the corresponding aggregation. We call this measure the dispersion of the particular aggregation graph. Let us assume that there are p leaf nodes (data items) in the graph and the user had already obtained m data items ($m < p$) say $(d_1, d_2, d_3, \ldots d_m)$. Then,

$$P = (\Sigma_{j=1}^{m} pr(t/d_j)) \times C$$

$$\text{and } \Delta_i = P log P$$

In the above equation of P, pr denotes probability function and C is a constant, which is application dependent. The value of C is set so as to make the least value of $pr(t/d)$ greater than or equal to 1. The constant C ensures that P is always greater than 1 and thus making sure that Δ_i always increases with the increase of P. Where d_j is any data item in the database and t is any target data item which depends on data items including d_j. Here, we are using the function $P log P$ to make the curve of Δ steeper as the threshold is approached. That is, even a small increase in the number of data items the user attained increases the Δ value by a high value as Δ approaches the threshold. But if the situation demands for a higher increase in Δ, a different function such as P^2 can be used.

Using the similar method, Δ_q is calculated for each of the aggregation graphs a_q, $1 \le q \le k$. Now, the inference dispersion Δ of the user is given by,

$$\Delta = max(\Delta_1, \Delta_2, \Delta_3, \ldots, \Delta_k)$$

where k is the number of aggregation graphs associated with the user.

Similarly the inference dispersion is calculated for all other users and is stored in the status table. Δ indicates the dispersion of the aggregation graph where the user is closest to obtaining a target data item. Therefore by setting a threshold over the value of Δ and by updating the value of Δ each time the user accesses a data item, the inference in the aggregation graph is controlled. The system maintains the same for all the users to guarantee an inference free environment across the entire database.

2.3   Updating the Value of (Δ)

Let us consider the aggregation graph shown in Figure 1 again. Now assume that the user u is requesting data item d_{m+1}. Before the user is given access to the data item, the inference interpreter recalculates the value of Δ_i using d_{m+1} in the calculation of P. That is, this value indicates how close the user u would be to infer the target data item t if the obtains the data item d_{m+1}. Next the interpreter calculates the value of Δ with the new value of Δ_i. It is important to note here that the interpreter only calculates the value of Δ; it does not update the status table with this new value. Now, the interpreter compares the calculated value to the threshold of Δ. If the value is greater than the threshold, then it does not allow the user to access the data item. If the value is less than or equal to the threshold, the user is given the requested data item and the value of Δ in the status table corresponding to this user u is updated with this new value of Δ.

In the case when the requested data item participates in multiple aggregation graphs, the inference interpreter runs the above check for all those aggregation graphs before allowing the user access to the data item. Obviously, Δ should be less than the threshold in all those tests. That is, before a data item is sent to the user, the system makes sure that the threshold for Δ is not being exceeded in any of the aggregation graphs, associated with the user, that involves the requested data item.

2.4 The Algorithm

The following variables are used in the algorithm. T: Threshold value for Δ, d: The data item the user is requesting, S: The set $(G_1, G_2, G_3, \ldots, G_k)$ of k aggregation graphs associated with the data item, G_i: The aggregation graph currently under consideration, m_i: The number of data items of G_i that have already been obtained by the user, and t_i: The data item which can be inferred using G_i.

The following algorithm describes the process which takes place at the inference interpreter when a user requests a data item d. The algorithm is self-explanatory; hence, no further explanations are provided here due to space constraints.

```
1    For each Aggregation graph G_i in S Loop;
2         Calculate the value: P = [(Σ^{m_i}_{j=1} pr(t_i/d_j)) + pr(t_i/d)] × C;
3         Δ_i = P log P;
4         if (Δ_i > T)
5              exit;
6         end if;
7    end loop;
8    Δ = max(Δ_1, Δ_2, Δ_3, ..., Δ_m);
9    send the data item to the user;
10   update m_i to reflect the fact data item d has been obtained;
11   exit;
```

3   A Lenient Model to Offer More Accessibility

In the model presented in the previous section, we observe that the interpreter maintains a single Δ value for each user. This means that once one of the aggregation graphs reaches the threshold, the user can access no other data item. Once this happens, even if the user tries to access the data items, which may not lead to any inference, the user's request will be denied. To solve this problem, we present a lenient model in this section.

3.1   The Lenient Model

This model stores separate Δ values for each aggregation graph of each user. Thus, the status table that the inference interpreter maintains looks as shown in Figure 2.

User	Domain	Data Items Accessed	Inference Dispersion (Δ)				
			a_1	a_2	a_3	$\cdots$	a_k

Fig. 2. The Status Table Used in the Lenient Model

The interpreter maintains separate Δ values for each aggregation graph. Whenever a user requests a data item, the interpreter finds which aggregation graphs the data item is present in and then sends the data item only if sending the data item does not lead to inference (Δ < threshold) in any of these aggregation graphs. In the previous model, if the threshold is reached in one of the aggregation graphs, then no other data item can be sent. In this improved model, sending of the data item depends only on the aggregation graphs associated with the particular data item. So, more data items will be sent in this model than in the previous one without leading to any kind of interference. But since we are maintaining separate Δ value for each aggregation graph, the size of the status table will be much larger than the one in the previous model. In databases where data items are constantly inserted and deleted, this model is not a good one to use. But for a static database where most of the operations are reads and updates, this model might be a better solution. Next, we present the algorithm for this model.

3.2   The Algorithm

In addition to the variables used in the previous algorithm, this algorithm uses the following variables.

- $(\Delta_1, \Delta_2, \ldots, \Delta_k)$: The Δ values associated with $(G_1, G_2, \ldots, G_k)$
- temp[ ]: A temporary array

The following process is performed at the inference interpreter.

```
1    For each Aggregation graph G_i in S Loop;
2         calculate the value: P = [(Σ^{m_i}_{j=1} pr(t_i/d_j)) + pr(t_i/d)] × C;
3         temp[i]= P log P;
4         if (temp[i]> T)
5              exit;
6         end if;
7    end loop;
8    for i from 1 to m loop
9         Δ_i =temp[i];
```

10   end loop;
11   send the data item to the user;
12   update m_i to reflect the fact data item d has been obtained;
13   exit;

4   Related Research

The basic need for inference control is to protect the privacy of a database. The major motivating domains for inference control have been the medical and military domains. Morgernstern [8] addressed the threat to multilevel security that emerged from logical inference and the semantics of the application. He provided an in depth description of the problem of inference, inference channels, degree of influence, and correcting potential inference channels. In [10], Thuraisingham has proved that it is impossible to identify all the inference channels. Chen and Chu [4] presented a modular architectural framework for the problem of inference control. In [11], Qian et. al. described a static model to eliminate inference. Burns [2], and Meadows and Jajodia [7] have claimed that integrity is in fundamental conflict with secrecy. In [6], Jajodia and Meadows presented an introduction to inference and aggregation. In [12], Yip and Levitt offered a data level inference detection system in which they identified and defined different types of inference. Chang and Moskowitz in [3] presented the study of inference problems in a distributed database environment. They used a Bayesian network to identify the inference. In [5], Hinke described a graph based inference aggregation detection scheme. In a recent paper, Simpson et. al [9] have discussed the information leakage problem in Healthcare systems in a Grid environment.

5   Conclusions

Inference control is a primary issue in databases that contain sensitive data. The key mode for inference in many databases is aggregation. In this research, we presented two models to solve the aggregation inference problem. Model 1 performs inference control by maintaining an inference dispersion (Δ) for each user. A threshold is set on the value of Δ, and users whose Δ value exceeds the threshold are not sent any more data items. The decision based on a single Δ value for each user leads to less accessibility. This problem was solved by introducing a separate Δ value for each aggregation graph associated with each user in Model 2. As a future research plan, we wish to study inference control in a collaborative environment.

Acknowledgement. The work performed by Brajendra Panda has been supported in part by US AFOSR under grant FA 9550-04-1-0429. We are thankful to Dr. Robert. L. Herklotz for his support, which made this work possible.

References

1. Anderson, R.: An integrated Survey of Medical Databases (1998),
   http://www.clcam.ac.uk/simrja14/caldicott/caldicott.html
2. Burns, R.K.: Integrity and Secracy: Fundamental Conflicts in the Database Environment. In: Proceedings of the Third RADC Database Security Workshop, pp. 37–40 (1990)
3. Chang, L.W., Mokowitz, I.: A Study of Inference Problems in Distributed Databases. In: Research Directions in Data and Applications Security, 16th Annual Edition, pp. 191–204
4. Chen, Y., Chu, W.: Database Security Protection via Inference Detection, Computer Science Department, University of California, Los Angeles, CA, USA
5. Hinke, T.H.: Inference Aggregation Detection in Database Management Systems. In: First IEEE Computer Security Foundations Workshop (1988)
6. Jajodia, S., Meadows, C.: Inference Problems in Multilevel Secure Database Management Systems. In: Abrams, M. (ed.) Information Security and Collection of Essays, IEEE Press, Los Alamitos (1995)
7. Meadows, C., Jajodia, S.: Integrity versus Security in Multilevel Secure Databases. In: Database Security: Status and Prospects (1988)
8. Morgernstern, M.: Security and Inference in Multilevel Database and Knowledge-Base Systems. SRI International Computer Science Laboratory, Menlo Park, CA (1987)
9. Simpson, A., Power, D., Slaymaker, M.: On Tracker Attacks in Health Grids. In: Proceedings of the 2006 ACM Symposium on Applied Computing, Dijon, France (April 2006)
10. Thuraisingham, B.: Recursion Theoritic Properties of the Inference Problem. In: Third IEEE Computer Security Foundations Workshop (1990)
11. Qian, X., Stickel, M., Karp, P., Lunt, T., Garvey, T.: Detection and Elimination of Inference Channels in Multilevel Relational Database Systems. In: IEEE Symposium on Security and Privacy (1993)
12. Yip, R.W., Levitt, K.N.: Data Level Inference Detection in Database Systeme. Department of Computer Science, University of California, Davis, CA, USA (1998)

An Efficient Certificate Authority for Ad Hoc Networks

Jaydip Sen and Harihara Subramanyam

Embedded Systems Innovation Lab, Tata Consultancy Services
96, EPIP Industrial Estate, Whitefield Road,
Bangalore-560066, India
{jaydip.sen,harihara.g}@tcs.com

Abstract. The attractiveness of the wireless ad hoc networks lies in the fact that these networks are self-organized: the hosts constituting the networks can communicate with each other without reliance on any centralized or specified entities such as base stations or access points. With these networks finding more applications, the need for adequate security mechanism is increasingly becoming important. Key management is an essential cryptographic primitive upon which other security protocols are built. However, most of the existing key management schemes are not feasible in ad hoc networks because public key infrastructures with a centralized certification authority are hard to deploy there. In this paper, we propose and evaluate a mechanism of distributed certification authority based on threshold cryptography that is suited for wireless ad hoc networks. In the proposed scheme, a collection of nodes acts as the certificate authority and provides the certification service. The feasibility of the proposed scheme is verified by simulation. The results show the effectiveness of the scheme.

1 Introduction

An ad hoc network is a group of mobile nodes without a centralized administration or a fixed network infrastructure. The mobility of the nodes and the fundamentally limited capacity of the wireless medium, together with wireless transmission effects such as attenuation, multi-path propagation and interference combine to create significant challenges for security in such networks. Due to lack of an underlying infrastructure, basic functionalities such as routing, configuration of the hosts, or security management cannot rely on predefined or centralized entities to operate and must be carried out in a distributed manner. However, due to this distributed nature, ad networks are vulnerable to various types of attacks. Wireless links can be eavesdropped on without noticeable effort and communication protocols on all layers are vulnerable to specific attacks.

Public Key Infrastructure (PKI) – an infrastructure for creating, distributing and managing digital certificates is a widely used mechanism for implementing security in wired networks and infrastructure-based wireless networks with

T. Janowski and H. Mohanty (Eds.): ICDCIT 2007, LNCS 4882, pp. 97–109, 2007.

access points and base stations. The heart of any PKI system is the *Certificate Authority* (CA). CA is a trusted entity that vouches for the authenticity of the digital certificates issued by PKI. The effectiveness of a PKI depends on the robustness, security and availability of the CA. Most of the solutions proposed in the literature (Section 2) for providing PKI services to ad hoc networks rely on distributing the CA functionality across multiple nodes using threshold cryptography. While these approaches increase the availability of the CA, they involve large communication overhead. Moreover, network partitioning can make a distributed CA nonfunctional.

In this paper, we propose and evaluate a key management scheme with a communication protocol that suits the dynamic nature of an ad hoc network. We extend the MOCA (Mobile Certificate Authority) framework as suggested by Yi and Kravets [1] and develop a highly reliable protocol for distributed CA. The proposed protocol has less communication overhead compared to MOCA framework. In the proposed mechanism, a set of nodes in an ad hoc network is first chosen based on certain parameters (Section 3.1) and the CA functionality is distributed on them. An efficient and robust communication protocol is developed between these CA nodes so that the certification facility is available even in presence of transient network partitioning scenario. Threshold cryptographic technique is utilized for distribution of CA functionalities. The communication overhead is minimized by avoiding flooding in the network and using multicasting for certificate requests. This is achieved by leveraging the information in the routing cache maintained in the nodes.

The rest of the paper is organized as follows. Section 2 discusses some of the related research works done in the area of key management and trust establishment in ad hoc networks. Section 3 describes the proposed CA framework. Section 4 depicts an outline of the communication protocol used in the proposed scheme. Section 5 presents the simulation results of the scheme. Finally, Section 6 concludes the paper while identifying some possible extensions of the present work.

2   Related Work

In this section, we discuss some of the currently existing works in area of key management and certificate distribution in ad hoc networks. We specifically discuss three major approaches in key management process, e.g., distributed trust model, ad hoc trust model based on threshold cryptography, and a self-organized trust model.

Abdul-Rahman and Hailes have proposed the Distributed Trust Model -a decentralized approach to trust management that uses a recommendation protocol to exchange trust-related information [2]. The model assumes that relationships are unidirectional and exist between two entities. The model is suited for establishing trust relationships that are less formal and temporary in nature, e.g., some ad hoc commercial transactions.

Zhou and Haas have introduced a key management system for ad hoc networks based on threshold cryptography [3]. A group of n servers together with a master public/private key pair are first deployed by a CA. Each server has a share of the master private key and stores the key pairs of all nodes. The shares of master private key are generated using threshold cryptography. Thus only n servers together can form a whole signature. If any node wants to join the network, it must first collect all of the n partial signatures. Then the node can compute the whole signature locally and thus get the certificate. This scheme has been extended in a mechanism proposed by Kong, Zefros, Luo, Lu and Zhang [7]. In this extended scheme, during the network bootstrapping phase, a centralized dealer is needed to issue certificates and private key shares to at least t nodes. A threshold cryptography system is also deployed in order to provide a (t, n) secret sharing service. Any t nodes can form a centralized dealer and can thus issue or revoke certificates. In this scheme, a node willing to join the network will have to collect t partial signatures in its local communication range. Although this method facilitates the joining and leaving of nodes to some extent, it increases the risk of leaking of private key of the centralized dealer.

Asokan and Ginzboorg have introduced several password-based key exchange methods to set up a secure session among a group of nodes without any support infrastructure [11]. In this scheme, only those nodes that know an initial password are able to obtain the session key. The session key is formed by combinations from all the nodes in the network. Initially, a weak password is sent to all the group members. Each member then contributes part of the key and signs this data by using the weak password. Finally, to establish a secure session key, a secure channel is derived without any central trust authority or support infrastructure.

Stajano and Anderson have proposed *Resurrecting Duckling* security protocol to establish trust in ad hoc networks [12]. The protocol is particularly suited for devices without display and for embedded devices that are too weak for public key operations. The fundamental authentication problem is solved by a secure and transient association between two devices establishing a master-slave relationship. It is secure in the sense that the master and the slave share a common secret. The protocol is transient because the master at any point of time can terminate the association. Also, a master can always identify its slave in a set of similar devices.

Hubaux, Buttyan and Capkun have proposed a self-organized public key infrastructure-based trust building scheme [4]. The scheme is similar to *Pretty Good Privacy* (PGP) [5] web of trust model. However, unlike in PGP, here are no central certificate directories for distribution of certificates. In order to find the public key of a remote user, a local user makes use of *Hunter Algorithm* [4] on the merged certificate repository to build certificate chain(s). A certificate trust chain should initiate from the local user's certificate and terminate at the remote user's certificate. The probability of finding such a certificate chain in this scheme is high, but is not guaranteed. However, this decentralized scheme leads to disclosure of too much information about the originating nodes, as it releases several unnecessary certificates.

Eshenaur, Gligor and Baras have proposed a trust establishment mechanism for ad hoc networks [6]. In this scheme, a node in the network can generate trust evidence about any other node. When a *principal* generates a piece of trust evidence, it signs the evidence with its own private key, specifying the lifetime and makes it available to others through the network. A principal may revoke a piece of evidence it produced by generating a revocation certificate for that piece of evidence and making it available to others at any time before the evidence expires. A principal can get disconnected after distributing trust evidence. Similarly, a producer of trust evidence does not have to be reachable at the time its evidence is being evaluated. Evidences can be replicated across various nodes to guarantee availability. Although the scheme seems conceptually sound, the authors have not provided any details about performance evaluation of the scheme.

However, most of the above mentioned key management protocols have limitations. In the distributed CA scheme involving threshold cryptography [7], the trust between a new node willing to join the network and t existing nodes in the network can be established by out-of-bound physical proofs, such as, human perception or biometrics. However, these methods will not be very practical in real world scenario. It may be very difficult, if not impossible, for a node to acquire t existing nodes in the network in its communication range for evaluation of its trust. Alternatively, there must be an off-line trust establishment mechanism between the new node and the t existing nodes. In an infrastructure-less ad hoc network environment, this may also be very difficult to realize in practice. In addition, threshold cryptography-based schemes suffer from the additional problems of high communication and computation overhead [8].

In self-organized scheme, trust is established through off-line trust relationships among the nodes. These offline trust relationships are generated from general social relationships. The initialization process depends on the issue of certificates among the nodes themselves and formation of a network of trust relationship between them. This process is very complex and slow in practice, because every issued certificate will require close contact between a pair of nodes. Moreover, ad hoc networks are formed at random by the member nodes, and thus, the trust relationships among the members are much sparse than those of general society.

3   The Proposed Framework

In this section, we describe the proposed key management scheme for ad hoc networks. The inherent heterogeneity of the nodes in a typical ad hoc network is utilized to choose the candidates for CA nodes. The nodes having more battery strength and computational power are deployed as the CA nodes, and threshold cryptographic technique is applied to realize a distributed CA framework. We have also identified some parameters that can be tuned to increase the efficiency and effectiveness of the proposed framework. Threshold cryptographic technique is applied to realize a distributed CA.

Before describing the salient features of the proposed scheme, we first identify some desirable characteristics of a key management system for ad hoc networks. A good key management system should ideally have the following properties: (i) High fault tolerance, (ii) High level of security, and (iii) High availability.

A system having high fault-tolerance will be able to keep its correct operation up even in presence of node failure and network partitioning. In the proposed scheme, we have introduced fault-tolerance by employing threshold cryptographic techniques.

Security is implemented in the certification scheme by cryptographic techniques and employing the nodes having more computing power as the certificate authorities.

In ad hoc networks availability is dependent on the connectivity of the network [1]. Thus, even if all the nodes in a network are up and running, due to connectivity problems a client may not be able to access a desired service or participate in a network activity. In the proposed scheme, availability of network services is maintained at a high level by design of an efficient and robust communication protocol based on caching and replication.

3.1   Heterogeneity of Nodes in Ad Hoc Networks

There are some applications of ad hoc networks (e.g., tactical battlefields) where the nodes constituting the network are intrinsically heterogeneous in terms of their computing and battery power, transmission range, and more importantly security characteristics [1]. These stronger nodes may be delegated with more sensitive information and more computing responsibilities for implementing security protocols in the network. However, if all the nodes in an ad hoc network are identical then the nodes for the distributed CA may be chosen randomly. Thus our proposed scheme is not dependent on the condition of heterogeneity of the nodes in ad hoc networks.

3.2   Analysis of Trust Relationships

The proposed framework uses threshold cryptography where n nodes in collaboration with each other act as the CA in the network. In threshold cryptography [9], each of these n nodes has a share of the master private key and stores the key pairs of all nodes in the networks. The n servers together can form the private key of the CA. If any new node wants to join the network, it must first collect all of the n partial signatures. The node can then compute the whole signature locally and thus get the certificate. As mentioned in Section 2, the scheme of threshold cryptography has been extended in [7].

In order to avoid the computation of the private key of the CA for each client request, the mechanism of threshold digital signature [10] is employed. For a (k, n) threshold cryptography system, a new node sends request to k CA nodes and each of these k CA nodes sends its own partial signature only. The computation of the whole signature is done by the new node locally after it receives all the k partial signatures from the CA nodes.

For consistency in certificate revocation, the distributed approach of *Certification Revocation List* (CRL) is followed. Like in case of generation of a certificate, the revocation of a certificate is only possible when at least k CA nodes put their partial signatures on it. Each of the k CA nodes broadcasts the certificate to be revoked after putting its own partial signature. When the certificate to be revoked gathers k-1 such partial signatures and reaches another CA node, it completes the signature and revokes the certificate and broadcasts the revoked certificate to other CA nodes for updating their local CRLs. Any node in the network may be chosen to store the global CRL as it must be publicly accessible. However, when a node storing the global CRL has to leave the network, it has to send the updated global CRL to an existing node in the network before it leaves. As the updating of the CRL is done by broadcast mechanism, there is a significant overhead associated with it. However, if the membership of nodes does not change very fast, the revocation will not be too frequent and the associated overhead will also be reduced. As with any threshold cryptography-based system, the proposed system has there parameters: (i) total number of nodes in the network at any given time (M), (ii) the number of nodes deputed with CA responsibility (n), and (iii) the minimum number of nodes for signature construction (k).

Choice of an optimum value of k is critical for efficient working of the proposed scheme. Higher the value of k, the more secure will be the system as more number of nodes will be involved in signature construction. However, it will also cause a large communication overhead. Thus a suitable trade-off is to be made. This is discussed in detail in Section 4.

4   The Certification Protocol

For joining the network and using network resources, a new node needs to contact at least k CA nodes and receive the replies from at least k of them. This is required for construction of the full signature. For this purpose, a client node (new node) sends a *Certificate Request* (CREQ) message. Every such CREQ is associated with a timer. Any CA node that receives such a CREQ message replies with a *Certificate Reply* (CREP) message that contains the partial signature of the CA node. If the client node is successful in receiving k valid CREPs, it constructs the full signature and the certification process succeeds. If the timer associated with CREQ expires before the client receives the requisite k CREPs, the certification process fails. In this case, the client has to start the certification process once again. These CREQ and CREP messages can be piggybacked on the routing packets thereby reducing the communication overhead of the protocol. For propagation of the CREQ messages in the network two methods may be followed: (i) CREQ message flooding and (ii) multiple CREQ message communication. We discuss these mechanisms in Section 4.1 and Section 4.2 respectively.

4.1   CREQ Flooding

To ensure that the CREQ from a node reaches all the CA nodes, flooding is the most reliable mechanism. However, in flooding, each message is transmitted multiple number of times by different nodes. Due to this large number of message transmissions, there will be a very high communication overhead in the network. In addition to this, as a single CREQ will reach many CA nodes, the client node will possibly receive many redundant responses for reconstruction of the signature. All these redundant responses (partial signatures) are subsequently discarded. This will lead to wastage of precious network bandwidth and computational resources of the nodes since all these redundant messages were processed by the CA nodes for signature reconstruction. In fact, CREQ flooding technique provides maximum reliability of message communication at the cost of high communication and computation overhead.

4.2   Multiple CREQ

If the client node has recently communicated with sufficient number of CA nodes (at least k) and those routing entries are present in the client's route cache then flooding can be avoided and multiple CREQ messages to those specific CA nodes may be sent. The use of multiple CREQ in place of flooding will dramatically reduce the overhead of message communication. As the route cache is sufficiently fresh, the multiple CREQ message propagation will not require any route discovery process to be initiated before it. This will enable us to reduce the number of messages in the network even further. However, naive use of multiple CREQs without having sufficient number of fresh route cache entries will make the situation worse compared to flooding. The reason for this is as follows. With insufficient route entries in cache, use of multiple CREQs will certainly lead to failure of certificate negotiation. The failure of certificate negotiation will result in a subsequent round of flooding of CREQs. Thus not only there will be a high overhead due to flooding, there will also be an unnecessary delay due to time lost for the failed multiple CREQ attempt. To avoid this situation, the proposed mechanism falls back on flooding when sufficiently large number of fresh route entries are not present in the route cache.

To avoid the large overhead of flooding and still ensure that certificate negotiation failure does not happen, we must always have fresh route entries for the CA nodes in all the nodes of the network. While we can afford to have occasional route errors and broken links in route discovery process for other ordinary nodes in the network, we must ensure that the route entries for the CA nodes are always very fresh and route failures to the CA nodes are kept at the minimum. To ensure this, the proposed scheme uses two timers associated to the route cache. The route entries for the CA nodes are kept in a special cache with a timer that is different from the normal timer associated with ordinary route entries. The timer associated with the route for the CA nodes times out faster, so that the CA routes are always more recent than the other routes. The whole objective is to emphasize the fact that a failure in certification process is more costly than a normal route discovery failure.

As regards the number of entries required in the route cache, it is very much dependent on the value of k, and the mobility of the nodes in the network. If the nodes in the network have less mobility, then the required number of cache entries may be very close to k (or just marginally greater than k), as in this case the client will receive k replies with a very high probability. However, with higher mobility of the nodes in the networks, it will be increasingly probable that the client will not receive CREPs against some CREQs because of route failures and packet drops due to broken links. Thus, the client should send more number of requests in this case. This additional number of CREQs (σ), is used to ensure success of the certification process while using multiple CREQs instead of flooding. As mentioned earlier, the number of additional CREQ messages (σ) depends on the mobility of the nodes in the network and rate of change of topology of the network. One rough idea of the mobility of the nodes in the network can be arrived at by noticing the number of broken routes and the number of failed route discovery process in the network in a given interval of time. The sum of k and σ is the threshold number (β) of CREQs that must be sent by a node for certification purpose to the CA nodes. If a client finds more than β entries in its route cache, it can choose the nearest CA entries or the most recently cached entries. The most recently cached entries will minimize the probability of failure of the certification process under a high mobility scenario. However, in a network with less mobility, communication to the nearest CA nodes will involve less communication overhead and less bandwidth consumption for the certification and authentication process.

4.3   Robustness to Network Partitioning

The proposed certification protocol requires at least k CA nodes for signature reconstruction. However, due to mobility of the nodes and unreliable character-istics of the wireless links in ad hoc networks, some of the nodes and links may fail in such a manner that it may lead to partitioning of the network. In such a scenario, if a partition happens to have less than k number of CA nodes, it will be impossible for a new node to acquire certificates from k CA nodes to recon-struct the signature. This will lead to non-availability of the CA mechanism. In the proposed scheme, we have handled this network partitioning problem by the mechanism of transitive delegation of CA responsibilities. In the proposed frame-work, if a network partitioning happens in such a way that a particular partition of the network falls short of k CA nodes, then an ordinary node that has re-cently authenticated itself by communicating to k CA nodes, will be temporarily delegated with the authority to act as a CA node till the partition problem gets over. This ensures that distributed CA framework will remain available even in presence of transient network partitioning and in the event of failures of a large number of CA nodes in the network.

5   Performance Evaluation

We have carried out simulations to evaluate the effectiveness and efficiency of the proposed scheme. Effectiveness is measured using the number of successful certificate requests (CREQs). For CREQ flooding, the success is dependent on the total number of received CREPs. For multiple CREQs, every CREQ that receives k or more CREPs is counted as a successful certificate request and the success ratio is defined as the ratio of the number of successful certificate request to the total number certificate requests sent. The efficiency of the protocol is evaluated by measuring the message overhead associated with the protocol. Three configuration parameters are identified for further investigation of the simulation results. They are: (i) k (crypto threshold), (ii) τ (time-out threshold), and (iii) β (CREQ threshold).

The crypto threshold (k) is the minimum number of CA nodes required for signature construction. In other words, k is the minimum number of CREPs required for a client to be able to reconstruct the full signature of the CA. A small value of k increases the probability of success (success ratio) of authentication and also reduces message overhead of the security mechanism. However, it reduces the security of the system as an adversary needs to compromise fewer number of CA nodes to break the security of the system. A high value of k, on the other hand, will make the system more secure but at the cost of increased communication overhead, as a client node will need to contact more number of CA nodes to authenticate itself.

The time-out threshold (τ) is the time for which a client node waits for receiving a CREP after sending a CREQ. If τ is reasonably large, the probability of receiving the CREP increases since the node waits longer for the CREP. However, if there is not a sufficient number of CREPs to reach the node, the certification request will eventually fail after an unnecessary wait. This will worsen the situation. On the contrary, if τ is set too small, there may be a possibility that the node may time out while the CREPs were on their way to the node. This will also lead to a subsequent flooding in the network.

As mentioned in Section 4.2, the CREQ threshold (β) is the sum of crypto threshold k and the number of additional CREQs sent (σ) for certification process. A large value of σ ensures successful certification but at the cost of a high communication overhead. This is due to the fact that a large value of σ leads to a large value of β and that leads to higher probability of CREQ flooding being used resulting in a high packet overhead. Choice of a lower value of σ may lead to the use of multiple CREQs. It may reduce the packet overhead provided there are not too many certification failures due to loss of CREPs.

5.1   Simulation Setup

The network simulator *ns-2* is used for simulation of the proposed protocol. The parameters used for simulation are depicted in Table 1. The simulation is run for 10 minutes duration. Each of 100 ordinary nodes (nodes that are not the CA nodes) is simulated to make 10 certification requests, resulting in a total of

Table 1. Simulation parameters

Total Number of nodes	150
Nuber of CA nodes	30
Simulated network area	1000 m * 1000 m
Total simulation time	600 seconds
Number of certificate requests	10 from each of 100 non-CA nodes
Node pause time	0, 10 seconds
Maximum speed of nodes	0, 5, 10 m/s
Mobility model	Random waypoint

Table 2. Effect of β on usage of multiple CREQs

	5	10	15	20	25
Multiple CREQs	368	256	208	176	123
Flooding CREQs	632	744	792	824	877

1000 certification requests in the network. Any node that wishes to communicate with any other node in the network first contacts the CA nodes to get the peer's certificate or to check the revocation status of the peer's certificate it acquired previously. Since each certification request precedes initiation of a new secure communication, we believe that the number of message communication in the simulated environment is more than adequate. The node movement is assumed to be random waypoint model with host pause times of 0 and 10 seconds and maximum speeds of 0, 5 and 10 m/s. The results are presented for host pause time of 0 second and the maximum speed of nodes 10 m/s to facilitate comparison with the results in MOCA [1] framework.

5.2   Percentage of Multiple CREQs and Flooding

We have simulated the mechanism with flooding and found that for all the speed of the nodes mentioned in the simulation, it works very effectively with almost all the CREQs reaching all the CA nodes and most of the CREPs returning to the source nodes. Table 2 presents the total number of requests made as well as the number of requests using flooding and multiple CREQs. As expected, the use of multiple CREQs decreases with larger value of β, since it is more likely that with higher values of β, there would not be sufficient number of routes to the CAs in the route cache of the node. The comparison of our results with those in MOCA [1] framework shows that there is a 10% average increase in the number of times multiple CREQs are used compared to flooding in our proposed scheme. It clearly shows that the proposed CA framework is more efficient than that proposed in [1].

5.3   Packet Overhead and Certification Delay

We have evaluated communication overhead, as measured by the total number of control packets used for certification services. Table 3 shows the overhead of flooding and multiple CREQ techniques with different values of β.

Results show that generally, multiple CERQ approach saves up to 30% of the control packet overhead with the configuration that we have used. This is mainly possible because the timer associated with the route cache for the CA route for certification purpose is set with a time interval that is half the timer interval for the ordinary route cache (typically 5 s for the CA route and 10 s for the ordinary routes). This leads to a high probability of success in the multiple CREQ based approach most of the time and does not lead to flooding. This savings on the communication overhead becomes even more prominent as smaller values of β are used. With larger values of β, there is no practical benefit of using multiple CREQs over flooding as most of the nodes may not be having sufficient number of CA routes in their cache and that eventually leads to flooding.

Table 4 shows the comparison of the overhead in our scheme with MOCA framework proposed in [1] for 30 CA nodes. Results clearly indicate that for all values of β and for both most recently cached CA-multiple CREQs and nearest CA-multiple CREQs, our scheme has less communication overhead compared to the MOCA [1] framework.

Any certification service relying on a PKI will have a start-up latency for establishing authentication and secure message communication among the nodes

Table 3. Packet overhead with 30 CA nodes

No. of packets	CREQ	CREP	Total	Ratio to flooding
Flooding	134576	89137	223713	100%
Most recently cached CA-multiple CREQs				
$\beta = 5$	89321	47591	136912	61.2
$\beta = 10$	103721	60036	163757	73.2
$\beta = 15$	112789	65287	178076	79.6
$\beta = 20$	120045	66979	187024	83.6
$\beta = 25$	127604	76601	204250	91.3
Nearest CA-multiple CREQs				
$\beta = 5$	96531	47316	143847	64.3
$\beta = 10$	103472	67445	170917	76.4
$\beta = 15$	116783	67333	184116	82.3
$\beta = 20$	122057	79732	201789	90.2
$\beta = 25$	125043	82563	207606	92.8

Table 4. Packet overhead-ratio of multiple CREQs to flooding with 30 CA nodes

Most recently cached CA-multiple CREQs		
CREQ threshold	MOCA [1] scheme	Proposed scheme
$\beta = 5$	71.2	61.2
$\beta = 10$	81.0	73.2
$\beta = 15$	87.6	79.6
$\beta = 20$	95.2	83.6
$\beta = 25$	95.3	91.3
Nearest CA-multiple CREQs		
$\beta = 5$	69.7	64.3
$\beta = 10$	80.5	76.3
$\beta = 15$	86.2	82.3
$\beta = 20$	89.8	90.2
$\beta = 25$	94.7	92.8

in an ad hoc network. To have an estimate about this latency in terms of communication delay in the network, we have observed the variation of the number of CREPs received with respect to time for flooding and nearest CA-multiple CREQs as has been done in MOCA [1] framework. It has been observed that the value of β does not affect the communication delay. The only factor that affects the communication delay is the density of the CA nodes in the neighborhood of the client node requesting the certification service.

6   Conclusions and Future Work

In this paper, we have presented a key management framework for ad hoc networks using a distributed CA, where a set of chosen nodes in the network collectively works using threshold cryptography. An efficient communication protocol has been proposed for the certification service. The simulation results show that with a proper timer associated with the route cache entries for the CA nodes, flooding can be avoided in most of the cases thus minimizing the communication overhead. The performance of our proposed framework is compared with the MOCA framework proposed by Yi and Kravets [1]. It has been observed that our scheme has less communication overhead because it avoids flooding most of the time. As a future scope of work, we will investigate deeper into the timer of the certificate route cache, so that the route entries can be even more reliably used with minimum certification failure. This will involve investigation of additional parameters e.g., the number of route discovery failure and the number of broken routes observed in a given interval of time. Browsing a neighbor node's cache to get more accurate information can be one mechanism for this. Another area of investigation could be dynamic selection of the time-out threshold (τ) depending on the density of the CA nodes in the neighborhood of the client node requesting certification service.

References

1. Yi, S., Kravets, R.: MOCA: Mobile Certificate Authority for Wireless Ad Hoc Networks. In: PKI 2003. 2nd Annual PKI Research Workshop Program, Gaithersburg, Maryland (2003)
2. Abdul-Rahman, A., Hailes, S.: A Distributed Trust Model. In: New Security Paradigms Workshop 1997, ACM Press, New York (1997)
3. Zhou, L., Haas, Z.: Securing Ad Hoc Networks. IEEE Network Magazine 13(6), 24–30 (1999)
4. Hubaux, J.-P., Buttyan, L., Capkun, S.: The Quest for Security in Mobile Ad Hoc Networks. In: ACM MobiHoc 2001, Long Beach, CA, USA (2001)
5. Zimmerman, P.: The Official PGP User's Guide. MIT Press, Cambridge (1995)
6. Eshenauer, L., Gligor, V.D., Baras, J.: On Trust Establishment in Mobile Ad Hoc Networks. In: Security Protocols Workshop, Cambridge (2002)
7. Kong, J., Zefros, P., Luo, H., Lu, S., Zhang, L.: Robust and Ubiquitous Security Support for Mobile Ad Hoc Networks. In: 9th International Conference on Network Protocols (ICNP), pp. 251–260 (November 2001)
8. Weimerskirch, A., Thonet, G.: A Distributed Light-Weight Authentication Model for Ad Hoc Networks. In: 4th International Conference on Information Security and Cryptology (ICISC), Seoul (December 2001)
9. Shamir, A.: How to Share a Secret. Communications of the ACM (1979)
10. Shoup, V.: Practical Threshold Signatures. Theory and Applications of Cryptographic Techniques, 207–220 (2000)
11. Asokan, N., Ginzboorg, P.: Key Agreement in Ad Hoc Networks. Computer Communications 23 (2000)
12. Stajano, F., Anderson, R.: The Resurrecting Duckling: Security Issues for Ad Hoc Wireless Networks. In: Malcolm, J.A., Christianson, B., Crispo, B., Roe, M. (eds.) Security Protocols. LNCS, vol. 1796, Springer, Heidelberg (2000)

Design and Analysis of a Game Theoretic Model for P2P Trust Management

M. Harish, N. Anandavelu, N. Anbalagan, G.S. Mahalakshmi, and T.V. Geetha

Department of Computer Science and Engineering, Anna University, Chennai
Tamilnadu, India
harishmanoharan@yahoo.com, {anandhavelu,anbalagan.n}@gmail.com,
{mahalakshmi,tvgeedir}@cs.annauniv.edu

Abstract. P2P networks provide a highly reliable way of sharing resources. But the peers have to manage the risk involved due to lack of knowledge about each other's trustworthiness. Peers could provide different types of services. For the peers to behave honestly, trust needs to be incorporated. The trust framework should enable assessing the peers based on the services provided by them. This paper discusses the design and implementation of a trust framework for evaluating the trust of peers in a network. The trust framework incorporates self experience and reputation to calculate trustworthiness of a peer. Various strategies like Game Tree strategy, Tit for Tat strategy, Self Trust strategy, Dynamic strategy and Auditing strategy are proposed for selecting peers for doing job and the performance is analysed.

1 Introduction

Peer to Peer networks can be seen as truly distributed computing applications in which peers (members) communicate directly with one another to exchange information, distribute tasks, or execute transactions. The issues with peer to peer network are that the resource is not centralized. Moreover, peers may not know about the trustworthiness of others. The resource has to be searched over the network. The peer who holds the resource may not be trustworthy. Thus the key challenge in creating peer-to-peer systems is to have a mechanism of accountability among peers. Only then the trustworthiness of the resource that has been identified can be assured. One way to address this problem is to develop strategies for establishing trust and to develop systems that can assist peers in assessing the level of trust they should place on a transaction. Reputation systems provide a way of assessing the trustworthiness of a peer using word of mouth information. Present reputation systems associate the trust value with the peer. But a peer could behave differently for each type of service it provides. So, the trust worthiness has to be associated with the type of job. Also they assume that the result provided by a peer could be evaluated for correctness. But there could be services for which the result cannot be evaluated.

T. Janowski and H. Mohanty (Eds.): ICDCIT 2007, LNCS 4882, pp. 110–115, 2007.

2   Related Work

Various trust models [1,2,8] have been proposed to bring in trustworthiness in P2P networks. [7]Proposes a polling scheme for calculating trust by using reputation. But the issue may be that, the peers might not 'vote' in order to avoid extra burden and risk. The trustworthiness of the 'vote' is not calculated and hence peers could collude. [9]Proposes various trust parameters and methods for evaluating trust.Game theory has widely been applied in trust mechanisms in P2P networks. [11] Proposes a framework for incentives in P2P systems. [10] Applies Bayesian game theory in trust calculation. Since this model combines both probability and game theory in trust evaluation, it is too computation intensive in trust calculation. [3]studies the node behavior in P2P networks by modeling it as an iterated prisoner's dilemma. This model minimizes the problem of free riders but the problem of collusion is not minimized. [4] proposes a model based on evolutionary game theory. This model assumes that the strategies of each other peer can be known. Under this assumption this model shows a good cooperation rate, but this assumption need not be true. In this paper, we develop a trust framework in which trust is associated with the type of job provided by the peer. We propose strategies like Tit for Tat, Self Trust Strategy, Dynamic Strategy and Game Tree Strategy in a P2P setting with peer groups for evaluating the trustworthiness of the result in places where result cannot be directly evaluated.

3   Architecture of Trust Management System

The architecture Fig.1 consists of Transaction Manager that takes care of submitting and doing jobs. It consists of the job submitter and the job doer. The job submitter [6] selects candidates and submits the jobs to them. When the job is completed by the member(s), result is evaluated based on job type, resource available and the evaluation strategies. The job doer [6]returns the results to submitter. The submitter then evaluates the result and submits a feedback, which is aggregated in the Trust Store, which can be implemented as a Distributed Hash Table (DHT). The Trust evaluator and the Group Manager use the Trust store. The Group Manager [6]takes care of group dynamics like nodes joining a group, nodes leaving a group, job submission from a node to a group and from a group to a node and also job performing.

When a member in a group submits a job to the group, it is submitted on the behalf of group depending on the reputation of the member within the group. When a job is submitted to the group from outside, a request is sent within the group, the job is submitted to one or more of the members who respond depending on their reputation and their previous contributions and the results are forwarded back. Members may join or leave the group, depending on the utility derived and behavior within the group.

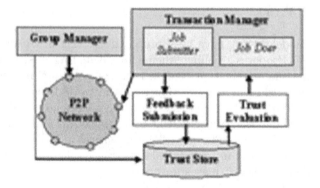

Fig. 1. P2P System Architecture

4   Design of Job Protocol

The design is shown in Fig.2. The job protocol will run in every member of
the network. It uses the decision maker to decide upon selection of candidates
for doing a job. For each job, it maintains list of candidates for whom job request was sent, list of nodes that have accepted the job and nodes for whom job
was submitted. Result evaluation strategy is used to evaluate submitted results.
If the result is known as in the case of file sharing, the result evaluation becomes unnecessary, but in places where result evaluation becomes very costly or

Fig. 2. Job protocol design

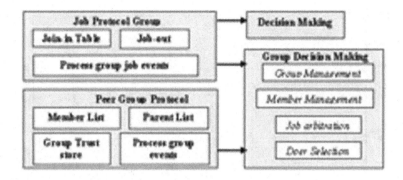

Fig. 3. Group Transaction Manager

impossible, we propose two different strategies: Redundant job submission strategy and Auditing Strategy.

In Redundant job submission strategy, the job is submitted to more than one node depending upon the criticality of the job and trust value of the nodes. The arrived results are compared for variations and job is resubmitted until variation reaches a tolerance factor. Redundant job submission may be ineffective in some cases because job has to be submitted to many nodes and large amount of network resources are utilized. This can be minimized by submitting job to a single node and evaluating the result randomly depending on trustworthiness of the node, which performed the job. This is known as the Auditing Strategy. Decision maker uses different strategies in order to select candidates for job submission and to arbitrate job. The policy-based strategies include tit for tat strategy, self trust strategy and dynamic strategy [5]. In Tit For Tat strategy, the decisions of each peer are based only on the previous moves of the other peer. In Self Trust Based Strategy, each node uses only its personal experience with other peers to make it decisions. In Dynamic Strategy, the peers use both self-trust and reputation of other peers to make decisions. In case of a network with peers forming groups the reputation of a peer within a group is also used. Game tree strategy makes job decisions by constructing a game tree and deciding on the best decision to maximize the peer's utility. Each level of a game tree corresponds to one job decision. The Group Transaction Manager (refer Fig.3) takes care of managing the transaction within and across the peer groups. Job protocol group deals with the job events in a group. It has to deal with jobs that come from outside the group and jobs that come from within the group. It uses group strategy to decide upon accepting or rejecting a job request within a group. Peer group protocol deals with group issues like joining and leaving a group and joining and ejecting a member. Group strategy is used to make decisions of a group. It is called upon while deciding on a job request, deciding on joining or leaving a group and deciding on joining or ejecting a member.

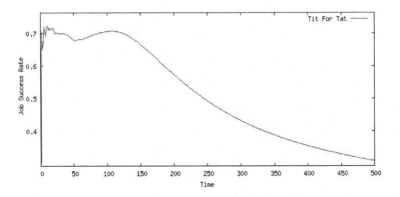

Fig. 4. Tit For Tat (TFT) Strategy- Results

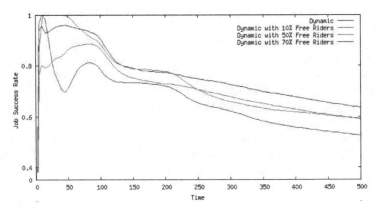

Fig. 5. Dynamic Strategy -Results

5   Results

Extensive simulations are done for different result evaluation strategies. Job success rate depends directly on the trustworthiness among the peers and increased job success rate is the major aim of creating trustworthiness among peers. The simulation is done for varying network sizes from 200 to 2000. Different levels of groups are also incorporated into the simulation. The simulation is done on peersim-1.0.1, java based P2P network simulator. The simulation is done for Tit for Tat and Dynamic strategies. The performance of these strategies is analyzed with different ratios of malicious nodes. In TFT strategy (Fig. 4), initially the peers tend to co-operate as they do not know about each other. So there is an initial peak in the job success rate. But, later, when all nodes adopt tit for tat strategy, job success rate is 30 percent. With increase in the number of free riders the job success rate decreases. In Dynamic strategy (Fig. 5), the peers use both self trust and reputation of other peers to make decisions. It can be observed that dynamic strategy provides a performance of 60 percent job success rate, which is higher than TFT strategy. The effect of free riders is also less pronounced, i.e. even in the presence of 70 percent free riders the job success rate is 50 percent.In this work, we have proposed various strategies for trust evaluation in P2P networks. Strategies for evaluating trustworthiness of result were also experimented in cases where correctness of the result cannot be directly known. In future, game tree strategy shall be considered to maximize the peer's utility.

References

1. Awan, A., Ferreira, R.A., Jagannathan, S., Grama, A.: Unstructured peer-to-peer networks for sharing processor cycles. Parallel Computing 32(2), 115–135 (2006)
2. Buragohain, C., Agrawal, D., Suri, S.: A game theoretic framework for incentives in p2p systems. In: Proceedings of 3rd International Conference on Peer-to-Peer Computing (2003)
3. Gupta, R., Somani, A.K.: Game theory as a tool to strategize as well as predict nodes' behavior in peer-to-peer networks. In: 11th International Conference on Parallel and Distributed System, pp. 244–249 (2005)
4. Hales, D., Arteconi, S.: Slacer: A self-organizing protocol for coordination in peer-to-peer networks. IEEE Intelligent Systems 21(2), 29–35 (2006)
5. Harish, M., Anandavelu, N., Anbalagan, N., Mahalakshmi, G.S., Geetha, T.V.: Strategies for peer selection with p2p trust management. International Journal of Communication Networks and Distributed Systems (2007)
6. Harish, M., Mahalakshmi, G.S., Geetha, T.V.: Game theoretic model for p2p trust management. In: Proceedings of International Conference on Computational Intelligence and Multimedia Applications, IEEE Computer Society Press, Los Alamitos (in press, 2007)
7. Manchala, D.W.: E-commerce trust metrics and models. IEEE internet computing 4(2), 36–44 (2000)
8. Morselli, R., Katz, J., Bhattacharjee, B.: A game-theoretic framework for analyzing trust-inference protocols. In: Workshop on Economics of Peer-to-Peer Systems (2004)
9. Resnick, P., Zeckhauser, R., Friedman, E., Kuwabara, K.: Reputation systems:facilitating trust in internet interactions. Communications of ACM 43(12), 45–48 (2000)
10. Xiong, L., Liu, L.: Building trust in decentralized peer-to-peer electronic communities. In: 5th International Conf. on Electronic Commerce Research (2002)
11. Xiong, L., Liu, L.: Peertrust: Supporting reputation-based trust for peer-to-peer electronic communities. IEEE Transactions on Knowledge and Data Engineering, Special Issue on Peer-to-Peer Based Data Management (2004)

Hasslefree: Simplified Access Control Management for XML Documents

Ashish Tripathi[1,*] and M.M. Gore[2,**]

[1] IBM Global Services(India) Ltd, Gurgaon, India
er.ashishtripathi@gmail.com
[2] Department of Computer Science and Engineering
Motilal Nehru National Institute of Technology, Allahabad, India
goremm@acm.org

Abstract. In this article we propose an approach which simplifies the task of DBAs in specifying the access constraints on a XML document. In the proposed methodology, for enforcing a security policy on a XML document, the DBA has to specify access constraints in terms of easy to understand Declarative Access Control Specification (DACS) language primitives. Once the constraints are specified, their corresponding security views are generated by the proposed implemented system. A working prototype based on above approach is also presented.

1 Introduction

XML(eXtensible Markup Language), a self-describing and semi-structured data format, is becoming a standard to represent and exchange data between applications across the web. It has kept researchers interested over a decade and half. Much of the research on XML has focussed on developing efficient mechanisms to store and query XML data. But as the sensitivity associated with data items is increasing with every passing day, the research interest in XML is switching towards access control and data management issues. XML access control aims at providing XML documents with a sophisticated access control model and access control specification language. With this access control technology, the access control policies control how an XML document appears. We illustrate the given point with an example in the following paragraph.

Suppose there is an online catalog document written in XML that lists available goods sold on the Internet. Consider an access control policy such that only premium members can view the special discount price information in the document. When a regular member views the catalog, any information provided for the premium members should be hidden. XML access control is capable of

---

* This work was carried at Motilal Nehru National Institute of Technology, Allahabad during his stay there as a Masters' student.
** Partially supported by the Information Security Education and Awareness (ISEA) Project of Ministry of Communication and Information Technology, Government of India.

T. Janowski and H. Mohanty (Eds.): ICDCIT 2007, LNCS 4882, pp. 116–128, 2007.

specifying such fine-grained access control policies for XML documents. A motivating example which will be discussed throughout the paper for illustrating our approach is given below.

Example 1. A simple XML document containing information related to a hospital is shown in Fig. 1(a). As the confidentiality of hospital information is very important hence the hospital enforces a security policy on this document which provides the 'public' with access to department's name, details of doctors working in the department, and details of patient admitted in each department, but the 'public' cannot find out the treatment details of individual patients. Also the 'public' is not allowed to access the salary information of doctors working in a department. This requires that the parent-child relationship between patient and treatment elements be blocked and salary element of doctor to be removed. The original XML hospital document and its corresponding security views which enforces the above mentioned security policy are shown in Fig. 1(a), 1(b) and 1(c).

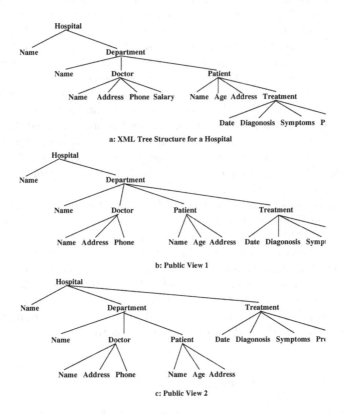

a: XML Tree Structure for a Hospital

b: Public View 1

c: Public View 2

Fig. 1. XML Tree and security view structures for given Example

1.1   Related Work

The literature possesses several approaches and models for providing access control in XML document. The concept and challenges in the area of XML security are briefly described in [4]. In [13] a framework for specifying and enforcing access constraints on XML document is proposed. This work is an extension of [14]. An access control system supporting selective distribution of XML documents among possibly large user communities is presented in [3]. Miklau [12] have studied cryptographic techniques for securing XML content. In [5] authors introduced a notion of specifying access constraints by annotating a DTD.

Other existing approaches [7,9,17] are limited to hiding nodes and subtrees except [6], which also hides ancestor and sibling relationship, making it a relationship-aware access control model. [20] presents an interesting and efficient access control methodology by combining role-based access control with an object-oriented database methodology. The literature also possesses several models for providing access control in XML documents. Prominent models are Author-X [2], XACL [10], XACML [11], ACXESS [13], and Xplorer [18]. XACL [10] and XACML [11] provide security to XML data by extending grant/revoke mechanism of relational databases. The shortcomings of [10] and [11] was removed in [16]. Author-X [2] approach for securing XML documents is based on encrypting a given document with different keys; the keys are determined according to the access control policies. In [8] a security model for regulating access to XML documents is presented. Most of the above mentioned approaches employ XPath[1] as the search and extraction language. The problem with above approaches is that all of them rely on the prowess of database administrators(DBAs) to specify access constraints correctly and efficiently. To relieve DBAs from this burden an interative approach for access control, IPAC [15] was presented. IPAC assists the DBA in specifying access control strategies and access constraints on XML data.

Our work focusses on assisting the DBAs in specifying access constraints on XML documents. In our approach the DBA specifies access constraints using primitives of DACS language [15]. Once the access constraints are specified, their corresponding views are generated. An algorithm for generating these views is also proposed. This algorithm makes use of existing declarative access constraint language used in IPAC [15] and concept of SSX(Security Specification Language for XML) used in ACXESS(Access Control for XML with Enhanced Security Specifications)[13]. These views are then ranked on the basis of ranking parameters specified by the DBA. The top ranked view is then made accessible to the end user.

1.2   Organisation of the Paper

The remainder of the paper is organized as follows. Preliminaries for this paper are discussed in section 2. It covers basic definitions related to XML, an introduction to Declarative access constraint specification(DACS) language, and Security specification language(SSX). Our approach for providing access control is presented in section 3. In section 4 the candidate security view generation methodology including the view generation algorithm and its implementation is discussed. Approach for ranking the generated security views is presented in section 5. Finally the paper is concluded in section 6.

2 Preliminaries

2.1 Basic Definitions

XML data is frequently represented as a rooted node-labeled tree structure, in which the nodes represent the objects (element (tags), element contents and attributes), and the edges represent the containment relationship among the objects. We create an understanding for an XML tree using following two definitions.

Definition 1. An XML document is a tree t $< V_t, E_t, r_t >$ over a finite alphabet Σ where
-V_t is the node set and E_t is the edge set.
-$r_t \in V_t$ is the root node of t.
-each node n $\in V_t$ has a label from Σ denoted as label(n).

Definition 2. Given an XML tree t $< V_t, E_t, r_t >$, s $< V_s, E_s, r_s >$ is a subtree of t if Vs $\subseteq$ Vt and Es $= $ (Vs $*$ Vt) $\cap$ Et .

2.2 Declarative Access Constraint Specication Language

The proposed approach makes use of a declarative access constraint specification (DACS) language presented in [15]. The goal of this language is to assist the DBAs in specifying access constraints to be implemented on a XML document. This language introduces a set of primitives as shown in Table 1. These primitives are used to (i) specify the nodes and subtrees to be revealed or hidden, and (ii) block the structural relationship between a node and its subtrees.

2.3 Security Specification Language for XML(SSX)

SSX is a security view definition language [13]. It consist of certain primitives. Each primitive takes an XML tree as input and outputs an XML tree. The semantics of the primitives used in this paper are defined as follows:

1) **delete(destXPath):** The delete primitive removes the subtrees rooted at the elemet that matches the 'destXPath' in the input tree.
2) **copy(sourceXPath,destSPE):** The copy primitive creates an identical copy of the subtrees rooted at the nodes that match the 'sourceXPath' in the original tree, and makes them the children of the elements that match the 'destSPE'.

Table 1. Primitives in Declarative Access Constraint Specication Language

Primitive	Explanation
deny(destPath)	deny access to the subtrees that match the destPath.
allow(destPath)	allow access to the subtrees that match the destPath.
blockStruct(ancsPath, relPath)	deny access to the structural relationship between nodes that match ancsPath and subtreess that match relPath.
allowStruct(ancsPath,relPath)	allow access to the structural relationship between nodes that match ancsPath and subtreess that match relPath.
dissociate(ancsPath,relPath1,..., relPathn)	deny access to the structural relationship among subtrees that match relPath1 to relPathn, with respect to the common ancestor that matches to ancsPath.
associate(ancsPath,relPath1,..., relPathn)	allow access to the structural relationship among subtrees that match relPath1 to relPathn, with respect to the common ancestor that matches to ancsPath.

3   Approach for Access Control

The proposed approach utilizes the concept of declarative access constraint specification(DACS) language proposed in [15]. All that a DBA need to do is to specify access contraints using this declarative access constraint specification language. So now the DBA don't have to specify the exact manner in which the access constraints are implemented as a security view, rather they just have to specify what the security constraints should be. On the basis of the specified access constraints several possible views of the XML document are generated according to a view generation algorithm. After several possible views had been generated we will rank these views on the basis of some ranking parameters as specified by the DBA. The top ranked view is then made visible to the authorized user which he uses to view and query.

Thus the goal of our work just like IPAC [15] is to assist DBAs in specifying access control strategies and access constraints on XML data. But unlike IPAC we have presented a formal algorithm for generating several possible views of an XML document from the specified DACS language constraints.

The core of the proposed approach is DACS language [15], which allows the DBAs to specify what to hide/reveal, rather than how the XML document is to be rearranged as in [5,6,13,14]. Once DBA specifies the access constraints using primitives of DACS language, then these primitives are converted to equivalent sequence of SSX primitives. [13]. From these SSX sequence we generate all

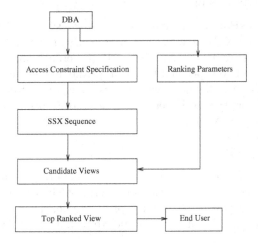

Fig. 2. Pictorial Description of Hasslefree Approach

possible Security views. The candidate security views are then ranked according to the ranking parameters as specified by the DBA. The pictorial description of this approach is shown in Fig. 2.

4   Candidate Security View Generation Methodology

We introduce an algorithm along with its implementation that generates all possible views of the XML document based on the specified access constraints. This view generation methodology assumes that a DBA has basic knowledge of DACS language primitives and realted XML technologies. So it is assumed that (s)he enters all the DACS primitives correctly.

4.1   Algorithm

Candidate Security View Generation Algorithm has two steps:

Step 1: Generation of Security Specification Language for XML (SSX) sequence corresponding to the specified declarative access constraints.
Step 2: Processing obtained sequences of SSX primitives to generate all possible security views.

Detailed Description of Step 1: For generating SSX sequence corresponding to the specified access constraints(written in DACS Language), we make use of a mapping algorithm. This algorithm maps the primitives in DACS language to corresponding primitives in SSX as per the following three rules:

1) **Deny(destPath):** This primitive can be mapped to delete(destPath).

2) **blockstruct(ancsPath, relPath):** To block the structural relationship between two nodes of an XML tree, several approaches are possible. One approach is to copy the node specified by Xpath ancsPath/relPath and associate it with nodes other than the node specified by ancsPath(i.e. its current parent). In this paper we are associating this node with all its ancestors. After associating this node with its ancestors this node need to be deleted. Hence an equivalent primitive of blockstruct in SSX can be :

i) copy(ancsPath/relPath, ancestors)

ii) delete(ancsPath/relPath)

3) **dissociate**(ancsPath,$relPath_1, relPath_2, ..., relPath_n$): Since a dissociate primitive is nothing but a combination of several blockstruct primitives. Hence its mapping will be similar to blockstruct primitive i.e. the corresponding primitives in SSX will be a series of copy and delete primitives in SSX.

Note that there is no need to map other primitives of DACS language because we assume that a DBA will only specify what to delete and what to block. So he will not make use of allow(destPath), allowStruct(ancsPath, relPath), associate(ancsPath, $relPath_1, relPath_2, .., relPath_n$) primitives of DACS Language. So there is no need to map these primitives. All the above mentioned mapping rules are summarized in the Table 3. A formal algorithm for this mapping process

Table 2. Mapping of DACS Language primitives To SSX primitives

Primitive in DACS Language	Equivalent Primitive in SSX
deny(destPath)	delete(destPath)
blockStruct(ancsPath, relPath)	copy(ancsPath/relPath,ancestors) delete(ancsPath/relPath)
dissociate(ancsPath,$relPath_1$,..,$relPath_n$)	a series of copy and delete primitives

is given below. It takes DACS language primitives as specified by the DBA as input and maps it to produce equivalent SSX primitives as output. The prespecified DACS language primitives are stored in a list, from where we sequentially access them with the help of a method called GetNextPrimitive.

MAP(DACS Language primitives)
```
1: currentprimitive=GetNextPrimitive();
2: while(currentprimitive != Null) do
3:        if(currentprimitive = 'Deny')
4:                Map it to delete(destPath);
5:        if(currentprimitive = 'BlockStruct')
6:                Map it to copy(ancsPath/relPath, ancestors)
7:                        delete(ancsPath/relPath);
8:        if(currentprimitive = 'Dissociate')
```

9:                    Map it to a series of copy and delete primitives;
10:        currentprimitive = GetNextPrimitive();
11: end while

The running time of mapping algorithm is O(p), where p is the number of DACS primitives specified by the DBA.

The SSX sequence for example 1 generated using MAP algorithm, corresponding to DACS Language primitives shown in Table 3 are shown in Table 4 and Table 5:

Table 3. Example Declarative Access Constraint Specications

S.No.	Access Contraint Specification
1	deny(hospital/department/doctor/ salary)
2	blockstruct(hospital/department/patient, treatment)

Table 4. Possible SSX Sequence

S.No	SSX sequence
1	delete(/hospital/department/doctor/salary)
2	copy(/hospital/department/patient/treatment, /hospital/department)
3	delete(/hospital/department/patient/treatment)

Table 5. Possible SSX Sequence

S.No.	SSX sequence
1	delete(/hospital/department/doctor/salary)
2	copy(/hospital/department/patient/treatment, /hospital)
3	delete(/hospital/department/patient/treatment)

Detailed Description of Step 2: Once sequences of SSX primitives are generated, they are processed to obtain possible candidate security views. The processing technique is simple. The delete(destXPath) primitive results in deletion of node specified by destXPath. For copy(sourceXPath,destSPE) primitive, a new node is first created having the same name, then it is moved to subtree specified by Xpath destSPE. Finally the copied node is deleted.

An algorithm which generates possible security views by processing sequence of SSX primitives is given below. It takes original XML document and SSX primitives as input and generates the corresponding security views as output. The input SSX primitives are stored in a list. A method named GetNextPrimitive is used to sequentially access these primitives from the list.

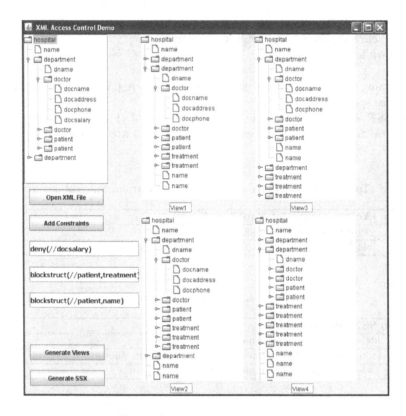

Fig. 3. Security View Generation

5   Candidate Security View Ranking

GenerateViews(XML Document, SSX primitives)
1: Copy original XML document to a new XML document.
// This new document will be modified according to SSX primitives to generate the security view.
2: curentprimitive=GetNextPrimitive();
3: while(currentprimitive != NULL) do
4:     if(currentprimitive = 'Delete(destXPath)')
5:         Delete the node specified by destXPath;
6:     if(currentprimitive = 'copy(sourceXPath,destSPE)')
7:         create a new node by copying sourceXPath
            and move it to destSPE and delete the node
            specified by sourceXPath;
8:     currentprimitive=GetNextPrimitive();
9: end while

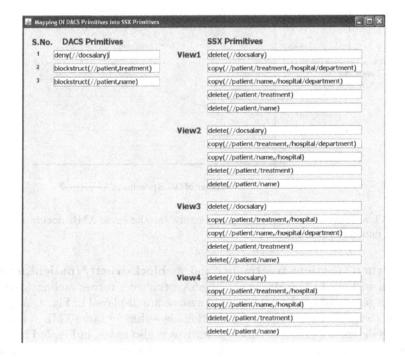

Fig. 4. Equivalent SSX Primitives

The complexity of this algorithm is O(s), where s in the number of equivalent SSX primitives as generated corresponding to the p DACS primitives specified by DBA. From Table 3, it is clear that corresponding to each DACS primitives there exists one or more SSX primitives. For example, for a deny primitive we have a delete primitive, for a single blockstruct primitive we have two SSX primitives copy and delete, and so on. Hence it can be implied that $s >= p$, as number of generated SSX primitives can be greater than or equal to the specified DACS primitives.

Hence the complexity of view generation algorithm is O(p+s) or O(c), where c is a constant dependent on number of specified primitives.

5.1 Implementation

We developed a GUI which generates all possible security views of an XML document based on the view generation approach discussed above. The view generation algorithm has been implemented using Java, DOM(Document Object model) and JAXP. For generating security views one has to only specify access constraints in the form of DACS primitives. The equivalent SSX primitives corresponding to the entered DACS primitives, as generated by Mapping algorithm can also be seen. A system snapshot showing all possible security views of hospital document corresponding to DACS primitives 1) **deny(//docsalary)** 2)

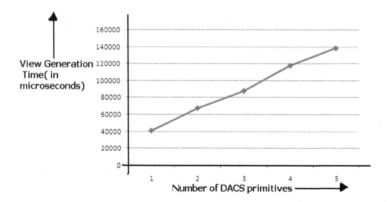

Fig. 5. View Generation Algorithm performance for the same XML document with different number of primitives

blockstruct(//patient,treatment) and 3) **blockstruct(//patient,name)** is shown in Fig. 3. Also sequences of SSX primitives corresponding to these views, as generated by the implemented system are displayed in Fig. 4. A graph showing the performance of view generation algorithm for same XML document but with different number of DACS primitives is also shown in Fig. 5. From the graph it is clear that time taken for view generation increases with the number of specified DACS primitives. Once all the possible security views are generated, they need to be ranked. The top ranked view is then made available to end user which he uses to view and query. Possible parameters for view ranking may be

1. The amount of information available to users.
2. The complexity of the view construction.
3. Potential information leakage(inference).

Out of all these parameters we are using the inference parameter to find the top-ranked view. The logic involved is that greater the depth difference between the blocked subtrees is, lesser information leakage is there and hence the view is more secure. For example in view1 of Fig. 1(b) patient and treatment are at the same level i.e. depth difference is zero, while in view2 shown in Fig. 1(c) the depth difference between these subtrees is 1. So view2 is more secure. This result is justified if we take the following scenario into consideration. Suppose a department has exactly one patient, then the information about association between patient and treatment can be easily inferred from security view1 as shown in Fig. 1(b), but not so easily from view2 as shown in Fig. 1(c). We are in process of developing a formal ranking algorithm based on inference and other ranking parameters.

6   Conclusion and Future Work

We proposed an approach that assist DBA's in specifying and enforcing access constraint on XML data. This approach uses a declarative language for access constraint specification. An algorithm which generates the security views corresponding to these security specification is presented in this paper. Finally to find the highest ranked view, inference parameter is used. The complete excercise is to make life of DBA hasslefree in enforcing access control on XML documents.

This work presumes that DBA has basic knowledge of DACS language primitives and related XML technologies. A more intelligent system having proper mathematical formal model can be developed. Such system will strengthen the security policy implementation and confidence in the implemented system from the DBA's point of view. Also a formal ranking algorithm can be developed based on the ranking approach discussed in this paper.

Acknowledgements. The Authors will like to thank Prof. B.D. Chaudhary, Ms. Reena Srivastava, Mr. Servesh Singh, Mr. Amul Jain, and Mr. Pankaj Kunmar for their valuable comments and suggestion during the development of work [19] and during the preparation of manuscript of the final draft.

References

1. Berglund, A., Boag, S., Chamberlin, D., Robie, J., Fernndez, M.F., Kay, M., Simon, J.: Xml path language(xpath) version 2.0. W3C Recommendation (2007), see http://www.w3.org/tr/xpath20
2. Bertino, E., Castano, S., Ferrari, E.: Securing xml documents with author-x. In: IEEE Internet Computing, pp. 21–31. IEEE, Los Alamitos (2001)
3. Bertino, E., Ferrari, E.: Secure and selective dissemination of xml documents. ACM Trans. Inf. Syst. Secur. 5(3), 290–331 (2002)
4. Bertino, E., Sandhu, R.: Database security-concepts, approaches, and challenges. IEEE Trans. Dependable Secur. Comput. 2(1), 2–19 (2005)
5. Fan, W., Chan, C.-Y., Garofalakis, M.: Secure xml querying with security views. In: SIGMOD 2004. Proceedings of the 2004 ACM SIGMOD international conference on Management of data, pp. 587–598. ACM Press, New York (2004)
6. Finance, A., Medjdoub, S., Pucheral, P.: The case for access control on xml relationships. In: CIKM 2005. Proceedings of the 14th ACM international conference on Information and knowledge management, pp. 107–114. ACM Press, New York (2005)
7. Fundulaki, I., Marx, M.: Specifying access control policies for xml documents with xpath. In: SACMAT 2004. Proceedings of the ninth ACM symposium on Access control models and technologies, pp. 61–69. ACM Press, New York (2004)
8. Gabillon, A., Bruno, E.: Regulating access to xml documents. In: Das 2001. Proceedings of the fifteenth annual working conference on Database and application security, Norwell, MA, USA, pp. 299–314. Kluwer Academic Publishers, Dordrecht (2002)
9. Kitagawa, N., Yoshikawa, M.: A study on efficient access control for xml ducuments. In: ICDEW 2005. Proceedings of the 21st International Conference on Data Engineering Workshops, p. 1230. IEEE Computer Society, Washington, DC, USA (2005)
10. Kudo, M., Hada, S.: Xml document security based on provisional authorization. In: CCS 2000. Proceedings of the 7th ACM conference on Computer and communications security, pp. 87–96. ACM Press, New York (2000)

11. Matheus, A.: How to declare access control policies for xml structured information objects using oasis' extensible access control markup language (xacml). In: HICSS 2005. Proceedings of the 38th Hawaii International Conference on System Sciences (2005)
12. Miklau, G., Suciu, D.: Controlling access to published data using cryptography. In: VLDB 2003. Proceedings of the 29th international conference on Very large data bases, pp. 898–909 (2004)
13. Mohan, S., Klinginsmith, J., Sengupta, A., Wu, Y.: Acxess - access control for xml with enhanced security specifications. In: ICDE 2006. Proceedings of the 2006 International Conference on Data Engineering, p. 171 (2006)
14. Mohan, S., Sengupta, A., Wu, Y.: Access control for xml: a dynamic query rewriting approach. In: CIKM 2005. Proceedings of the 14th ACM international conference on Information and knowledge management, pp. 251–252. ACM Press, New York (2005)
15. Mohan, S., Wu, Y.: Ipac: an interactive approach to access control for semi-structured data. In: VLDB'2006: Proceedings of the 32nd international conference on Very large data bases, VLDB Endowment, pp. 1147–1150 (2006)
16. Murata, M., Tozawa, A., Kudo, M., Hada, S.: Xml access control using static analysis. In: CCS 2003. Proceedings of the 10th ACM conference on Computer and communications security, pp. 73–84. ACM Press, New York (2003)
17. Qi, N., Kudo, M., Myllymaki, J., Pirahesh, H.: A function-based access control model for xml databases. In: CIKM 2005. Proceedings of the 14th ACM international conference on Information and knowledge management, pp. 115–122. ACM Press, New York (2005)
18. Steele, R., Gardner, W., Dillion, T.S., Eradi, A.: Xml-based declarative access control. In: Vojtáš, P., Bieliková, M., Charron-Bost, B., Sýkora, O. (eds.) SOFSEM 2005. LNCS, vol. 3381, pp. 310–319. Springer, Heidelberg (2005)
19. Tripathi., A.: Hasslefree: Simplified access control management for xml documents. Master's Thesis: Department of Computer Science and Engineering, Motilal Nehru National Institute of Techology, Allahabad, Uttar Pradesh, India (2007)
20. Wang, J., Osborn, S.L.: A role-based approach to access control for xml databases. In: SACMAT 2004. Proceedings of the ninth ACM symposium on Access control models and technologies, pp. 70–77. ACM Press, New York (2004)

LISA: LIghtweight Security Algorithm for Wireless Sensor Networks

Somanath Tripathy

Department of Information Technology,
North Eastern Hill University, Shillong
stripathy@nehu.ac.in

Abstract. Confidentiality and authenticity are two important security services required for almost every WSN application. However, small memory, weak processor and limited battery power of the sensor nodes are the major obstacles to implement traditional security primitives in them. Owing to both, the requirement as well as the obstacles, this paper proposes a LIghtweight Security Algorithm (LISA) tailored to implement in resource restrained sensor nodes. The novelty of this scheme is that it achieves both, confidentiality and authenticity of data, without using traditional encryption algorithm.

1 Introduction

Wireless Sensor Network (WSN) [1] is an emerging technology that plays a role in sensing, gathering and disseminating information about environmental phenomena. It comprises of a large number of sensor nodes deployed in an ad-hoc fashion. These sensing devices are well equipped with a processor, a communication module, and a battery supply, and the one equipped with all the three is called *mote* [2]. Mote, in a WSN, acts as a source to report the environmental events to the subscriber *sink*. The sink acts upon these information. Let us assume an application of WSN for fire detection to actuate sprinklers. In this application, a situation may arise, when false message may activate the sprinkler too. This may result in a larger damage than that due to the fire itself. Therefore, authentication becomes necessary to enable sensor nodes for detecting maliciously injected or spoofed packets.

Confidentiality, integrity and freshness of data as well as source authentication are the essential security parameters in WSN [4,6,7]. Zheng et.al [10] proposed a security architecture for WSN, based on lightweight public key cryptography, yet the available memory and processing power may not even be sufficient to hold the variables of an asymmetric cryptosystem. Perrig et.al. [6] proposed a security component called SNEP that can be used for mote-sink message authentication in WSN. A link layer security architecture for WSN called TINYSEC is proposed in [3] to provide authentication and maintain confidentiality. Both these techniques [3,6] use symmetric key encryption which severely drains energy from the sensor nodes.

T. Janowski and H. Mohanty (Eds.): ICDCIT 2007, LNCS 4882, pp. 129–134, 2007.

This paper proposes a *LIghtweight Security Algorithm (LISA)* for WSN. LISA is to achieve the same security services as proposed in SNEP [6] but in a reduced implementation complexity. LISA uses cellular automata (CA) -based operations because of the simple, regular and modular structure of the CA based component. LISA is presented after giving a brief overview of CA.

2   Cellular Automata (CA)

Cellular Automata (CA) is a dynamic system consists of a grid of identical finite state machines, whose states are updated synchronously at discrete time steps according to a local update rule f. The evolution of the ith cell, in a 3-neighborhood CA can be represented as a function of the present state of $(i-1)^{th}, i^{th}$, and $(i+1)^{th}$ cells as in equation (1).

$$x_i(t+1) = f(x_{i-1}(t), x_i(t), x_{i+1}(t)) \tag{1}$$

A CA is said to be reversible, if the initial configuration can be obtained from the evolved configuration. Second order CA is a reversible class CA (RCA) in which the future configuration of the ith state on clock cycle $t+1$, is determined by the states of the neighborhood configuration at clock cycle t and the configuration of ith state at t-1 clock cycle as expressed in (2).

$$x_i(t+1) = f(x_{i-1}(t), x_i(t), x_{i+1}(t), x_i(t-1)) \tag{2}$$

RCA exhibits the interesting property shown in equation (3), denoting respectively X and Y for the previous and current configuration (for more details about CA the reader can refer to [9]).

$$RCA(RCA(X,Y),Y) = X \tag{3}$$

3   LIghtweight Security Algorithm (LISA)

A commonly used WSN constitutes of a large number of *motes* or *sensor nodes* which are randomly dispersed in the *monitoring area*. Each of these nodes has the capability of collecting data and routes them to the *Sink* or *Base Station (BS)*. The sink is a central point of control within the network and disseminates control information back to the network. Since sensor network uses a shared wireless communication medium, the job of an attacker to inject spurious information becomes easier. Therefore, the source authentication *i.e.* the verification of the origin of a packet as well as the data authentication *i.e* the conformation of no change in the data become necessary. This paper refers authentication for both source and data authentication. Limited resources in sensor nodes are the major obstacles to implement the traditional cryptographic primitives for achieving authentication. The solution LISA is to overcome such obstacle while achieving authentication.

3.1   Designing Goal

Sending the randomized data over wireless channel, requires more energy. Therefore, Perrig et.al [6] proposed a protocol to achieve semantic security using symmetric key encryption with the help of counter (CTR) shared between the sink and the mote. Karlof et.al [3] argued that if each counter requires 4-bytes and 100 bytes RAM available for the neighbor table, networks with larger than 25 nodes would be vulnerable. However, the careful observation makes clearer that neighbor table is to hold the counter shared with its neighbors only, but not with all the nodes in the network. Therefore, the CTR-based schemes do not face the scaling problem. Moreover, TINYSEC [3] consumes extra computation and communication overhead. So, the proposed scheme LISA opts to use the counter (CTR).

The implementation of intensive computations involved in traditional cryptographic mechanisms severely drain energy from the sensor nodes. Simple binary operations are more suitable and therefore, the CA based components (second order RCA) are being chosen in designing the proposed scheme.

3.2   Operational Details

The whole operation of LISA comprises of two basic phases: *Initialization phase* and *Data authentication phase*. Besides these, LISA has a *Counter re-initialization phase* to re-initialize the counter value.

Initialization Phase: The sink and a mote (identity ID_m) are shared with a secret key S_m and counter value CTR_m during deployment.

Data authentication Phase: This phase executes as follows.

Step 1. While transmitting data, mote uses the format of Ψ_m as expressed in equation (4).

$$\phi_m = H(ID_m \oplus CTR_m)$$
$$\Psi_m = RCA(data \parallel \phi_m, S_m \parallel CTR_m). \tag{4}$$

Where, $\oplus$ and $\parallel$ respectively denote for Boolean XOR and string concatenation operation. The mote increments the counter value CTR_m. It is assumed that size of data and that of secret is $l-$bits, while the size of CTR_m, ID_m and that of hash-digest is $k-$bits.

Step 2. Sink determines the S_m and CTR_m of corresponding mote ID_m. It may maintain a table to hold these values (S_m, CTR_m and ID_m). Sink assures the data to be authentic if

$$H(ID_m \oplus CTR_m) = RT_k(RCA(\Psi_m, S_m \parallel CTR_m)). \tag{5}$$

Where, $RT_k(\alpha)$ and $LT_l(\alpha)$ respectively represent the last $k-$ bits and first $l-$ bit of α.

Step 2a. If equation (5) holds, it proceeds to execute Step 3. Otherwise, sink increments the CTR_m value and verifies the equation (5) again. Sink discards the data if the equality in equation (5) fails for both consecutive iterations.

Step 3. The sink retrieves the data as

$$data = LT_l(RCA(\Psi_m, S_m \parallel CTR_m)). \tag{6}$$

Finally, the sink increments CTR_m value.

Counter re-initialization Phase: If de-synchronization of counter value shared between the sink and a mote occurs, counter needs to be re-initialized by a new value. To perform this, sink executes the following steps.

Step 1. The sink randomly chooses a counter CTR_n value. It sends Ψ_{sm} (as expressed in equation (7) to the mote.

$$\phi_{sm} = H(S_m \oplus CTR_n)$$
$$\Psi_{sm} = RCA(S_m, \phi_{sm} \parallel CTR_n) \tag{7}$$

Step 2. The mote assures the CTR_n is authentic if the equation (8) holds.

$$H(S_m \oplus CTR_n) = RT_k(RCA(S_m, \Psi_{sm})) \tag{8}$$

The mote updates its counter value to CTR_n if authentic.

Since size of data must be equal to that of secret key, while transmitting a large message a large secret needs to be generated from the shared secret key. For this purpose, any lightweight key expansion algorithm [8] can be used.

3.3   Important Security Features

The proposed scheme achieves the following security properties.

- *Semantic Security:* Since the counter value is incremented after each data, the same data gives the different results even though with the same secret key. Therefore, the scheme achieves semantic security.
- *Mote (source) Authentication:* The equation (5) verifies correctly that the message has been generated from the correct mote. Thus sink authenticates the mote.
- *Replay Protection:* The counter value in the message of equation (4) prevents the replay of old messages.
- *Weak Freshness:* Sink correctly verifies that the message has been generated after the previous message. This assures the weak freshness.
- *Cut and Paste Attack Resistant:* If the attacker changes a part of message while flows from mote to sink, sink rejects the message as the implicit message integrity checking is carried out at Step 2 of data authentication phase. Therefore, LISA is robust against Cut and Paste attack.

– *Message lost tolerant:* Since both the sink and mote use a common counter value and update without their confirmation, de-synchronization occurs if the message flows from mote to sink in the Step 2 gets lost. In this situation, counter value at the mote that has incremented is not equal to that value stored at sink. In the next instance, Step 2a of the protocol takes care of and therefore LISA is tolerant towards message lost.

– *Counter value de-synchronization protection:* If the message flows has been dropped more than once it is considered as intentional. Therefore, sink may take some appropriate actions and counter re-initialization phase is executed. Thus, the protocol is robust against de-synchronization attack.

4 Discussion

Though LISA is discussed for mote-sink authentication, it can also be used during mote-mote communication (treating receiver node as sink) to achieve the security services proposed in SNEP and TINYSEC.

Table 1. Efficiency Comparison

	Scheme	LISA	SNEP
	Semantic security	Achieves	Achieves
	Source authentication	Achieves	Achieves
Features	Data Integrity	Achieves	Achieves
	Message Loss	Tolerant	Not tolerant
	De-synchronization	Tolerant	Not tolerant
	DoS	Resistant	Not Resistant
Implementation Complexity	Data authentication Phase	1H + 1 RCA (at either end)	1E + 1 MAC (at either end)

As discussed in previous section, LISA achieves all the security services as in SNEP. On the other hand, SNEP being not a message-loss tolerant de-synchronization of the counter value shared between the mote and sink may occur. Moreover, counter exchange protocol of SNEP needs more computation as well as communication resources. If attacker blocks the message flows between the mote and sink; Sink becomes busy to execute the counter exchange protocol between the mote. This leads to DoS attack. Using novel idea in LISA, both the de-synchronization and DoS are avoided.

Both TINYSEC [3] and SNEP [6], use symmetric key encryption for achieving the same security features. At the same time, TINYSEC requires extra computations to pre-encrypt the IV (initialization vector) and extra communication overhead in sending IV. Therefore, we compare the proposed scheme with SNEP. Table 1 compares the features and the implementation complexity of LISA with SNEP.

LISA requires only one Hash operation and one RCA operation at both the ends. RCA is 3-neighborhood second order CA is simple bitwise procedures, which can be executed independently for every bit. This inherent parallelism provides for a very fast and efficient implementation. Secondly, our protocol does not require any encryption unlike SNEP [6]. This adds to the speed at which the authentication procedure can be completed. This also prevents from the chocking up of computation power on the motes. This protocol needs very low communication over heads that is of $k-$ bit overhead on $l-$ bits data. $k-$ value can be chosen as 32-bit for any value of l. SNEP needs 1 encryption and 1 MAC computation at both the ends.

5   Conclusion

Sensor networks play an important role in military applications as well as our day to day life. However, security concerns constitute a potential stumbling block to the impending wide deployment of sensor networks. Meanwhile, the limited resources are considered as a major obstacle to implement traditional security primitives in sensor nodes. This paper proposed a lightweight sensor node authentication mechanism to achieve semantic security, data freshness and data integrity security services with minimum computation and communication overhead. The protocol is tolerant against message lost also. Because the protocol is not using any traditional cryptographic intensive computations, the scheme is considered to be more suitable towards sensor networks.

References

1. Akyildiz, A.F., Su, W., Sankarasubramaniam, Y., Cayiric, E.: A survey on Sensor Networks. IEEE Communication Mag. 20, 102–114 (2002)
2. Hill, J., Culler, D.: Mica: A wireless platform for deeply embedded networks. IEEE Micro 22(6) (2002)
3. Karlof, C., Sastry, N., Wagner, D.: TinySec: A Link layer security SArchitecture for Wireless Sensor Networks. In: SENSYS 2004. Proc of ACM Intl conference on Sensor networks security (2004)
4. Luk, M., Perrig, A., Whillock, B.: Seven Cardinal Properties of Sensor Network Broadcast Authentication. In: SASN 2006. Proc. of ACM conference on Security of Ad Hoc and Sensor Networks, pp. 147–156 (2006)
5. Perrig, A., Stankovic, J., Wagner, D.: Security in wireless sensor networks. Commnication of ACM 47(6), 53–57 (2004)
6. Perrig, A., Szewczyk, R., Wen, V., Culler, D., Tygar, J.D.: SPINS: Security Protocols for Sensor Networks. Wireless Networks 8(5), 521–534 (2002)
7. Shi, E., Perrig, A.: Designing Secure Sensor Networks. IEEE Wireless Communications, 38–43 (2004)
8. Stinson, D.R.: Cryptography theory and practice, 2nd edn. CRC Press, Boca Raton, USA (2002)
9. Wolfram, S.: A New kind of Sciences. Wolfram media Inc (2002)
10. Zheng, J., Li, J., Lee, M.J., Anshel, M.: A lightweight encryption and authentication scheme for wireless sensor networks. Int. J. Security and Networks 1(3/4) (2006)

An Optimal Weighted-Average Congestion Based Pricing Scheme for Enhanced QoS

Koteswara Rao Vemu[1], Shalabh Bhatnagar[1], and N. Hemachandra[2]

[1] Indian Institute of Science,Bangalore 560012, India
{eshwar,shalabh}@csa.iisc.ernet.in
[2] Indian Institute of Technology Bombay, Mumbai, 400076, India
nh@iitb.ac.in

Abstract. Pricing is an effective tool to control congestion and achieve quality of service (QoS) provisioning for multiple differentiated levels of service. In this paper, we consider the problem of pricing for congestion control in the case of a network of nodes under a single service class and multiple queues, and present a multi-layered pricing scheme. We propose an algorithm for finding the optimal state dependent price levels for individual queues, at each node. The pricing policy used depends on a weighted average queue length at each node. This helps in reducing frequent price variations and is in the spirit of the random early detection (RED) mechanism used in TCP/IP networks. We observe in our numerical results a considerable improvement in performance using our scheme over that of a recently proposed related scheme in terms of both throughput and delay performance. In particular, our approach exhibits a throughput improvement in the range of 34 to 69 percent in all cases studied (over all routes) over the above scheme.

1   Introduction

Most of the literature on pricing of network resources considers a model for rate control by users where the network adjusts the prices according to the demand, and the users respond by adjusting their transmission rates to optimize a (possibly local) utility function. Some works [1] and [2] describe a family of window-based allocation schemes that can be used to achieve a proportionally fair allocation or approximate a max-min fair allocation arbitrarily closely. These schemes were motivated by TCP, the Internet congestion control protocol. This paper does not consider the rate control of sources. Rather, it assumes that each link in the network can accommodate multiple classes of service by defining the desired average per hop behavior for each of these classes on the link. Traditional pricing models for Internet services have been fairly simple such as flat rate or connect time charges for the retail user and a flat rate depending on the interconnection bandwidth for the bulk user. Allocating resources during periods of congestion is a complex problem. Appropriate usage and congestion based pricing could lead to efficient usage of network resources. As a result, the overall quality of service that the network provides can be improved.

T. Janowski and H. Mohanty (Eds.): ICDCIT 2007, LNCS 4882, pp. 135–145, 2007.

In the differential service model the basic idea is to divide the available bandwidth among the various competing classes of traffic in a static or dynamic manner. In [3], the work conserving Tirupati Pricing (TP) scheme is proposed as an alternative to the Paris Metro Pricing (PMP) [4] scheme. In [5], an adaptive stochastic approximation based pricing scheme for the case of a single-node system that is based on actual congestion levels in queues is analyzed and its performance studied numerically. In [6], the performance of TP is compared with the PMP scheme for a single-node model and it is observed that TP performs better than PMP, the latter being non-work conserving. A stochastic approximation based adaptive pricing methodology is considered in [7] in order to bring the congestion along any route (from source to destination) on the network to a prescribed nominal level. The objective function there depends on the price values and not actual congestion levels as with [5]. Moreover, prices for the entire routes are considered for simplicity, and not of individual queues on each link along the route. In [8], we adapt the algorithm of [7] to the case when prices for individual queues on each link along a route are separately considered. This allows for much greater flexibility in implementation as customers from one service grade at a link can shift to another service grade on another link (a scenario not allowed in [7]). The scheme in [8] is seen to exhibit much better performance over that in [7].

In this paper, we consider pricing in a single class service system and adopt the TP pricing scheme. We consider prices for individual queues on each link as with [8] and present a state-dependent multi-layered pricing methodology whereby states in each queue are clustered together into various levels and prices are assigned to individual state or queue length levels. Thus each queue 'manager' charges a price to an incoming customer joining that queue on the basis of the level of congestion in the queue. We adopt a stochastic approximation based gradient search methodology for finding the 'optimal' price levels at each queue on each link in the network. This is unlike most other schemes in the literature that compute one price per queue. In fact, the scheme in [7] computes one price for an entire route comprising of a sequence of link-queue tuples. In our scheme, the price charged to an incoming customer at a given queue on a link is a function of the weighted average queue length. This is in the spirit of the random early detection (RED) mechanism in TCP/IP based networks. The idea in this scheme is to avoid changing prices too often (as would happen if instantaneous queue lengths are used instead) as to prevent rapid fluctuations or volatility in traffic flows. For finding the optimal pricing policy within the given class of policies we adapt a simultaneous perturbation stochastic approximation (SPSA) algorithm that uses two-timescales and deterministic perturbation sequences [9]. We compare the performance of our scheme with that of [8]. We observe that our scheme shows much better performance over the algorithm in [8]. As already stated, the algorithm of [8] shows considerable performance improvements over the scheme in [7]. We thus do not show performance comparisons of our algorithms with the scheme of [7] and refer the reader to [8] for those details. Our state-dependent pricing methodology reduces congestion considerably, increases utilization and minimizes delays in comparison to the methodology in [8]. In particular our scheme shows an improvement in throughput performance in the range of 34 to 69 percent over the scheme in [8]. In our model, as with [8], each node in the network maintains a separate logical queue for each service class on each outgoing link and services packets according to the rules of the pricing scheme. However, as expected the amount of computational effort required using our approach is marginally higher than that in [8].

The rest of the paper is organized as follows: In Section 2, we briefly discuss the link route pricing methodology and present the network and user model. In Section 3, we describe the price adaptation scheme that we adopt. Section 4 presents our simulation studies. Finally, Section 5 presents the concluding remarks.

2   Link Route Pricing and Our Model

We assume each link in the network offers multiple grades of services [10]. A set of routes are defined on the network where a route r is defined as a sequence of n_r 2-tuples of the form (i, j), where i is a link on the route and j is the service grade for that route on link i. The nominal congestion levels in our scheme are prescribed a *priori* for each of the link-service grade tuples on the routes. Arriving packets are allowed to choose any of the service grades that are available on a link.

We propose and use in this paper an adaptive multi-level feedback control scheme based on the SPSA methodology. In our scheme, the prices are varied based on a weighted average queue length at each link, with the queue managers or controllers periodically announcing a price for incoming customers to join the queue. The price for each of the levels in our scheme is updated using SPSA. We thus obtain a state-based closed loop pricing scheme that periodically updates prices of individual queues on each link according to the level-of-congestion in these. We present our pricing scheme in the next section. The utility function in our scheme could take any form and the network does not require knowledge of it. As mentioned above, the nominal congestion levels in our scheme are prescribed a *priori*. A link state protocol can be used to exchange congestion and pricing information required by the pricing scheme. This scheme provides (a) well defined guarantees on the grades of services, (b) congestion control and traffic management, and (c) is easy to implement and requires minimal measurements.

Our basic model is similar to that in [7] even though we use a different price structure from [7]. Consider a packet communication network having N links with the ith link having a transmission capacity of μ_i and providing J_i possible grades of service to the packets. We assume that a separate queue is maintained for packets corresponding to each of the service grades. Thus, the ith link has J_i queues, each of them used by packets desiring service of the corresponding class. We let $b_{i,j}$ denote the buffer size in the jth queue on the ith link. By a route r, we mean a sequence of tuples of the form $r := [(i_1, j_1), (i_2, j_2), \cdots, (i_{n_r}, j_{n_r})]$ comprising of n_r links and the corresponding service grade used on each of these. Let R denote the entire set of routes and let $| R | \stackrel{\triangle}{=} K > 0$ is the total number of routes. The J_i queues at link i can be serviced according to any arbitrary policy that provides the required QoS, e.g., strict round robin, weighted fair queuing etc. Let $y(t) \triangleq [y_1(t), \ldots, y_N(t)]$ denote the state of the network at time t, with each $y_i(t)$ in turn being a vector of the form $y_i(t) \triangleq [y_{i,1}(t), \cdots, y_{i,J_i}(t)]$. Here, $y_{i,j}(t)$ corresponds to buffer occupancy in the jth queue on the ith link at time t. Thus $y_i(t)$ is the vector of buffer occupancies of all queues on the ith link.

Let $z_{i,j}(t)$ denote the amount of congestion in service grade j on link i at time t. Let $z^r(t) \in \Re$ denote the congestion on route r at time t defined as

$$z^r(t) = \sum_{k=1}^{n_r} z_{i_k, j_k}(t), \text{ where the route } r \text{ corresponds to } r = [(i_1, j_1), \ldots, (i_{n_r}, j_{n_r})].$$

Let $z(t) \triangleq [z^1(t), z^2(t), \ldots, z^K(t)]$ be the overall congestion vector along all possible routes in the network. In order to provide the required QoS, the network service provider selects operating points y^* and z^* for the service classes and the tuples of links and service grades, respectively. Here, in particular, $z^* = [z_1^*, \ldots, z_K^*]$ with each $z_i^* = [z_{i,1}^*, \ldots, z_{i,J_i}^*]$.

Next, we describe the price structure used. We assign here prices to the tuples of links and service grades, unlike [7] that does so directly for the whole route. This is seen to, result in improved overall performance. We let $p^i(t)$ denote the price vector for unit traffic on link i at time t. Specifically, $p^i(t) = [p^{(i,1)}(t), \ldots, p^{(i,J_i)}(t)]$ with $p^{(i,j)}(t)$ denoting the price for unit traffic on link i for service class j at time t. We assume that $p^i(t)$ is posted by the service provider for each link $i = 1, 2, \ldots, N$. It is computed based on the current level of congestion and is made available to the users. However, $p^i(t)$ is updated periodically every T time instants for some $T > 0$ fixed. We update the price vector $p^i(t)$ by using an SPSA based methodology. This is described in the next section. A user typically sends packets along the route with the least cost. In order to compute the least cost route, the user computes along each possible i^{th} link on a feasible route, the appropriate least cost service grade to use. Let $C_s(x, z_{i,j}(t), p^{(i,j)}(t))$ denote the cost for user s in sending x units of traffic on link i using service grade j. We assume here that instantaneous values of quantities $Z_{ij}(t)$ and $p^{ij}(t)$ for all tuples (i,j) along a route are known to user s. Let

$$j^i = \arg \min_{j \in \{1, \ldots, J_i\}} C_s(x, z_{i,j}(t), p^{(i,j)}(t))$$

denote the least cost service grade on the ith link for the sth user. Note that j^i is in general a function of t. We have suppressed this dependence here for notational simplicity. The sth user would then select its least cost route according to

$$\arg \min_{r=[(1,j^1), \ldots, (n_r, j^{n_r})]} \sum_{i=1}^{n_r} C_s(x, z_{i,j^i}(t), p^{(i,j^i)}(t)).$$

We have assumed here (by an abuse of notation) for simplicity that the links on route r are numbered $1, \ldots, n_r$. The minimum above is over all feasible routes from the source to destination for the sth user. An example of a cost function $C_s(\cdot, \cdot, \cdot)$ could be $C_s(x, z_{i,j}(t), p^{(i,j)}(t)) = x(p^{(i,j)}(t) - U_s(x, z_{i,j}(t)))$, where

$U_s(x, z_{i,j}(t))$ is the sth user's utility in sending x units of traffic using the jth service grade on the ith link when the congestion level there is $z_{i,j}(t)$. Note that in general both the cost function and utility are different for different users. Thus the optimal routes for two users sending packets from the same source node to the same destination node under identical conditions of congestion could in general be different.

3   The Price Update Scheme

We first formulate the problem in the simulation based parameter optimization setting and then present our multi-layered price adaptation scheme that obtains optimal state-dependent price levels using the simultaneous perturbation stochastic approximation (SPSA) methodology. The aim here is to update prices associated with each link-service grade tuple (i, j) in a manner as to reduce an associated long-run average cost for the queue that serves customers of class j on link i. As stated previously, we assume that on each link, different classes of customers are serviced by different queues. Let $Z_{ij}(t)$ denote the queue length (or level of congestion) at queue j on link i at time t. Let $\overline{Z}(t) \stackrel{\Delta}{=} (Z_{ij}(t), j = 1, \ldots, J_i; i = 1, \ldots, N)$ denote the vector of all queue lengths at individual queues on each link in the network. Let $\theta \in C \subset \mathbb{R}^d, d \geq 1$, be a tunable parameter that governs the state $\overline{Z}(t)$ of the system at any time t. We assume that C is in fact a set of the form $C = [\underline{A}, \overline{A}]^d$. In particular, $d = \gamma L$ where γ is the dimension of $\overline{Z}(t)$ and L denotes the number of parameter levels at each queue (assumed same for simplicity) that is defined below. We assume that C is a compact subset of $\mathbb{R}^d$ and that $\{\overline{Z}(t), t \geq 0\}$ is an ergodic Markov process for any fixed $\theta \in C$. In our numerical experiments, we consider Poisson arrivals and exponential service times at all nodes. For such a system, $\overline{Z}(t)$ itself is Markov for any given θ and is trivially ergodic as well since it is finite state and irreducible.

We assume in our model that controllers at individual queues update the prices associated with their own queues. This they do by using congestion information that pertains (or is local) to only their queues. Let $h_{ij}(.)$ denote the single-stage cost associated with link-service grade tuple (i, j) that depends at any instant t only on the state $Z_{ij}(t)$ of the queue. Let $Z_{ij}(k) \stackrel{\Delta}{=} Z_{ij}(kT)$ denote the queue length at the jth queue on the ith link at instant kT, where $T > 0$ is a fixed time element. We assume in our model that queue lengths are observed every T instants of time and based on this information, prices at individual queues are instantly updated. For any given $\theta \in C$, let

$$J(\theta) = \sum_{\substack{j \in \{1, \ldots, J_i\} \\ i \in \{1, \ldots, N\}}} J_{ij}(\theta) \quad \text{with} \quad J_{ij}(\theta) = \lim_{n \to \infty} \frac{1}{n} \sum_{k=1}^{n} h_{ij}(Z_{ij}(k)) \qquad (1)$$

Let $\theta_{ij} \stackrel{\Delta}{=} (\theta_{ij}^1, \ldots, \theta_{ij}^L)$ be the parameter vector associated with j^{th} queue on i^{th} link, and $\theta = (\theta_{ij}, j = 1, \ldots, J_i, i = 1, \ldots, N)$. In the above, L corresponds to the number of levels for the parameter, that may in general vary from one queue to another. We however keep L fixed (for all queues) for simplicity. We now present our optimization scheme that is based on the SPSA methodology.

Consider a system for which the queue length $Z_{ij}(n)$ of the jth queue on i^{th} link at any instant nT is governed by the parameter $(\theta_{ij}(n) + \delta\Delta_{ij}(n))$ where $\delta > 0$ is a 'small' constant. Also $\Delta_{ij}(n) \triangleq (\Delta_{ij}^1(n), \ldots, \Delta_{ij}^L(n))$ is a vector of ± 1 - valued perturbations obtained via a Hadamard matrix based construction described in [9]. Then, for all $j = 1, \ldots, J_i; i = 1, \ldots, N; k = 1, \ldots, L$, we have

$$Y_{ij}(n+1) = Y_{ij}(n) + b(n)\left(h_{ij}\left(Z_{ij}(n)\right) - Y_{ij}(n)\right) \tag{2}$$

$$\theta_{ij}^k(n+1) = \Gamma\left(\theta_{ij}^k(n) - a(n)\frac{Y_{ij}(n)}{\delta\Delta_{ij}^k(n)}\right). \tag{3}$$

Here $\Gamma(.)$ is a projection operator that projects each price update to the interval $[\underline{A}, \overline{A}]$, with $\underline{A}, \overline{A}$ as before. Also, $\{a(n)\}$ and $\{b(n)\}$ are two step-size sequences that satisfy

$$\sum_n a(n) = \sum_n b(n) = \infty; \quad \sum_n a(n)^2, \sum_n b(n)^2 < \infty; \quad a(n) = o(b(n)).$$

We now describe our scheme SPSA-WA-LRP (SPSA Based Weighted Average Link Route Pricing) below.

SPSA-WA-LRP: Let $\widehat{Z}_{ij}(n)$ denote the 'weighted average' congestion on the jth queue at i^{th} link at instant nT, $n \geq 1$. This is obtained according to the relation

$$\widehat{Z}_{ij}(n) = (1 - w_z)\widehat{Z}_{ij}(n) + w_z Z_{ij}(n).$$

Here w_z is a small constant. The price assignment policy in this case corresponds to

$$p_{ij}(n+1) = \widehat{g}_{ij}(\theta_{ij}(n), Z_{ij}(n), \widehat{Z}_{ij}(n))$$

where $\widehat{g}(\cdot, \cdot)$ are measurable functions and $\theta_{ij}(n)$ are obtained using (2)-(3).

Remark. In our numerical experiments, we let $L = 3$ viz., we consider a three-layered pricing scheme at each of the queues. We let the single-stage cost $h_{ij}\left(Z_{ij}(k)\right)$ to be $h_{ij}\left(Z_{ij}(k)\right) = |Z_{ij}(k) - Z_{ij}^*|$, where Z_{ij}^* are prescribed thresholds. The prices $p_{ij}(n+1)$ in our scheme are then set as follows.

SPSA-WA-LRP:

$$p_{ij}(n+1) = \begin{cases} \theta_{ij}^1 & \text{if } \widehat{Z}_{ij}(n) > Z_{ij}^* + \overline{N}_{ij} \\ \theta_{ij}^2 & \text{if } Z_{ij}^* - \overline{N}_{ij} \leq \widehat{Z}_{ij}(n) \leq Z_{ij}^* + \overline{N}_{ij} \\ \theta_{ij}^3 & \text{if } \widehat{Z}_{ij}(n) < Z_{ij}^* - \overline{N}_{ij} \end{cases} \tag{4}$$

Here, $\overline{N}_{ij}$ is another queue length threshold. Thus for purposes of pricing, we split the entire queue length buffer of each queue into three regions or intervals

$[\,0,\,Z_{ij}^{*}-\overline{N}_{ij}-1]$, $[Z_{ij}^{*}-\overline{N}_{ij},\,Z_{ij}^{*}+\overline{N}_{ij}\,]$ and $[\,Z_{ij}^{*}+\overline{N}+1,\,B]$, respectively, where B denotes the buffer size (for simplicity assumed constant for all queues). In SPSA-WA-LRP, we assign prices based on the region in which the weighted average queue length $\widehat{Z}_{ij}(n)$ lies. The parameter to be tuned then corresponds to $\theta_{ij}=(\theta_{ij}^{1},\,\theta_{ij}^{2},\,\theta_{ij}^{3})$, $j=1,\ldots,J_i$, $i=1,\ldots,N$, in both cases. We then use algorithm (2)-(3) to tune the above parameter. Upon convergence of the algorithm, we obtain corresponding optimal three-layered policy within the class of policies (4). The measurable function $\widehat{g}_{ij}(.)$ that specifies the pricing mechanism is then given by (4). One expects that upon convergence in the above scheme, $\theta_{ij}^{1,*}>\theta_{ij}^{2,*}>\theta_{ij}^{3,*}$, where $\theta_{ij}^{1,*}$, $\theta_{ij}^{2,*}$, $\theta_{ij}^{3,*}$ correspond to converged values of those quantities. We however do not impose the above constraint on the system. One thus has three different grades of prices in this scheme depending upon the level of congestion. We assume, however, that quantities Z_{ij}^{*} and $\overline{N}_{ij}$ are known a priori. The task of finding 'optimal' values for these quantities is highly nontrivial as they depend on various factors that affect QoS. SPSA-WA-LRP is motivated by the random early detection (RED) mechanism used in TCP/IP based networks. The idea in this scheme is to avoid changing offered prices too often so as to present rapid fluctuations or volatility in traffic flows. As with the original RED mechanism proposed in [11], we set the weighting parameter w_z in our experiments to 0.01. We also observed this to be a good choice in our experiments. In [12], an SPSA based algorithm for RED is presented where in the parameter w_z is also tuned along with other RED parameters in order to find its optimum value. A similar procedure can also be used in our SPSA-WA-LRP algorithm for finding the optimal weight parameter w_z, in addition.

4   Simulation Results

This section describes the simulation results for a four-node network shown in Fig. 1. This setting is similar to the one considered in [7] and [8]. We show here performance comparisons of our scheme with that in [8]. We, however, do not

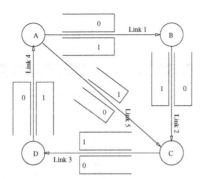

Fig. 1. A four node network for simulation

show performance comparisons with the scheme in [7] since as stated before, the scheme in [7] considers prices for entire routes and not for individual link-service grade tuples along a route. As a result, the scheme in [8] shows much better performance than the one in [7]. We refer the reader to [8] for details of experimental comparisons with the scheme in [7]. We refer to the scheme in [8] below as RA-LRP (Regulation Approach Based Link Route Pricing). Our network consists of five links. Each link receives traffic from a single class and each class can be served by two queues. The buffer capacity of each queue is 30 and the target value for congestion on either queue at each link is 10. The routes are shown in Table 1.

Table 1. The Set of Routes used in Experiments

Src-Dstn	Routes
A→B	[(1, 0)]
A→C	[(1,0),(2,0)];
A→D	[(1, 0), (2, 0), (3, 0)];
B→D	[(2, 0), (3, 0)];

We consider 1Mbps links across the network with a packet size of 210 bytes with each link being duplex. We assume that customers in each link arrive according to independent Poisson processes with rates 0.5. Also, the service time for each link is exponential but with parameter 0.7. We assume there are no delays in transmitting feedback on price information to users. The simulation is run for one thousand time units. As with [7] and [8], we let $z_{i,j}^* = 10$ for all links in all routes. The price data is collected at regular instants. Fig. 2 shows the prices across link $B \to C$ for all three regions.

The congestion data is collected at arrival instants. The long-term average of the congestion at any time t is calculated by taking the sample average of the

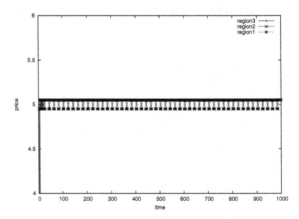

Fig. 2. Price across all three regions of link $B \to C$ for $\lambda = 0.5$ and $\mu = 0.7$

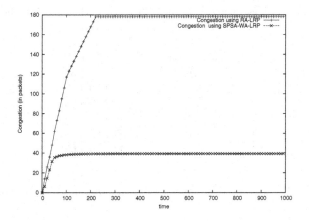

Fig. 3. Congestion on route $A \to D$ for $\lambda = 0.5$ and $\mu = 0.7$

congestion seen by the arrivals upto time t. Fig. 3 shows a plot of variation of instantaneous congestion as a function of time using the two schemes.

Table 2 gives a comparison between the two schemes of the mean and variance in congestion across all four routes. The above metrics are obtained over a time window of 1000 seconds. From Fig. 3 and Table 2, it can be seen that SPSA-WA-LRP shows significantly better performance as compared to RA-LRP.

Table 2. Comparison of mean and variance of congestion across all routes

Algorithm	Route AB		Route AC		Route AD		Route BD	
	Mean	Var	Mean	Var	Mean	Var	Mean	Var
SPSA-WA-LRP	8.29	1.18	21.63	8.44	38.09	27.58	29.80	17.46
RA-LRP	49.60	439.13	105.20	993.43	161.93	1485.91	112.33	481.13

We also obtain here the short-term average of the congestion seen by arrivals by using a shifting window and obtain the sample average over arrivals in the window. The short term averages for the last 1000 time units of simulation are also calculated. These are found to be reasonably close to the corresponding prescribed values. We observed some fluctuations in the instantaneous values while the averages seem to stabilize near the prescribed nominal values. For the various link-queue tuples along the route $A \to D$ in the network, we show in Table 3, the converged values for all three price levels when the SPSA-WA-LRP scheme is used.

In Table 4, we show performance comparisons between the two algorithms in terms of throughput and delay metrics along various routes in the network. From the table, it can be seen that SPSA-WA-LRP exhibits a throughput improvement in the range of 34-69 percent over all routes compared to RA-LRP. This happens because SPSA-WA-LRP utilizes network resources in a better manner

Table 3. Optimal values of prices using SPSA-WA-LRP across all the links in the route $A \to D$

Link-queue tuple(i,j)	$\theta_{ij}^{1,*}$	$\theta_{ij}^{2,*}$	$\theta_{ij}^{3,*}$
(1,1)	4.95	4.80	4.65
(1,2)	4.85	4.70	4.65
(2,1)	5.10	5.00	4.90
(2,2)	5.05	4.95	4.85
(3,1)	4.95	4.80	4.75
(3,2)	4.90	4.85	4.65

Table 4. Comparison of the two schemes for Throughput and Delay Performances over all Routes

Src-Dstn	Route	Throughput (*in kbps*)		Delay (*in ms*)	
		SPSA-WA-LRP	RA-LRP	SPSA-WA-LRP	RA-LRP
A→B	[(1, 0)]	8728.12	5442.6936	478.27	573.5
A→C	[(1, 0),(2,0)]	7954.73	4727.5744	784.53	882.22
A→D	[(1, 0), (2, 0), (3, 0)]	3214.83	2102.6128	827.83	922.72
B→D	[(2, 0),(3,0)]	7193.28	4580.289	812.46	873.43

as compared to RA-LRP. However, we observe that this is achieved at the cost of a slight increase in the overall computational effort using our scheme.

5   Conclusions and Future Work

We proposed in this paper a two state-dependent multi-layered link-route inter-net based pricing approach. Our scheme uses an efficient SPSA based gradient search and converges to an optimal pricing policy within a prescribed class of these. Our scheme is seen to perform significantly better than the regulation pricing methodology in [8] that was in turn adapted from the scheme in [7]. The link-route pricing approach used in [8] that we also adapt in our current work has been observed to show considerably better performance than the route based pricing approach in [7]. There are various directions that one may pursue in future. For instance, one may try out other variants of the price adaptation scheme. One may also experiment with different arrival processes, service time distributions and user models. An implementation over larger networks with many routes and service classes should also be tried.

Acknowledgments

S. Bhatnagar was supported in part by Grant No. SR/S3/EECE/011/2007 from the Department of Science and Technology, Government of India.

References

1. La, R.J., Anantharam, V.: Charge-sensitive TCP and rate control in the internet. In: Proc. of INFOCOM, vol. 3, pp. 1166–1175 (March 2000)
2. La, R.J., Anantharam, V.: Utility-based rate control in the internet for elastic traffic. IEEE/ACM Trans. Netw. 10(2), 272–286 (2002)
3. Dube, P., Borkar, V.S., Manjunath, D.: Differential join prices for parallel queues: Social optimality, dynamic pricing algorithms and application to internet pricing. In: Proceedings of IEEE Infocom, N.Y., vol. 1, pp. 276–283 (2002)
4. Odlyzko, A.: Paris metro pricing for the internet. In: EC 1999. Proceedings of the ACM Conference on Electronic Commerce, pp. 140–147. ACM Press, N.Y. (1999)
5. Borkar, V.S., Manjunath, D.: Charge-based control of diffserv-like queues. Automatica 40(12), 2043–2047 (2004)
6. Tandra, R., Hemachandra, N., Manjunath, D.: Diffserv node with join minimum cost queue policy and multiclass traffic. Perform. Eval. 55(1-2), 69–91 (2004)
7. Garg, D., Borkar, V.S., Manjunath, D.: Network pricing for QoS: A 'regulation' appproach. In: Abed, E.H. (ed.) Advances in Control, Communication Networks, and Transportation Systems (in honour of Pravin Varaiya), pp. 137–157 (2005)
8. Vemu, K.R., Bhatnagar, S., Hemachandra, N.: Link-Route Pricing for Enhanced QoS. Technical Report 2007-8, Department of Computer Science and Automation, Indian Institute of Science, Bangalore (2007), http://archive.csa.iisc.ernet.in/TR/2007/8/
9. Bhatnagar, S., Fu, M.C., Marcus, S.I., Wang, I.-J.: Two timescale simultaneous perturbation stochastic approximation using deterministic perturbation sequences. ACM Transactions on Modelling and Computer Simulation 13(2), 180–209 (2003)
10. Carlson, D., Davies, E., Wang, Z., Blake, S., Black, M., Weiss, W.: An architecture for differential services. Technical Report RFC 2475, IETF (1998)
11. Floyd, S., Jacobson, V.: Random early detection gateways for congestion avoidance. IEEE/ACM Trans. Netw. 1(4), 397–413 (1993)
12. Vaidya, R., Bhatnagar, S.: Robust optimization of random early detection. Telecommunication Systems 33(4), 291–316 (2006)

Distributed Resource Adaptation for Virtual Network Operators

Con Tran, Jahangir Sarker, and Zbigniew Dziong

École de Technologie Supérieure, University of Quebec, Montréal, Canada
con.tran.1@ens.etsmtl.ca, zdziong@ele.etsmtl.ca

Abstract. Virtual Network Operators lease bandwidth from different data carriers to offer well managed Virtual Private Networks. By using proprietary algorithms and leased resource diversity they can offer Quality of Service, at competitive prices, which is difficult to attain from traditional data network operators. In this paper, we describe a novel distributed resource management approach, based on an economic model, that allows continuous optimizing of the network profit, while keeping network blocking constraints. The approach integrates leased link capacity adaptations, based on measurements, with connection admission control and routing policies. This is done in the framework that applies decomposition of Markov Decision Process. Our numerical analysis validates the approach and shows the convergence and stability of the adaptation as functions of measurement parameters.

1 Introduction

Internet is formed by numerous interconnected Autonomous Systems (AS) operating independently and therefore real time applications such as Voice over Internet (VoIP), Streaming Multimedia and Interactive Games are often unable to get their required end-to-end Quality of Service (QoS) guarantee. One possible approach to overcome the problem is to use global Service Overlay Networks (SON) [1,2], where a set of overlay routers (or overlay nodes, ON), owned and controlled by one Virtual Network Operator (VNO), is interconnected by virtual overlay links realized by leasing bandwidth from the AS's via Service Level Agreements (SLA) [3].

In general, there are two approaches to provide QoS in the SON. In the first approach, the VNO that manages the SON leases the best effort access to the AS's. In this case, to ensure availability of required bandwidth and QoS, the SON has to monitor continuously its links established over best effort Internet and react fast when QoS of some links deteriorates, e.g., by rerouting the connections on the paths with acceptable QoS. In the second approach, the VNO leases the overlay links with appropriate bandwidth and QoS guarantees (e.g., based on the MPLS-TE technology). In this case, user end-to-end QoS connections are realized through the SON admission control and routing policy. Obviously, the VNO can use both types of leased bandwidth in a flexible and controlled way to reduce cost since best effort bandwidth is less expensive.

T. Janowski and H. Mohanty (Eds.): ICDCIT 2007, LNCS 4882, pp. 146–157, 2007.

The above arguments indicate that Virtual Network Operators can potentially offer well managed QoS Virtual Private Network (VPN) at competitive prices, by using economically-sound SONs that can be managed by sophisticated proprietary control mechanisms adaptable towards the needs of particular clients. Note that VNOs can lease bandwidth from several different operators that removes the geographical barriers and also offers much better architecture for reliability and failure protection. These advantages led to creation of several VNOs like Internap (internap.com), Mnet (mnet.co.uk), Sirocom (sirocom.com), Vanco (vanco.co.uk), Virtela [4] (virtela.net), Vanguard (vanguardms.com), Netscalibur (netscalibur.com).

In this paper, we focus on distributed resource management in SONs based on leased bandwidth with QoS guarantees. The approach is based on decomposition of the Markov Decision Process that is also used for efficient routing. The theoretical base for this approach was presented in [5] where also some analytical results were given. Here we propose a distributed implementation of this approach that is based on measurements. We analyze convergence and stability of the distributed algorithm under non-stationary conditions. It is important to underline that the approach integrates leased link capacity adaptations with connection admission control (CAC) and routing policies by using coherent economic framework derived from Markov Decision Process theory.

The paper is organized as follows. In Section 2, we describe in short the main results presented in [5], providing a theoretical background for the proposed measurements based distributed implementation. The distributed implementation is presented in Section 3 together with stability and convergence metrics used to assess the adaptation algorithm performance. Numerical analysis illustrating the convergence and stability of the proposed approach is given in Section 4.

2 Analytical Model for Resource Adaptation

The monetary and provided goods flows between the users, SON and Autonomous Systems are illustrated in Fig. 1 for the considered system. We assume

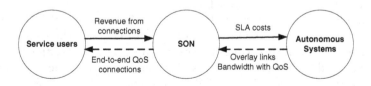

Fig. 1. SON economic framework

that the objective of the SON operator is to maximize the profit expressed as:

$$P = R - \sum_{s \in S} C_s = \sum_{j \in J} \bar{\lambda}_j r_j - \sum_{s \in S} C_s \qquad (1)$$

where: R - SON average revenue rate, $\bar{\lambda}_j$ - average rate of admitted class j connections, r_j - average revenue (price) for class j connections, C_s - overlay link costs, S - set of overlay links, and J - set of user connection classes.

In this formulation, the maximization of the revenue profit can be achieved by leased bandwidth adaptation that influences the admission rate $\bar{\lambda}_j$ and cost C_s, and by adjusting the service prices r_j. The profit maximization should be done in such a way that the connection blocking probabilities B_j of all classes do not exceed the constraints B_j^c.

In general, demand for SON services is variable due to factors like periodic variability in scale of a day, week, month, year, and variability caused by trends of varying demand for certain services. Since the leased bandwidth amount within SLA can be adapted from time to time or even dynamically (on line), it is natural that the VNO needs a mechanism that can indicate when and how to adapt the SLA's to maximize profit while respecting the required blocking constraints.

2.1   Models Derived from Markov Decision Theory

In this section we describe a model for resource adaptation for given connection arrival rates. First, the applied CAC and routing policy based on Markov decision theory is presented. Then, the mechanism for bandwidth adaptation for given reward parameters is described. Finally, we discuss the issue of adaptation of reward parameters in order to achieve the required blocking constraints. While the proposed framework is applicable to multi-class services with different bandwidth requirements, in this paper we will consider a network with homogeneous connections where all classes have the same bandwidth requirement and the same mean service time.

CAC and Routing Policy. For a network with given links dimensions and reward parameters, optimizing profit is realized with efficient use of available resources, through a CAC and routing policy which admits the connections on the most profitable routes. The policy used is a state dependent CAC and routing based on Markov Decision Process (MDP) theory [6]. In addition to dynamic link costs, defined in [6] as shadow prices, we integrated the costs of leasing the SON overlay links, C_s, in the model.

As shown in [6,7], for given reward rate, one can find an optimal CAC and routing policy that maximizes the average profit by using one of the standard MDP solution algorithms. In this paper, this exact approach is called the MDP CAC and routing model. Since this model is too complex for realistic size networks, a decomposition technique, called MDPD, described in [6,7], was proposed. The technique uses a link independence assumption to decompose the network reward process into separable link reward processes with link arrival and service rates λ_j^s, μ_j, and link connection reward parameters r_j^s. In this paper, this approach is called the MDPD CAC and routing model. In this model, to integrate monetary link costs into the CAC and routing policy, we propose to divide connection reward into link connection rewards proportionally to the used resources cost:

$$r_j^s = r_j.(C_s/N_s)/(\sum_{o \in S^k} C_o/N_o) \tag{2}$$

where: N_s - link s capacity (max number of connections), S_k - set of links on path k. Then, analogously to (1), the link expected profit is:

$$\bar{P}_s = \bar{R}_s - C_s = \sum_{j \in J} \bar{\lambda}_j^s r_j^s - C_s \tag{3}$$

where $\bar{\lambda}_j^s$ is the rate of admitted class j connections on link s.

In the MDPD model, a link s net gain $g_j^s(X)$ is defined as the expected link reward increase from accepting an additional connection of class j in link state X. A state dependent link shadow price is then defined as the difference between the link reward and net gain. It represents the cost of accepting the class j call on link s in state X:

$$p_j^s(X) = r_j^s - g_j^s(X) \tag{4}$$

During network operation, the link shadow prices can be calculated based on measurement of link connection arrival rates [6,7]. Then the optimal CAC and routing policy will choose the path with the maximum positive net gain:

$$g_{max} = max_{k \in W_j}[r_j - \sum_{s \in S^k} p_j^s(X)] \tag{5}$$

where W_j is the set of possible class j paths. If no path produces a positive gain, the connection is rejected.

Link Bandwidth Adaptation for Given Reward Parameters. With changing network conditions, such as traffic level or leased bandwidth cost, SON parameters should be adapted to continuously realize the reward profit maximization objective. As mentioned, the SON operator can control overlay links capacities (by modifying the SLAs) and reward parameters r_j . In this section, we concentrate on overlay link capacity adaptation with given reward parameters.

Profit Sensitivity to Link Capacity. In the MDPD model the network profit sensitivity to a link capacity can be approximated by the link profit sensitivity to the link capacity. Following (3) we have:

$$\partial \bar{P}_s/\partial N_s = (\partial \bar{R}_s/\partial N_s - \partial C_s/\partial N_s) \tag{6}$$

It has been shown in [7] that the average reward sensitivity to link capacity can be approximated by the average link shadow price of a connection class with unit bandwidth requirement, $\partial \bar{R}_s/\partial N_s = \bar{p}_s(N_s)$. Assuming that C_s is a linear function of N_s, $C_s = cN_s$, where c is the bandwidth unit cost, we arrive at requirement that

$$\bar{p}^s(N_s) - c = 0 \tag{7}$$

since the link profit is maximized when $\partial \bar{P}_s/\partial N_s = 0$. (7) constitutes the base for the capacity adaptation procedure.

Bandwidth Adaptation Model. An iterative procedure is used to converge to the solution for (7) that gives the optimized link capacity. In [5], we use Newton's successive linear approximations, in which the capacity new value N_{n+1} at each iteration step n is given by (link index s is omitted to simplify the notation):

$$N_{n+1} = N_n - \frac{\bar{p}_n(N) - c}{[\partial(\bar{p}_n(N) - c)/\partial N]} \qquad (8)$$

Details of the procedure can be found in [5]. It is important to underline that the bandwidth adaptation procedure and the CAC and routing procedure (described earlier) are integrated by the fact that link shadow prices obtained in the latter procedure are used in the capacity adaptations. In turn, CAC and routing policies adapt to changes in link capacities and to bandwidth costs.

Reward Parameter Adaptation to Meet the Blocking Constraints. The CAC algorithm rejects connection requests when bandwidth is not available or the connection is not profitable. The resulting blocking probabilities can be defined for each connection class j as:

$$B_j = (\lambda_j - \bar{\lambda}_j)/\lambda_j = 1 - (\bar{\lambda}_j/\lambda_j) \qquad (9)$$

Then we define the network average blocking probability as:

$$B_T = \sum_j (\lambda_j - \bar{\lambda}_j)/\sum_j \lambda_j = 1 - (\sum_j \bar{\lambda}_j / \sum_j \lambda_j) \qquad (10)$$

As mentioned in Section 2, blocking probabilities should not exceed the network and/or class blocking constraints B_T^c and B_j^c. To achieve this objective, we propose an adaptation of reward parameters, since in general the increase of r_j will cause a decrease of B_j and B_T, and vice versa. Note that a change of r_j may influence the optimal solution for link bandwidth allocation. Therefore adaptation of reward parameters should be integrated with adaptation of link bandwidths. One relatively simple solution is to apply the two adaptation algorithms iteratively, as illustrated in Fig. 2. Network blocking constraint can be met by multiplying all class reward parameters $\{r_j\}$ by a common factor γ.

Once the network constraint has been met, class blocking probabilities can be readjusted to meet class constraints by varying relatively the class reward parameters between them (while preserving average network reward parameter). In this paper, we only consider meeting the network blocking constraint.

Let $r_T = \sum_j \bar{\lambda}_j r_j / \sum_j \bar{\lambda}_j$ and $r_s = \sum_j \bar{\lambda}_j^s r_j^s / \sum_j \bar{\lambda}_j^s = \sum_j \bar{\lambda}_j^s r_j^s / \bar{\lambda}_s$ be the current average network and link reward parameters. To achieve $B_T(r_T) = B_T^c$, one can apply Newton's iterations with an approximation for the derivative $\partial B_T / \partial r_T$. More details of the procedure for reward parameters adaptation can be found in [5].

3   Distributed Adaptation Based on Measurements

The analytical model presented in the previous section is not practical for application in realistic size networks due to the cardinality of the problem. Namely,

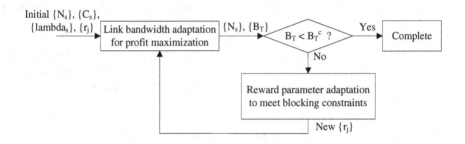

Fig. 2. SON adaptation algorithm

while the resource adaptation problem is decomposed into the link problems, this decomposition requires knowledge of the connection flow distribution in the network. This distribution was achieved from the exact network performance model that is prohibitive in complexity for any realistic size network. One could apply a simplified model based on the link decomposition, as indicated in [5], but even in this case the complexity is quite large. To cope with the problem we propose a distributed implementation of the adaptation algorithm. In this case, instead of using the analytical performance model, the required parameters are measured. By avoiding complexity of the performance model, this approach can be easily implemented in a distributed fashion in each overlay node.

The measurement process can be realized by using different filtering methods. For the initial study we have chosen a simple approach based on moving average. In Subsection 3.1 we describe details of the measurement model and the resulting changes in the distributed adaptation model. To assess the stability and convergence of the distributed adaptation, we also propose a set of metrics presented in Subsection 3.2.

3.1 Measurements, Estimations and Model Modifications

By using distributed approach, we need to estimate only connection flows offered to links. Then these flows are used to calculate state dependent shadow prices for routing and average shadow price for adaptation. This gives opportunity to further simplify the link model since, as indicated in [7], for the purpose of link performance and shadow price model, we can aggregate all classes with the same bandwidth requirements offered to link s into one class i having reward parameter defined by:

$$r_i^s = \frac{\sum_{j \in J_i} r_j^s \bar{\lambda}_j^s}{\sum_{j \in J_i} \bar{\lambda}_j^s} \tag{11}$$

where J_i is the set of connection classes j aggregated into class i. Since in this paper we consider examples with homogeneous bandwidth requirements, we arrive at the case with one link connection class for the purpose of link bandwidth adaptation. Then we need to estimate, based on measurements, the following parameters needed in our routing and adaptation models: link connection arrival rate, λ_s, link connection service rate, μ_s, average link connection reward parameter, r^s, and link average shadow price, $\bar{p}_s$.

Note that the measurement and estimation of average number of link connections in service is much more straightforward than measurement of link arrival rates. Therefore, our estimation approach is based on measured link s connection occupancy averages $\bar{A}_s$.

Estimation Approach. For estimation of $\bar{A}_s$ we apply moving average approach. The link occupancy samples are taken at regular sampling sub-intervals and the moving average estimate is obtained by averaging over the measurement window interval. As time advances, the window slides by an interval t_m at a time. In the simulations, we used sampling interval of $0.25t_s$ and $t_m = 2.5t_s$, where t_s denotes average service time.

Link Connection Arrival Rate Estimation. Link connection arrival rates are evaluated from average link occupancies $\bar{A}_s$ using the following relation:

$$\lambda_s = A_s\mu_s = \frac{\bar{A}_s\mu_s}{1 - E_b(A_s, N_s)} \qquad (12)$$

where: A_s is the link offered traffic and $E_b(A_s, N_s)$ is the Erlang B formula for link s with capacity N_s. With N_s given, A_s and $E_b(A_s, N_s)$ are obtained by interpolation of the equation:

$$A_s[1 - E_b(A_s, N_s)] = \bar{A}_s \qquad (13)$$

Estimation Adjustment Following Link Capacity Change. When a link capacity is adjusted by the adaptation algorithm, this event induces a corresponding change in the link carried traffic. To account in part for this change, all occupancy samples in the current sliding window are re-adjusted to become:

$$\bar{A}_{adj} = A[1 - E_b(A, N + \Delta N)] = \frac{\bar{A}}{1 - E_b(A, N)}[1 - E_b(A, N + \Delta N)] \qquad (14)$$

where ΔN is the capacity change and $\bar{A}_{adj}$ is the adjusted link carried traffic.

Average Shadow Price Evaluation. The average link shadow price $\bar{p}_s$ used to determine optimal link capacity can be evaluated from A_s and $\bar{A}_s$ [7]:

$$\bar{p}_s = \frac{A_s}{\bar{A}_s}[E_b(A_s, N_s - 1) - E_b(A_s, N_s)]\bar{A}_s\mu_s r^s \qquad (15)$$

Then, by using

$$A_s[E_b(A_s, N_s - 1) - E_b(A_s, N_s)] = \bar{A}_s(A_s, N_s) - \bar{A}_s(A_s, N_s - 1) \qquad (16)$$

where $\bar{A}_s$ is expressed as a function of A_s and N_s (13), we arrive at:

$$\bar{p}_s = \left[1 - \frac{\bar{A}_s(A_s, N_s - 1)}{\bar{A}_s(A_s, N_s)} \right] \bar{A}_s \mu_s r^s \tag{17}$$

With N_s given and A_s interpolated from (13), $\bar{p}_s$ can be determined from (17).

3.2 Capacity Adaptation Performance Metrics

To evaluate capacity adaptation performance, we have chosen a traffic scenario that consists of two phases. In the first phase the offered traffic is stationary and the length of this phase is long enough to achieve the capacity adaptation algorithm convergence. In the second phase, the offered traffic level is changed significantly and kept at this new level for a long period of time so the capacity adaptation mechanisms converges to the new optimal values. An example of such a scenario is shown in Fig. 3, where the link offered traffic level is increased at time $t_0 = 500 t_s$ and the link capacity converges at time $t_f = 688 t_s$. Convergence time is defined as the time when the capacity enters the range delimited by stationary capacity fluctuations ($75 - 79$ in the example). The second phase itself can be divided into two periods: convergence period of duration $d_C = t_f - t_0$, and stationary period after t_f. For each of these periods we propose metrics that characterize the quality of the adaptation convergence in the first period and the adaptation stability under stationary conditions for the second period.

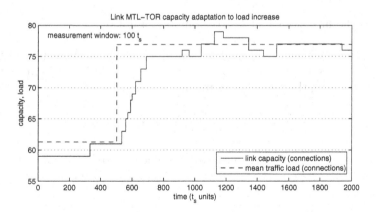

Fig. 3. Link adaptation example

Stability Metrics. Let us consider first the second period for a given link. This period consists of several time intervals during which the capacity remain fixed and let t_n be duration of the nth such time interval. Adaptation stability can be characterized by the number and amplitude of deviations from the average capacity value, where smaller values represent better stability. As a metric for amplitude deviation we propose the relative standard deviation from the rounded link capacity mean that represents the converged capacity:

$$\sigma_S = \frac{1}{\bar{N}} \sqrt{\frac{1}{\sum_n t_n} \sum_n (N_n - \bar{N})^2 t_n} \tag{18}$$

where: n is the interval index in the stationary period, t_n is interval n duration, N_n is link capacity in interval n, $\bar{N}$ is link capacity average, rounded to an integer.

The other stability measure is the number α of link capacity changes per time unit. The two measures can optionally be integrated in a combined parameter S_S, with a weight k applied to α to account for its relative importance:

$$S_S = \sigma_S + k\alpha \tag{19}$$

Overall network stability measures $\bar{\sigma}_S, \bar{\alpha}, \bar{S}_S$, corresponding to the link stability measures, are obtained by averaging the measures over all links in the network:

$$\bar{\sigma}_S = \frac{1}{\sum_s \bar{N}_s} \sum_s \sigma_{S,s} \bar{N}_s \tag{20}$$

$$\bar{\alpha} = \frac{1}{L} \sum_s \alpha_s \tag{21}$$

$$\bar{S}_S = \bar{\sigma}_S + k\bar{\alpha} \tag{22}$$

where s is the link index and L is the number of links in the network.

Convergence Metrics. Adaptation convergence can be characterized by the convergence period duration d_C and the link capacity deviation from converged capacity $\bar{N}$ during the convergence period defined as:

$$\sigma_C = \frac{1}{\bar{N}} \sum_n |N_n - \bar{N}| t_n \tag{23}$$

where n is the interval index during convergence period. Network convergence measures $\bar{\sigma}_C, \bar{d}_C$ are obtained by averaging link metrics similarly to (20,21).

4   Numerical Analysis

In this section, we evaluate our resource adaptation model using event driven simulations. Connection requests with exponentially distributed inter-arrival and service times are offered to the network. The requests are admitted and routed following the profit maximization CAC and Routing policy presented in Section 2. As traffic condition changes are introduced during the simulation, links capacity and reward parameters are adapted to maintain profit maximization while meeting blocking constraints, according to the adaptation model presented in Sections 2 and 3.1.

Simulation Scenario. Simulations are performed on a network example called ANE_20L, representing a SON implemented in North East America major cities. This SON includes 10 overlay nodes with 20 overlay links which yields 45 possible origin-destination (OD) pairs, each representing a connection class.

All connections have bandwidth requirement of 1 unit and mean service time t_s of 200 seconds. Connection arrival rates are initially set at 0.1 per second for a third of the classes, and at 0.067 per second for the remaining classes. In this paper, we will use t_s as the time unit. The SON links are sized initially for optimal profit under initial network conditions, with capacities of 25 to 62 bandwidth units. The first stationary phase of simulations is run for a period of 500 t_s under the initial traffic levels. Then in the second phase at 500 t_s, all arrival rates are increased by 20%.

Simulation Results. Overall network adaptation performance is presented in Table 1, where network averages for convergence duration $\bar{d}_C$, convergence deviation $\bar{\sigma}_C$, stability deviation $\bar{\sigma}_S$ and stability rate of changes $\bar{\alpha}$ are given. The results show that a good convergence is achieved for small measurement window at the expense of lower stability.

Table 1. Network ANE_20L capacity adaptation evaluation, 20% traffic increase

Window size(in t_s)	d_C	$\bar{\sigma}_C$	$\bar{\sigma}_S$	$\bar{\alpha}$
20	35	4.66	0.0325	0.0859
50	74	9.03	0.0232	0.0209
100	239	22.65	0.0126	0.0055

To give more insight into the behavior of the adaptation algorithm as a function of the measurement window size, Fig. 4 and 5 show capacity adaptations for one of the links, with window size of respectively 20 t_s and 100 t_s. Link capacity is adapted to optimal value of 70 in both cases, but the 20 t_s case shows much faster convergence with its steep capacity ramp up. On the other hand, its stability is significantly worse, as shown by both the amplitude and frequency of capacity changes.

To illustrate variation of adaptation performance among different links, Fig. 6 includes results for all links and for the three window sizes. Each point on the figure corresponds to one link and its location corresponds to link adaptation convergence σ_C and stability deviation σ_S.

In general the points are grouped by the window size, though it can be noticed that for large window size of 100 t_s, the variation of convergence deviation among the different links is quite large.

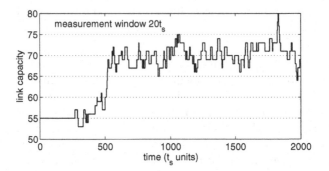

Fig. 4. Link MTL-QUE capacity adaptation qualities, window size 20 t_s

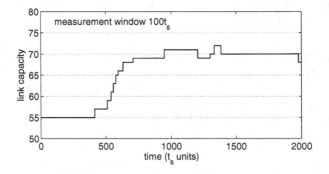

Fig. 5. Link MTL-QUE capacity adaptation qualities, window size 100 t_s

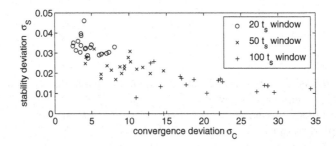

Fig. 6. Link capacities adaptation performance, network ANE_20L

5   Conclusion

In this paper, we proposed a distributed resource adaptation approach for Virtual Network Operators that manage Service Overlay Networks. The objective is to adapt leased bandwidth in order to maximize network profit subject to connection blocking constraints. The framework uses Markov decision theory for integration of the CAC and routing model with the link bandwidth and reward parameter adaptation models. The key element of this integration is the concept of link shadow price that provides consistent economic framework for the whole problem. The distributed algorithm is based on decomposition of the whole problem into a set of link problems, that can be solved based on measurements and estimation of the link parameters. To assess the convergence and stability of the adaptation process, we proposed several metrics. Using these metrics and the simulation model, we demonstrated the convergence and stability of the proposed scheme. The results show that in the applied estimation, based on moving average, the measurement window is a key parameter that determines the trade-off between convergence and stability. Future work will include more sophisticated filtering mechanism to verify whether the convergence can be improved without significant reduction of stability level.

Acknowledgments. This work is supported in part by grants from NSERC.

References

1. Li, B., et al.: Guest Editorial, Recent Advances in Service Overlay Networks. IEEE Journal on Selected Areas in Communications 22(1), 1–5 (2004)
2. Sen, A., et al.: On Topological Design of Service Overlay Networks. In: de Meer, H., Bhatti, N. (eds.) IWQoS 2005. LNCS, vol. 3552, pp. 54–68. Springer, Heidelberg (2005)
3. Duan, Z., Zhang, Z.-L., Hou, Y.T.: Service Overlay Networks: SLAs, QoS, and Bandwidth Provisioning. IEEE/ACM Transactions on Networking 11, 870–883 (2003)
4. Allen, D.: Virtela's IP VPN Overlay Networks. Network Magazine (January 2002)
5. Tran, C., Dziong, Z., Pioro, M.: SLA Adaptation for Service Overlay Networks. In: Networking 2007. 6th International IFIP-TC6 Networking Conference Proceedings. LNCS, vol. 4479, pp. 691–702. Springer, Heidelberg (2007)
6. Dziong, Z., Mason, L.G.: Call Admission and Routing in Multi-Service Loss Networks. IEEE Transactions on Communications 42(234), part 3, 2011–2022 (1994)
7. Dziong, Z.: ATM Network Resource Management. McGraw-Hill, New York (1997)
8. Fulp, E.W., Reeves, D.S.: Bandwidth Provisionning and Pricing for Networks with Multiple Classes of Service. Computer Networks 46(1), 41–52 (2004)
9. Yannuzzi, M., et al.: On the Challenges of Establishing Disjoint QoS IP/MPLS Paths Across Multiple Domains. IEEE Communications Magazine 44(12), 60–66 (2006)

Maximum Lifetime Tree Construction for Wireless Sensor Networks

G.S. Badrinath[1], Phalguni Gupta[1], and Sajal K. Das[2]

[1] Department of Computer Science and Engineering,
Indian Institute of Technology Kanpur, Kanpur, India
{badri,pg}@cse.iitk.com
[2] Department of Computer Science and Engineering,
The University of Texas at Arlington, Arlington, USA
das@cse.uta.edu

Abstract. This paper proposes a centralized tree structure based routing protocol. It is based on a greedy heuristic to maximize wireless sensor network lifetime. The proposed heuristic results in greater lifetime has been compared with naive heuristic used earlier in literature. The proposed design uses residual energy for the construction of tree which makes high energy sensor nodes nearer to base station. Rigorously the algorithm is tested using simulation and found that the lifetime is improved significantly compared to the available well known greedy solutions respectively.

1 Introduction

Multi-hop, ad hoc, wireless sensor networks (WSNs) have received increasing research attention due to its technology to observe changes in physical environment. Applications of WSNs [1] include battlefield surveillance, biological detection, home appliance, smart spaces, and inventory tracking. Sensor nodes are equipped with sensing device, computing processor, short range wireless transmitter-receiver, and limited battery supply. The observation of sensor devices which can communicate over short range is delivered to base station (i.e. sink) over multiple hops which is out of reach of data source sensor nodes. The observation in sensor network may be Time driven or Event driven. In case of Time driven network, the environment is sensed periodically at a constant rate and sends the data to the sink while in Event driven [2] network the environment is sensed only on some event or changes.

In WSN, lifetime and connectivity stands out as the major challenges, because sensor nodes[1] have limited battery power, and directly related to lifetime. Amount of energy utilized to transmit packets [3] is significant compared to sensing and computing. Energy spent by the system for each transmission depends on transmitter-receiver distance, and cost to receive. So these factors demand to develop efficient routing protocol to increase network lifetime and to maintain network connectivity as far as possible.

---

[1] Sensor nodes, sensor and nodes are used interchangeably.

T. Janowski and H. Mohanty (Eds.): ICDCIT 2007, LNCS 4882, pp. 158–165, 2007.
© Springer-Verlag Berlin Heidelberg 2007

To address this issue several protocols have been indirectly aimed [5-7, 10], which aimed at minimizing the total energy consumption, and hence improving the lifetime. The network lifetime of a wireless sensor network is defined as the time of the first node failure in the network [9]. Some researchers have directly aimed at improving the lifetime [8, 9, 11, 12, 15].

The conventional routing protocol [13], for all-to-one data routing problem on a multi hop WSN is Minimum Transmission Energy (MTE) path. MTE protocol reduces the transmiting power of all the nodes in the network, all nodes choose the minimum length edge to reach the next destination node and stay connected. In most of the routing protocols [6, 14, 15] in literature for WSNs, the data is routed ons minimum hop (MH) path to the base stations. Typical protocols use shortest path algorithms based on hop count, or transmission power.

This paper considers time driven wireless sensor networks which asssumes a base station and hundreds or thousands of sensors equipped with omni-directional antenna. The data from sensors at each time unit (known as round) is sent to the base station for further processing. The problem is to construct a routing tree to route data from all sensors to the base station, which maximizes the lifetime of the sensor network. In other words, the problem is to maximize the number of rounds before any sensor node exhausts from energy.

In this paper, a novel greedy heuristic method is proposed to construct Maximum Lifetime Tree (MLT) to maximize the lifetime of wireless sensor network in terms of rounds metric. A round is a process where data is gathered from all sensor nodes to base station, which have relatively powerful computing and communication capabilities. Number of packets that the node can relay is considered as the cost metric for the edge [13], which includes the cost due to transmission, receiving and remaining energy.

2 Problem Statement and System Models

The wireless sensor network can be modeled as a directed graph $G = (V, E)$, where V is a set of n distinct sensor nodes with $Id \in \{1, 2, \cdots |V|\}$, and the base station having $Id\, 0$. There exists a directed edge (i, j) in E associated with weight as $Flow_{ij}$, if node j is within the transmission range of i (i.e. $d_{ij} < \Im$). Since data from all the nodes is moves towards base station for further processing, any minimally connected graph structure can support this routing scheme for data accumulation from all the sensor nodes to base. It can be seen intitutively that a tree is the minimal graph structure rooted to base as supporting structure for network connectivity. Hence the routing structure for data gathering is a tree.

2.1 Radio Model

The energy dissipation for sensors is based on the first order radio model presented in [13]. In this model, to run the radio transmitter or receiver circuitry, $E_{elec} = 50nJ/bit$ of energy is dissipated while $E_{amp} = 100pJ/bit/m^2$ is dissipated to run the transmit amplifier. Therefore, energy spent by the transmitting sensor node i to transmit a k-bit packet to the receiving node j at distance d is

$$E_T(k, d) = E_{Elec} * k + E_{amp} * k * d^2 \qquad (1)$$

and energy spent by the receiving node j to receive a k-bit packet is

$$E_r(k) = E_{Elec} * k \qquad (2)$$

It is also important to note that the cost incurred to the sensor node i for transmitting a k-bit packet is either:

$$C_{ij}(k) = 2 * E_{Elec} * k + E_{amp} * k * d_{ij}^2 \qquad (3)$$

or

$$C'_{ij}(k) = E_{Elec} * k + E_{amp} * k * d_{ij}^2 \qquad (4)$$

where C_{ij} is the cost of transmission between node i and node j for the *relay packet*, and C'_{ij} is the cost of the transmission for the generated data packet after sensing the environment, and d_{ij} is the distance between node i and node j.

2.2   Definitions and Notations

For the nodes in the routing tree T at round t , let $\Re_i(t)$, $E_T^i(T)$, $E_R^i(T)$ and $P_i(T)$ represent the remaining battery energy level, the transmitting power, receiving power, and the number of packets received by i for relaying respectively.

3   Maximum Lifetime Tree Construction

The strategy followed to deal with maximum lifetime data gathering problem is to maximize the residual energy of the tree constructed at each round. Minimizing the total energy consumed which increases the residual energy. By maximizing the residual energy in each round, a cumulative effect on series of trees improves the lifetime of the network.

The information of energy available across the nodes is used to achieve maximum lifetime tree, and to balance the energy consumption across all sensor nodes. Nodes that have less energy would be the first one to die. So node with less energy can be added later and tries to have fewer children in the tree. Hence, fewer packets should be relayed to its neighbor which maximize its lifetime. Nodes with high residual energy are penalized to relay more packets. Also, high energy nodes would have many children. With the goal to achieve this, the wieght $Flow_{ij}$ of the edge (i, j) is computed in terms of number of bit size packets that can be relayed from the node i to the node j.

$$Flow_{ij} = \frac{EnergyAvailable(i)}{Energyfor(RelayPacket)} \qquad (5)$$

$$= \frac{\Re_i(t)}{E_T^i(t) + E_R^i(t)} \qquad (6)$$

$$= \frac{\Re_i(t)}{2 * E_{Elec} * k + E_{amp} * k * d_{ij}^2} \qquad (7)$$

Table 1. Maximum Lifetime Tree Algorithm

Input: Given directed weighted graph where : set of nodes and : set of edges
Intialization: set $T := B$, where B is the base station of the sensor network. Set $Cost(i) := 0$, for all $0 < i < |V|$, where $Cost(i)$ is the cost to reach the base station.
Procedure:
while $|T| \neq |V|$
do find an edge$(i, j) \in T \times (V - T)$ such that incremental cost $\delta Cost(j) = Cost(i) + 1/Flow_{ji}$ is Minimum
add node j to T, i.e. $T := T \cup j$
set $Cost(j) = Cost(i) + 1/Flow_{ji}$

3.1 Description of MLT Algorithm

The routing tree is computed using variant of Prim's Minimum Spanning Tree algorithm, shown in Table 1. The idea behind the algorithm is that every new node added to the tree has the minimum cost to reach the base station. The algorithm works as follows: Initially, we assume base station is in the tree, and cost of all the nodes is zero. The tree structure T to represent the sub routing tree that has been built for for the graph G at a round. A new edge $(i, j) \in T \times (V - T)$ is added to T if

$$\Delta Cost(j) = Cost(i) + 1/Flow_{ji} \tag{8}$$

is minimum. The procedure is continued until all sensors in V have been added to T. The running time of the algorithm is $\bigcirc(n^2)$.

From the definition of edge cost, the following holds the proposed strategies about the maximum lifetime tree construction problem:

- If the distance between the sending sensor j and the receiving sensor i is low, the edge weight $Flow_{ji}$ tends to be high. Hence it lowers the value $1/FLow_{ji}$. Thus the sensor j has high possibility to be added to T and connects to i. It meets the strategy to minimize the energy spent by a node, and hence residual energy is maximized in each round;
- If the residual energy of the node j is high, the edge weight $Flow_{ji}$ tends to be high. Hence it lowers the value $1/Flow_{ji}$. The strategy of greedy heuristic lowers the $1/Flow_{ji}$, the cost to reach the base station would be lower and higher the possibility of the node i being added to T. It meets the strategy to transmit data packets on behalf many nodes, hence the lifetime of a routing tree is maximized.

Since base station knows the location of nodes, energy and routing tree, it can estimate the remaining energy levels of the nodes after Δt rounds using the cost model. After passing t rounds (e.g. 100) the new routing tree is computed and the base station sends the required information for every node.

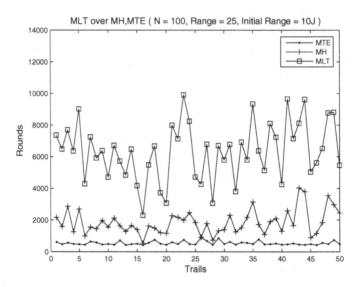

Fig. 1. Lifetime of MTE, over MH and MLT for $\Im = 25$, $\Re(0) = 10J$, $\Delta t = 100$

4   Performance Evaluation

In this section, the performance of the algorithm is evaluated through experimental simulations using MATLOG [4]. Three different routing protocol schemes are simulated: MH, MTE, and the proposed MLT. Networks of size 100 nodes in a (100×100) region are randomly generated with uniform distribution. Simulations for the same network are repeated for different transmission ranges and different position of the base station. Network is assumed to be static without node mobility and energy spent at unintended receiver within the transmission range due to overhearing is ignored.

In Fig.1, the network lifetime of MH, MTE, and MLT are compared for transmission range $\Im = 25$, initial energy $\Re(0) = 10J$, $N = 100$ and for update interval of $\Delta t = 100$ rounds. 50 different network topologies are generated and network lifetime has been calculated for each case. Table 2 summarizes the performance in terms of network lifetime for the above 50 trails. Using MLT, the network lifetime is roughly prolonged by a factor of three (200%) and by factor of eleven (1000%) compared to MH and MTE respectively.

4.1   Effect of Transmitting Range

Increasing the transmission range of the nodes increases the number of one hop neighbors, so the topology of the sensor network changes. To study the impact of transmission range on performance of proposed protocol MLT, 24 experiments have been conducted with transmission range $\Im, \Im = 15, 20, \cdots, 80$. Fig. 2, shows the plot of the results.

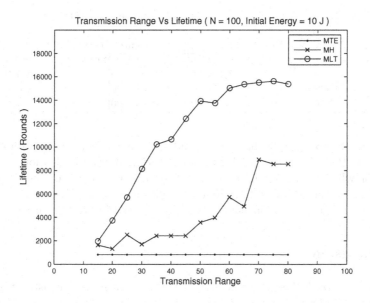

Fig. 2. Impact of transmission range on lifetime for $N = 100$, $\Re(0) = 10J$, $\Delta t = 100$

Table 2. Mean Lifetime and Standard Deviation of MTE, MH and MLT

Protocol	Mean Lifetime	Standard Deviation
MTE	540.80	116.843
MH	1849.200	765.303
MLT	6358.4000	1833.650

It has been observed that varying transmission range with constant energy and constant node density the lifetime of MLT increases. The routing structure for MTE does not change irrespective of transmission range of the nodes. Hence lifetime remins constant. MH lifetime improves gradually because the nodes in one hop length increases, and each node at base station which is first one to die [13] forwards less number of data packets on behalf of other nodes. But the topology remains same through out, so nodes on the shortest path exhaust early. MLT lifetime increases significantly because the tree is constructed dynamically, and as the transmission range increases the number of nodes within the range of one hop length increases. So there is more chance to switch the nodes near base station for forwarding, based on the residual energy.

4.2   Impact of Base Station Location

In this paper, the performance of the system based on location base station in the network is also tested. Table 3. gives the mean lifetime of the system for same network with initial energy (10J) for two locations of base stations once at

Table 3. Lifetime for center and distance base station

Protocol	Distance Base $(0,0)$		Center Base $(50,50)$	
	Mean Lifetime	Standard Deviation	Mean Lifetime	Standard Deviation
MST	273.4000	200.6480	391.400	323.040
MH	550.60000	458.74456	1612.4000	790.60
MLT	964.4000	901.2148902	5240.800	3870.676

middle ($(50,50)$ position) of the network and again at rear end ($(0,0)$ position) of the network. Performance of MLT with base station at distant location is found to be poor when it is compared to base station at the center of the network, because there is more chance to switch the nodes near to the base station when placed at center, but MLT outperforms MTE and MH in both the cases.

5   Conclusion

In this paper, greedy heuristics algorithm for the routing tree construction for the problem of lifetime maximization in wireless sensor networks is proposed. Extensive experiments are conducted by simulation to evaluate the performance of the proposed algorithm varying parameters transmission range and base station position. The experimental results show that MLT outperforms MH and MTE by 3× and 12× times respectively, if the tree is updated dynamically after Δt rounds. Experimental evaluation shows that increase in the transmitting range increases the lifetime of the sensor network, when it is infeasible to recharge batteries, deploying sensor nodes with high transmitting range increase the lifetime.

References

1. Akyildiz, I.F., Su, W., Sankarasubramaniam, Y., Cayirci, E.: Wireless Sensor Network: A Survey. Comp. Networks J. 38(4), 393–422 (2002)
2. Mdden, S., Franklin, M.J., Hellerstein, J.M., Hong, W.: The Design of an Acquisitional Query Processor for Sensor Networks. In: Proc. ACM SIGMOD 2003, pp. 491–502 (2003)
3. Kahn, J.M., Katz, R.H., Pister, K.S.J.: Next century challenges: Mobile networking for smart dust. In: ACM MobiCom, pp. 271–278 (August 1999)
4. http://www.ise.ncsu.edu/kay/matlog/
5. Clementi, A.E.F., Crescenzi, P., Penna, P., Rossi, G., Vocca, P.: A worst-case analysis of an MST-based heuristic to construct energy efficient broadcast trees in wireless networks, Technical Report 010 of the Univ. of Rome Tor Vergata (2001)
6. Gao, J., Zhang, L.: Load Balanced Short Path Routing in Wireless Networks. In: Proc. IEEE INFOCOM (2004)
7. Kar, I.K., Kodialam, M., Lakshman., T.V., Tassiulas, L.: Routing for Network Capacity Maximization in Energy constrained Ad-hoc Networks. In: Proc. IEEE INFOCOM (2003)

8. Sankar, A., Liu, Z.: Maximum Lifetime Routing in Wireless Ad-hoc Networks. In: IEEE INFOCOM (2004)
9. Chang, J.H., Tassiulas, L.: Routing for maximum system lifetime in wireless ad hoc networks. In: 37th Annu. Allerton Conf. Communication, Control, and Computing, Monticello, IL (September 1999)
10. Chang, J.H., Tassiulas, L.: Energy conserving routing in wireless ad hoc networks. In: IEEE INFOCOM (March 2000)
11. Chang, J.H., Tassiulas, L.: Maximum lifetime routing in wireless sensor networks. In: ATIRP Conf., College Park, MD (March 2000)
12. Chang, J.H., Tassiulas, L.: Maximum lifetime routing in wireless sensor networks. IEEE/ACM Trans. on Network 12(4), 609–619 (2004)
13. Heinzelman, W.R., Chandrakasan, A., Balakrishnan, H.: Energy efficient communication protocol for wireless microsensor networks. In: 33rd Annual Hawaii International Conference on System Sciences, pp. 3005–3014 (2000)
14. Woo, A., Tong, T., Culler, D.: Taming the Underlying Challenges of Reliable Multihop Routing in Sensor Networks. In: ACM SenSys (2003)
15. Luo, J., Hubaux, J.P.: Joint Mobility and Routing for Lifetime Elongation in Wireless Sensor Networks. In: IEEE INFOCOM (2005)

Overlay Network Management for Scheduling Tasks on the Grid

Kovendhan Ponnavaikko and D. Janakiram

Distributed and Object Systems Lab
Department of Computer Science and Engineering
Indian Institute of Technology Madras, Chennai, India
kovendhan@cs.iitm.ernet.in, djram@iitm.ac.in

Abstract. In this paper, we address the problem of building and maintaining dynamic overlay networks on top of physical networks for the autonomous scheduling of divisible load Grid applications. While autonomous scheduling protocols exist to maximize steady-state throughputs for given overlay networks, not much work has been done on building the most efficient overlay. In our work, nodes use the bandwidth-centric principle to select other nodes with which overlay edges must be formed dynamically. The node which has the entire dataset initially (the scheduler) starts forming the overlay and the nodes which receive tasks at rates greater than their task execution rates further expand it. We use simulation studies to illustrate the functioning of our overlay forming mechanism, and its robustness to changes in the characteristics of the system resources.

1 Introduction

The amount of data processed by Grid applications has been continuously increasing over the past few years and is expected to increase even more rapidly in the years to come [1]. A large number of Grid applications are divisible load applications [2], which usually involve a large dataset and an associated computation that needs to be performed on the entire dataset. The dataset can arbitrarily be divided into several pieces, and computations can be performed on the different pieces independently. The problem of finding the optimal schedule that minimizes the makespan of such applications is known to be NP-complete [3]. A recent approach has been to focus on maximizing the steady-state task completion rate since it is less hard.

Usage of autonomous scheduling protocols has been gaining popularity since the scheduler cannot have global knowledge of the system [4][5][6]. The network of nodes formed or used by the protocols is referred to as the Overlay Network. An edge in the overlay network represents the communication path between a source node and the corresponding destination node. Our work focuses on the problem of building and maintaining dynamic overlay networks on top of physical networks, such that the steady-state execution rate of the application is maximized. The rest of the paper is organized as follows – Section 2 discusses

T. Janowski and H. Mohanty (Eds.): ICDCIT 2007, LNCS 4882, pp. 166–171, 2007.

some background and the related work done in this area. The details of how the overlay network is built and managed are presented in Sect. 3. Section 4 discusses our simulations and Sect. 5 summarizes our findings.

2   Background and Related Work

Most of the scheduling strategies for divisible load applications assume the presence of a centralized scheduler and the availability of significant amounts of global knowledge. However, such strategies do not scale well in a typical complex system such as the Internet. Some of the autonomous scheduling strategies that have been developed to schedule divisible load applications are [4], [5] and [6].

In the Organic Grid project [5], computations are done by mobile agents. Agent behavior ensures that well-performing nodes are pushed closer to the source and poorly performing nodes are pushed farther away. In the autonomous scheduling protocol proposed in [6], the authors take motivation from fluid flow networks. A node transfers a task to another only if the number of back-logged tasks (pressure in fluid flow) is greater than that of the requesting node. An autonomous scheduling protocol for a given tree overlay based on a bandwidth-centric principle is proposed in [4]. The authors show that autonomous scheduling protocols that adopt an interruptible communication model help in achieving the maximum steady-state performance for a tree overlay. The request for a task from a higher priority child (lesser communication time) can interrupt a task transfer to a lower priority child (higher communication time) in an interruptible communication model. In [4] as well as [6], it is assumed that the overlay is known beforehand and the protocols try to maximize the throughput for that overlay. However, the problem of how to build the most efficient overlay is not addressed in the current literature.

In [7], the authors show that it is possible to achieve the optimal steady-state execution rate for a divisible load application on a set of nodes, connected in the form of a tree, by using a bandwidth-centric approach. In a bandwidth-centric approach, nodes with which communication speeds are high are prioritized ahead of the others. Consider a subtree in which the nodes $P_1, P_2, ..., P_k$ are the children of P_0. The time taken to execute a task at a node (P_i) is represented by w_i and the time taken to transfer the data required for one task from a parent to a child (P_i) is represented by c_i. The algorithm used by the authors (we refer to it as the *Optimal Steady-State Throughput* Algorithm) is given below [7]:

1. Sort the children by increasing communication times and renumber such that $c_1 \le c_2 \le ... \le c_k$.
2. Find p such that $\sum_{i=1}^{p} \frac{c_i}{w_i} \le 1$.
3. If $p < k, \epsilon = 1 - \sum_{i=1}^{p} \frac{c_i}{w_i}$, otherwise $\epsilon = 0$.
4. Then, the maximum steady-state execution rate is given by:

$$min\left(\frac{1}{c_0}, \frac{1}{w_0} + \sum_{i=1}^{p} \frac{1}{w_i} + \frac{\epsilon}{c_{p+1}}\right)$$

The idea is that maximum steady-state throughput is achieved by maximizing the rate at which tasks are sent out from P_0 such that all the receiving nodes execute the tasks at the rate at which they receive them.

3   Overlay Network Management

For building the overlay network, we require each node to maintain a list of its neighbors in the system. The list must include up-to-date estimates on the communication and processing capabilities of each neighbor, and must be sorted in the descending order of the communication speeds between the two nodes. In the case of similar communication speeds, the neighbor with better processing capability is listed ahead of the other.

The entire dataset that is required by the application is assumed to be initially available at a repository local to one node, the scheduler. We assume that a node can simultaneously receive tasks from other nodes, perform computations locally and send tasks to its children. Nodes maintain buffers to store application tasks and request their parents for a new task whenever a buffer is emptied. Moreover, nodes use an interruptible communication model to send tasks to their children.

The idea behind our strategy is that, while forming the overlay network, nodes use the bandwidth-centric approach to maintain their set of children dynamically. Nodes select their initial set of children based on the *Optimal Steady-State Throughput* algorithm. However, this set has to be periodically updated in order to achieve maximum throughput values and this is done in our approach.

In the *Optimal Steady-State Throughput* algorithm, one of the assumptions is that a parent can communicate with only one node at a time. However, in a practical scenario, multiple task transfers can take place simultaneously without affecting each other in any significant fashion because the communication paths from the source to the multiple destinations are usually, largely independent. Thus, the number of children that can be served tasks by the parents, and hence the steady-state throughput, is larger than what is computed by the original algorithm. We address this issue by making the nodes periodically check if their uplinks are being used to full potential or not. If the uplink is found to be idle at regular intervals, such nodes can include additional children.

The scheduler (S) starts forming the overlay by selecting an initial set of children to serve tasks to, and then continuously tries to optimize the set so as to maximize its processing rate. A task getting processed by a node refers to either the task being executed at that node or it being forwarded to a child for getting processed. A node (other than S) that starts receiving tasks at a rate greater than its execution rate expands the overlay further. Due to the changing processing rates of the nodes and the inherent dynamism in the characteristics of the different system resources, the overlay must keep adapting itself dynamically.

3.1   Selecting the Initial Set of Children

Suppose the set of neighbors of S is $\{P_0, P_1, ..., P_n\}$, with the neighbors listed in the increasing order of the time required to transfer a single task from S. Let the set of task transfer times be $\{c_0, c_1, ..., c_n\}$ and the set of task processing times of the neighbors be $\{w_0, w_1, ..., w_n\}$. The task processing time for each neighbor will initially be the time required by that neighbor to execute one task.

S must include the first p available nodes from its neighbors list as its initial set of children, such that $\sum_{i=1}^{p} \frac{c_i}{w_i} < 1$.

Nodes other than S, when they start receiving tasks, start executing them. If the rate at which tasks are being sent to a node is higher than its execution rate, the node attempts to increase its task processing rate by serving tasks to few other nodes. Let us assume that the task input rate of node P_k is I_k. When I_k exceeds P_k's execution rate, P_k selects as its initial set of children the first p available nodes starting from the top of its neighbors list such that $\sum_{i=1}^{p} \frac{c_i}{w_i} < 1$ and $I_k > \frac{1}{w_k} + \sum_{i=1}^{p} \frac{1}{w_i}$.

3.2 Updating the Overlay

The typical scenarios that call for overlay changes are discussed below:

- Parents must keep adding children as long as their uplinks are not being used to full potential. However, parents other than the scheduler are constrained by their task input rates. They can add more children only when their task input rates are greater than their task processing rates.
- A parent must ensure that it is serving tasks to its closest neighbors. A close neighbor may not have been made a child earlier since it may have been unreachable then. Thus, a parent must keep checking if there is any neighbor which is closer to it than some of its children. Such a neighbor must be added as a child in the place of the farthest child.
- A child may sometimes get tasks from its parent at a rate lesser than its task execution rate. Such a child is allowed to accept additional parents, when requested by them. Therefore, our overlay is structured as a Directed Acyclic Graph (DAG).
- On the other hand, children must not have more parents than what is necessary. An increase in the task input rate from a parent can invalidate the need for other parents. In such cases, children must disconnect from surplus parents.
- Since nodes are allowed to have more than one parent, cycles can get formed in the overlay. A node can detect that a cycle has been formed if it gets back a task that it had previously sent to one of its children. The cycle can be broken by disconnecting from the parent that sent the repeating task.

4 Simulation

We simulated a system of nodes along with the required switches, routers and communication channels. Our simulation consisted of 150 nodes distributed among 30 switches. The nodes were assigned random processor speeds (uniformly distributed between 3 GHz and 6 GHz) which kept changing dynamically. The communication links among the nodes, switches and routers were assigned speed values equivalent to those seen in actual networks. The uplink capacity of the scheduler was set to 100 Mbps, the size of a task was set to 6 MB, and the number of processor cycles required for a task was set to $8 * 10^9$.

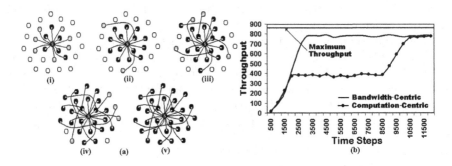

Fig. 1. (a) Growth of the Overlay (b) Bandwidth-Centric Vs. Computation-Centric

The throughput achieved by a scheduler is the number of results received, for the tasks sent earlier, during a particular time interval. For our setup, the maximum value for the throughput was theoretically computed to be 862 tasks in 50 seconds.

The growth of our overlay can be seen in Fig.1a. The states of the nodes at five different points of execution are displayed for a portion of the system. A node shaded in black receives tasks at a rate greater than or equal to its task execution rate and a grey node gets tasks at a rate lesser than its task execution rate. We can see that the scheduler (S) starts supplying tasks to the nodes closest to it and when it realizes that it can serve more nodes, it adds more children. In a similar way, when a node (P_i) starts receiving tasks at a rate greater than its task execution rate, it expands the overlay by adding children to itself. When this happens, the color of P_i in Fig.1a turns to black from grey.

In Fig.1b, we can see that, after the start-up phase, the throughput remains almost constant in spite of the dynamism in resource characteristics. The steady-state throughput reaches values of around 790. This value is lesser than the theoretical maximum of 862 because of the control messages being sent and the local network load on the scheduler's uplink.

Our overlay forming mechanism was also compared with a computation-centric strategy. In the computation-centric strategy, processing capabilities of the nodes are used to prioritize them. While forming the overlay, nodes with higher processing capabilities are added as children first, irrespective of their communication times. It can be seen in Fig.1b that our mechanism achieves steady-state throughput values in much lesser time than the computation-centric strategy. The behavior of our overlay was found to be similar for different values of the task size and the number of processor cycles required for a task.

It is obvious that the average network distance between a parent and a child is lesser in bandwidth-centric overlays than in computation-centric overlays. The total load added to the network by the application is, therefore, lesser in the first case. This is an added benefit of using a bandwidth-centric approach to form the overlay.

5   Conclusions

In this paper, we have worked out the details of a mechanism to build and maintain dynamic overlays over large physical networks, which assist in maximizing the steady-state throughput of divisible load applications. The overlay continuously adapts itself to changes in the resource characteristics. Using simulations, we show that high steady-state throughput values can be reached using such overlays, comparable to theoretical maximum values. We also show that forming the overlay using our mechanism results in achieving steady-state throughput in much lesser time than using a computation-centric approach.

Acknowledgement

This work has been supported by the Department of Science and Technology (DST), Ministry of Science and Technology, Government of India.

References

1. Kosar, T., Livny, M.: Stork: Making data placement a first class citizen in the grid. In: Proc. of ICDCS 2004, IEEE Computer Society, pp. 342–349. IEEE Computer Society Press, Los Alamitos (2004)
2. Bharadwaj, V., Robertazzi, T.G., Ghose, D.: Scheduling Divisible Loads in Parallel and Distributed Systems. IEEE Computer Society Press, Los Alamitos (1996)
3. Ullman, J.: NP-complete scheduling problems. Journal of Computer and Syst. Sciences 10, 384–393 (1975)
4. Kreaseck, B., Carter, L., Casanova, H., Ferrante, J.: Autonomous protocols for bandwidth-centric scheduling of independent-task applications. In: Proc. of IPDPS 2003, pp. 23–25. IEEE Computer Society, Los Alamitos (2003)
5. Chakravarti, A.J., Baumgartner, G., Lauria, M.: The organic grid: Self-organizing computational biology on desktop grids. Parallel Computing for Bioinformatics (2005)
6. Nandy, S., Carter, L., Ferrante, J.: A-fast: Autonomous flow approach to scheduling tasks. In: Bougé, L., Prasanna, V.K. (eds.) HiPC 2004. LNCS, vol. 3296, pp. 363–374. Springer, Heidelberg (2004)
7. Beaumont, O., Carter, L., Ferrante, J., Legrand, A., Robert, Y.: Bandwidth-centric allocation of independent task on heterogeneous platforms. In: Proc. of IPDPS 2002, IEEE Computer Society, Los Alamitos (2002)

An End-Systems Supported Highly Distributed Content Delivery Network

Jaison Paul Mulerikkal and Ibrahim Khalil

Distributed Systems and Networking
School of Computer Science, RMIT University,
Melbourne 3000, Australia
{jmulerik,ibrahimk}@cs.rmit.edu.au

Abstract. Commercial Content Delivery Networks (CDN) compete each other and are forced to set up costly infrastructure around the globe to effectively deliver Web content to the end-users. Huge financial cost involved in setting up commercial CDN compels the commercial CDN providers to charge high remuneration from their clients (the content providers). Academic models of peer-to-peer CDNs aim to reduce the financial cost of content distribution by forming volunteer group of servers around the globe. But their efficiency is at the mercy of the volunteer peers whose commitment is not ensured in their design. We propose a new architecture that will make use of the existing resources of common Internet users in terms of storage space, bandwidth and Internet connectivity to create a Distributed Content Delivery Network (DCDN). The profit pool generated by the infrastructure savings will be shared among the participating nodes (DCDN surrogates) which will function as an incentive for them to support DCDN.

1 Introduction

The growth of the World Wide Web and new modes of Web services have triggered an exponential increase in Web content and Internet traffic [1,2,3]. As the Web content and the Internet traffic increases, individual Web servers find it difficult to cater to the needs of end-users. In order to store and serve huge quantities of Web content, Web server farms - a cluster of Web servers functioning as a single unit - are introduced [4]. Even those Web server farms find it difficult to deal with flash crowds - large number of simultaneous requests for a popular content - that are frequently experienced in Web traffic [5].

Replication of same Web content around the globe in a net of Web servers is a solution to the above issue. However, it is not financially viable for individual content providers to set up their own server networks. An answer to this challenge is the concept of Content Delivery Network (CDN) that was initiated in 1998 [6,2]. CDN allows a number of content providers to upload their Web content into the same network of Web servers and thereby reduce the cost of content replication and distribution [2].

In a typical CDN environment (Figure 1), the replicated Web server clusters are located at the edge of the network to which the end-users are connected.

T. Janowski and H. Mohanty (Eds.): ICDCIT 2007, LNCS 4882, pp. 172–183, 2007.
© Springer-Verlag Berlin Heidelberg 2007

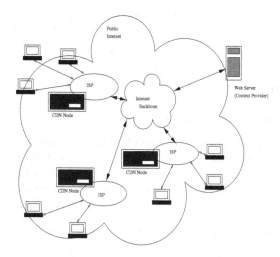

Fig. 1. CDN and Web Content Distribution

There are a number of CDNs available around the globe [6,2] and are collectively called as *Conventional CDN architectures* in this paper. Conventional CDN architectures - Commercial CDN and Academic CDN - have got their own advantages and disadvantages, but the marjor pitfalls of them are:

- High rental rates resulting from huge infrastructural cost.
- Efficiency of academic CDNs is at the mercy of the volunteer peers whose commitment is not ensured in their design.

A lot of work has been done in this area aimed at these ends. An academic CDN, Globule, which is envisaged as Collaborative Content Delivery Network (CCDN) [7] aims to provide performance and availability through Web servers that cooperate across a wide area network. J. Coppens *et al* proposes the idea of a self-organizing Adaptive Content Distribution Network (ACDN), where they introduce a less centralized replica placement algorithm - (COCOA - Cooperative Cost Optimization Algorithm) which will push the content more to the clients [8] . Though most of these works seem to be theoretically sound, they never challenged the efficiency and reliability of commercial client-server architecture for they were purely peer-to-peer architecture which will be effective only at the mercy of participating peers, whose performance is not under the control of suggested architecture.

This paper proposes a new architecure for CDN to overcome the major limitations of Commercial and Academic models. According to the proposed Distributed Content Delivery Network (DCDN) common Internet users become content space providers (they are called DCDN surrogates). It will empower Internet users to fetch revenue from their existing resources (bandwidth, processing power and Internet connectivity) which they share in support of DCDN.

In the rest of the sections, first we discuss the background of and the rationale behind DCDN. Then we introduce the proposed DCDN architecture. Then we discuss the major DCDN challenges and suggest possible solutions.

2   Background

2.1   Conventional CDN Architectures

Commercial (Client-Server) Architecture. The classical example is of Akamai. Akamai offers content delivery services to content providers by offering worldwide distributed platform to host their content. It is done by installing a worldwide network of more than twenty thousand Akamai Surrogate Servers [9]. A typical approach by which Akamai provides this service is as follows:

1. The client's browser requests the default Web page at the Content Provider's site. The site returns the Web page index.html.
2. The HTML code contains link to some content (eg: images) hosted on the Akamai owned server.
3. As the Web browser parses the HTML code, it pull the content from Akamai server [10].

Akamai uses a simple tool called *Free Flow Launcher* for its customers that they use to Akamaize their pages [11]. The users will specify what content they want to be served through Akamai and the tool will go ahead and Akamaize the URLs. This way the customers still have complete control of what gets served through Akamai and what they still are in charge of [12].

Academic (Peer-to-Peer) Architecture. Distributed computer architectures labelled *peer-to-peer* are designed for the sharing of computer resources (content, storage, CPU cycles) by direct exchange, rather than requiring the intermediation or support of a centralized server or authority. The same technique has been proposed and adopted for creating reliable CDN for the propagation of Web content. A peer-to-peer (P2P) CDN is a system in which the users get together to forward contents so that the load at a server is reduced.

A classical example would be the academic peer-to-peer CDN - Globule, developed by Vrije University in Amsterdam. It is implemented as a third-party module for the Apache HTTP server that allows any given server to replicate its documents to other Globule servers. This improves the site's performance; maintain the site available to its clients even if some servers are down, and to a certain extent help to resist flash-crowds [13]. S. Sivasubramanian, B Halderen and G. Pierre rightly observe that 'a peer-to-peer CDN aims to allow Web content providers to together and operate *their own* worldwide hosting platform [14] .

2.2   Limitations of Existing CDN Architectures

Despite the many advantages of commercial CDNs, they suffer from some major limitations. Commercial CDN providers compete each other and forced to set up costly infrastructure around the globe. Since they want to meet the QoS standards agreed with the clients they are constantly in a process of installing and updating new infrastructure. This process gives rise to the following issues:

1. *Network cost* : Increase in total network cost in terms of new set of servers and corresponding increase in network traffic.
2. *Economic cost*: Increase in cost per service rate for the distribution of Web content, resulting from increase in initial investment and running cost of each commercial CDN.
3. *Social cost*: Content distribution is been centralized to a couple of CDN providers and the possible issues of monopolization of revenue in this area.

The huge financial cost involved in setting up a commercial CDN compels the commercial CDN providers to charge high remuneration from their clients (the content providers). Usually this cost is so high that only large firms can afford it. As a result, Web content providers of medium and small sizes are not in a position to rent the services of commercial CDN providers.

Moreover, the revenue from content distribution is monopolized. Only large CDN providers with huge infrastructure around the world are destined to amass revenue from this big business. At the same time, the resources in terms of processing power, storage capacity and the network availability of large number of common Internet users are ignored who would support a content delivery network for proportionate remunerations.

On the other hand, the academic CDNs are non-profitable initiatives in a peer-to-peer fashion. But they serve only the content providers who own *their own* network of servers around the globe. Or they have to become a part of a voluntary net of servers. However, the academic CDNs do not provide a built-in network of independent servers around the globe. That means, the risk and responsibility of running content distribution network ultimately goes back to the content providers themselves. The content providers, who are generally not interested in taking such big risks and responsibility, do not find academic CDNs as attractive alternatives.

2.3 Distributed Content Delivery Network - An Effective Alternative

The above discussion proves that there is a need for much reliable, responsible and scalable CDN architecture, which can make use of the resources of a large number of general Web users. A unique architecture of Distributed Content Delivery Network (DCDN) is proposed in this thesis to meet these ends.

DCDN aims at involving general Web users with comparatively high bandwidth of Web connection (broadband or higher) to form a highly distributed content delivery network. Those who become the part of DCDN network are called DCDN surrogates. A cluster of those DCDN surrogates that are distributed very much to the local levels around the globe, will replace the conventional CDN server pushing the content very much near to the end-users. Since the content is pushed very much into the local levels, the efficiency of the content retrieval in terms of response time is expected to increase considerably. It will also reduce network traffic, since clients can access the content from locally placed surrogates. A local DCDN server, which is mainly a redirector and load balancer, is designed to redirect the client requests to the appropriate DCDN surrogate servers.

Since DCDN is aimed at using the available storage space and Web connectivity of existing Web users, it will not demand the installation of fresh new infrastructure. This approach is supposed to reduce the economic cost. This acquired new value (profit pool) could be shared between the DCDN surrogates through proper accounting and billing mechanism and through highly attractive business models. It will serve as an incentive for the DCDN surrogates to share their resources to support DCDN network.

3   Architecture: Distributed Content Delivery Network

In order to provide a highly distributed network of DCDN surrogates a basic structure of commercial client-server CDN is adopted with novel peer to peer concepts.

3.1   DCDN Framework

A collection of Local DCDN Servers and innumerable DCDN Surrogates are networked together to deliver requested Web content to the clients. The main elements of DCDN architecture Content providers, DCDN servers and DCDN surrogates are arranged in a hierarchical order as depicted in Figure 2

Content Provider: It is that entity that request to distribute its Web content through DCDN.

DCDN Administrators: Rather than a technical entity, it is a managerial/ business entity. The entire DCDN network is managed, supported and run by a team of administrators.

DCDN Servers: DCDN servers are basically redirectors that will only have the knowledge about the location of the content. They do not store any content as such. They monitor, keep log of and regulate the content flow from providers to the surrogates.

In the proposed architecture, DCDN servers are of two types: Master and Local.

1. *DCDN Master Servers*: Master DCDN servers are the first point of contact of a content provider. A global network of Master DCDN servers are set up in such a way that every network region will have at least one Master DCDN server. Content providers deal with administrators through Master DCDN servers and reach terms and conditions with DCDN administrators for the service provided by DCDN. They monitor, regulate and control the content flow into DCDN servers and surrogates.

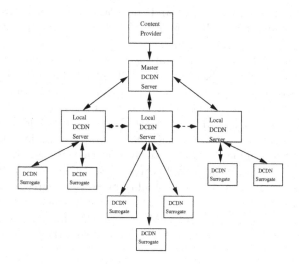

Fig. 2. DCDN Content Distribution Architecture

2. *DCDN Local Servers*: They are placed very near to the end-users (virtually they reside among the end-users). A number of Local servers can come under the service of a single Master server. They have got two major functions. Firstly, they decide where to place the content (among the surrogates) and keep log of it. Secondly, they find out and return the IP address of the best available surrogate a client on request for a particular content under the care of DCDN. In doing so, they also function as a load balancer that will protect the surrogates in the network from being overloaded.

DCDN Surrogates: As explained before, DCDN surrogates are the large number of Web users who offers resources in terms of storage capacity, bandwidth and processing power to store and make available DCDN Web content. A requested client Web content is ultimately fetched from DCDN surrogates.

DCDN Client: The client refers to an end user, who makes a request for a particular Web content using a Web browser.

3.2   Distribution of Content - The Process

The aim is to place the replica of content as close as possible to the clients. In this process, firstly, the content providers approach DCDN administrators. Once the Service Level Agreement is reached, content providers can upload their content to DCDN net. This can be done either through the Master DCDN servers or through the Local DCDN servers assigned by the Master DCDN servers. If they are uploading the content through the Master servers, they will push it to the Local servers. The Local servers push replicas to the surrogates in their own region and keep a track of these records. The Master servers will have more universal knowledge about it (Like, what are the network areas in which a particular content is distributed) and the Local servers will have more local knowledge of the location of the content (That is, which are the surrogates that actually holding a particular content).

On request from a Local server, a surrogate may share the replicas with other surrogates in a peer-to-peer fashion. This will offload the Local severs from additional workload. The process will make sure that the Local server still has the knowledge about the replicated content in the new surrogate/s.

However, the content providers need not choose to distribute their content in a true global manner. If they want DCDN to support only for some region(s), they can request for regional support too. In that case, the administrators (with the help of Master servers) choose only those Local DCDN servers, which are set by the parameters given in the QoS (Quality of Service) agreement. In order to keep sync with the updates and modifications, or in the event of *termination of service* to a specific content provider, Master DCDN through the Local DCDN servers request the DCDN surrogates to update/delete the content.

Partial Replication. Because of the unlikelihood of being online at the time of request of a specific content in a specific surrogate, the same content is replicated in large number of surrogates. Moreover, DCDN does not expect individual surrogates to host a huge volume of content, for they are only general Web users with low storage capacity.So, partial replication of a Website shall be anticipated in DCDN model. In case of partial replication, the knowledge about the remaining content is kept in the respective surrogate to facilitate HTTP redirection in case of query for the rest of the content.

3.3   Content Delivery to a User

The DCDN Local server, which is envisaged as a redirector, will follow the DNS protocol. It will take care of the queries related to the Websites under the care of DCDN. This information is shared with other DNS servers too. So, when there is a request for a Website under the care of DCDN, the DNS redirectors will redirect it to the nearest available Local DCDN server. The DCDN Local server searches the log of active surrogates holding those files using a suitable technique (Eg. Distributed Hash Table (DHT) algorithm). It will then make a decision based on the other relevant parameters (availability of full or partial replica content, bandwidth, physical/online nearness, etc) and will return the IP addresses of the best suitable surrogate to the client.

Now the client fetches the content from the respective surrogate. The participating surrogates will have a client daemon program running on their machines, which will handle the requests from the clients and the parent DCDN server. If the surrogate is having only a partial content of the Website under request, it has to get the rest from other surrogates. The surrogate may use HTTP redirection to fetch the content from other surrogates.

Diagrammatical representation of the above process is given in Figure 3 and the following interactions between different entities of DCDN are identified.

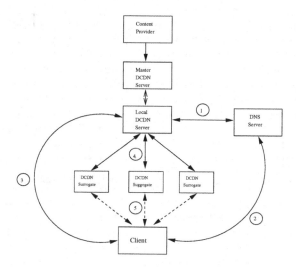

Fig. 3. DCDN Content Delivery

1. *Local DCDN Server - DNS Server Interaction*: The Local DCDN server updates the DNS server with the list of content providers under DCDN care and request DNS server to map corresponding URL requests to the IP address of the Local DCDN server. DNS Server queries the Local DCDN server from time to time to update its library.
2. *Client - DNS Server Interaction*: Client requests for a particular content (Website) under DCDN care. The DNS server directs the request to the Local DCDN server, using DNS protocol.
3. *Client - Local DCDN Server Interaction*: Local DCDN server finds out the best possible surrogate to cater to the request of the client and returns the IP address of that particular surrogate.
4. *Local DCDN Server - Surrogate Interaction*: There is a constant interaction going between the Local server and the surrogates. The content from the content providers are stored in the surrogates through the Local DCDN servers. The surrogates inform their availability and non-availability to the Local server as and when they become online or offline in terms of connectivity. Local servers keep a track of it. Local DCDN servers direct the surrogates to add, delete, update or modify the content according to the decisions made from time to time.
5. *DCDN Surrogate - Client Interaction*: Once the Local DCDN server returns the IP address of the most suitable surrogate, the client contacts that surrogate to fetch the requested content. On request from the client, surrogate delivers the content to the client.

The transition diagram (Figure 4) clubs the major two flows of interactions in DCDN, namely, content distribution and the content delivery.

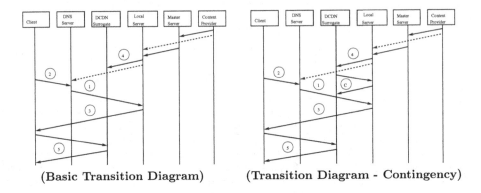

(Basic Transition Diagram)   (Transition Diagram - Contingency)

Fig. 4. Transition Diagrams

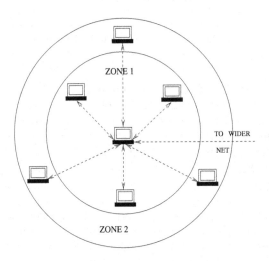

Fig. 5. Server Zones

3.4   Contigency Plans

The special design of DCDN suggests the possibility of a number of unavailable surrogates at any instance. So, it becomes a high priority to assess the availability of surrogates at every moment. Asking the surrogates to notify the Local server as and when they become online and offline, DCDN achieve this end. At the same time the Local servers issue ping commands at regular intervals to make sure the availability of surrogates, if at all they fail without notifying the Local server. So, the sequence diagram is modified as in Figure 4.

Another scenario is, when specific Web content is not available within a local DCDN Network. In order to cope up with this scenario, each DCDN local surrogate will be classifying the nearby DCDN Local servers into *zones* in the representative order of network proximity (Figure 5). That is, the nearby Local DCDN servers with least cost accessibility will fall in *zone 1*, and so on. When a specific content is not found in a Local DCDN net, the DCDN server will first search its availability in the nearby zone 1 DCDN servers. If its found, the request is redirected to the specific Local DCDN server. If its not found in the lower zones the search is extended to the higher zones, till the specific content is found.

4   DCDN Design Challenges

In spite of all its advantages, DCDN architecture arouses its own unique set of challenges. The major challenges would be:

- Security
- Efficient algorithm for the effective load balancing and DNS redirection.
- Development of Billing and SLA (Service Level Agreement) Verification Software.

4.1   Security

The security requirements for a DCDN service environment will be driven by the general security issues such as:

1. Authentication of a content provider (who is recognized by the administrators to use the service of DCDN) while uploading its content to DCDN through Master/Local servers.
2. Authentication of Master and Local DCDN server when they contact each other (for sharing/updating content information and so on).
3. Authentication of Local Servers by the surrogates to authenticate pushed content.

Maintaining integrity of the content provided by the content provider throughout the DCDN surrogate replicas will become a crucial criteria in the business success of DCDN. This is because, the large number of surrogates suggest possible vulnerability of the content being manipulated by vicious surrogates or hackers.

The DCDN daemon running on the surrogates are supposed to ensure security of the content stored in it. The DCDN surrogate daemon authenticates the injected content from the Local DCDN server and make sure that they receive original replicas. Different security measures can be employed to block any attack from the hackers or even from surrogate owner itself to tamper the content within the DCDN daemon. One of the solutions is to make sure that we track down the anomalies when the content is tampered and delivered to the end-users. If that can be identified, the respective surrogate can be put on alert, corrected or even eliminated from DCDN.

This can be achieved by stamping all content injected to the surrogate with a digital stamp like md5. The Local server will keep a record of these digital stamps. On each delivery of content, the surrogate daemon shall calculate the digital stamp of the delivered content and send it back to the Local server. The Local server compares it with its database and makes sure that there is no anomaly. If an anomaly is found, content manipulation is identified and the Local server takes appropriate action. Verification of digital stamp for each and every transaction can create a huge volume of traffic between surrogates and the Local server. In order to moderate this traffic, this security measure can be done in a random basis.

4.2 Effective Redirection and Load-Balancing Algorithm

The key to the success of DCDN would rely on the success of an effective redirection algorithm. The DCDN will be having multiple replications of the same content within a local DCDN set up to ensure scalability of the system. This replication may exponentially increase as the number of local DCDN networks increase throughout the globe. A combination of DNS- HTTP address redirection system as mentioned in 6.1 has to be a developed as a possible solution in this regard.

The DCDN server has to distribute the load within a local system. It should also take care of the availability or non-availability of peer nodes. If the requested content is not within the local DCDN system, DCDN server should be able to make the right decision to get it from the other local DCDN systems without causing network congestion. Effective load-balancing algorithms have to be developed in this regard.

4.3 Billing and SLA (Service Level Agreement) Verification Software

DCDN has to provide content providers with accounting and access-related information. This information has to be provided in the form of aggregate or detailed log files. In addition, DCDN should collect accounting information to aid in operation, billing and SLA verification. The DCDN Master surrogates deal with these content provider related issues. At the same time, DCDN has to quantify proper remuneration for surrogates according to their availability, performance, storage space, etc. There is a need for generalized system or protocol in the calculation of the contributions of surrogates and a local DCDN servers, on the basis of the business model adopted for DCDN.

5 Conclusion

The DCDN architecture addresses the main pitfalls of conventional CDN architectures by ensuring a more scalable and reliable content delivery system without the installation of fresh infrastructure. It is supposed to make content delivery more cheaper by allowing the common Internet users to take their share of responsibility in maintaining DCDN and thereby inheriting their share of revenue.

References

1. Molina, B., Ruiz, V., Alonso, I., Palau, C., Guerri, J., Esteve, M.: A closer look at a content delivery network implementation. In: MELECON 2004. Electrotechnical Conference, 2004. Proceedings of the 12th IEEE Mediterranean, Dept. of Commun., Univ. Politecnica de Valencia, Spain, vol. 2, pp. 685–688 (2004)
2. Vakali, A., Pallis, G.: Content distribution networks - status and trends. IEEE Internet Computing, 68–74 (2003)
3. Presti, F., Bartolini, N., Petrioli, C.: Dynamic replica placement and user request redirection in content delivery networks. In: IEEE International Conference on Communications, vol. 3, pp. 1495–1501. Dubrovnik, Los Alamitos (2005)
4. Burns, R., Rees, R., Long, D.: Efficient data distribution in a web server farm. IEEE Internet Computing 5(5), 56–65 (2001)
5. Pan, C., Atajanov, M., Shimokawa, T., Yoshida, N.: Design of adaptive network against flash crowds. In: Proc. Information Technology Letters, pp. 323–326 (2004)
6. Douglis, F., Kaashoek, M.: Scalable internet services. IEEE Internet Computing 5(4), 36–37 (2001)
7. Pierre, G., van Steen, M.: Globule: A collaborative content delivery network. IEEE Communications Magazine, 127–133 (2006)
8. Coppens, J., Wauters, T., Turck, F.D., Dhoedt, B., Demeester, P.: Design and performance of a self-organizing adaptive content distribution network. In: IEEE/IFIP Network Operations and Management Symposium 2006, Vancouver, Canada (2006)
9. Dilley, J., Maggs, B., Parlkh, J., Prokop, H., Sitaraman, R., Welhl, B.: Globally distributed content delivery. IEEE Internet Computing, 50–56 (2002)
10. Wikipedia: Content Delivery Networks (cdn) (2007), Web Page:
    http://en.wikipedia.org/wiki/Content_Delivery_Network
11. Mahajan, R.: How akamai works (2004), Web Page:
    www.cs.washington.edu/homes/ratul/akamai.html
12. Reitz, H.: Cachet Technologies, p. 2163. Harward Business School Publishing, Boston, MA (2000)
13. Pierre, G., van Steen, M.: Design and implementation of a user-centered content delivery network (2003)
14. Sivasubramanian, S., Pierre, B.H.: Globule: a user-centric content delivery network. In: 4th International System Administration and Network Engineering Conference (2004)

An Analytical Estimation of Durability in DHTs

Fabio Picconi[1], Bruno Baynat[2], and Pierre Sens[3]

[1] University of Bologna, Italy
picconi@cs.unibo.it
[2] LIP6, Paris, France
Bruno.Baynat@lip6.fr
[3] INRIA Rocquencourt, France
Pierre.Sens@inria.fr

Abstract. Recent work has shown that the durability of large-scale storage systems such as DHTs can be predicted using a Markov chain model. However, accurate predictions are only possible if the model parameters are also estimated accurately. We show that the Markov chain rates proposed by other authors do not consider several aspects of the system's behavior, and produce unrealistic predictions. We present a new analytical expression for the chain rates that is condiderably more fine-grain that previous estimations. Our experiments show that the loss rate predicted by our model is much more accurate than previous estimations.

1 Introduction

Large-scale distributed storage systems such as DHTs [1,3,4,2] can provide a low-cost alternative to expensive persistent storage solutions such as Storage Area Networks (SANs) and dedicated servers. DHTs guarantee persistence by replicating the same data object on several nodes, and regenerating replicas that are lost after a disk crash. However, unlike local-area storage systems, object replicas in a DHT are usually stored on geographically dispersed nodes, so communications between replicas have usually low bandwidth.

A low-bandwidth environment limits the rate at which lost replicas can be regenerated. For instance, if each node stores 100 GB, has a 1 Mbit/s connection to the Internet, and allocates one third of its total bandwidth to restore failed replicas, then repairing a crashed hard disk will take approximately one month. Long repair times, in turn, increase the probability of permanent data loss. Assuming random failures, there's a non-zero probability that all replicas of a given object will fail within a short period of time. Since it takes so long to restore the whole contents of a failed disk, the last replica of an object may be lost before the system can restore at least one copy of it. Adding more replicas decreases the probability of irrecoverable data loss, but can never completely eliminate it.

In practice, the number of replicas per object is chosen so that the probability of data survival is kept above a desired value. However, care must be taken when choosing the replication factor. An excessively high value will reduce the usable

T. Janowski and H. Mohanty (Eds.): ICDCIT 2007, LNCS 4882, pp. 184–196, 2007.

storage capacity and increase the network overhead. Conversely, a low replication factor may result in poor durability.

Recent work has shown that object durability can be predicted by modeling the state of the system using a continuous-time Markov chain [6,7]. The chain models the number of replicas of a given object that are present in the system at a given time. Although this model is relatively simple, the difficulty resides in estimating the chain's transition rates accurately. Incorrect estimations of these model parameters will result in the probability of data survival being underestimated, or, worse, overestimated. This, in turn, will lead the system's designer into choosing a replication factor based on poor model predictions.

Although the failure rate may be estimated rather easily (using the disk MTBF, for instance), modeling the repair rate is much more difficult, as this depends on a myriad of factors such as the number of available replicas, the amount of data per node, the available bandwidth, and even the failure rate. In this paper we provide an analytical expression for system's repair rate that takes into account all these factors.

This paper makes the following contributions. First, it shows that estimating the Markov chain repair rates to predict durability in DHTs is a hard problem, as these rates depend on a large number of factors. Second, it presents an analytically-derived expression of the system's repair rate that is much more accurate than previous estimations. This increased accuracy directly translates into a much better prediction of the probability of object loss in the system.

The rest of this paper is organized as follows. Section 2 lists our assumptions and describes the Markov chain model. Section 3 discusses previous approximations of the chain repair rates, and presents our new analytical expression to estimate these rates. Section 4 evaluates the model's predictions through long-term simulations, and Section 5 concludes the paper.

2   Model

2.1   Assumptions and Definitions

We consider a Distributed Hash Table composed of thousands of nodes connected to the Internet by low-bandwidth links, e.g., 1 Mbit/s links. Each object is associated with a unique key, and is replicated on k adjacent nodes which are close to the key in the DHT address space. This is a common replication scheme used by DHTs such as PAST [1] and OpenDHT [14]. We assume a ring address space as this is the easiest to visualize, but our results also apply to other geometries such as XOR [3] and d-torus [5]. We assume that each node stores thousands of objects, and a capacity from tenths to hundreds of gigabytes per node.

The contents of a node may be lost due to a hard disk crash or a destructive operating system reinstall. We make no difference between the two, and we will use the terms node *failure* and *crash* to refer to the same event. We also assume that failures are random and uncorrelated. We assume that failed hard disks are replaced by an empty disk quickly after the crash (i.e., within a few hours). We ignore this replacement time as it is negligible compared to the time needed to regenerate a disk's contents. The node then starts regenerating the objects it stored before the crash using the following repair procedure: first, since replicas are stored on ring neighbors, the node determines which objects are to be restored by querying its neighbors. Then, the node starts transferring the objects sequentially from the remaining replicas. This is basically what existing DHTs do to regenerate replicas after a crash.

We assume highly stable nodes, i.e., that the disconnection and churn rate are low. Contrary to P2P file-sharing systems, which are characterized by high churn [8,9], storage systems must rely on nodes which stay connected for long periods of time (i.e., weeks or months) in order to guarantee data persistence [10]. These could be, for example, the workstations of a corporate network (in a system that federates several networks), users who leave their P2P client running continuously, or residential set-top boxes equipped with hard disks and running a P2P storage service. Because of this, churn and temporary disconnections will not be considered in our current analysis. A more refined model that takes these into account is left for future work. Also, since we assume high availability, our analysis will only consider systems that use replication, rather than erasure codes, as the former has been shown to be more efficient for highly available nodes [16].

Finally, we list some important definitions that will be used throughout the following sections:

- MTBF. Mean time between failures of a given node. This figure may be smaller than the hardware failure rate of a disk because of destructive operating system reinstalls.
- b. Average number of bytes stored per node.
- bw_{max}. Maximum bandwidth per node allocated to regenerate lost replicas. We assume symmetric upstream and downstream bandwidths.
- θ. The value of θ gives the ratio between the MTBF and the minimum time needed to restore the contents of a hard disk. It is defined as follows:

$$\theta = \frac{MTBF}{b/bw_{max}}$$

θ is a key parameter of our model. High values of θ indicate that a node will finish restoring its hard disk long before it crashes again, and that it only spends a small fraction of its total uptime regenerating replicas lost after a crash. Conversely, a small θ means that is likely that the node will fail again shortly after it finishes restoring its disk from the previous crash, or even before the disk is completely restored.

2.2   Markov Chains

In order to estimate data durability, we model the state of a data object using a continuous-time Markov chain [6,7]. Each state in the chain represents the number of replicas for a particular object that exist in the system at time t after

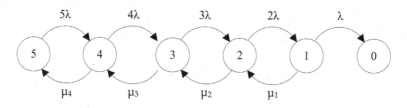

Fig. 1. The number of live replicas of a given object is modeled using a continuous-time Markov chain

its insertion into the DHT. Therefore, the chain has $k + 1$ states, 0 to k, where k is the replication factor. Figure 1 shows the Markov chain for $k = 5$. State transitions correspond to replicas being lost or restored. Once state 0 is reached, there are no more copies left and the object is lost. The probability of being in state i as a function of the time t can be obtained by solving a system of $k + 1$ linear differential equations. The probability of losing the object permanently is simply the probability of reaching state 0 at time t.

Failure rates, i.e., transitions to lower states, are caused by hard disk crashes or system reinstalls, so they can be approximated using the disk MTBF provided by the manufacturer or the destructive reinstall rate observed on the real system. As usual, we will assume that the time between failures of the same node is exponentially distributed with mean MTBF$= \lambda^{-1}$ [11,6,7]. Thus, if each disk fails with MTBF, then the time between two failures in a set of i independent disks becomes MTBF$/i = (i\lambda)^{-1}$. This yields a failure rate $i\lambda$ from state i to state $i - 1$.

The repair rate μ_i, i.e., from state i to state $i+1$, is much harder to determine. Intuitively, it corresponds to the inverse of the mean time needed by the system to restore a *single* copy of the object when $k - i$ replicas are missing. However, the average time needed to regenerate *one* replica is not independent of the number of replicas being repaired. As the number of failed replicas increases, fewer sources become available to download from. This means that two or more nodes may contact the same source, congesting its upstream link and decreasing the average transfer rate.

3   Analytical Expression for the Transitions Rates μ_i

3.1   Previous Estimations

Chun et al. [7] have presented a system for persistent data storage called Carbonite, in which they predict durability using the same model of Figure 1. They suggest using a constant repair rate $\mu_i = \mu'$, and propose a simple approximation for μ'. Their estimation for the value of μ' is as follows[1]: if each node stores

---

[1] We refer to this value as μ' to differentiate it from our estimation of μ which will be presented in the next section.

b bytes of data in its hard disk, and has allocated a maximum repair bandwidth of bw_{max} bytes/sec, then the time needed to restore a crashed hard disk is $T'_r = b/bw_{max}$. Therefore, the model repair rates are:

$$\mu'_i = \mu' = \frac{1}{T'_r} = \frac{bw_{max}}{b} \tag{1}$$

In a different approach, Ramabhadran et al. [6] suggest that the repair rate μ_i grows with the number of missing replicas, and propose the following linear expression:

$$\mu''_i = (k - i)\mu \tag{2}$$

However, the authors do not provide any expression for μ, as they consider it to be a tunable system parameter, dependent on how aggressively the system reacts to failures.

As we will see in the next sections, the expression for μ' is too simple and provides a poor estimation of the real mean repair rate. The expression for μ'' assumes a parametrable repair rate, but the authors do not provide any expression for its maximum value.

3.2   Theoretical Analysis

In this section we present a new analytical expression for the mean repair rate μ. The value of μ represents the rate at which, in average, one copy of a given object is regenerated after a crash. We then use this value to approximate μ_i using the linear equation 2 presented in Section 3.1.

Estimating μ. We define μ as the mean rate at which one object replica is restored after a disk crash, or equivalently, as the inverse of the mean time $\overline{t_r}$ required to restore an object replica:

$$\mu = \frac{1}{\overline{t_r}} \tag{3}$$

To estimate $\overline{t_r}$, we start by noticing that each hard disk does not store a single object of b bytes, but rather thousands of smaller objects. Thus, assuming that the crash occurs at t_{crash}, that restoring the contents of the hard disk takes a time T_r, and that the node does not crash again while the disk is being restored, then each object i will be restored at some time $t_{crash} + t_{r,i}$, with $0 < t_{r,i} \leq T_r$. Second, when more than one replica of the same object is missing, it becomes highly likely that the remaining replicas will receive concurrent download requests from several nodes. Since the uploader's upstream bandwidth must be shared by several downloaders, the effective bandwidth available to each restoring node will be lower than the maximum bandwidth bw_{max}.

Finally, depending on the amount of data stored per node, the time needed to restore a hard disk may not be negligible compared to the MTBF. In such cases (i.e., for small values of θ), there is a small but non-zero probability that the same

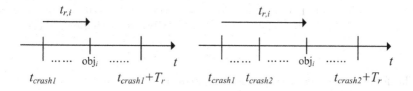

Fig. 2. A premature crash occurs when the node fails before it has finished restoring its hard disk. As a result, the repair time for that object is significantly increased.

node will fail a second time before it has finished restoring the contents of its hard disk, as shown in Figure 2. The probability of premature crashes depends on the value of θ. For $\theta \gg 1$, the hard disk restore time is negligible compared to the mean time between failures, and premature crashes will be rare. In practice, however, the system may exhibit values of θ for which premature crashes cannot be ignored. For instance, Chun et at. show that storing 500 GB per node on Planetlab nodes yields $\theta = 6.85$ [7]. With this value of θ, the probability of a premature crash is around 14%.

Analytical expression for $\overline{t_r}$. We now obtain an analytical expression for $\overline{t_r}$ by taking into account the issues described above. Our theoretical analysis is based on the following key assumption: the nodes that are restoring their hard disk consume a portion of the bandwidth allocated for replica regeneration. Therefore, when a node contacts another node to transfer an object back to its hard disk, the available bandwidth will be less than bw_{max}.

Before we detail our analysis, a few definitions are in order:

- T_r. Time required to restore the whole contents of a hard disk (i.e., b bytes), assuming that no premature crashes occur during the restore process. This is not simply b/bw_{max}, as the actual available bandwidth will be lower than bw_{max} due to nodes downloading from the same sources concurrently.

- b_e. Average amount of bytes transferred per node between two successive crashes. For $\theta \gg 1$, we have $b_e \approx b$. However, for smaller values of θ we have $b_e < b$ due to the effect of premature crashes. In fact, when a premature crash occurs, the amount of bytes transferred between those two crashes will be less than b (e.g., between t_{crash1} and t_{crash2} in Figure 2), resulting in an average value which is lower than b.

- bw_b. Average background bandwidth consumed by each node due to replica regeneration. This is simply the average amount of bytes b_e transferred between crashes, divided by the MTBF:

$$bw_b = \frac{b_e}{MTBF} \tag{4}$$

- bw_r. Effective bandwidth available to each node for replica regeneration. This is obtained by substracting the background bandwidth bw_b consumed by other nodes from the maximum repair bandwidth bw_{max}:

$$bw_r = bw_{max} - bw_b \tag{5}$$

- X. Random variable representing the time between two successive crashes of the same node. X follows an exponential distribution with mean MTBF$=\lambda^{-1}$:

$$f_X(x) = \lambda e^{-\lambda x} \text{ for } x \geq 0$$

The following analysis contains two parts. First, we find the value of T_r as a function of the system parameters b, bw_{max}, MTBF. Second, we obtain an expression for $\overline{t_r}$ as a function of T_r.

Let $Z = \tau(X)$ be the time that the node spends downloading objects between two successive crashes separated by a time X. We then have:

$$Z = \tau(X) = \begin{cases} X \text{ for } X < T_r \\ T_r \text{ for } X > T_r \end{cases}$$

Clearly, if $X < T_r$ then a premature crash has occurred, so the time spent downloading objects is equal to the time between the two crashes. Conversely, for $X > T_r$ the hard disk is completely restored in a time T_r, after which the node remains idle until the next crash.

Since X is exponentially distributed with parameter λ, the expected value of Z, which we will call T_e, is:

$$T_e = \int_0^\infty \tau(x) f_X(x) dx = \int_0^{T_r} x \lambda e^{-\lambda x} dx + \int_{T_r}^\infty T_r \lambda e^{-\lambda x} dx = \frac{1 - e^{-\lambda T_r}}{\lambda} \quad (6)$$

The value of T_e can be interpreted as the average time a node spends transferring objects between two consecutive crashes, taking into account the probability of premature crashes. Notice from equation 6 that T_e depends on T_r, which is not known yet.

We then notice that b_e is the amount of bytes transferred during the time interval T_e using a repair bandwidth bw_r. Similarly, a node will transfer b bytes during a time T_r using a bandwidth bw_r. Therefore, we have:

$$bw_r = \frac{b_e}{T_e} = \frac{b}{T_r} \implies b_e = \frac{T_e}{T_r} b \quad (7)$$

Combining equations 4, 5 and 7 we have the following two equations:

$$bw_b = \frac{b_e}{MTBF} = \frac{T_e}{T_r} \frac{b}{MTBF} \quad (8)$$

$$T_r = \frac{b}{bw_r} = \frac{b}{bw_{max} - bw_b} \quad (9)$$

Notice that in equations 6, 8 and 9 the only unknown variables are T_e, bw_b and T_r (b, bw_{max}, and MTBF are known). Therefore, we can find their values by solving a system of three equations. This can only be done numerically, as T_r appears in the exponent of equation 6.

From this point we will assume that the value of T_r is known (as it can be computed numerically from the system of equations we just described). We will now use T_r to find an expression for $\overline{t_r}$.

Let Y be a random variable representing the time at which a given object is restored after a given crash. According to this definition, the mean object repair time $\overline{t_r}$ is simply the expected value of Y, i.e., $\overline{t_r} = E[Y]$.

In order to find $E[Y]$, we must consider several cases:

1. The node finishes restoring its disk before the next crash occurs, i.e., $X > T_r$. In this case, the object will be restored at some time y with $0 < y < T_r$. Assuming that the variable Y is uniformly distributed in the interval $[0, T_r]$, the average object restore time for this case is:

$$\overline{t_{r1}}(x) = E[Y|X = x, x > T_r] = \frac{T_r}{2}$$

2. A premature crash occurs, i.e., $X < T_r$. We must distinguish between two more cases:

   (a) The object is restored before the node crashes again, i.e., $Y < X$. The probability of this occuring, given that a premature crash has taken place at $t = x$, is:

$$p_{2a}(x) = P(Y < X|X = x, x < T_r \wedge x > Y) = \frac{x}{T_r}$$

   In this case, the average object repair time will be uniformly distributed in the interval $[0, x]$. Thus, we have:

$$\overline{t_{r2a}}(x) = E[Y|X = x, x < T_r \wedge x > Y] = \frac{x}{2}$$

   (b) The node crashes again before the object is restored, i.e., $Y > X$. As before, we obtain the probability that this occurs:

$$p_{2b}(x) = P(Y > X|X = x, x < T_r \wedge x < Y)$$
$$= 1 - P(Y < X|X = x, x < T_r \wedge x > Y) = 1 - \frac{x}{T_r}$$

   In this case, however, the node crashes again before the object is repaired, and restarts a new repair procedure from stratch. All we can say is that the object will be repaired after some average time $\overline{t_r} = E[Y]$ from the beginning of this new repair procedure. Thus, in this case we have:

$$\overline{t_{r2b}}(x) = E[Y|X = x, x < T_r \wedge x < Y] = x + \overline{t_r}$$

Finally, the mean object repair time $\overline{t_r}$ is obtained as the expected value of Y:

$$\overline{t_r} = E[Y] = \int_0^\infty E[Y|X = x] f_X(x) dx$$
$$= \int_0^{T_r} \left[\overline{t_{r2a}}(x) p_{2a}(x) + \overline{t_{r2b}}(x) p_{2b}(x) \right] f_X(x) dx + \int_{T_r}^\infty \overline{t_{r1}}(x) f_X(x) dx$$
$$= \int_0^{T_r} \left[\frac{x}{2} \frac{x}{T_r} + (x + \overline{t_r})(1 - \frac{x}{T_r}) \right] \lambda e^{-\lambda x} dx + \int_{T_r}^\infty \frac{T_r}{2} \lambda e^{-\lambda x} dx$$

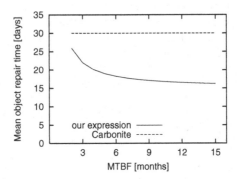

Fig. 3. Mean repair time predicted by our expression, as well as Carbonite's, for different values of the MTBF

After computing the integrals, we obtain $\overline{t_r}$ as a function of λ and T_r:

$$\overline{t_r} = \frac{1}{\mu} = \frac{1 + e^{\lambda T_r}(\lambda T_r - 1)}{\lambda(e^{\lambda T_r} - 1)} \tag{10}$$

Figure 3 shows the variation of the mean repair time (i.e., $\overline{t_r} = 1/\mu$) as a function of the MTBF for a system storing 300 GB per node and allocating 1 MBit/s per node as maximum repair bandwidth bw_{max}. Notice that Carbonite's expression for μ does not depend on the MTBF (cf. equation 1), thus resulting in the constant value shown in Figure 3.

First-order approximation of μ_i. Although we have obtained an analytical expression for the value of μ, the Markov chain requires $k - 1$ repair rates, one for each state i in the chain, with $0 < i < k$. As a first approximation, we will consider that μ_i increases linearly with each state, i.e., $\mu_i = (k - i)\mu$. Notice that this linear form has already been suggested by other authors (cf. equation 2). However, their model lacked a general expression for μ, considering it as a tunable parameter. As we will see in the next section, simulations show that a linear expression provides a good approximation of the real μ_i when the system uses a small number of replicas (i.e., $k = 3$).

4   Validation

In order to evaluate the expressions of Section 3, we use a discrete-event simulator that implements a simplified version of the PAST protocol [1]. Each node has a unique identifier in the integer interval $[0, 2^{160}]$, thus adopting a ring geometry. Data objects are replicated on the k nodes which are closest to the object key.

We assume a symmetric repair bandwidth of 1.5 Mbit/s, as was previously done by other authors [7]. Each node stores b bytes, which can vary from tenths to hundreds of gigabytes of data, according to the experiment. In all cases the data stored by each node is divided into 1000 objects, so each object has a size $b/1000$ bytes. We assume high node availability (cf. Section 2.1), so temporary node disconnections are ignored by our simulator.

All our simulations use a DHT of 100 nodes, as our simulations show that increasing the network size does not qualitatively change the results. The reason is that objects are replicated on adjacent nodes on the ring, so restoring a node's hard disk only affects a small number of other nodes. We generate synthetic traces of failures by obtaining node inter-failure times from an exponential distribution of mean MTBF [7]. Whenever the last replica of an object is lost, the simulator logs the time elapsed since the insertion of that object into the DHT, and inserts a new object of the same size. This ensures that the amount data in the DHT remains constant during the experiment.

Unless otherwise noted, we use an MTBF of two months. Although this is small for a hardware failure rate, it is not far from the failure rate observed in a study conducted on Planetlab nodes [12]. Also, the durability of a system depends on the key parameter θ, i.e., the ratio between the MTBF and the node capacity. For instance, a system with $\theta = 10$ will exhibit the same durability whether it stores 100 GB per node with a MTBF of 2 months, 500 GB per node with an MTBF of 10 months, or any other equivalent combination of b and MTBF. By choosing a MTBF of 2 months and varying the node capacity b between 50 and 500 GB per node, we can test our model for $2 \le \theta \le 20$, thus covering the configurations most likely found in real systems.

4.1   Mean Repair Rate μ

In this experiment we measure the mean repair rate μ and compare it to that obtained through the analytical expression of Section 3.2. Each time a node crashes, we measure the time t_r it takes for each lost object replica to be recreated. Since transfers are serialized, some objects will be recreated shortly after the crash, whereas other will be pending until almost the end of the restore process of that node. We measure μ as the inverse of the average of all repair times t_r for all objects restored in the system. We use a constant MTBF of two months, and we vary the amount of data per node b from 50 GB ($\theta = 20$) to 500 GB ($\theta = 2$).

Figure 4 shows the mean object repair time $\overline{t_r} = 1/\mu$ measured by the simulator for $k = 3$ and $k = 7$, that obtained with our analytical expression, and the one produced by Carbonite's expression (cf. equation 1). The repair time increase with smaller values of θ, as this corresponds to a higher storage capacity per node. The figure also shows the error between the measured and predicted values. Our expression stays always within 20% of the measured μ, and in most cases within 5%. Conversely, Carbonite's value deviates considerably from the measured μ for large values of θ.

4.2   Probability of Object Loss

In Section 3.2 we suggested using the linear approximation $\mu_i = (k - i)\mu$, where μ is the value produced by our analytical expression. To evaluate the accuracy

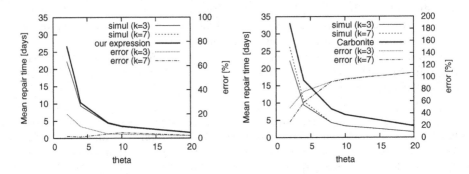

Fig. 4. Mean repair time measured by simulation, compared to the value predicted by our estimation (left) and Carbonite's expression (right)

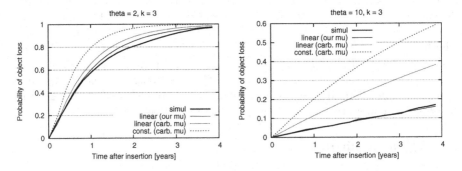

Fig. 5. Probability of object loss measured by simulation and predicted by the Markov chain

of this approximation, we measure the probability of object loss predicted by the Markov chain, and compare it with the loss rate observed on the simulator.

The loss rate predicted by the Markov chain is obtained by solving a system of $k + 1$ differential equations. For simplicity, we find a numerical solution using Mathematica's NDSolve [13]. The loss probability measured by simulation is obtained by counting the percentage of objects that are lost at time t after their insertion. In order to smooth the curve we run 5 simulations and average the results.

Figure 5 shows the probability of object loss over time, using $k = 3$ and two values of θ. Our linear approximation $\mu_i = (k-i)\mu$ produces a good prediction of the probability of object loss over time. Conversely, using the value μ' suggested in the Carbonite paper [7] overestimates the probability of object loss, regardless of the approximation used to obtain μ_i (linear or constant). The error when using μ' is higher for the higher value of θ, which is consistent with Figure 4.

Unfortunately, for larger values of k (i.e., $k > 3$) the predicted loss rate is no longer accurate (the curves are not shown for space reasons). This is not due to our analytical estimation of μ, but to the first-order approximation of μ_i, which produces poor results for $k > 3$. In fact, our measurements show that the values of μ_i grow sublinearly with i. We are currently working on deriving an analytical expression for the values of μ_i, which will prove useful for $k > 3$.

5 Conclusions and Future Work

In this paper we have focused on finding an accurate prediction of data durability in DHTs. Recent work has suggested that this can be achieved by modeling the system's behavior using Markov chains. However, our experiments show that the repair rates suggested previously produce inaccurate predictions of the object loss probability. We have presented a new analytical estimation for the mean repair rate which produces much more accurate results. We have also shown that a first-order approximation of the chain's repair rates yields good predictions for a small replication factor (i.e., $k = 3$). For higher values of k, a higher-order approximation must be found to produce accurate predictions of the system's durability. Future work will include considering the impact of churn, as well as deriving an analytical expression for all repair rates of the chain.

References

1. Rowstron, A., Druschel, P.: Storage management and caching in PAST, a large-scale, persistent peer-to-peer storage utility. In: Proc. of SOSP (2001)
2. Rhea, S., Godfrey, B., Karp, B., Kubiatowicz, J., Ratnasamy, S., Shenker, S., Stoica, I., Yu, H.: OpenDHT: A Public DHT Service and Its Uses. In: Proc. of SIGCOMM (2005)
3. Maymounkov, P., Mazieres, D.: Kademlia: A Peer-to-peer Information Systems Based on the XOR Metric. In: Proceedings of IPTPS (2002)
4. Dabek, F., Kaashoek, M.F., Karger, D., Morris, R., Stoica, I.: Wide-area cooperative storage with CFS. In: Proc. of SOSP (2001)
5. Ratnasamy, S., Francis, P., Handley, M., Karp, R., Shenker, S.: A Scalable Content-Addressable Network. In: Proc. of SIGCOMM (2001)
6. Ramabhadran, S., Pasquale, J.: Analysis of long-running replicated systems. In: Proc. of INFOCOM (2006)
7. Chun, B., Dabek, F., Haeberlen, A., Sit, E., Weatherspoon, H., Kaashoek, F., Kubiatowicz, J., Morris, R.: Efficient Replica Maintenance for Distributed Storage Systems. In: Proc. of NSDI (2006)
8. Saroiu, S., Gummadi, P.K., Gribble, S.D.: A measurement study of peer-to-peer file sharing systems. In: Proc. of MMCN (2002)
9. Gummadi, K.P., Dunn, R.J., Saroiu, S., Gribble, S.D., Levy, H.M., Zahorjan, J.: Measurement, modeling, and analysis of a peer-to-peer file-sharing workload. In: Proc. of SOSP (2003)
10. Blake, C., Rodrigues, R.: High availability, scalable storage, dynamic peer networks: Pick two. In: Proc. of HotOS (2003)
11. Patterson, D., Gibson, G., Katz, R.: A case for redundant arrays of inexpensive disks (RAID). In: Proc. of SIGMOD (1988)
12. Dabek, F.: A Distributed Hash Table. Ph.D. thesis (2005)
13. Tam, P.: A Physicist's Guide to Mathematica. Elsevier, Amsterdam (1997)

14. Rhea, S.: OpenDHT: A Public DHT Service. Ph.D. thesis (2005)
15. Zhao, B., Huang, L., Stribling, J., Rhea, S., Joseph, A., Kubiatowicz, J.: Tapestry: A Resilient Global-Scale Overlay for Service Deployment. IEEE Journal on Selected Areas in Communications 22(1) (January 2004)
16. Rodrigues, R., Liskov, B.: High Availability in DHTs: Erasure Coding vs. Replication. In: Castro, M., van Renesse, R. (eds.) IPTPS 2005. LNCS, vol. 3640. Springer, Heidelberg (2005)

A Multiple Tree Approach for Fault Tolerance in MPLS Networks

Sahel Alouneh, Anjali Agarwal, and Abdeslam En-Nouaary

Department of Electrical and Computer Engineering,
Concordia University, Montreal, Canada
{s_aloune,aagarwal,ennouaar}@ece.concordia.ca

Abstract. This paper presents a new approach to provide fault tolerance in MPLS multicast networks. MPLS has been used to provide faster forwarding; combining with multicasting it further supports applications with improved service. Fault tolerance is therefore important for such networks. Our strategy for fault tolerance is to divide and encode the traffic into multiple disjoint trees using a modified (k, n) Threshold Sharing scheme. Our scheme can reconstruct the original traffic from any k out of n trees available. Therefore, in the event of node/link failure(s) of any $(n\text{-}k)$ trees, our approach provides fault tolerance without introducing any recovery delay and packet loss. Moreover, our objective is also to minimize bandwidth utilization for protection purposes.

1 Introduction

Many service providers use MPLS technology [5] as a solution to address the problems faced by conventional IP networks (speed, scalability, quality-of-service (QoS), and traffic engineering). Several applications like web services, video/audio on demand services, and teleconferencing consume a large amount of network bandwidth. Multicasting is a useful operation for supporting such applications. Using multicasting services, data can be sent from one or more sources to several receivers at the same time. The data is distributed with the use of a multicast tree structure. The establishment and maintenance of multicast trees make multicast routing more challenging than unicast routing.

Several approaches have been proposed to deploy multicasting over MPLS networks. Moreover, many approaches have been proposed to employ MPLS based failure recovery methods in multicast trees [1,2,3,4]. Most of these approaches satisfy only some of the quality of service requirements. The existing schemes can be grouped in two categories: pre-planned and on-demand. On-demand approaches do not need to compute backup routes beforehand, the computational and maintenance cost is therefore low. However, these schemes usually experience longer recovery delay. In contrast, preplanned failure restoration predefines the backup routes, which introduces a large amount of computational and maintenance cost when there are large number of groups ongoing in the network. The big advantage of this type of fault tolerance is the much shorter recovery delay. In this paper we propose a novel approach for fault tolerance for MPLS

T. Janowski and H. Mohanty (Eds.): ICDCIT 2007, LNCS 4882, pp. 197–202, 2007.

network based on multiple trees. Our scheme falls in the category of preplanned protection, and is based on the Threshold Sharing Scheme (TSS) [6]. We show that our scheme introduces no recovery delay and handles packet loss or node failure in up to $(n\text{-}k)$ trees.

2   Proposed Algorithm

We use a modified version of TSS to suit MPLS networking requirements such as bandwidth. Threshold sharing scheme is a very well known concept used to provide security. However, the idea to use the threshold sharing for providing fault tolerance in networks has never been studied, and especially for MPLS networks to the best of our knowledge. We are using a *modified* version of the threshold sharing scheme because the original algorithm is not suitable for network resource utilization as it will be explained later in this section. The detailed discussion about our proposed algorithm is presented along in this section.

The idea behind the TSS is to divide a message into n pieces, called shadows or shares, such that any k of them can be used to reconstruct the original message. Using any number of shares less than k will not help to reconstruct the original message. Adi Shamir polynomial approach [6] will be used to show this concept. The Shamir's *(k,n)* threshold scheme is based on the Lagrange interpolation for polynomials. The polynomial function is shown as in equation 1. Let p be a prime number, then a polynomial with intermediate x values over the finite field Z_p has the following expression form:

$$f(x) = (a_{k-1}x^{k-1} + \ldots a_2x^2 + a_1x + a_0) \; mod \; p \tag{1}$$

where the coefficients $a_0, \cdots, a_{k-1}$ are unknown elements of Z_p, and $a_0 = M$ is the original message.

Our approach uses the (k,n) threshold sharing algorithm with multiple tree routing wherein k out of n trees are required to reconstruct the original message. For example, if we are using a (2,3) threshold sharing algorithm, then it is enough for the egress router to receive MPLS packet shares coming from two trees to reconstruct the original message which was divided at the ingress router.

2.1   Modified TSS and Integration with MPLS Multicast Model

Our proposed algorithm works as follows. When IP multicast packets enter the MPLS network at the ingress router, a distributor process is used to generate the n share messages/packets that will become the payloads for MPLS packets. These n MPLS packets are allocated over n disjoint multicast trees. The control unit is responsible to build the disjoint multicast trees for the participating groups. The IP packet is divided into L byte blocks $S_0, S_1, \cdots, S_m$. The n shares are calculated using the n different x_i values as agreed between the sender(s) and the receiver(s). As an example we show in Figure 1 a (3,4) modified version of the TSS to divide the IP multicast packet.

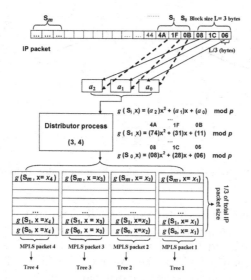

Fig. 1. Processing an IP Multicast packet by Distributor process for (3,4) TSS

It is important to mention here that we consider all coefficients of the polynomial function to be part of packet division. Unlike the original definition used in the Threshold Sharing Scheme [6], a_1 and a_2 values are provided from each block (not by assigning random values). The number of coefficients of polynomial function as used in Figure 1 is $k = 3$, and hence, each L bytes block is divided into three equal parts. These parts will be mapped to the polynomial's three coefficients a_0, a_1, a_2. To reconstruct the original message, the receiver needs to receive shares from $k = 3$ trees.

3   Scenario Examples

The well-known NSF (National Science Foundation) network is chosen as shown in Figure 2. In the first scenario, we consider the subset of egress routers $E_1 = \{N_4, N_9\}$ as receivers, which have the same source N_0. For this subset, we can build three disjoint trees T_1, T_2, and T_3 as shown in Figure 2-a, which also shows the delay costs on the links. At the source router (ingress N_0), the original traffic f is split into three different shares based on a modified (2,3) TSS model. Each share f_n will carry an encoded traffic of amount equal to the half of the original traffic f and allocated to any one of the three trees T_1, T_2, and T_3. Accordingly, each receiver in E_1 should receive at least two shares from any two trees to be able to reconstruct the original traffic f. A failure in one tree (node(s) or link(s)) or any share lost along any of the tree will not affect the reconstruction of the original traffic as long as the other two trees have no failure and receive their shares correctly. The second scenario is similar to the previous scenario except that the subset E_1 now contains more participating receivers in

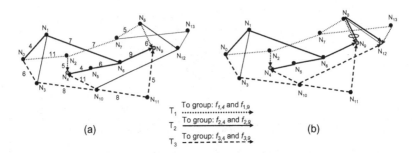

Fig. 2. (a) Complete disjoint trees coverage, (b) maximally disjoint trees coverage

the group $E_1 = \{N_4, N_9, N_{12}\}$. Indeed, we call these trees maximally disjoint trees. Figure 2-b shows a possible establishment of maximally disjoint trees that cover E_1. Note that T_1 and T_2 are sharing the link between N_8 and N_9. However, if a failure occurred on this link, neither N_9 nor N_{12} will be affected because N_9 and N_{12} are still able to reconstruct the original traffic from T_2 and T_3 and T_1 and T_3 respectively.

4   Performance Analysis

4.1   Recovery Delay and MPLS Packet Loss

Due to the way the proposed TSS works, the egress router just needs to receive at least k out of n shares from any k trees. Therefore, even if a failure occurs or a MPLS packet share is lost in any of the $(n\text{-}k)$ trees, the egress is able to reconstruct the original message without any additional recovery delay. This is compared to traditional pre-planned recovery approaches where a notification message is sent from the failed node/link to the ingress router to switch to the predefined backup paths.

4.2   Bandwidth Requirement

Assuming an IP packet of size $P_{size} = Q$ bytes, and using the original (k,n) Threshold Sharing scheme. The total size of n MPLS packets is:

$$Total\ n\ packets\ size\ T_{originalTSS(n)} = n \times P_{size} \qquad (2)$$

Using the modified TSS algorithm, where all coefficients values are considered to be *part of* the original IP packet it results in:

$$Total\ n\ packets\ size\ T_{modifiedTSS(n)} = \frac{n}{k}\ P_{size} \qquad (3)$$

Assuming a (3,4) modified Threshold Sharing scheme used and IP packet of 3 Kbytes entering the MPLS network. Referring to Figure 1, the distributor process

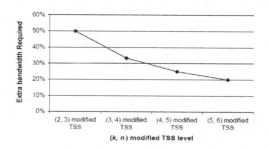

Fig. 3. The effect of Number of Shares on Extra Bandwidth Required

will generate four MPLS packets, each share size in this case is ≈ 1 Kbytes (i.e., 1024 bytes + MPLS packet header). The total size of four MPLS packet shares created is therefore equal to ≈ 4 Kbytes. Depending on the modified (k, n) TSS level used, extra bandwidth needed to provide fault tolerance is shown in Figure 3. The highest extra bandwidth is 50 % when a (2,3) TSS level is used. The extra bandwidth needed goes down as higher (k, n) TSS level is used.

4.3   Receiver Buffer Requirement

The proposed scheme may require packets reordering at the receiving nodes due to the possibility of having different propagation delays for the multiple trees considered. Therefore, buffer allocation is required to synchronize packets received from shorter paths. Consider an original traffic flow f with n subflows or shares f_n. The end-to-end delay for each share towards an egress node e is given by:

$$d^{f_n,e} = \sum_{(i,j) \in T_n} d_{ij} \qquad (4)$$

where according to our model, d_{ij} is the delay of each link (i,j) in a tree T_n. The delay for the slowest f_n belonging to f toward egress node e is:

$$d_{slowest}^{f_n,e} = max\left(\{d^{f_n,e}\}\right) \ \forall \ T_n \in T \qquad (5)$$

Therefore, the buffer size $B^{f_n,e}$ required for each f_n flow is:

$$B^{f_n,e} = (d_{slowest}^{f_n,e} - d^{f_n,e}) \cdot b_{f_n} \qquad (6)$$

where b_{f_n} is the bit rate arrival for node e from flow f_n. Note that a buffer for the slowest path is not required. The total buffer size in an egress router e for an original traffic flow f is:

$$B^{f_e} = \sum_{\forall T_n \in T} B^{f_n,e} \qquad (7)$$

Table 1. Buffer allocation required at each egress router

	$d^{f_{n,e}}$ ms	max	Partial Buffer (bits)	Total buffer size (bits)
$f_{1,4}$	16		(25-16).128 = 1152	
$f_{2,4}$	21		(25-21).128 = 512	1664
$f_{3,4}$	25	25	0	
$f_{1,9}$	29	29	0	
$f_{2,9}$	20		(29-20).128 = 1152	1408
$f_{3,9}$	27		(29-27).128 = 256	

To illustrate more on how to calculate the required buffer size at the egress router we present this example. A modified (2,3) TSS model is used as seen in Figure 2-a.

Each egress router (N_4 and N_9) receives shares from three disjoint trees T_1, T_2 and T_3. In this case, $d^{f_{1,4}} = \sum_{(i,j)\in T_1} d_{ij} = d_{0,2} + d_{2,4} = 11 + 5 = 16$. In the same way we obtain the values for the rest in Table 1 where the bit rate used for all links is 128Kbps.

5   Conclusion

In this paper, we used a modified (k,n) TSS model to provide fault tolerance in MPLS multicast environment. Our approach is novel and takes new approach for protecting the network from failure. The concept of sending failure notification to reroute the primary traffic into a backup tree is not used in our approach. Our scheme can reconstruct the original traffic from any k out of n trees available. Therefore, in the event of node/link failure, our approach provides fault tolerance without introducing recovery delay, packet loss while at the same time with reasonable resource utilization.

References

1. Cui, J., Faloutsos, M., Gerla, M.: An architecture for scalable, efficient, and fast fault-tolerant multicast provisioning. IEEE Networks 18(2), 26–34 (2004)
2. Deshmukh, R., Agarwal, A.: Failure recovery in MPLS multicast network using segmented backup approach. In: International Conference on Networking (2004)
3. Kodialam, M., Lakshman, T.: Dynamic routing of bandwidth guaranteed multicasts with failure backup. In: Proceeding 10th IEEE International Conference on Network Protocols (2002)
4. Pointer, Y.: Link Failure Recovery for MPLS Networks with Multicasting. PhD thesis, University of Virginia, Master thesis (2002)
5. Rosen, E.: Multiprotocol label switching architecture. RFC 3031 (2001)
6. Shamir, A.: How to share a secret. Commun. ACM 22(11), 612–613 (1979)

Selective Querying and Other Proposals for a Less Congested Gnutella Network

K.G. Srinivasa[1], Anuj Bhatt[1], Sagnik Dhar[1], K.R. Venugopal[2],
and L.M. Patnaik[3]

[1] Data Mining Laboratory, M S Ramaiah Institute of Technology
kgsrinivas@msrit.edu, anuj.bhatt@gmail.com, sagnik.dhar@gmail.com
[2] Dept. of CSE, University Visvesvaraya College of Engineering, Bangalore University
[3] Microprocessor Applications Laboratory, Indian Institute of Science, Bangalore

Abstract. Network congestion and look-up times are of prime concern in peer-to-peer networks and Gnutella is no exception to this problem. A number of proposals and suggestions have been made to improve the scalability and performance and to reduce the congestion in Gnutella networks. An improvement would be to query a subgroup of positive respondents of the PING message that is exchanged among peers prior to the QUERY message. We discuss possible ways in order to determine "profitable" peers which could result in a successful transfer of a requested file and further highlight issues which we think would reduce congestion in the network.

1 Overview

Peer-to-peer (P2P) systems do away with the traditional client-server model and enable each of the participating systems to act as a server, providing requested services (if available) as well as a client, making use of the services provided by other peer(s).

P2P systems discussed so far fall into two categories: centralized and decentralized. As the name suggests, centralized systems are those which have certain central entities providing services to the remaining peers. Napster [1], as an example, provided media hungry users to exploit digital content by sharing files through a central indexing server, which provided a map between files and users (who possess those files). Decentralized systems, on the other hand, do not have any such central entities. Peer request and render services to and from other peers. Gnutella is an example of such a P2P system.

2 Introduction: Gnutella Basics

Gnutella is a decentralized P2P system which consists of members referred to as *servents*. According to the Gnutella Protocol Specification [3], the servents communicate with each other by using *Ping, Pong, Query, QueryHit, Push* messages.

T. Janowski and H. Mohanty (Eds.): ICDCIT 2007, LNCS 4882, pp. 203–208, 2007.

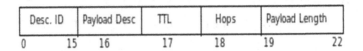

Desc. ID	Payload Desc	TTL	Hops	Payload Length
0 15	16	17	18	19 22

Fig. 1. Packet header

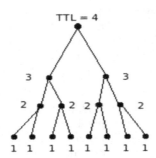

Fig. 2. TTL pattern through hops

Each of the packets in the Gnutella network contains header with the format as shown in Figure 1. The fields [3] are Descriptor ID, Payload Descriptor, Time To Live(TTL), Hops, Payload length.

3   Contributions

We address the following main issues related to the Gnutella system

- **Selecting profitable peers:** Initially a peer, on recognizing and registering with neighboring peers, broadcasts the PING message to them with an initial TTL value (= 7). This PING message is then broadcasted to adjacent peers on each level as indicated in Figure 2. Peers which are alive, respond back with a PONG message. The QUERY message then follows. Since TTL=7 will consequently incur a large number of PONGS [4], we propose a method to select a subset of the positive respondents, referred to as *profitable* peers in order to reduce the network congestion.
- **PONG packet header changes:** The typical PONG message consists of the fields: Port, IPAddress, No. of shared files, No. of Kb shared. We modify this header to *reveal* more information while preserving the information reflected by the original PONG header. This modification will help us make better judgments of assigning specific TTL values being sent to a node.
- **Handling Asymmetric Peers:** [2] indicates the problem associated with "downloading" files from hosts which utilize ADSL or cable connections. The download speed for such a host is three to eight times faster than the

upload speed. When the PUSH command is used to download a file from a host guarded by a firewall, the queried host is made to *upload* the file to the querying host, making the transfer rate considerably low.

4   Selecting Profitable Peers

We propose a new field, Information String, in the Pong packet, replacing the "Number of files" field in the previously used system.

We refer to this new field, Information String, as "IString". The IString, indicates not just the number of fields, but also indicates the number of shared files beginning with a particular alphabet. An example of an IString is *2a4b3c14p23r*. This has the implication that the respondent, has 2 files beginning with the letter 'a', 4 with 'b' and so on. With this knowledge, the host receiving the PONG message can decide to selectively query a subset of the respondents. The following steps indicate the validity of assumptions based on the IString:

If the IString is of the format: $w_1 a_1 w_2 a_2 ... w_n a_n$ where w_i is the number of files beginning with the alphabet a_i. Now:

- After a host receives a number of PONG messages we compute

$$W_{tot} = \Sigma_{i=1}^{i=k} w_i \text{ for a given } a_i$$

  Where k is the number of Pongs received. Each of the w_i corresponds to a particular a_i. This a_i is the first alphabet of the file being requested by a peer.
- Now, the peer querying the other peers, from which it received a PONG, can assume that the probability of finding a file beginning with the the alphabet a_i in a node that responded is:

$$P(F_i) = \frac{w_i}{W_{tot}}$$

  where $i \epsilon \{1, 2...k\}$
- Now, selecting a profitable peer becomes a function of the probability and the hop count as shown below:

$$M_i = f(P(F_i), hops_i)$$

4.1   Discussion

Consider that a PING results in the PONGs as indicated by Table 1. The host desires to QUERY, for example, an MP3 file with the title beginning with 'p'. Let the file be *pxxxxxx.mp3*. We obtain $W_{tot} = 44$. Thus, the probability of finding *pxxxxxx.mp3* in:

$$IP_A \text{ is } P(F_1) \sim 0.39$$
$$IP_B \text{ is } P(F_2) \sim 0.52$$
$$IP_C \text{ is } P(F_3) \sim 0.09$$

Table 1. Eg. Received PONG Messages

Port	IP	IString	Size
$xxxx$	IP_A	3a4b...17p	$xxXB$
$xxxx$	IP_B	2a4b...23p	$xxXB$
$xxxx$	IP_C	3b4c...4p	$xxXB$

Now, say IP_A and IP_B are both 10 hops away. The function f selects IP_B in order to query it and the packet follows a trace to the peer, temporarily ignoring IP_A. If a QUERYHIT is received, then a successful initiation of a file transfer follows. If a negative response is received, the requesting peer queries IP_A. This results in selective querying which reduces network utilization and in the worst case causes intermittent querying of all peers who responded with a PONG earlier.

This process is simultaneously executed for a *profitable* node at every hop, thereby selecting the most apparent profitable peer at each hop. This is illustrated in *Algorithm 1*.

Algorithm 1. *Algorithm to select probable profitable peers*

1: $N \leftarrow$ Number of respondents
2: $N_h \leftarrow$ Number of respondents for each hop h
3: $M_h \leftarrow$ Most profitable peer at hop h
4: $M_h' \leftarrow$ Most profitable after M_h for a certain hop
5: **for** $i \leftarrow 1$ to h **do**
6:    SELECT M_h
7: **end for**
8: QUERY M_h for all h
9: **while** M_h for any h not profitable **do**
10:    **if** M_h not profitable for *thish* **then**
11:       $M_h = M_h'$
12:    **end if**
13: **end while**

4.2   Algorithm Example

Consider a network, where the nodes are arranged as shown in Figure 3. The node at the top, queries for a particular file, while the remaining nodes respond to that query. We have 3 nodes which are 1 hop away, i.e. $N_h = 3$ for $h = 1$, while there are 4 nodes which are 2 hops away, i.e. $N_h = 4$ for $h = 2$, with request to the querying node.

On selecting the most probable profitable peer M_h: QUERY M_h. We repeat the process for all values of h. The diagram shows us that the second node at hop $h = 1$, has maximum probability of possessing the queried file, in that hop. The QUERY message to this node, returns a positive response and hence the file download starts. A dashed circle shows the node which has the highest

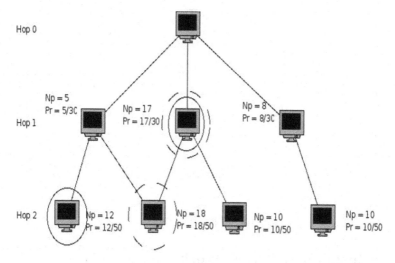

Hop 0

Np = 5
Pr = 5/3C
Hop 1

Np = 17
Pr = 17/30

Np = 8
Pr = 8/3C

Hop 2

Np = 12
Pr = 12/50

Np = 18
Pr = 18/50

Np = 10
Pr = 10/50

Np = 10
Pr = 10/50

Fig. 3. Selecting a subset of positive respondents. The dashed circle indicates the M_h and the solid circle indicates final selected M_h

probability of being the most 'profitable' peer, while the solid circle denotes the node which is actually the most 'profitable'.

A similar process is simultaneously initiated in the second hop. The second node in the second hop, has the maximum probability of being the most 'profitable' peer. A QUERY sent to that node, returns a negative response. The node with the second highest probability is queried, which happens to have a positive response. This example demonstrates that the node with maximum probability of being the most 'profitable' need not always be the most profitable. As the most profitable peer at each hop is selected, the queried file is downloaded simultaneously from several hosts, and merged.

5   Experimental Setup and Results

We simulated the Gnutella network by using multiple processes which acted as peers across systems on our network. The hops were preset and delays were inserted accordingly. The processes exchanged messages as per the protocol specification and we recorded the results related to look-up and QUERY success-failure analysis based on our selective querying approach. It was also noted that the average time decreases considerably if we use a $n - threaded$ look-up approach, where n is the number of words which make up the filename being queried.

Figure 4 shows the number of positive respondents and the number of times we had to reselect another peer based on our approach. The success rate will be higher if we include approximate string matching for our look-up method. The result here is only for exact matching.

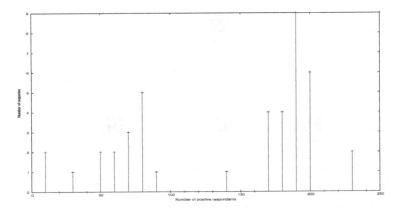

Fig. 4. QUERY results

6   Conclusion and Future Work

We analyzed various approaches based on the results obtained from other publications. Our approach converges closer to the desired result with respect to the filename being queried. The concept was simulated using multiple objects which acted as peers for our study. Future work will involve further analysis and study of a distributed hash table (DHT) mechanism for the Gnutella. DHT based P2P systems require hosts to store content based on the hash calculated on a file object. Such systems provide a *structured* feature to the P2P networks and requires cooperation among participating peers. Future work will include investigating a way in which we could include such a feature in an otherwise decentralized ad-hoc network such as Gnutella.

Acknowledgments

The Project is partially supported by the AICTE, as a part of Career Award of Young Teachers(AICTE File No.: F. No.1-51/FD/CA/(9)2005-06) to Mr.K.G. Srinivasa, who is presently working as a faculty in Department of Computer Science and Engineering, M. S. Ramaiah Institute of Technology, Bangalore – 560 054, India.

References

1. Napster. http://www.napster.com/
2. Minar, N., Hedlund, M.: Peer-to-Peer: Harnessing the Power of Disruptive Technologies, ch. 1. O'Reilly
3. The Gnutella Protocol Specification v0.4, Document Revision 1.2.
   http://dss.clip2.com/GnutellaProtocol04.pdf
4. Markatos, E.P.: Tracing a larger scale Peer-to-Peer System: an hour in the life of Gnutella. In: 2nd IEEE/ACM Int. Symposium on Cluster Computing and the Grid (2002)

Language Support and Compiler Optimizations for STM and Transactional Boosting

Guy Eddon and Maurice Herlihy

Computer Science Department, Brown University, Providence RI 02912, USA
herlihy@cs.brown.edu

Abstract. We describe compiler optimizations for object-based Software Transactional Memory (STM) systems designed to make STM more accessible and efficient than is possible in the context of a purely library-based approach. Current object-based STM libraries are faced with a difficult tradeoff: offer an efficient but complex programming model or, as some recent libraries have done, sacrifice efficiency for ease-of-use. In this paper, we show that this dichotomy is not necessary. Our research suggests that an STM-enabled optimizing compiler can achieve performance comparable to that of the most efficient STM algorithms coded by a programmer, while still supporting a nearly transparent programming model. We also propose novel language extensions to support transactional boosting, a powerful new technique for transforming existing linearizable objects into transactional objects, thus permitting highly concurrent objects such as those found in the java.util.concurrent package to participate in STM transactions. When applied in conjunction with compiler support, we show that transactional boosting is both a flexible and natural way to escape the standard transactional model, and thus offers a promising alternative to existing "expert" approaches, such as open nesting and early release. Based on our results, we conclude that appropriate language support and high quality compiler optimizations are necessary parts of any STM system.

1 Introduction

Software transactional memory systems can be classified as word-based, synchronizing on uninterpreted regions of memory, or object-based, synchronizing on language-level objects. Much recent research has focused on word-based systems [1,4,6,5,8,19], which are well-suited for "unmanaged" languages such as C or C++. If, however, we turn our attention to "managed" languages such as Java or C#, object-based STM systems have a number of attractive features. Because memory accesses are routed through method calls, it is feasible to provide strong atomicity [17,20], ensuring that transactional and non-transactional code are properly synchronized, thus avoiding a class of difficult-to-detect synchronization errors. Moreover, object-based designs support transactional boosting [12], a safe alternative to open nested transactions that can be used to enhance concurrency for "hot-spot" shared objects. Finally, object-based STMs offer better opportunities

T. Janowski and H. Mohanty (Eds.): ICDCIT 2007, LNCS 4882, pp. 209–224, 2007.

for optimization because the semantics of object-oriented languages naturally provide the context for each field, allowing for a higher level understanding of memory access patterns.

The most straightforward way to provide an object-based STM is as a library [14,13,16,21]. However, it has been our experience, and the experience of others [3], that it is difficult to implement object-based STM libraries that are both efficient and provide a simple programming interface, because a simplified interface usually requires a high level of abstraction that does not permit non-local optimizations. As a programming model, transactions have a pervasive influence on both data and control flow. For example, the DSTM library [14], the first library of this kind, required programmers to express data and control structures in an idiosyncratic way, explicitly opening and closing shared atomic objects, and hand-coding retry loops. One important advantage of the DSTM2 [13] and SXM [21] libraries, which build on DSTM, was that they offered a more natural programming interface than their predecessor, automatically generating transactional "wrappers" around fields of shared atomic objects, and automatically retrying failed transactions. Nevertheless, while transactionalwrappers led to a simpler, less error-prone programming style, overheads could be high, since libraries did not know how they were used by clients, and there was little or no opportunity for non-local optimization. Dalessandro et al. [3] report similar dissatisfactions with the RSTM2 library.

It is the premise of this paper that compiler support is the key to making object-based STM systems achieve both a simple programming interface and adequate performance. Fortunately, we will show that relatively straightforward measures can be very effective. Underlying these measures is an STM model that uses annotations to describe atomic types and methods. Annotations are an attractive way to prototype languaage features because they are easily extensible, familiar to programmers, and do not require introducing new syntactic structures.

We describe an STM compiler that performs a dataflow analysis to determine whether an atomic object is accessed in read or write mode and whether a specific atomic field access is guaranteed to occur subsequent to a previous use of that object. Based on this information, the compiler makes more efficient use of the STM library, inlining much of the transactional machinery directly in the user's code in the form of bytecode instructions. The compiler supports a natural and largely transparent programming interface, and, to date, offers a performance improvement of between four and ten times compared with the same algorithms implemented solely with an STM library. This performance improvement helps close the gap between STM systems and conventionally synchronized concurrent algorithms.

This paper makes the following contributions:

- To the best of our knowledge, we are the first to apply whole object dataflow analysis to track the state of open transactional objects.
- We show that subsequent reads and writes can be made entirely lock-free, even in the context of a blocking STM that relies on short-lived locks for initial reads and writes.

- Based on this application, we demonstrate that compiler optimization can yield non-blocking, obstruction-free STMs that perform at least as well as comparable blocking systems.
- We propose the first language extensions and compiler support for transactional boosting.

Section Two describes the language interface we have developed to support STM and transactional boosting. Section Three covers the compiler and library optimizations that enable significant performance gains and Section Four describes important improvements in the handling of arrays. Finally, Section Five summarizes the current state of the project.

2   The Language Interface

Our compiler supports transactional programming features to alleviate the difficulty of programming directly with an STM library. By supporting atomic types and transactionally-boosted objects in the programming language, and transparently rewriting field accesses for those objects, the compiler hides the transformations required to convert a sequential algorithm into one that uses STM. Because our compiler support exists at the backend, all our language proposals are expressed as annotations. While such annotations could be also implemented as first-class language keywords, we have not found this to be a disadvantage; in fact, to the extent that programmers are comfortable with annotations from other contexts this seems a natural way of introducing such support.

2.1   Atomic Classes, Methods and Blocks

The fundamental annotation is the Atomic attribute, which can be used on both classes and methods. When applied to classes, the Atomic attribute indicates that all the fields of that type must always be accessed from within a transaction. The compiler verifies that code accessing atomic objects is always executed in the context of a transaction. The code fragment below shows an atomic Node class from the List benchmark:

```
[Atomic] public class Node {
    public int value;
    public Node next;
}
```

The only restriction is that the field types must either be value types, or, in the case of reference types, the reference types must themselves by marked as atomic. Certain special pre-existing objects that are known to be safe for transactional use but are not marked with the Atomic attribute are permitted when the field reference is tagged with the TxSafe attribute, which informs the compiler that the field is in fact safe for transactional use. Finally, the compiler supports inheritance of atomic types, such that atomic types can derive from other atomic types or types marked with the TxSafe attribute.

Although all methods of an atomic type are automatically assumed to support transactions, methods can also be explicitly annotated with the Atomic attribute to indicate that the entire method requires a transaction. By default, methods simply support but do not require or create a transaction. If a transaction exists on the current thread when the method is called, the atomic method's work will become part of that transaction. If, on the other hand, no transaction exists, the method will run unsynchronized.

To ensure that a method is always run in the context of a transaction, the programmer can provide a parameter to the Atomic attribute indicating the desired semantics. The available options are Uses (this is the default behavior when no parameter is specified), Requires, and Starts. The Requires option indicates that the method must always run in a transaction. If no transaction exists on the current thread, the method will automatically begin a new transaction before executing the user's code. However, if a transaction already exists, a "Requires" method will simply use it. In contrast, the Starts option indicates that the method will always begin a new transaction. In cases where a transaction already exists before the method is called, a "starts" method will begin a nested transaction. The Contains method shown below always runs in a new transaction:

```
[Atomic(XKind.Starts)]
public bool Contains(int v) {
    Neighborhood hood = Find(v);
    return hood.currNode != null;
}
```

In addition to the method-based approach to transaction creation represented by the Atomic annotation, the compiler also supports block-level creation of transactions through the using(new XAction())   block. This approach allows for dynamic control of transaction creation at the call site, so that a method can be called at different times, with or without a transaction. Importantly, local variables used inside the atomic using block are saved and restored on abort, so that the block is semantically idempotent:

```
using(new XAction()) {
    // code here runs in a tx
}
```

Our underlying STM library supports a retry [10] operation that waits until the current transaction has been aborted before re-attempting execution of the transaction. This is useful when the value read in one transaction depends on another transaction to modify that value for its success. The canonical example is that of a shared buffer, where one transaction is reading a value from the buffer while another is writing a value to it. The code below shows the Put method, which retries whenever the buffer's size reaches its maximum capacity. The retry operation then waits for another transaction to read and remove a value from the buffer (thereby invalidating and aborting this transaction), before retrying:

```
// Put a value into the buffer
[Atomic(XKind.Starts)]
public void Put(int v) {
    // check for the condition
    if(buffer.size + 1 ==
                    buffer.capacity)
        XAction.Retry();
        buffer.data[++buffer.size] = v;
}
```

The compiler offers an alternate way of expressing this behavior. Instead of coding an explicit check for a condition and then executing the retry function, the condition can be more elegantly expressed as a parameter of the using block that accepts a boolean condition. This overloaded version of the XAction constructor causes the compiler to generate code rather similar to that shown above. The programmer, however, can express the functionality as shown here:

```
// Put a value into the buffer
[Atomic(XKind.Uses)]
public void Put(int v) {
                    // condition
    using(new XAction(buffer.size +
            1 != buffer.capacity))
        buffer.data[++buffer.size] = v;
}
```

In this case the compiler overloads the meaning of the using block. Normally, the value passed to the XAction constructor would only be evaluated once. In this context, however, the compiler generates code that reevaluates the entire expression every time the transaction is executed; the body of the using block is executed only when the boolean condition evaluates to true.

2.2 Transactional Boosting

Transactional boosting [12] is a technique that transforms highly-concurrent linearizable objects into transactional objects. Each method call is associated with an abstract lock, and locks for non-commuting calls conflict. Each method call must also have an inverse, which is logged and applied to the object when a transaction aborts. As discussed elsewhere, transactional boosting can enhance both the concurrency and performance of shared objects. Finally, transactional boosting is a safe alternative to open nested transactions [18].

Consider, for example, a shared set providing methods to add and remove integer items. Calls with distinct arguments commute (say, add(4) and remove(5)). When add(4) is called, the inverse remove(4) call is logged, in case the add operation must later be undone. Operating at this level of abstraction has advantages over more traditional STM models of word-based or object-based conflict detection and resolution. For example, consider a standard STM implementation of a sorted integer list containing the elements 1, 3, 5. While there is no reason that operations to add(2) and add(4) cannot execute concurrently, these operations will in fact conflict in standard STM systems, since one transaction will always write to a node read by the other.

By exploiting the programmer's understanding of an object's semantic properties, transactional boosting makes it possible introduce concurrency where traditional STMs do not. The initial proposal for transactional boosting, however, required that the programmer write special wrapper classes for existing linearizable objects in order to build the undo logs. We effectively obviate this process, by introducing language and compiler support for specifying method inverses and abstract locks. Rather than writing code to express the locking and undo logging, our approach uses annotations to specify the behavior of transactional boosting via a contract technique.

We support transactional boosting through three new annotations: TxBoosting, Inverse and AbstractLock. The TxBoosting attribute is applied to a class instead of the Atomic attribute; it signifies to the compiler that the type is safe for transactional use, but that its data does not need to be protected in the traditional manner because the object is already linearizable. The Inverse attribute is applied to a method in order to identify its logical inverse, which must have the same signature as the marked method. The Inverse annotation also accepts a parameter specifying under what circumstances the inverse call should be logged for undo purposes. While custom handlers can be specified, generally a boolean return value is sufficient to indicate that the method has successfully altered the abstract state of the object, thus requiring that the inverse operation be logged. In the example below, the ReturnsTrue flag indicates the corresponding method inverse, Remove, should only be logged when the Insert method executes successfully (i.e., if the Insert method fails, the Remove method is not logged, as there is no change in the object's state that must be undone):

```
[TxBoosting]
public class RBTree {
    [Atomic(XKind.Starts)]
    [Inverse(InverseKind.Method,
     "Remove",
     InverseCondition.ReturnsTrue)]
    public bool Insert(
        [AbstractLock] int key) {
        // ...
    }

    [Atomic(XKind.Starts)]
    [Inverse(InverseKind.Method,
     "Insert",
     InverseCondition.ReturnsTrue)]
    public bool Remove(
```

```
[AbstractLock] int key) {
    // ...
  }
}
```

The optional AbstractLock attribute identifies the parameter that defines the abstract lock that must be acquired by this method. Without the AbstractLock annotation, transactional boosting automatically acquires an exclusive lock, resulting in the serialization of all Insert calls. With the addition of the Abstract-Lock attribute, however, the abstract lock acquired only blocks on the Insert operations for this particular value. Note that such key-based locking may block commuting calls (e.g., two calls to Insert(3) where 3 is in the set), but it provides sufficient concurrency for practical purposes.

Abstract locks are automatically released when the transaction commits or, where it aborts, after the undo log has been executed. For cases where the Inverse and AbstractLock attributes are not sufficiently flexible to capture the desired concurrency semantics of a transactionally boosted object (see, e.g., the HeapRW example [12]), the model permits programmers to invoke helper methods that perform the customized inverse operation. The striking performance improvements (reported in [12]) achieved by transactional boosting are unaffected by our compiler and language support.

3   Optimizations

Today's STM systems can be broadly divided into two categories depending on the underlying progress condition they support (i.e., a non-blocking progress condition such as obstruction-freedom, or a blocking model that uses short-lived locks). The compiler and the underlying STM library support both approaches. Conventional wisdom holds that although non-blocking algorithms have nicer theoretic properties (e.g., no deadlock or priority inversion), they are nearly always significantly outperformed by functionally equivalent blocking algorithms. We find that with good compiler and library optimizations this no longer holds true-our obstruction-free mode outperforms the blocking mode in nearly all cases.

We have approached optimizations at two levels: traditional flow-based compiler optimization directed towards generating more efficient code and direct optimizations in the underlying STM library. Both have turned out to be extremely valuable in achieving our overall performance results. The compiler supports a whole object view of dataflow analysis that builds on our object-based language interface for STM. In the underlying STM library, we made a number of improvements to the transactional synchronization and validation algorithms that maintain the transactional state of each atomic object

3.1   Whole Object Analysis

As noted in [11], library-based STM systems blindly redirect all heap access through the STM interface, without first checking whether the object is thread-local or has been opened previously. Thus, using dataflow analysis can help determine whether an atomic object must be accessed transactionally, or is guaranteed to be thread-local. Second, it can determine when a field is accessed for a first or second (i.e., subsequent) time, guaranteeing that the object is already open for reading or writing. This is possible primarily because the compiler is built on top of an object-based STM, not a word-based one as in [9].

The observation that field reads performed on atomic objects that the transaction has previously read or written can proceed without any locks can be exploited by the compiler to significantly reduce the overhead of STM. By employing a PRE dataflow analysis algorithm based on the Static Single Assignment (SSA) format [2,22], the compiler can determine which reads and writes are guaranteed to be executed subsequent to a full open. In such cases, the subsequent reads and writes can be of the fast-path variety and are fully inlined in the user's code. This improves performance significantly, as only a lightweight "open" is performed and no method invocation is required.

Note that this is quite different from the peephole optimizers described in [11] and [1], which seem to rely primarily on the compiler's existing CSE optimizer to reduce the overhead of STM. The STM in [19] is cache line-based rather than object-based, which means it can't assume that all fields of an object are accessible after one field of that object has been accessed. The log-based system in [11] does not appear to support a non-blocking model. Finally, our dataflow analysis looks deeper into an object's use of atomic references, such that even where a reference to an open atomic object is stored in a field of another atomic object, the compiler tracks its open state.

Dataflow analysis is able to detect many of the instances where an object is first read and later written in the same transaction. In such cases, it is more efficient to open the object in write mode initially, and therefore OpenRead calls are automatically promoted to OpenWrites. Where the dataflow analysis detects that an atomic object is used across basic blocks, a special Phi node is inserted at the point where two or more object references merge. If an atomic object will be accessed two or more times subsequent to a Phi node, the compiler inserts a pre-open call at the Phi node. Where the object will only be read, the OpenRead call is inserted; otherwise the compiler inserts a call to the OpenWrite method. This optimization makes it possible for all actual field accesses to be inlined as subsequent accesses with the fast-path code.

Since a pre-open is inserted at a point where no object access existed in the user's code, the compiler must be careful not to introduce any new exception paths at the pre-open points. For example, if an atomic object reference is null when the pre-open call is made, it would be incorrect to have a null reference exception thrown at that point, since the programmer has no reason to believe that such an exception might be thrown at that place in the code. As a result, if a target object reference is null at the time the pre-open call is made, it will fail silently, as shown below.

```
if(target != null)
    target.synch.OpenRead/Write(me);
```

The compiler also inserts a special startup instruction at the top of each atomic method that retrieves and stores the current transaction in a local variable. This simple, but significant, optimization avoids later field accesses from needing to retrieve the current transaction (an expensive thread-local read). Where the methods of the atomic object are non-virtual, our object-based model makes it possible for the compiler to pass the cached transaction reference among methods of the atomic object.

3.2   Blocking Optimizations

In the STM model that uses short locks, the compiler generates a shadow field for each field of an atomic type to store the backup value during the transaction's execution. In addition, the compiler automatically generates code implementing the two methods of the IRecoverable interface, Backup and Restore, which copies the value of the "real" fields to the "shadow" fields and vice versa. Backup, which is invoked on the first attempt to write to an atomic object in the current transaction, copies the real fields to the shadow fields. Restore, which is invoked when the previous writer to the object is found to have aborted, copies the last known good values from the shadow fields back to the real fields. Const, final (or readonly), and TxSafe-annotated fields are considered idempotent, so no shadow fields need to be generated for them.

In this model, we optimized the OpenRead and OpenWrite methods to acquire a lock only when absolutely necessary. Before acquiring the lock, then, all possible conditions that can be handled without a lock are dealt with first. For example, in the OpenRead algorithm, if the reading transaction also turns out to be the "owner" (the current writer) of the object, the read can proceed in a completely non-blocking fashion. After the desired field is read, the algorithm simply checks to see whether the current transaction has been aborted. If not, it can be certain that the value read was correct and can be returned to the user's code. The relevant portion of the OpenRead algorithm, which is executed without an object-wide lock, is shown below:

```
// do i already own the object?
if(me == writer) {
    value = field; // do the read
    // is the value good?
    if((XStates)me.state ==
                  XStates.ABORTED)
        throw new AbortedException();
    return value; // yes, return it
}
```

This is correct even where, by the time the value is returned to the user's code, the transaction has been aborted and the field overwritten with a new value. Consistency does not require that we report the current value of the field. In fact, quite the opposite: transactions require that the client see only those values that are consistent with some linearizable execution of the active transactions.

These insights into the blocking model makes it possible for the compiler to inline fast-path versions of the read and write algorithms that do not require locks, where it is certain that the object has already been opened in read or write mode. In the case of subsequent reads, executed after an earlier read or write, the inlined code need only determine whether the value read is valid. If the transaction wasn't aborted at the time the value was read, then we can safely return the value to the user's code (note that no CAS is required):

```
// inlined for subsequent reads
[stack] = [target].field;
if(me.state == XStates.ABORTED)
    throw new AbortedException();
```

Unlike subsequent reads, the algorithm for safely writing to a field of an atomic object cannot proceed entirely without a CAS operation. In the case where the target object is already owned by the writing transaction, we still must ensure that the transaction is not aborted prior to the write operation. Unfortunately, checking whether the transaction has been aborted before doing the write is not effective, since an abort might occur asynchronously immediately after the check but before the write; checking the transaction's status after the write is too late-another transaction's value might already have been overwritten. To address this problem, the compiler must ensure that the transaction cannot be aborted during the update operation. By incrementing a special transaction-wide abortCounter, a fast-path write prevents the transaction from being aborted during this critical period. The algorithm is wait-free, but two CAS operations are required per write:

```
// inlined for subsequent writes
[FieldType] value = [stack1];
[AtomicType] target = [stack2];

// prevent a null ref exception
if(target == null)
    throw new NullRefException();

// make sure that no one aborts me
if(Interlocked.Increment(
        ref me.abortCounter) < 1) {
    // i've already been aborted!
    Interlocked.Decrement(
            ref me.abortCounter);
    throw new AbortedException();
}

target.field = value; // the update

// release the pro-life lock
```

```
Interlocked.Decrement(
        ref me.abortCounter);
```

The inlined code for subsequent writes shown above specifically checks for a null reference so that this exception cannot be thrown after the abortCounter is incremented (An exception thrown at this point would cause the corresponding decrement to be skipped.). The actual waiting, if any, occurs in the Abort method, which must check whether a transaction's abortCounter is zero before aborting it. While it is not, the Abort method blocks, as shown here:

```
// abort this tx
public void Abort() {
    XState targetTx = this;
    // wait, during a write...
    while(
        Interlocked.CompareExchange(
            ref targetTx.abortLock,
            int.MinValue, 0) > 0)
        ; // try again...

    ...
```

Figure 1 compares the performance of several standard benchmark algorithms as implemented with a library-based STM and as optimized by the compiler. (These results were obtained from 30 second runs using 1 thread, 30% modifiers,

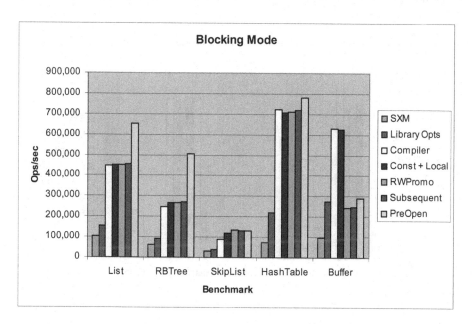

Fig. 1. Blocking mode results

and the aggressive contention manager on a 4-way machine.) Note in particular that the HashTable benchmark uses large arrays and thus benefits greatly from the hybrid array implementation described in section 4.

The STM-only results give the performance for the un-optimized SXM library [21]; Library Opts shows the improvements of our optimized transactional synchronization algorithms; the Compiler bar shows the results of inlining and automating the generation of STM code; Const + Local is the result of the dataflow analysis that eliminates STM accesses for those objects that are provably local; RWPromo includes the optimization that promotes read accesses to write mode open operations for atomic objects that are both read and written; the Subsequent optimization exploits our understanding of the difference between the first and subsequent accesses of an atomic object (see section 3.1); finally, the PreOpen optimization shows the results of our full interprocedural PRE analysis. Note that the bars are cumulative (i.e., each more advanced optimization includes all the prior ones).

4   Obstruction-Free Optimizations

The compiler optimizations implemented for the obstruction-free mode are slightly different from those that apply to the blocking STM. In the obstruction-free model, in place of shadow fields the compiler implements the ICloneable interface's Clone method to create a new, speculative, copy of the object. Interestingly, the obstruction-free STM cannot support static fields, since they cannot be cloned in an object-based STM. Instead, the compiler manages static fields

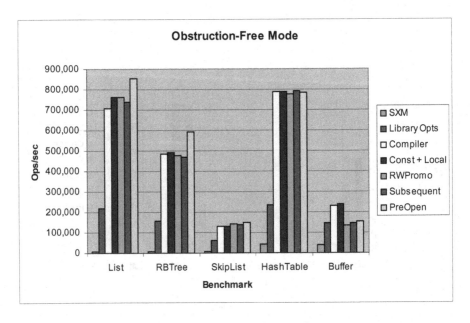

Fig. 2. Obstruction-free results

of an atomic object as in the blocking mode, where their values are copied to static shadow fields.

In its obstruction-free mode, the compiler generates local variables to cache the "open" version of atomic objects. In contrast to the blocking mode, subsequent reads do not need to check whether the transaction has been aborted, and subsequent writes need not temporarily delay aborts during the write. This means that subsequent reads and writes are completely inlined and have no transactional overhead whatsoever. These optimizations are possible because the obstruction-free STM creates clones of atomic objects, such that a subsequent read or write may see or update an inactive copy of the object, but linearizability is not compromised. Figure 2 shows the performance results of the compiler using the obstruction-free STM mode. Overall, the graphs show that the obstruction-free STM performs slightly better than the blocking mode using short-lived locks.

4.1   The CASe Primitive

The complexity involved with implementing a wait-free subsequent write in the blocking STM mode led us to identify a potential use for short hardware transactions. While much previous work has focused on the feasibility of efficiently implementing various types of multi-compare and swap (MCAS) operations [15], we observe that a very slight modification to the existing CAS primitive would greatly simplify the implementation of subsequent write operations in object-based STM systems: simply atomically comparing one location (the transaction's status) and swapping another (the target field) would obviate the need for our approach to delaying aborts during write operations.

We call this new primitive Compare and Swap elsewhere (CASe). Its only real added complexity, from a hardware perspective, is the fact that the compare location and the swap location might fall in different cache lines, necessitating that both lines be locked. With this new primitive, the algorithm for subsequent writes shown above can be rewritten as shown here:

```
if(!CASe(ref me.state, // compare A
    XStates.ACTIVE,   // with this
    ref target.field, // swap B
    value))           // with this
  throw new AbortedException();
```

5   Array Algorithms

One aspect of the runtime system that turned out to be a significant performance bottleneck for some benchmarks was the array implementation provided by the STM library. In the initial release of SXM [21], the basic array support was not typed (all array elements were of type object), and the backup and restore operations performed complete copies of the array. To optimize the performance of array-based data structures, we investigate several alternate array implementations. First, the atomic array type was parameterized using generics so that casts are not needed when reading or writing array elements. Second, in addition to the basic copying array described above, we developed a number of experimental array algorithms that are more efficient in terms of space or time.

The log array is typically more space efficient than the copying array. It defines a list of ArrayElement structures that store the value and index number of an array entry. The log array stores the backup log in a list of array elements. To limit the maximum size of the backup log to the size of the array, a bit array is used to determine whether the client has accessed this array element previously. Each array write operation first checks the bit array to see whether the user has modified the specified element previously. If the index's bit is not set, the array element must be added to backup list; if the index's bit is set, the array element has already been backed-up previously.

The log array is more efficient than the copying array when accessing larger arrays, since the entire array is not copied on each backup operation (a far more common operation than a restore). However, when working with small arrays consisting of several elements, copying the array is can be more efficient compared with the overhead of creating the backup log in a piecemeal fashion as part of every update. The hybrid array combines the strengths of both approaches. For arrays consisting of ten elements or fewer, the hybrid array simply creates a copy of the entire array on each backup/restore. Larger arrays are handled in the manner of the log array. This array algorithm provides the best overall performance, although it does require a runtime check to determine whether it is in copying or logging mode.

6   Summary

We have presented an optimizing compiler designed specifically for an object-based STM library to show that compiler support is extremely beneficial in terms of improving performance and programmability. By introducing atomic types, methods, and blocks as annotation-based language features, the compiler supports a natural and nearly transparent language interface, thus easing the burden an STM library places on the programmer. By applying object-based dataflow optimizations and improving the underlying STM library, the compiler achieves significant performance gains over a purely library-based approach. Our work reveals that in STM models that use short locks, only the initial access to an atomic object requires the acquisition of a lock; subsequent accesses can be made wait-free. We also show that, contrary to recent thinking [7], obstruction-free STM systems do not perform worse than those that employ short locks. Finally, we introduce the first compiler support for transactional boosting, a methodology for transforming highly concurrent linearizable object into highly-concurrent transactional objects.

References

1. Adl-Tabatabai, A.-R., Lewis, B.T., Menon, V., Murphy, B.R., Menon, V., Saha, B., Shpeisman, T.: Compiler and runtime support for efficient software transactional memory. In: PLDI 2006: Proceedings of the 2006 ACM SIGPLAN conference on Programming language design and implementation, pp. 26–37. ACM Press, New York (2006)
2. Chow, F., Chan, S., Kennedy, R., Liu, S.-M., Lo, R., Tu, P.: A new algorithm for partial redundancy elimination based on ssa form. In: PLDI 1997. Proceedings of the ACM SIGPLAN 1997 conference on Programming language design and implementation, pp. 273–286. ACM Press, New York (1997)
3. Dalessandro, L., Marathe, V.J., Spear, M.F., Scott, M.L.: Capabilities and limitations of library-based software transactional memory in c++. In: Proceedings of the 2nd ACM SIGPLAN Workshop on Transactional Computing, Portland, OR (August 2007)
4. Damron, P., Fedorova, A., Lev, Y., Luchangco, V., Moir, M., Nussbaum, D.: Hybrid transactional memory. In: ASPLOS-XII. Proceedings of the 12th international conference on Architectural support for programming languages and operating systems, pp. 336–346. ACM Press, New York (2006)
5. Dice, D., Shavit, N.: What really makes transactions faster. In: Proc. of the 1st TRANSACT, workshop, 2006. Electronic (2006)
6. Dice, D., Shalev, O., Shavit, N.: Transactional locking ii. In: Dolev, S. (ed.) DISC 2006. LNCS, vol. 4167, pp. 194–208. Springer, Heidelberg (2006)
7. Ennals, R.: Software transactional memory should not be obstruction-free. Intel Research Cambridge (unpublished manuscript)
8. Felber, P., Fetzer, C., Müller, U., Riegel, T., Süßkraut, M., Sturzrehm, H.: Transactifying applications using an open compiler framework. In: TRANSACT (2007)
9. Harris, T., Fraser, K.: Language support for lightweight transactions. In: OOPSLA 2003. Proceedings of the 18th ACM SIGPLAN conference on Object-oriented programing, systems, languages, and applications, pp. 388–402. ACM Press, New York (2003)
10. Harris, T., Marlow, S., Peyton-Jones, S., Herlihy, M.: Composable memory transactions. In: PPoPP 2005. Proceedings of the 10th ACM SIGPLAN symposium on Principles and practice of parallel programming, pp. 48–60. ACM Press, New York (2005)
11. Harris, T., Plesko, M., Shinnar, A., Tarditi, D.: Optimizing memory transactions. In: PLDI 2006. Proceedings of the 2006 ACM SIGPLAN conference on Programming language design and implementation, pp. 14–25. ACM Press, New York (2006)
12. Herlihy, M., Koskinen, E.: Transactional boosting: A methodology for highly-concurrent transactional objects. Technical Report CS-07-08, Brown University (July 2007)
13. Herlihy, M., Luchangco, V., Moir, M.: A flexible framework for implementing software transactional memory. In: OOPSLA, pp. 253–262 (2006)
14. Herlihy, M., Luchangco, V., Moir, M., Scherer III, W.N.: Software transactional memory for dynamic-sized data structures. In: PODC 2003. Proceedings of the 22nd annual symposium on Principles of distributed computing, pp. 92–101. ACM Press, New York (2003)
15. Luchangco, V., Moir, M., Shavit, N.: Nonblocking k-compare-single-swap. In: SPAA 2003. Proceedings of the fifteenth annual ACM symposium on Parallel algorithms and architectures, pp. 314–323. ACM Press, New York (2003)

16. Marathe, V.J., Spear, M.F., Heriot, C., Acharya, A., Eisenstat, D., Scherer III, W.N., Scott, M.L.: Lowering the overhead of software transactional memory. In: ACM SIGPLAN Workshop on Transactional Computing (June 2006) Held in conjunction with PLDI 2006. Expanded version available as TR 893, Department of Computer Science, University of Rochester (March 2006)
17. Martin, M., Blundell, C., Lewis, E.: Subtleties of transactional memory atomicity semantics. IEEE Computer Architecture Letters 5(2) (2006)
18. Ni, Y., Menon, V.S., Adl-Tabatabai, A.-R., Hosking, A.L., Hudson, R.L., Eliot, J., Moss, B., Saha, B., Shpeisman, T.: Open nesting in software transactional memory. In: PPoPP 2007. Proceedings of the 12th ACM SIGPLAN symposium on Principles and practice of parallel programming, pp. 68–78. ACM Press, New York (2007)
19. Saha, B., Adl-Tabatabai, A.-R., Hudson, R., Minh, C.C., Hertzberg, B.: Mcrt-stm: A high performance software transactional memory system for a multi-core runtime. In: PPoPP (2006)
20. Spear, M.F., Marathe, V.J., Dalessandro, L., Scott, M.L.: Privatization techniques for software transactional memory. In: Proceedings of the 26th PODC ACM Symposium on Principles of Distributed Computing (August 2007)
21. http://research.microsoft.com/research/downloads/Details/6cfc842d-1c16-4739-afaf-edb35f544384/Details.aspx
22. VanDrunen, T., Hosking, A.L.: Anticipation-based partial redundancy elimination for static single assignment form. Software: Practice and Experience 34, 1413–1439 (2004)

Unifying Denotational Semantics with Operational Semantics for Web Services*

Huibiao Zhu, Jifeng He, and Jing Li

Software Engineering Institute, East China Normal University
3663 Zhongshan Road (North), Shanghai, China
{hbzhu,jifeng,jli}@sei.ecnu.edu.cn

Abstract. Web Services have become more and more important in these years, and BPEL4WS (BPEL) is a de facto standard for the web service composition and orchestration. It contains several distinct features, including the scope-based compensation and fault handling mechanism.

The denotational semantics and operational semantics have been explored for BPEL. The two approaches should be consistent. This paper considers the unifying of these two semantics. Our approach is to derive the denotational semantics from operational semantics for BPEL, which aims for the consistency of the two models. Moreover, the derivation can be applied in exploring the program equivalence easily, especially for parallel programs.

1   Introduction

Web services and other web-based applications have been becoming more and more important in practice. In this blooming field, various web-based business process languages have been introduced, such as XLANG, WSFL, BPEL4WS (BPEL) and StAC [8,6,2,1], which are designed for the description of services composed by a set of processes across the Internet. The important feature of BPEL is that it supports the long-running interactions involving two or more parties. Therefore, it provides the ability to define fault and compensation handing in application-specific manner, resulting in a feature called *Long-Running (Business) Transactions (LRTs)*. BPEL provides two kinds of synchronization techniques. In our model, shared-labels are introduced for the synchronization between a process and its partners within a single service, while channel communications are introduced for message transmission between different services.

Three different styles of mathematical representation are normally used for a programming language: operational, denotational and algebraic one [7,5,4]. Moreover, the unifying theories [9] between different semantic models for a language are particularly interesting, which can provide the correct understanding for one semantics based on the viewpoint of another. For BPEL, the denotational semantics [3] and operational semantics [10] have already been explored. This paper considers the derivation of denotational semantics from operational semantics, which aims at the consistency of these two semantic models.

---

* Partially supported by National Basic Research Program of China (No. 2005CB321904) and Shanghai STCSM project (No. 06JC14058).

T. Janowski and H. Mohanty (Eds.): ICDCIT 2007, LNCS 4882, pp. 225–239, 2007.
© Springer-Verlag Berlin Heidelberg 2007

The remainder of this paper is organised as follows. Section 2 introduces the language BPEL and proposes the denotational semantic model. Program states are classified into five types. Section 3 explores the strategy of deriving denotational semantics from operational semantics for BPEL. The concepts of transition condition and phase semantics are introduced. Based on this strategy, section 4 is to derive the denotational semantics from operational semantics for every statement of BPEL. The derived denotational semantics gives us confidence for the consistency of these two semantic models.

2   The Denotational Semantic Model

2.1   The Syntax of BPEL

We have proposed a BPEL-like language, which contains several interesting features, such as scope-based compensation and fault handling mechanism. Our language contains the following categories of syntactic elements:

$$BA ::= \mathtt{skip} \mid x := e \mid \mathtt{rec}\ a\ x \mid \mathtt{rep}\ a\ x \mid \mathtt{throw}$$

$$A\ ::= BA \mid g \circ A \mid b \triangleright l \mid A; A \mid A \triangleleft b \triangleright A \mid b * A \mid A \parallel A$$
$$\mid A \sqcap A \mid \mathtt{undo} \mid \{A\,?\,A, A\}$$

where:

- $x := e$ assigns the value of e to local variable x. skip behaves the same as $x := x$. Activity throw indicates that the program encounters a fault immediately. In order to implement the communications between different services, two statements are introduced; i.e., rec $a\ x$ and rep $a\ x$. Command rec $a\ x$ represents the receiving of a value through channel a, where rep $a\ x$ represents the output of value of x via channel a.
- Several constructs are similar to those in traditional programming languages. $A; B$ stands for sequential composition. $A \triangleleft b \triangleright B$ is the conditional construct and $b * A$ is the iteration construct. $A \sqcap B$ stands for the nondeterministic choice.
- Shared-labels are introduced to implement the synchronization between a process and its partner. $g \circ A$ awaits the Boolean guard g to be set true, where g is composed of a set of source links; i.e., a set of read only shared-labels. $b \triangleright l$ assigns the value of b to label l.
- $\{A\,?\,C, F\}$ stands for the scope-based compensation statement, where A, C and F stand for the primary activity, compensation program and fault handler correspondingly. If A terminates successfully, program C is installed in the compensation list for later compensating. On the other hand, if A encounters a fault during its execution, the fault handler F will be activated. Further, the compensation part C does not contain scope activity. On the other hand, statement "undo" activates the execution of the programs in the compensation list under the reverse order of their installed sequence.
- $A \parallel B$ stands for the parallel composition. Its local variable set is the union of the corresponding sets for the two components. For a shared label, it can

be owned by one parallel component; i.e., it can only be written by one parallel component.

For exploring the parallel expansion laws, our language is enriched with the concept of guarded choice, expressed in the form:

$$\{h_1 \rightarrow P_1\} [\!] \ldots \ldots [\!] \{h_n \rightarrow P_n\}$$

where, (1) h_i can be a skip guard, expressed as $b_i \& \text{skip}$, where b_i is a Boolean expression and satisfies the condition "$\vee_i b_i = true$". (2) h_i can also be a communication guard, expressed as rec a x and rep a x. (3) h_i can also be a Boolean guard $@(g_i)$; i.e, waiting for g_i to be fired.

2.2   Denotational Semantic Model for BPEL

This section considers the denotational semantic model for BPEL. Our approach is based on the relational calculus [5]. In order to represent the execution state of a program, we introduce a variable st in our semantic model. A program may have five execution states: (1) *divergent state*, (2) *completed state*, (3) *waiting state*, (4) *error state*, (5) *undo state*. The first three states are similar to those in reactive systems. For "*error state*", a program may encounter a fault during its execution, where compensation may be executed via fault handling. Further, "*undo state*" is introduced to distinguish the termination of a process itself and the termination of the execution of compensating programs.

  For a parallel process, messages can be transformed from one service to another. A Boolean guard can be fired by the update of its associated links. For considering these two mechanisms in parallel composition, a trace variable tr is introduced, whose elements have two forms: (1) the message transmission between different services; (2) the update of the shared-labels. For the message transmission, the element recorded in the trace variable can be expressed in the form $a.m$. Here, a is the channel name where communication may go through and m is the message for transmitting. For the update of a shared-label, the associated element recorded in the trace variable can be expressed as a snapshot in the form "$l : (\overleftarrow{l}, \overrightarrow{l})$", where l is the label name. Here $\overleftarrow{l}$ and $\overrightarrow{l}$ stand for the initial and final values of label l respectively.

  Further we introduce a variable $Cpens$ in our model, which records a sequence of programs in the form of *stack* (i.e., first installing last compensating). For channel communication, we apply set type variable ref in our semantic model, which indicates that the elements in the set are refused by the process currently.

  As in relational calculus, for any variable x in our model (e.g., st, tr, $Cpens$ and ref), we use $\overleftarrow{x}$ to represent the initial value of variable x before activation and $\overrightarrow{x}$ to represent the final value of variable x during the current observation.

  Next we give the definition for $\mathcal{H}$-function, which can be used in defining the denotational semantics for BPEL programs.

$$\mathcal{H}(X) =_{df} (X \wedge R1 \; ; \; I\!I\!I) \lhd \overleftarrow{st} = completed \rhd (R1 \lhd \overleftarrow{st} = div \rhd I\!I\!I)$$

where:

(1) $P \lhd b \rhd Q =_{df} b \wedge P \vee \neg b \wedge Q$
(2) $R1 = \overleftarrow{tr} \preceq \overrightarrow{tr}$. Here, $s \preceq t$ denotes that sequence s is a prefix of sequence t.
(3) $III =_{df} (\overleftarrow{st} = div \Rightarrow R1) \wedge (\overleftarrow{st} \neq div \Rightarrow Id)$. Here Id is the identity relation.

Next we explore the refinement calculus for the BPEL semantic model. Let

$$F(X_1, X_2, X_3, X_4, X_5)$$
$$= \mathcal{H} \left(\begin{matrix} \overrightarrow{st} = div \wedge X_1 \ \vee \ \overrightarrow{st} = wait \wedge X_2 \ \vee \ \overrightarrow{st} = error \wedge X_3 \ \vee \\ \overrightarrow{st} = undo \wedge X_4 \ \vee \ \overrightarrow{st} = completed \wedge X_5 \end{matrix} \right)$$

For formula $F(X_1, X_2, X_3, X_4, X_5)$, X_1 stands for the divergent behavior and X_2 stands for the waiting behaviour. X_3 stands for the behaviour when the process encounters a fault and X_4 stands for the behaviour that the process is at the undo state. Moreover, X_5 is the terminating behaviour for the process. Now we can have a theorem about the refinement calculus.

Theorem 2.1

(1) $F(X_1, X_2, X_3, X_4, X_5) \ ; \ F(Y_1, Y_2, Y_3, Y_4, Y_5)$
  $= F(X_1 \vee (X_5; Y_1), \ X_2 \vee (X_5; Y_2), \ X_3 \vee (X_5; Y_3), \ X_4 \vee (X_5; Y_4), \ X_5; Y_5)$
(2) $F(X_1, X_2, X_3, X_4, X_5) \ \vee \ F(Y_1, Y_2, Y_3, Y_4, Y_5)$
  $= F(X_1 \vee Y_1, \ X_2 \vee Y_2, \ X_3 \vee Y_3, \ X_4 \vee Y_4, \ X_5 \vee Y_5)$
(3) $F(X_1, X_2, X_3, X_4, X_5) \ \wedge \ F(Y_1, Y_2, Y_3, Y_4, Y_5)$
  $= F(X_1 \wedge Y_1, \ (X_1 \vee X_2) \wedge (Y_1 \vee Y_2), \ (X_1 \vee X_3) \wedge (Y_1 \vee Y_3),$
      $(X_1 \vee X_4) \wedge (Y_1 \vee Y_4), \ (X_1 \vee X_5) \wedge (Y_1 \vee Y_5))$
(4) $F(X_1, X_2, X_3, X_4, X_5) \lhd b \rhd F(Y_1, Y_2, Y_3, Y_4, Y_5)$
  $= F(X_1 \lhd b \rhd Y_1, \ X_2 \lhd b \rhd Y_2, \ X_3 \lhd b \rhd Y_3, \ X_4 \lhd b \rhd Y_4, \ X_5 \lhd b \rhd Y_5)$ □

This theorem can help us in reasoning about program equivalence, especially in deriving the denotational semantics from operational semantics for BPEL.

3   Strategy for Deriving Denotational Semantics from Operational Semantics for BPEL

3.1   Operational Model for BPEL

For the operational semantics of BPEL, its transitions are written in a special notation SOS (Structural Operational Semantics) [7], which are of the five types:

$$C \xrightarrow{\tau} C' \quad or \quad C \longrightarrow C' \quad or \quad C \xrightarrow{v} C' \quad or$$
$$C \xrightarrow{a.m}_{\alpha} C' \quad or \quad C \xrightarrow{e}_A C'$$

where C and C' are the configurations describing the states of an execution mechanism before and after a step respectively. The first type models a process does the nondeterministic selection. The second type is mainly used to model the assignment of a local variable, whereas the third type models the update of a shared-label.

The fourth type is used to model the message communication between different services through channel a, where m stands for the message for communication. Here, the subscript α can be r or s. $\xrightarrow{a.m}_r$ stands for the message receiving transition, and $\xrightarrow{a.m}_s$ stands for the message sending transition. If there are no subscripts for message communication transition, it means that the parallel process completes the transition; i.e., the sending and receiving commands are two components of the parallel process. The fifth transition stands for the case that the environment performs the updates of shared-variables, while the channels in set A are ready for communication.

The configuration can be expressed as $\langle P,\ \sigma,\ L,\ Cpens \rangle$. The first component P is a program that remains to be executed. The second element σ is the state for all local variables. The third element L stands for the state for all labels. The fourth element $Cpens$ stands for a compensation list; i.e., a sequence of programs to be executed as compensation.

Regarding the program P in configuration $\langle P,\ \sigma,\ L,\ Cpens \rangle$, it can either be a normal program. Further, it can also be one of the following special forms:

Π : A program completes all its execution and terminates successfully. Π is used to represent the empty program.

$\boxtimes$: A program may encounter a fault and stops at the fault state. $\boxtimes$ is used to represent the fault state.

$\boxminus$: The installed compensation programs for the current process can be activated for execution. After the termination of the compensating programs, the control will not be passed to the subsequent activity of the current process. This is the difference between the termination of the compensating programs and the termination of the current process. We use $\boxminus$ to represent the *undo* state; i.e., the terminating state for the execution of programs in the compensation list of the current process.

3.2 Transition Condition and Phase Semantics for Operational Semantics

For the aim of unifying the operational semantics and denotational semantics for BPEL, we define a transition condition for each type of transition. Based on this, the concept of phase semantics will be defined, which is the denotational view of the transitions of operational semantics.

Firstly we introduce the alphabet for command c, which is denoted as:

$$(\mathbf{Var}(c),\ \mathbf{SLink}(c),\ \mathbf{TLink}(c))$$

where: (1) $\mathbf{Var}(c)$ is the set of local variables owned by c. (2) $\mathbf{SLink}(c)$ stands for the set of links which can only be read by c; i.e., the set containing all the source links of command c. (3) $\mathbf{TLink}(c)$ represents the set of links which can only be updated by c; i.e., the set containing all the target links of command c. Sometimes, without causing confusions, $\mathbf{Var}(c)$, $\mathbf{SLink}(c)$ and $\mathbf{TLink}(c)$ are simply written as $\mathbf{Var}$, $\mathbf{SLink}$ and $\mathbf{TLink}$ for command c respectively.

Further, we use $\mathbf{Comm}(C)$ to record all the snapshots which stand for the update of all the links in set C; i.e., $\mathbf{Comm}(C) =_{df} \{l : (e_1, e_2) \mid l \in C\}$. Next we give some preliminary definitions.

(1) $Rec\_Comm =_{df} \exists t \in \mathbf{Comm(SLink)}^* \bullet \overrightarrow{tr} = \overleftarrow{tr}\frown t$

(2) $same(A) =_{df} \bigwedge_{x \in A} \overrightarrow{x} = \overleftarrow{x}$

(3) $VTC =_{df} \mathbf{Var} \cup \mathbf{TLink} \cup \{Cpens\}$

Formula Rec_Comm indicates that the source links of the process may receive updates from other parallel components. These updates are recorded in the trace variable. Formula $same(A)$ indicates that all variables in set A remain unchanged during the execution of the program. Further, VTC stands for the set of the union of all local variables, target links of a process, together with the denotational variable $Cpens$.

Now we start to explore the transition condition and phase semantics for each type of transition.

(1) Non-communication transition
   (a) Local variable assignment

   $\langle P, \sigma, L, Cpens \rangle \longrightarrow \langle P', \sigma[e/x], L, Cpens \rangle$

   The corresponding transition should record the assignment of local variable x, while leaving other variables unchanged.

   $Cond_1 =_{df} \overrightarrow{x} = e \wedge \overrightarrow{tr} = \overleftarrow{tr} \wedge same(VTC \setminus \{x\})$

   (b) Shared-label update

   $\langle P, \sigma, L, Cpens \rangle \xrightarrow{v} \langle P', \sigma, L[b/l], Cpens \rangle$

   Similarly, the corresponding transition condition only makes the update of shared-labels.

   $Cond_2 =_{df} \overrightarrow{l} = b \wedge \overrightarrow{tr} = \overleftarrow{tr} \wedge same(VTC \setminus \{l\})$

   (c) Compensation program recording

   $\langle P, \sigma, L, Cpens \rangle \longrightarrow \langle P', \sigma, L, Cpens\frown\langle C \rangle \rangle$

   Its transition condition needs to record the compensation program C at the end of the compensation list $Cpens$.

   $Cond_3 =_{df} record(C) \wedge \overrightarrow{tr} = \overleftarrow{tr} \wedge same(VTC \setminus \{Cpens\})$

   where,

   $$record(C) =_{df} \left(\begin{array}{l} (O(C) \Rightarrow O(\mathtt{skip})) \Rightarrow \overrightarrow{Cpens} = \overleftarrow{Cpens} \\ \neg(O(C) \Rightarrow O(\mathtt{skip})) \Rightarrow \exists p \bullet \left(\begin{array}{l} (O(p) \Rightarrow O(C)) \wedge \\ \overrightarrow{Cpens} = \overleftarrow{Cpens}\frown\langle p \rangle \end{array} \right) \end{array} \right)$$

   Here, $O(p)$ stands for the derived denotational semantics for program p (see page 232 for the definition).

   On the other hand, we also have the transition for making the last recorded process in the compensation list ready to execute.

   $\langle P, \sigma, L, Cpens\frown\langle C \rangle \rangle \longrightarrow \langle P', \sigma, L, Cpens \rangle$

   Its transition condition can be expressed as:

   $\overrightarrow{Cpens} = \mathbf{front}(\overleftarrow{Cpens}) \wedge \overrightarrow{tr} = \overleftarrow{tr} \wedge same(VTC \setminus \{Cpens\})$

   Here, $\mathbf{front}(s)$ stands for all but the final element of sequence s.

Besides the above three non-communication transitions, there remains another transition; i.e., non-deterministic choice transition. Its transition condition is just $same(VTC \cup \{tr\})$.

For the above types of non-communication transitions, we can define its phase semantics as below.

If $\langle P, \sigma, L, Cpens \rangle \xrightarrow{\beta} \langle P', \sigma', L', Cpens' \rangle$, then the corresponding phase semantics can be defined as below.

$$phase_i =_{df} \mathcal{H}(\overrightarrow{st} = state(P') \wedge Cond_i), \quad i = 1, 2, 3$$

where,

$$state(X) =_{df} \begin{cases} error & \text{if } X = \boxtimes \\ undo & \text{if } X = \boxminus \\ completed & \text{otherwise} \end{cases}$$

(2) Communication transition

(d) Message sending

$$\langle P, \sigma, L, Cpens \rangle \xrightarrow{a.m}_s \langle P', \sigma, L, Cpens \rangle$$

The transition condition needs to record the sent message at the end of the trace variable tr, while leaving other variables unchanged.

$$Cond_4 =_{df} \overrightarrow{tr} = \overleftarrow{tr}^{\frown}\langle a.m \rangle \wedge same(VTC)$$

(e) Message receiving

$$\langle P, \sigma, L, Cpens \rangle \xrightarrow{a.m}_r \langle P', \sigma[m/u], L, Cpens \rangle$$

The corresponding transition condition needs to model the process receiving a message via the channel.

$$Cond_5 =_{df} \exists m \in \mathbf{Type}(a) \bullet \overrightarrow{u} = m \wedge \overrightarrow{tr} = \overleftarrow{tr}^{\frown}\langle a.m \rangle \wedge same(VTC \backslash \{u\})$$

Below is the communication transition whose sending and receiving parts are two components of a parallel process.

$$\langle P, \sigma, L, Cpens \rangle \xrightarrow{a.m} \langle P', \sigma[m/u], L, Cpens \rangle$$

Its transition condition can be described as below:

$$\overrightarrow{u} = m \wedge \overrightarrow{tr} = \overleftarrow{tr}^{\frown}\langle a.m \rangle \wedge same(VTC \backslash \{u\})$$

For the above communication transitions, their phase semantics can be defined as:

$$phase_i =_{df} \mathcal{H}(\overrightarrow{st} = state(P') \wedge Cond_i), \quad i = 4, 5$$

where, $Cond_i$ is the transition condition of the corresponding transition.

(3) (f) Environment label update

$$\langle P, \sigma, L, Cpens \rangle \xrightarrow{e}_A \langle P', \sigma, L', Cpens \rangle$$

Environment can perform the update of shared-labels. A snapshot needs to be appended at the end of the trace variable tr. Further, if the current command is channel communication related, the channel should be ready for communication.

$$Cond_6 =_{df} \left(\begin{array}{c} \exists s \in \mathbf{Comm}(\mathbf{SLink}) \bullet \overrightarrow{tr} = \overleftarrow{tr}^{\frown}s \wedge \\ same(VTC) \wedge (\forall x \in A \bullet x \notin \overrightarrow{Ref}) \end{array} \right)$$

If the environment performs the update of a shared-variable, the current process can observe it and the transition completes. However, if the current process is channel communication related, before the current transition takes place, the current process is in the waiting state. Below is its phase semantics.

$$phase_6 =_{df} \mathcal{H} \begin{pmatrix} (Cond_6 \wedge \overrightarrow{st} = completed) \vee \\ (A \neq \emptyset \wedge same(VTC \cup \{tr\}) \wedge \\ (\forall x \in A \bullet x \notin \overrightarrow{Ref}) \wedge \overrightarrow{st} = wait) \end{pmatrix}$$

3.3 Strategy for Deriving Denotational Semantics from Operational Semantics for BPEL

This section aims to provide the strategy of deriving the denotational semantics from operational semantics for BPEL. Our approach only limits to finite programs. Firstly we introduce the concept of computation sequence. It is crucial in deriving the denotational semantics from operational semantics.

Definition 3.1. $C_0 \xrightarrow{\beta_0} C_1 \cdots\cdots \xrightarrow{\beta_n} C_n$ is a computation sequence, where $n \geq 1$. □

Next we introduce the semantics for a computation sequence, which can assist the derivation of denotational semantics from operational semantics.

Definition 3.2. Let seq stand for a computational sequence. Its semantics can be defined as:

$$sem(seq) =_{df} sem(seq[1]) ; \cdots\cdots ; sem(seq[n])$$

where, (1) $seq[i]$ stands for the i-th transition of computation sequence seq. (2) $sem(seq[i])$ stands for the phase semantics of the i-th transition of computation sequence seq. □

Now we give the definition of the strategy for deriving denotational semantics from operational semantics. We use $O(P)$ to stand for the derived denotational semantics from operational semantics for program P. Let $cp[P]$ stand for the set containing all the computational sequences leading program P to the *terminating* state, *error* state, or *undo* state.

Definition 3.3. (Derivation Strategy)

$$O(P) =_{df} \bigvee_{seq \in cp[P]} sem(seq) \qquad \square$$

Further, we classify the computation sequence into three classes, the set containing the computation sequences leading a program to the terminating state, undo state and error state respectively.

- $cp[P]_{ter}$ is the set containing all the computation sequences leading program P to the terminating state.
- $cp[P]_{undo}$ is the set containing all the computation sequences leading program P to the undo state.

- $cp[P]_{err}$ is the set containing all the computation sequences leading program P to the error state.

Based on these notations, we can have an alternative way to calculate the denotational semantics from operational semantics.

$$O(P) = \bigvee_{seq \in cp[P]_{ter}} sem(seq) \vee \bigvee_{seq \in cp[P]_{undo}} sem(seq) \vee$$
$$\bigvee_{seq \in cp[P]_{err}} sem(seq)$$

Now we consider the calculation of the semantics of computation sequences. Let $L1(i)$ stands for the notation:

$$C_0 \xrightarrow{e}_\emptyset C_1 \cdots\cdots \xrightarrow{e}_\emptyset C_i$$

$L1(i)$ stands for the computation sequence which performs the update of source links i times by the environment, and channels do not involve in these transitions. Then we can have the corresponding semantics of this type of computation sequences.

Theorem 3.4

$$\bigvee_{i \geq 0} sem(L1(i)) = \mathcal{H}(\overrightarrow{st} = completed \wedge Rec\_Comm \wedge same(VTC)) \qquad \square$$

Further, we introduce a new type of computation sequence $L2(i, A)$, where A is a nonempty set.

$$C_0 \xrightarrow{e}_A C_1 \cdots\cdots \xrightarrow{e}_A C_i$$

$L2(i, A)$ not only stands for the computation sequence which performs the update of source links i times by the environment, but also indicates that all channels in A are ready for communication. We can also have a theorem for calculating the semantics of this type of computation sequence.

Theorem 3.5

$$\bigvee_{i \geq 0} sem(L2(i, A)) = \mathcal{H}\left(\begin{array}{c} Rec\_Comm \wedge same(VTC) \wedge (\forall x \in A \bullet x \notin \overrightarrow{Ref}) \\ \wedge (\overrightarrow{st} = completed \vee \overrightarrow{st} = wait) \end{array} \right)$$
$$\square$$

From the definition of phase semantics, we know that the phase semantics of a computation sequence normally does not depend on the processes in the configuration. It only depends on the other elements of configurations in the computation sequence. Therefore, we have the following lemma.

Lemma 3.6

Let $seq1 : \langle P, \alpha \rangle \xrightarrow{\beta_1} \langle P_1, \alpha_1 \rangle \cdots\cdots \xrightarrow{\beta_n} \langle P_n, \alpha_n \rangle$,

$seq2 : \langle Q, \alpha \rangle \xrightarrow{\beta_1} \langle Q_1, \alpha_1 \rangle \cdots\cdots \xrightarrow{\beta_n} \langle Q_n, \alpha_n \rangle$.

(1) If $P_n \neq \boxtimes, \boxminus$ and $Q_n \neq \boxtimes, \boxminus$, then $sem(seq1) = sem(seq2)$.

(2) If $P_n = Q_n = \boxtimes$ or $P_n = Q_n = \boxminus$, then $sem(seq1) = sem(seq2)$. $\qquad \square$

4 Deriving Denotational Semantics from Operational Semantics for BPEL by Strict Proof

In this section we will derive the denotational semantics for every BPEL statement by strict proof. Therefore our denotational semantics is considered as consistent to the corresponding operational semantics.

4.1 Basic Commands

The execution of $x := e$ assigns the value of expression e to variable x, and leaves other variables unchanged. Furthermore, before the execution of assignment, the environment can make the contribution of the update of source links.

$$\langle x := e, \sigma, L, Cpens \rangle \longrightarrow \langle \Pi, \sigma[e/x], L, Cpens \rangle$$
$$\langle x := e, \sigma, L, Cpens \rangle \xrightarrow{e}_\emptyset \langle x := e, \sigma, L', Cpens \rangle$$

Theorem 4.1

$$O(x := e) = \mathcal{H} \left(\begin{array}{c} \overrightarrow{st} = completed \wedge Rec\_Comm \wedge \\ \overrightarrow{x} = \overleftarrow{e} \wedge \bigwedge_{y \in VTC \setminus \{x\}} \overrightarrow{y} = \overleftarrow{y} \end{array} \right)$$

Proof. Let $seq(i)$ be the computation sequence below:

$$\langle x := e, \sigma, L, Cpens \rangle \quad \xrightarrow{e}_\emptyset \quad \langle x := e, \sigma, L_1, Cpens \rangle$$
$$\cdots \qquad\qquad \cdots$$
$$\xrightarrow{e}_\emptyset \quad \langle x := e, \sigma, L_i, Cpens \rangle$$
$$\longrightarrow \quad \langle \Pi, \sigma[e/x], L_i, Cpens \rangle$$

The phase semantics of the last transition can be described as formula X, where:

$$X = \mathcal{H}(\overrightarrow{st} = completed \wedge \overrightarrow{x} = e \wedge same(\{tr\} \cup (VTC \setminus \{x\})))$$

Therefore, we have:

$$\begin{array}{lll} & LHS & \{\text{Derivation Strategy}\} \\ = & \bigvee_{i \geq 0} sem(seq(i)) & \{\text{Above Analysis, PL}\} \\ = & (\bigvee_{i \geq 0} sem(L1(i))) \ ; \ X & \{\text{Th 3.4}\} \\ = & RHS & \qquad\qquad\qquad\quad \square \end{array}$$

For communication commands, statement "**rec** a x" receives message m through channel a.

$$\langle \textbf{rec a x}, \sigma, L, Cpens \rangle \xrightarrow{a.m}_r \langle \Pi, \sigma[m/x], L, Cpens \rangle,$$
$$\langle \textbf{rec a x}, \sigma, L, Cpens \rangle \xrightarrow{e}_{\{a\}} \langle \textbf{rec a x}, \sigma, L', Cpens \rangle,$$

Theorem 4.2

$$O(\textbf{rec a x}) = \mathcal{H} \left(\begin{array}{l} \overrightarrow{st} = wait \wedge Rec\_Comm \wedge same(VTC) \wedge a \notin \overrightarrow{ref} \quad \vee \\ \overrightarrow{st} = completed \wedge same(\textbf{VTC} \setminus \{x\}) \wedge \\ \exists s \in \textbf{Comm}(\textbf{SLink})^*, \exists m \in \textbf{Type}(a) \bullet \\ \quad (\overrightarrow{x} = m \wedge \overrightarrow{tr} = \overleftarrow{tr}\hat{\ }s\hat{\ }\langle a.m \rangle) \end{array} \right)$$

Proof. Let $seq(i)$ be the computation sequence below:

$$\langle \mathbf{rac}\ a\ x, \sigma, L, Cpens \rangle \quad \xrightarrow{e}_{\{a\}} \quad \langle \mathbf{rac}\ a\ x, \sigma, L_1, Cpens \rangle$$

$$\cdots \qquad\qquad \cdots$$

$$\xrightarrow{e}_{\{a\}} \quad \langle \mathbf{rac}\ a\ x, \sigma, L_i, Cpens \rangle$$

$$\xrightarrow{a.m}_r \quad \langle \Pi, \sigma[m/x], L_i, Cpens \rangle$$

The phase semantics of the last transition can be described as formula Y, where:

$$Y = \mathcal{H} \left(\begin{array}{l} \overrightarrow{st} = completed \wedge \bigwedge_{z \in VTC \setminus \{x\}} \overrightarrow{z} = \overleftarrow{z} \wedge \\ \exists m \in \mathbf{Type}(a) \bullet \overrightarrow{x} = m \wedge \overrightarrow{tr} = \overleftarrow{tr}^\frown \langle a.m \rangle \end{array} \right)$$

Therefore, we have:

$$
\begin{array}{lll}
LHS & & \{\text{Derivation Strategy}\} \\
= \bigvee_{i \geq 0} sem(seq(i)) & & \{\text{Above Analysis, PL}\} \\
= (\bigvee_{i \geq 0} sem(L2(i, \{a\}))) \ ; \ Y & & \{\text{Th 3.5, PL}\} \\
= RHS & & \qquad\qquad \square
\end{array}
$$

Similarly, the denotational semantics for the shared-label update "$b \triangleright l$" and the sending command of channel communication "$\mathbf{rep}\ a\ x$" can also be derived. Moreover, for sequential composition, nondeterministic choice, conditional choice, Boolean guard and guarded choice, we can also derive the corresponding denotational semantics [3] based on their operational semantics [10].

4.2 Compensation

$\mathbf{throw}$ encounters a fault immediately after activation, while leaving all variables and the compensation list unchanged.

$$\langle \mathbf{throw}, \sigma, L, Cpens \rangle \longrightarrow \langle \boxtimes, \sigma, L, Cpens \rangle$$

$$\langle \mathbf{throw}, \sigma, L, Cpens \rangle \xrightarrow{e}_{\emptyset} \langle \mathbf{throw}, \sigma, L', Cpens \rangle$$

Theorem 4.3

$$O(\mathbf{throw}) =_{df} \mathcal{H}(\overrightarrow{st} = error \ \wedge \ Rec\_Comm \ \wedge \ same(\mathbf{VTC}))$$

Proof. Let $seq(i)$ be the computation sequence shown below:

$$\langle \mathbf{throw}, \sigma, L, Cpens \rangle \quad \xrightarrow{e}_{\emptyset} \quad \langle \mathbf{throw}, \sigma, L_1, Cpens \rangle$$

$$\cdots \qquad\qquad \cdots$$

$$\xrightarrow{e}_{\emptyset} \quad \langle \mathbf{throw}, \sigma, L_i, Cpens \rangle$$

$$\longrightarrow \quad \langle \boxtimes, \sigma, L_i, Cpens \rangle$$

The phase semantics of the last transition can be described as formula X, where:

$$X = \mathcal{H}(\overrightarrow{st} = error \ \wedge \ same(VTC \cup \{tr\}))$$

Similar to the proof of assignment, together with the help of predicate calculus, we can achieve the denotational semantics for $\mathbf{throw}$. $\square$

Statement $\mathbf{undo}$ activates the execution of compensating programs. The execution sequence is in the reverse order of the installed sequence. Its transition rules are shown below.

$$\langle \mathbf{undo}, \sigma, L, Cpens \rangle \longrightarrow \langle X; \mathbf{undo}, \sigma, L, Y \rangle,$$

$$\langle \mathbf{undo}, \sigma, L, \varepsilon \rangle \longrightarrow \langle \boxminus, \sigma, L, \varepsilon \rangle \quad \text{and} \quad \langle \mathbf{undo}, \sigma, L, \varepsilon \rangle \xrightarrow{e}_{\emptyset} \langle \mathbf{undo}, \sigma, L', \varepsilon \rangle,$$

Here, $X = \mathbf{final}(Cpens)$ and $Y = \mathbf{front}(Cpens)$. $\mathbf{final}(s)$ stands for the last element of sequence s.

Now we consider the derivation of denotational semantics for undo. For simplicity, here we assume $Cpens = \langle X \rangle \widehat{\ } \langle Y \rangle$ and both X and Y terminates successfully. Firstly we consider the following three computation sequences.

Let $\quad seq1 : \langle Y, \sigma, L, \varepsilon \rangle \xrightarrow{\beta_1} \cdots\cdots \xrightarrow{\beta_1} \langle II, \sigma', L', \varepsilon \rangle,$

$\quad\quad seq2 : \langle X, \sigma', L', \varepsilon \rangle \xrightarrow{\gamma_1} \cdots\cdots \xrightarrow{\gamma_1} \langle II, \sigma'', L'', \varepsilon \rangle,$

Then, $seq3$ is a computation sequence for undo shown below.

$$seq3 : \langle \mathbf{undo}, \sigma, L, Cpens \rangle \longrightarrow \langle Y; \mathbf{undo}, \sigma, L, X \rangle \tag{1}$$

$$\xrightarrow{\beta_1} \cdots\cdots \xrightarrow{\beta_n} \langle \mathbf{undo}, \sigma', L', X \rangle \tag{2}$$

$$\longrightarrow \langle X; \mathbf{undo}, \sigma', L', \varepsilon \rangle \tag{3}$$

$$\xrightarrow{\gamma_1} \cdots\cdots \xrightarrow{\gamma_m} \langle \mathbf{undo}, \sigma'', L'', \varepsilon \rangle \tag{4}$$

$$\xrightarrow{e}_{\emptyset} \cdots\cdots \xrightarrow{e}_{\emptyset} \langle \mathbf{undo}, \sigma'', L''', \varepsilon \rangle \tag{5}$$

$$\longrightarrow \langle \boxminus, \sigma'', L''', \varepsilon \rangle \tag{6}$$

The phase semantics of transition (1) can be described as:

$$\mathcal{H}(\overrightarrow{st} = completed \wedge same(\{tr\} \cup (VTC \setminus \{Cpens\})) \wedge \overrightarrow{Cpens} = \mathbf{front}(\overleftarrow{Cpens}))$$

The phase semantics of computation sequence (2) is the same as $sem(seq1)$.

Moreover, the phase semantics of transition (3) can be described as:

$$\mathcal{H}(\overrightarrow{st} = completed \wedge same(\{tr\} \cup (VTC \setminus \{Cpens\})) \wedge \overrightarrow{Cpens} = \varepsilon)$$

On the other hand, the phase semantics of computation sequence (4) is the same as $sem(seq2)$. Meanwhile, the phase semantics of computation sequence (5) and (6) can be described as below respectively.

$$\mathcal{H}(\overrightarrow{st} = completed \wedge Rec\_Comm \wedge same(VTC)),$$
$$\mathcal{H}(\overrightarrow{st} = undo \wedge \overrightarrow{tr} = \overleftarrow{tr} \wedge same(VTC))$$

Based on the above analysis, we can achieve the denotational semantics for undo shown as below.

Theorem 4.4 $\quad O(\mathbf{undo}) = \mathbf{exec}(\overleftarrow{Cpens})$, where

$$\mathbf{exec}(\overleftarrow{Cpens}) =_{df} \overleftarrow{Cpens} = \varepsilon \Rightarrow \mathcal{H}(\overrightarrow{st} = undo \wedge Rec\_Comm \wedge same(VTC)) \wedge$$
$$\overleftarrow{Cpens} \neq \varepsilon \Rightarrow O(\mathbf{final}(\overleftarrow{Cpens})) ; \mathbf{exec}(\mathbf{front}(\overleftarrow{Cpens})) \qquad \square$$

4.3   Scope

For scope $\{A? C, F\}$, its transition rules are below:

(1) if $\langle A, \sigma, L, Cpens \rangle \xrightarrow{\beta} \langle A', \sigma', L', Cpens' \rangle$ and $A' \neq II, \boxtimes$

$\quad$ then $\langle \{A? C, F\}, \sigma, L, Cpens \rangle \xrightarrow{\beta} \langle \{A'? C, F\}, \sigma', L', Cpens' \rangle$

(2) if $\langle A, \sigma, L, Cpens \rangle \xrightarrow{\beta} \langle II, \sigma', L', Cpens' \rangle$

$\quad$ then $\langle \{A? C, F\}, \sigma, L, Cpens \rangle \xrightarrow{\beta} \langle \{II? C, F\}, \sigma', L', Cpens' \widehat{\ } \langle C \rangle \rangle$

(3) if $\langle A, \sigma, L, Cpens \rangle \xrightarrow{\beta} \langle \boxtimes, \sigma', L', Cpens' \rangle$

$\quad$ then $\langle \{A? C, F\}, \sigma, L, Cpens \rangle \xrightarrow{\beta} \langle F, \sigma', L', Cpens' \rangle$

(4) if $\langle A,\ \sigma,\ L,\ Cpens \rangle \xrightarrow{\beta} \langle \boxminus,\ \sigma',\ L',\ Cpens' \rangle$

   then $\langle \{A?\,C,\ F\},\ \sigma,\ L,\ Cpens \rangle \xrightarrow{\beta} \langle \boxminus,\ \sigma',\ L',\ Cpens' \rangle$

Furthermore, we give two auxiliary transitions shown below.

$\langle \{II?\,C,\ F\},\ \sigma,\ L,\ Cpens \rangle \xrightarrow{e}_{\emptyset} \langle \{II?\,C,\ F\},\ \sigma,\ L',\ Cpens \rangle$

$\langle \{II?\,C,\ F\},\ \sigma,\ L,\ Cpens \rangle \longrightarrow \langle II,\ \sigma,\ L,\ Cpens{}^{\frown}\langle C \rangle \rangle$

Now we analyse the derivation of denotational semantics for scope activity.

(1) Let $seq1:\ \langle A,\ \sigma,\ L,\ Cpens \rangle \xrightarrow{\beta_1} \langle A_1,\ \sigma_1,\ L_1,\ Cpens_1 \rangle \cdots \xrightarrow{\beta_n} \langle II,\ \sigma_n,\ L_n,\ Cpens_n \rangle$

   $seq1':\ \langle \{A?C,F\},\ \sigma,\ L,\ Cpens \rangle \xrightarrow{\beta_1} \langle \{A_1?C_1,F_1\},\ \sigma_1,\ L_1,\ Cpens_1 \rangle \cdots$

$$\xrightarrow{\beta_n} \langle T,\ \sigma_n,\ L_n,\ Cpens_n \rangle$$

$$\xrightarrow{e}_{\emptyset} \cdots \cdots \xrightarrow{e}_{\emptyset} \langle T,\ \sigma_n,\ L'_n,\ Cpens_n \rangle \longrightarrow \langle T,\ \sigma_n,\ L'_n,\ Cpens_n{}^{\frown}\langle C \rangle \rangle$$

where, $T =_{df} \{II?\,C,\ F\}$. Moreover, let

$$install(C) =_{df} \mathcal{H} \left(\begin{array}{l} \overrightarrow{st} = completed \wedge record(C)\ \wedge \\ smae(VTC \setminus \{Cpens\}) \wedge Rec\_Comm \end{array} \right)$$

Then we can have: $\ sem(seq1')\ =\ sem(seq1)\ ;\ install(C)$

(2) Let $seq2:\ \langle A,\ \sigma,\ L,\ Cpens \rangle \xrightarrow{\beta_1} \langle A_1,\ \sigma_1,\ L_1,\ Cpens_1 \rangle \cdots \xrightarrow{\beta_n} \langle \boxtimes,\ \sigma_n,\ L_n,\ Cpens_n \rangle$

   $seq2':\ \langle \{A?C,F\},\ \sigma,\ L,\ Cpens \rangle \xrightarrow{\beta_1} \langle \{A_1?C_1,F_1\},\ \sigma_1,\ L_1,\ Cpens_1 \rangle \cdots$

$$\xrightarrow{\beta_n} \langle F,\ \sigma_n,\ L_n,\ Cpens_n \rangle$$

Then we can have: $\ sem(seq2')\ =\ sem(seq2)\ ;\ Id[completed/\overleftarrow{st}]$

(3) Let $seq3:\ \langle A,\ \sigma,\ L,\ Cpens \rangle \xrightarrow{\beta_1} \langle A_1,\ \sigma_1,\ L_1,\ Cpens_1 \rangle \cdots \xrightarrow{\beta_n} \langle \boxminus,\ \sigma_n,\ L_n,\ Cpens_n \rangle$

   $seq3':\ \langle \{A?C,F\},\ \sigma,\ L,\ Cpens \rangle \xrightarrow{\beta_1} \langle \{A_1?C_1,F_1\},\ \sigma_1,\ L_1,\ Cpens_1 \rangle \cdots$

$$\xrightarrow{\beta_n} \langle \boxminus,\ \sigma_n,\ L_n,\ Cpens_n \rangle$$

Then we can have: $\ sem(seq3')\ =\ sem(seq3)$.

Based on the above analysis, we can achieve the denotational semantics shown as the theorem below.

Theorem 4.5

$$O(\{A?\,C,\ F\})\ =\ O(A)\ ;\ \left(\begin{array}{l} \overleftarrow{st} = completed \Rightarrow install(C) \\ \overleftarrow{st} = error \Rightarrow O(F)[completed/\overleftarrow{st}] \\ \overleftarrow{st} \in \{wait,\ undo\} \Rightarrow II \end{array} \right)$$

4.4   Parallel Process

Although we have not derived the universal formula representing the denotational semantics for a parallel BPEL process, we can write down its transition system. Its semantics can be calculated based on its transition steps. We use the example below to illustrate how the denotational semantics for a parallel process can be derived from its operational semantics [10].

Example 4.6

Let $\quad P_1\ =\ \{(x := 3\ ;\ \mathbf{rep}\ a\ x\ ;\ (l = 1) \circ x := x + 3)?\ C,\ \mathbf{skip}\}$,

$\qquad\quad P_2\ =\ \mathbf{rec}\ c\ z\ ;\ z := z + 4\ ;\ 1 \triangleright l$,

$\qquad\quad P_3\ =\ \mathbf{rec}\ a\ u\ ;\ v := u + 5\ ;\ \mathbf{rep}\ c\ v, \qquad P\ =\ P_1 \parallel P_2 \parallel P_3.$

Now we consider the derivation of the denotational semantics for program P. Below is the computation sequence for program P.

$$\langle P, \sigma, L, Cp\rangle \uparrow \longrightarrow \langle P_1' \parallel P_2 \parallel P_3, \sigma_1, L, Cp\rangle \qquad \uparrow \xrightarrow{a.3} \langle P_1'' \parallel P_2 \parallel P_3', \sigma_2, L, Cp\rangle$$

$$\uparrow \longrightarrow \langle P_1'' \parallel P_2 \parallel \mathbf{rep}\ c\ v, \sigma_3, L, Cp\rangle \uparrow \xrightarrow{c.8} \langle P_1'' \parallel P_2', \sigma_4, L, Cp\rangle$$

$$\uparrow \longrightarrow \langle P_1'' \parallel 1 \rhd l, \sigma_5, L, Cp\rangle \qquad \uparrow \xrightarrow{v} \langle P_1'', \sigma_5, L', Cp\rangle$$

$$\longrightarrow \langle P_1''', \sigma_5, L', Cp\rangle \qquad\qquad \uparrow \longrightarrow \langle II, \sigma_6, L', Cp^\frown\langle C\rangle\rangle$$

where, $P_1' = \{(\mathbf{rep}\ a\ x\ ;\ (l=1) \circ x := x+3)?\ C,\ \mathbf{skip}\}$,

$P_1'' = \{(l=1) \circ (x := x+3)?\ C,\ \mathbf{skip}\}$,

$P_1''' = \{(x := x+3)?\ C,\ \mathbf{skip}\}$,

$P_2' = z := z+4\ ;\ 1 \rhd l$, $\qquad P_3' = v := u+5\ ;\ \mathbf{rep}\ c\ v$

$\sigma_1 = \sigma[3/x]$, $\quad \sigma_2 = \sigma_1[3/u]$, $\quad \sigma_3 = \sigma_2[8/v]$, $\quad \sigma_4 = \sigma_3[8/z]$,

$\sigma_5 = \sigma_4[12/z]$, $\quad L' = L[1/l]$, $\quad \sigma_6 = \sigma_5[6/x]$.

Here, $\uparrow$ indicates that the environment can perform the update of source links several times before the current transition takes place. Based on the derivation strategy, we can achieve the denotational semantics for parallel program P.

$$O(P) = O(x := 3)\ ;\ O(u := x)_a\ ;\ O(v := u+5)\ ;\ O(z := v)_c\ ;$$

$$O(z := z+4)\ ;\ O(1 \rhd l)\ ;\ O(x := x+3)$$

where, the derived denotational semantics of assignment and shared-variable update can be found in the previous sections. Further,

$$O(u := x)_a =_{df} O(u := x)\ ;\ \mathcal{H}(\overrightarrow{st} = completed \wedge same(VTC) \wedge \overrightarrow{tr} = \overleftarrow{tr}^\frown\langle a.\overleftarrow{u}\rangle)$$

5   Conclusion

In this paper we have considered the derivation of denotational semantics from operational semantics for BPEL, which aims for the consistency of the two semantic models. Compared with traditional programming languages, two new execution states have been introduced; i.e., *error* state and *undo* state. In order to do the semantic unifying, the concepts of tradition condition and phase semantics have been introduced. Based on the two new concepts, the derivation strategy has been introduced and the denotational semantics for every BPEL statement has been derived from the corresponding operational semantics.

For the future, we continue to explore the unifying theories of web services, as well as the further web services models. It is interesting to integrate the two essential features; probability and security, into our web services models.

References

1. Butler, M.J., Ferreira, C.: An operational semantics for StAC, a language for modelling long-running business transactions. In: De Nicola, R., Ferrari, G.L., Meredith, G. (eds.) COORDINATION 2004. LNCS, vol. 2949, pp. 87–104. Springer, Heidelberg (2004)
2. Curbera, F., Goland, Y., Klein, J., Leymann, F., Roller, D., Satish Thatte, M., Weerawarana, S.: Business Process Execution Language for Web Service (2003), http://www.siebel.com/bpel

3. He, J., Zhu, H., Pu, G.: A model for BPEL-like languages. Frontiers of Computer Science in China 1(1), 9–19 (2007)
4. Hoare, C.A.R., Hayes, I.J., He, J., Morgan, C., Roscoe, A.W., Sanders, J.W., Sorensen, I.H., Spivey, J.M., Sufrin, B.: Laws of programming. Communications of the ACM 38(8), 672–686 (1987)
5. Hoare, C.A.R., He, J.: Unifying Theories of Programming. Prentice Hall, Englewood Cliffs (1998)
6. Leymann, F.: Web Services Flow Language (WSFL 1.0). IBM (2001), http://www-3.ibm.com/software/solutions/webservices/pdf/WSDL.pdf
7. Plotkin, G.: A structural approach to operational semantics. Technical Report 19, University of Aahus (1981) Also published in The Journal of Logic and Algebraic Programming 60(61),17–139 (2004)
8. Thatte, S.: XLANG: Web Service for Business Process Design. Microsoft (2001), http://www.gotdotnet.com/team/xml_wsspecs/xlang-c/default.html
9. Zhu, H.: Linking the Semantics of a Multithreaded Discrete Event Simulation Language. PhD thesis, London South Bank University (February 2005)
10. Zhu, H., He, J., Pu, G., Li, J.: An operational approach to BPEL-like programming. In: Proc. SEW-31: 31st IEEE Software Engineering Workshop, IEEE Computer Society Press, Los Alamitos (2007)

PHAC: An Environment for Distributed Collaborative Applications on P2P Networks

Adnane Cabani[1], Srinivasan Ramaswamy[2], Mhamed Itmi[1,2],
and Jean-Pierre Pécuchet[1]

[1] INSA de Rouen BP 08, LITIS Laboratory, 76131 Mont Saint Aignan, France
{Adnane.Cabani,Mhamed.Itmi,Jean-Pierre.Pecuchet}@insa-rouen.fr
[2] Computer Science Department, University of Arkansas at Little Rock, USA
srini@acm.org

Abstract. Using Peer-to-Peer networks is a way to distribute large scale scientific problems. But the P2P networks are very heterogeneous, highly dynamic and volatile. The objective of our work is to offer one P2P network based on high availability. We propose our PHAC framework to improve the dependability of applications. And we present the first results with case π computing.

1 Introduction

The use of Peer-to-Peer networks is fastgrowing due to the popularity of file sharing. Hence Peer-to-Peer networks have sparked a great deal of interdisciplinary excitement and research in recent years [1]. The majority of these works have concentrated on topology and search algorithms [2,3]. We can distinguish two different types of P2P networks: structured networks (CAN [4], Chord [5], Viceroy [6]) and unstructured networks (PRU [7], Hypergrid [8]). P2P networks are formed without any particular intention of a peers' capability. This means that all the peers in the network are highly heterogeneous in their characteristics (CPU, memory, bandwidth). This capability is very important for collaborative applications. But, only few works have been concerned of applications of this kind. Hence it is important that the capability of each peer be used as a determining factor so that tone can strive to increase an application's dependability.

In this paper, we will illustrate the use P2P network to distributed collaborative applications while improving their dependability characteristics. We give some solutions with our PHAC framework. We discuss the use of our approach for computing the results of using P2P computing. And finally, we conclude and present the next step in this research.

2 Background

As contrasted with the Client/Server model, a P2P network is formed by peer nodes which function as both clients and servers. Peer nodes may differ in processing speed, RAM, network bandwidth, and storage quantity. The P2P model

T. Janowski and H. Mohanty (Eds.): ICDCIT 2007, LNCS 4882, pp. 240–247, 2007.

consists of several topologies: hybrid and pure [1]. Hybrid systems are characterized by presence of some servers. The server corresponds to a single group which provides an index and data of available groups. Such systems overcome some drawbacks, such as the communication bottleneck occurred in the systems with the Client/Server topology. Decentralized systems are called P2P pure. In this kind, all peers communicate symmetrically and have equal roles. They are no bottleneck because there is no special centralized server. However, the inconvenience is when searching for other peers. This topology can be further classified by the manner in which decentralization is realized: structured or unstructured.

Structured systems [4,5] adapts efficiently as nodes join and leave the system and can answer queries even whether the system is continuously changing. Unstructured systems are characterized by a complete lack of constraints on resource. In the literature, one may find different structured networks, such as CAN [4], Chord [5] and Viceroy [6], which emerged in an attempt to address the scalability issues. In structured P2P systems, the overlay network topology is tightly controlled and objects are placed at precisely specified locations. These systems use a distributed routing or hash table (DHT) [9] to provide the mapping between the identified object and its location. Queries can be efficiently routed to the node where the desired data object is located. With the advent of this class of structured systems, different research groups have explored a wide variety of applications, services, and infrastructures built on top of a DHT abstraction. Examples of such proposals include systems for wide-area distributed storage, indexing, search, querying [10]. All of the aforementioned structured networks assume that all peers are uniform in resources and capabilities and hence are equally desirable to store prospective objects. We propose to improve the performance of associated algorithms by taking into account the heterogeneity nature of P2P systems.

All existing lookup algorithms in structured P2P systems assume that all peers are uniform in the availability of resources. Messages are routed on the overlay network without considering the capabilities differences among participating peers. However, measurement studies [11,12] have shown that the heterogeneity in deployed P2P systems is quite extreme. The bottleneck caused by very limited capabilities of some peers therefore could lead to inefficiency of existing lookup algorithms. Existent structure formations do not take into account the heterogeneity of peers and resources asked by the user. In following paragraph, we introduce our methodology for structuring which takes into account the needs of the users and their applications as well as heterogeneity of peers.

3   Problem Description

Until now, existent structured P2P network solutions ignored the heterogeneity and volatility of peers. But these two characteristics are very important for the deployment of efficient collaborative applications. Heterogeneity can influence the execution times and hence effect volatility. Besides if one peer leaves the network, the application may become suspended and may require restarting the application. For these reasons, we define the notion of a Job and Redundacy Peer Groups.

Definition 1. *The JobPeerGroup (JPG) is a group of peers. The role of the JPG is to make the necessary calculations through the appropriate choice of peers which can directly influence calculations times, the reliability and the robustness of the application system.*

Definition 2. *The RedundacyPeerGroup is another group of peers group defined to increase the reliability of P2P systems by using a method of data redundancy.*

3.1   Description

Overall a peer group is made up of entities that consist of all the available peers:

$$P = \bigcup_{1 \le i \le n} P_{ci} = \bigcup_{l \in \{1,2,3\}} P_l \ . \tag{1}$$

where

P_{ci} is a peer group based by criterion capability

P_1 : all peers at level 1

P_2 : all peers at level 2

P_3 : all peers at level 3

$$P_l = \bigcup_{\substack{cc \in \{H,M,L\} \\ 1 \le i \le n}} P_{ci}^{cc}$$

Peers can be grouped by specific capability criteria and by their immediate

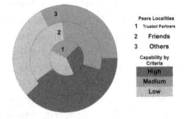

Fig. 1. Organization P2P network

locality (see Fig.1). It is assumed that there are three principles localities of peers: trusted partners, friends, and others.

For each criterion, peers may again can be grouped into three sub-groups. These are related to the specific criterion capability (cc) which can be high (H), medium (M) or low (L).

Property 1. Some peers may have access to specialized resources that may be required for the completion of a job.

$$\exists_{0 \le t \le m} R_t : R_t \in P \ . \tag{2}$$

$|P|$ is the number of peers in the system.

We define P_{R_t} a set of all peers with access to R_t.

Property 2. P_{ci} is made up of all peers that meet the specific capability criterion.

$$P_{ci} = \bigcup_{\substack{j \in \{H,M,L\} \\ l \in \{1,2,3\}}} P_{ci}^{j,l} \ . \tag{3}$$

Property 3. A JobPeerGroup is made up of peers that meet specially stated criteria for a job. Problem is defined by the user requesting peers meeting some minimum value of chosen criteria called ExpectedJobPeerGroup (E_{JPG}).

$$E_{JPG} = \left\{ |E_p|, \bigcup_{\substack{1 \leq i \leq n \\ l \in \{1,2,3\}}} E_{P_{ci}^{j,l}} / j = \{H, M, L, Undefined\} + \sum_{t=0,1,\dots,m} E_{R_t} \right\} . \quad (4)$$

where

$|Ep|$ is a number of peers requested.

E_{R_t} is a set of resources required to complete the job.

3.2 Objective

The problem is to find ActualJobPeerGroup (A_{JPG}) such that cost is minimized and performance is maximized.

$$A_{JPG} \approx E_{JPG} . \quad (5)$$

Subject to:

Cost(A_{JPG}) is minimum.

Perf(A_{JPG}) is maximum.

So, the ActualJobPeerGroup is equal at:

$$A_{JPG} = \left\{ |E_p| \leq |A_{JPG}|, A_{JPG}^R + A_{JPG}^{P_{ci}} \right\} . \quad (6)$$

To find ActualJobPeerGroup (A_{JPG}), we use algorithm 1. And to form the RedudancyPeerGroup, we use algorithm 2.

Algorithm 1. Formation of ActualJobPeerGroup

---

        begin

REM   /* Initialization */

        $A_{JPG}^R \leftarrow \{\}$

        $A_{JPG}^{P_{ci}} \leftarrow \{\}$

REM   /* Choice of peers that have specifics ressources */

        forall *elements of* E_{R_t} **do**

            $P_i \in P_{R_t} : \forall i, j; i \neq j; 0 \leq i, j \leq |P|; l, l' = \{1, 2, 3\}$ such as $P_i^l \leq P_j^{l'}$;

            $A_{JPG}^R \leftarrow A_{JPG}^R \cup P_i$;

        end

REM   /* Choice of peers that have required ressources */

        foreach $E_{P_{ci}} <> "undefined"$ **do**

            $P_x \in P_{ci} : \forall x, y; x \neq y; k = \{H, M, L\}; P_x^{ci} \leq P_y^{ci} et P_x^{ci} = k$;

            $A_{JPG}^{P_{ci}} \leftarrow A_{JPG}^{P_{ci}} \cup P_x$;

        end

        return $A_{JPG}^R \cup A_{JPG}^{P_{ci}}$

        end

Algorithm 2. Formation of unclustered RedundancyPeerGroup

---

        begin

        | **return** $P - AJPG$

        end

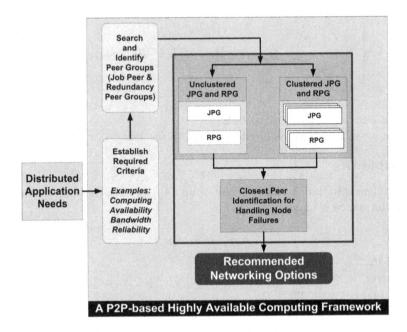

Fig. 2. PHAC framework

3.3   The PHAC Framework

To offer to users a P2P network based on high availability, we will the P2P-based
Highly Available Computing Framework (see Fig.2). The user needs to define the
criteria which his application has needed. Our framework - which is implemented
on JXTA [13,14] - will search and identify peer groups (JobPeerGroup and RedundancyPeerGroup) [15]. Until now, we have implemented the unclustered JobPeer-
Group and RedundancyPeerGroup and are working to implement and try the
case that clustered JopPeerGroup and RedundancyPeerGroup. Once the groups
of peers are identified, it identifies the closest peer for handling node failures. Finally, it proposes to user a recommended network for the proposed job. The user
can modify the structure of network before using it to distribute their application.

4   Study Case

In this section, we introduce some acquired results by implementing our methodology. We chose to calculate π by using the expression BBP (Bailey-Borwein-
Plouffe) which allows calculating umpteenth decimal of π.

$$\pi = \sum_{k=0}^{\infty} \frac{1}{16^k} \left(\frac{4}{8k+1} - \frac{2}{8k+4} - \frac{1}{8k+5} - \frac{1}{8k+6} \right) . \tag{7}$$

We have implemented this algorithm with collaborative approach on multia-
gent system [16]. Each agent has a role to calculate iteratively π between two

indices. Our choice is justified by made that it is easier to interpret the result of our framework forasmuch this example is determinist. The implementation was on 10 computers interconnected by a Fast Ethernet 100 Mbps network where eight computers have a processor of 2 Ghz and 512 MB of random access memory. And two computers are equipped with a processor of 600 Mhz and 256MB of random access memory.

The first step is the building of network. The JobPeerGroup is formed of the eight computers of 2Ghz and the RedundancyPeerGroup is composed of the two other computers. The calculation is divided into sub-tasks defined in a XML file. This decomposition takes into account a load balancing.

Figure 3 represents the precision of π computing on X axis. A precision of 3000 means the calculation of the 3000th decimal of π. The Y axis represents the calculation time. We tested different configurations: the only machine, four peers and eight peers. For every precision (500 to 5500) we performed calculation on each of configurations. We point out that the time of calculation increasing according to precision. Fact of distribute calculation allows to gain time almost linear in comparison with the number of peers. This is owed to the load balancing between different peers. In the following, we represent the speed-up, figure 4, and efficiency, figure 5, in cases of 4 and 8 peers.

Speed-up is an important indication. It reflects the degree of improvement of the calculation time in a parallel approach in comparison with a sequential approach. Let us note that a lower acceleration than 1 means that iterative calculation gives better results than parallel calculation.

The efficiency is an indication which links up speed-up to the number of peers participating in calculation. In our case, speed-up is divided by four or eight according to the number of used peers. So, for a precision of 5500, the processors of four peers are used in 97%. They are it in 96% in the case of 8 peers.

Acquired results show that the calculation time is better than in the case of sequential calculation.

To end the test process of our approach, we are going to study the scenario of a fault on participating computers in calculation. Peers being volatile, it is necessary to consider the fault tolerance. We present in what follows results acquired for a precision of 5500 with eight peers for calculation. In the figure 6, we observe three curves: the first one for case without fault, the second and the third represent the calculation at the time of a fault respectively after three seconds and twenty seconds of the starting of the calculations.

We can see when the fault was provoked after three seconds the calculation time reached one hundred seconds. Whereas in case fault occurred after twenty seconds, the calculation is finished in 61s. This is due to peers belonging to RedunduncyPeerGroup which are not powerful (Pentium 600Mhz). They put much more time than of peers belonging to JobPeerGroup. However, acquired results are better than in the case of sequential calculation. And, it's better than repeat the calculation again with parallel approach. To note that in case of presence of RequestPeers, i.e. it exist free peers belonging to JobPeerGroup, the restart of calculation would have been made by these peers kind by recovering

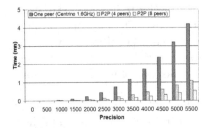

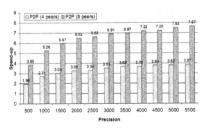

Fig. 3. Calculation time of π computing

Fig. 4. Speed-up

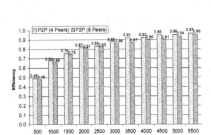

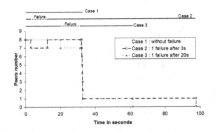

Fig. 5. Efficiency

Fig. 6. Calculation time of π with fault tolerance

the replication of the peer belonging to RedundancyPeerGroup. The calculation time would be necessarily better than acquired results in this experience where one RedundancyPeer became ExecutantPeer.

5 Conclusion

In this article, we presented a framework (PHAC) to improve the dependability of applications executing over a P2P network. We showed its need and feasibility using a simple application for demonstration purposes. The selection of peers to form JobPeerGroup and RedundancyPeerGroup allows increasing the dependability of applications such as that envisaged for the π calculation. These results are encouraging. We continue the study of this framework and its applicative value in other types of applications. We also plan to extend this with structured peer groups and the case with increasing the number of peers in larger-scale peer clusters.

References

1. Milojicic, D.S., Kalogeraki, V., Lukose, R., Nagaraja, K., Pruyne, J., Richard, B., Rollins, S., Xu, Z.: Peer-to-peer computing. In: External HPL-2002-57, HP (2002)
2. Faloutsos, M., Faloutsos, P., Faloutsos, C.: On power-law relationships of the internet topology. In: Applications, technologies, architectures, and protocols for computer communication (ACM SIGCOMM), Cambridge, Massachusetts, United States, pp. 251–262 (1999)

3. Newman, M.: The structure and function of complex networks. SIAM Review 45, 167–256 (2003)
4. Ratnasamy, S., Francis, P., Handley, M., Karp, R., Shenker, S.: A scalable content-adressable network. In: ACM SIGCOMM 2001, San Diego, California, United States, pp. 161–172 (2001)
5. Stoica, I., Morris, R., Karger, D., Kaashoek, F., Balakrishnan, H.: Chord: A scalable peer-to-peer lookup service for internet applications. In: ACM SIGCOMM 2001, pp. 149–160. ACM Press, New York (2001)
6. Malkhi, D., Naor, M., Ratajczak, D.: Viceroy: A scalable and dynamic emulation of the butterfly. In: 21st ACM Symposium on Principles of Distributed Computing, Monterey, California, United States (2002)
7. Pandurangan, G., Raghavan, P., Upfal, E.: Building low-diameter p2p networks. IEEE Journal on Selected Areas in Communications 21(6), 995–1002 (2003)
8. Saffre, F., Ghanea-Hercock, R.: Beyond anarchy: self-organized topology for peer to peer networks. Resilient and adaptive defense of computing networks 9(2), 1076–2787 (2003)
9. Yoshikawa, C., Chun, B., Vahdat, A.: Distributed hash queues: Architecture and design. In: 3rd International Workshop on Agents and Peer-to-Peer Computing, New York City, USA (2004)
10. Hari, B., Kaashoek, M.F., David, K., Robert, M., Ion, S.: Looking up data in p2p systems. Communications of the ACM 46(2), 43–48 (2003), http://doi.acm.org/10.1145/606272.606299
11. Saroiu, S., Gummadi, P.K., Gribble, S.D.: A measurement study of peer-to-peer file sharing systems (2002)
12. Andersen, D., Balakrishnan, H., Kaashoek, F., Morris, R.: Resilient overlay networks. ACM SIGOPS Operating Systems Review 35(5), 131–145 (2001), http://doi.acm.org/10.1145/502059.502048
13. JXTA-v2.0 (Jxta v2.0 protocols specification)
14. JXTA-v2.3.x: (Jxta v2.3.x: Java programmer's guide)
15. Cabani, A., Itmi, M., Pécuchet, J.P.: Improving collaborative jobs in p2p networks. In: ICECS 2005. 12th IEEE International Conference on Electronics, Circuits and Systems, Gammarth, Tunisia, pp.135–138 (2005)
16. Cabani, A., Itmi, M., Pécuchet, J.P.: Multi-agent distributed simulation: Discussions and prototyping a p2p architecture. In: Computer Simulation Conference (SCSC'05), Philadelphia, Pennsylvania, United States, pp. 281–286 (2005)

Webformer: A Rapid Application Development Toolkit for Writing Ajax Web Form Applications

David W.L. Cheung[1,2], Thomas Y.T. Lee[1,2], and Patrick K.C. Yee[1,2]

[1] Department of Computer Science, University of Hong Kong
[2] Center for E-Commerce Infrastructure Development, University of Hong Kong
{dcheung,ytlee,kcyee}@cs.hku.hk

Abstract. Web forms are commonly used to capture data on the web. With Asynchronous Javascript and XML (Ajax) programming, interactive web forms can be created. However, Ajax programming is complex in a way that the model-view-controller (MVC) code is not clearly separated. This paper discusses about a MVC-oriented web form development called "Webformer" that we develop to simplify and streamline web form development with Ajax. We introduce a scripting language called Web Form Application Language (WebFAL) for modeling web forms. Webformer hides the programming complexity by generating Ajax code directly from the web form models.

1 Introduction

Web forms are one of the mostly used applications for data capture on the web. In early days, a web form was presented as a static HTML page, which requires page reload for the web server to perform data validation. The long page reload time made web applications not as interactive as stand-alone applications. The recent use of the Asynchronous JavaScript and XML (Ajax) [12] programming pattern supports the browser to contact the server to validate the data on a web page dynamically without reloading the whole page. With Ajax, software developers write JavaScript to handle the user interface (UI) events of an HTML component (e.g. when a character is typed in a text box). The JavaScript handler can perform dynamic data validation by sending an XMLHttpRequest to the server. A JavaScript callback function is assigned to process the server response and render the validation results on the web page asynchronously. This approach reduces frequent page reloads in web applications and largely improves their interactivity. However, there is a price to pay in using Ajax. The browser incompatibility and the programming complexity are two pitfalls of Ajax commonly recognized [12,14,15,16].

Model-View-Controller (MVC) [13] is a design pattern commonly used for UI application development. MVC factors a UI application into three aspects: (1) the data model that represents the application context, (2) the view of the application that is presented to the user, and (3) the application controller that controls the user interactions. Although an Ajax application has the code for handling MVC interactions, the code is not modularly separated for the three

T. Janowski and H. Mohanty (Eds.): ICDCIT 2007, LNCS 4882, pp. 248–253, 2007.

aspects, i.e. the MVC code in HTML and JavaScript is mixed together in a web document. Also, Ajax applications are programmed in different languages, e.g. HTML, JavaScript, Java, etc. This makes developing and maintaining Ajax applications very difficult [12].

We have designed a rapid application development (RAD) toolkit called "Webformer", which provides a MVC framework for web forms to simplify the Ajax programming and streamline the development process.

In Sect. 2, we give an overview of the architecture of Webformer. Section 3 elaborates a scripting language called "Web Form Application Language" (WebFAL) that provides MVC specification for web forms. We introduce a tool called "Webformer Compiler" (wfc) in Sect. 4 and outline how a WebFAL script is complied into a web form runtime. The related work is discussed in Sect. 5. Section 6 concludes the paper.

2   Webformer Architecture

We have designed an XML-based scripting language called "Web Form Application Language" (WebFAL) for modeling web forms. A web form model written in WebFAL is complied by our "Webformer Complier" (wfc) to generate the JavaScript/HTML source to run on the browser. Webformer also provides a JavaScript engine called "webformer.js" that provides the common JavaScript routines to handle the MVC interactions, e.g. data validation and auto-completion, XML document object model (DOM) management, and Ajax messaging.

There are two types of message exchange between the server and the browser: Ajax messaging and web form submission. The Ajax messages will be exchanged when a server validation event is triggered. When a web form is submitted, the form data will be packaged in an XML document conforming to the XML Schema Definition (XSD) file generated from the WebFAL script at the design time. While the message formats are pre-defined, a Java library called "webformer.jar" is provided for parsing and composing the messages in these formats to ease the programming the Java Servlet handlers on the server-side.

The life-cycle of developing a web form using Webformer consists of two phases. The software developer first specifies the model and controller of a web form in WebFAL. The model is then compiled into an HTML template for the web designer to enhance the UI view. This two-phase life-cycle facilitates the segregation of duties between software developers and web designers to streamline the web development process.

Sample Web Form Application. We use a simple web form application as an example to illustrate the use of WebFAL and other Webformer components. This application provides a web form for the user to upload photo files to an online album. A use case of the application is described in Fig. 1.

1. The user enters his username. The entered username is validated on-the-fly against the server database.
2. The user enters the album name while the server suggests the possible names that match what the user types.
3. The user can upload multiple photos. He can click on the [**Add Photo**] or the [**Delete Photo**] link to add or delete a upload entry.
4. In each upload entry, the user specifies the photo file name, whether he wants to share the photo, and the number of prints of the photo he wants to order.
5. The user clicks on the **Submit** button to send the form data to the server.

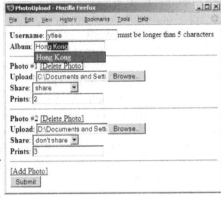

Fig. 1. Use case of the sample web form application

3   Web Form Application Language (WebFAL)

WebFAL is an XML-based scripting language to express the MVC specifications for web forms. A WebFAL document has a root element `<WebForm/>` and consists of five kinds of child elements: `<Model/>`, `<Validation/>`, `<Selection/>`, `<Event/>`, and `<SubmitUrl/>`.

`<Model/>` **Element.** The `<Model/>` specifies the data model of the web form, which is a hierarchical structure of data groups (`<Group/>`) and data fields (`<Field/>`). Each `<Field/>` is associated with a name and a data type. Possible data types include: `String`, `Number`, `Date`, `DateTime`, `Time`, `File` and `Boolean`. A `<Group/>` contains a list of `<Field/>`s or other `<Group/>`s. The minimum and maximum occurrence for a `<Field/>` or `<Group/>` on the web form can be specified. See Fig. 2 for the sample code.

`<Validation/>` **Element.** A `<Validation/>` specifies a set of validation rules for a `<Field/>` or a `<Group/>`. There are two types of validation rules: browser validation rules and server validation rules. Browser validation rules are some static constraints for `<Field/>`s that can be checked by the browser without contacting the server. Available static validation constraints are `<RegExp/>`, `<Length/>`, `<MinLength/>`, `<MaxLength/>`, `<TotalDigits/>`, `<FractionDigits/>`, `<MinInclusive/>`, `<MaxInclusive/>`, `<MinExclusive/>`, and `<MaxExclusive/>`. An error message may be specified so that that message is reported on the HTML page when the validation fails. A server validation is dynamically performed by the server. The `<HandlerUrl/>` specifies the URL of the server handler that performs the validation. At runtime, when the server validation event is triggered, an Ajax request containing the data field content is sent to the specified handler. The server validates the content dynamically and responses to the browser with the validation result. See Fig. 2 for the sample code.

```
<Model>
    <Field name="Username">String</Field>
    <Field name="Album">String</Field>
    <Group name="Photo" minOccurs="1" maxOccurs="unbounded">
        <Field name="File">File</Field>
        <Field name="Share">String</Field>
        <Field name="Prints">Number</Field>
    </Group>
</Model>
<Validation id="ValPrints">
    <FractionDigits errorMsg="must be integer">0</FractionDigits>
    <MinInclusive errorMsg="must be greater than 0">0</MinInclusive>
    <MaxInclusive errorMsg="must be less than 10">10</MaxInclusive>
</Validation>
<Validation id="ValUser">
    <MinLength errorMsg="must be longer than 6 characters">6</MinLength>
    <MaxLength errorMsg="must be shorter than 20 characters">20</MaxLength>
    <HandlerUrl>/ajax/userval</HandlerUrl>
</Validation>
```

Fig. 2. Sample code for <Model/>'s and <Validation/>'s.

<Selection/> **Element.** A <Selection/> provides either a static set of coded values for a <Field/> or specifies the URL of a server handler that provides some suggested values. Coded values are a set of permissible values for a data field. Each code value must be unique within a <Selection/>. A <Code/> can be optionally given a text attribute, which is a description for presenting on the web page. Suggested values are dynamically generated by a server handler through an XMLHttpRequest. <HandlerUrl/> specifies the URL of the server handler. See Fig. 3 for the sample code.

<Event/> **Element.** An <Event/> specifies an event that can take place in a <Field/> in order to trigger some validation or selection operations. Each <Event/> binds a <Field/> to one or more <Validation/>s or <Selection/>s. The reference to a <Field/> is the path of <Group/> and <Field/> names,

```
<Selection id="SelShare">
  <Code text="Share">public</Code>
  <Code text="Don't share">
    private
  </Code>
</Selection>
<Selection id="SelAlbum">
  <HandlerUrl>
    /ajax/albumsuggeset
  </HandlerUrl>
</Selection>

<Event>
  <FieldRef>Username</FieldRef>
  <ValidationRef>ValUser</ValidationRef>
  <Trigger>FocusOff</Trigger>
</Event>
<Event>
  <FieldRef>Album</FieldRef>
  <ValidationRef>SelAlbum</ValidationRef>
  <Trigger>KeyUp</Trigger>
</Event>
```

Fig. 3. Sample code for <Selection/>s and <Event/>s

delimited by a dot, from the root of the `<Model/>` to that `<Field/>`, e.g. `Photo.Description`. A `<Trigger/>` specifies the event type of the data field that triggers the specified validations/selections. For example, a text field can be validated while when a pressed key is released (i.e. `KeyUp`,). See Fig. 3 for the sample code.

`<SubmitUrl/>` **Element.** The `<SubmitUrl/>` specifies the URL of the server handler that processes the data submission. When a user clicks on the submit button in the web form, the form data will be re-validated, packaged in an XML document, and submitted to that URL.

4 Compilation of WebFAL Scripts

The Webformer Compiler (wfc) compiles the WebFAL script into an JavaScript/ HTML file that provides the basic layout of a web page. The wfc picks the HTML component that best represents a `<Field/>`. For example, a `String` `<Field/>` is translated into a text box, or a selection box (when the `<Field/>` is bound to a code selection). JavaScript code is embedded to handle the validation and selection events for the component. The web designer may modify this HTML file to enhance the view and content of the web page. The wfc also generates an XSD file from the WebFAL script that specifies the XML format of the web form data for submission to the server. The `<Model/>` and `<Validation/>`s are converted into XSD types and elements. In the `<Model/>`, the structure of `<Group/>`s and `<Field/>`s determines the XML structure while the data type of a `<Field/>` determines its XSD data type. For example, the WebFAL `Number` type is mapped to the XSD `xs:decimal` type. Moreover, the `<Validation/>` definitions are translated into the restriction facets of the XSD type.

5 Related Work

XForms. XForms is a W3C specification [9] for representing web forms in XML. XForms provides a sophisticated processing model, a large set of data types based on W3C XML Schema [8], and a rich collection of form controls and user interface. Addressing the same problem of web form modeling, XForms takes a different approach. Instead of providing a separate language, XForms is built on top of XHTML [6] in a way that XForms mark-ups are used with the XHTML mark-ups in the web document. The advantage of this approach is that the XForms statements do not require compilation and can directly run on an XForms-enabled browser. However, XForms also has some shortcomings. Firstly, XForms statements cannot be natively interpreted by popular browsers. Installation of an XForms plug-in is required to enable the browsers to run XForms. Secondly, Instead of being a self-contained language, XForms is used with other standards, such as XHTML, XPath [11], and XML Schema, which results in mixing different language constructs within a web document. This potentially leads to more implementation complication [10] and browser incompatibility.

Ajax frameworks. A variety of frameworks have been developed to simplify Ajax programming. Google Web Toolkit [4], ASP.NET AJAX [1], Yahoo UI Library [7], Dojo [2], Prototype [5], and DWR [3] are among the popular Ajax frameworks. These frameworks typically provide the JavaScript engines and server libraries to save programming efforts in coding sophisticated web UIs and Ajax messaging. In contrast, Webformer focuses on RAD of web forms using its own WebFAL language.

6   Conclusion

The key contributions of our research are the WebFAL web form modeling language, and the wfc compiler that generates the runtimes of the web forms from their models. Moreover, Webformer provides the webformer.js and webformer.jar libraries, as well as the standard Ajax message formats, to simplify Ajax programming. We also propose a two-phase web development life-cycle to segregate the duties of software developers and web designers and streamline the development process. We anticipate that Webformer will serve the developer community as a useful RAD toolkit for interactive web form programming.

References

1. ASP.NET AJAX Website. http://ajax.asp.net
2. Dojo Website. http://dojotoolkit.org
3. DWR Website. http://getahead.org/dwr
4. Google Web Toolkit Website., http://code.google.com/webtoolkit
5. Prototype Website., http://www.prototypejs.org
6. XHTML2 Working Group Home Page., http://www.w3.org/MarkUp
7. Yahoo User Interface Library., http://developer.yahoo.com/yui
8. Biron, P.V., Malhotra, A.: XML Schema Part 2: Datatypes Second Edition. W3C Recommendation (28 October 2004) 2 (2001), http://www.w3.org/TR/xmlschema-2/
9. Boyer, J.M. XForms 1.0 (Second Edtion). W3C Recommendation 14 March 2006 14 (2003), http://www.w3.org/TR/xforms/
10. Cagle, K.: Understanding XForms: In: The Model. O'REILY, xml.com (2006)
11. Clark, J., DeRose, S.: et al. XML Path Language (XPath) Version 1.0. W3C Recommendation 16 November 1999 16 (1999), http://www.w3.org/TR/xpath
12. Garrett, J.J.: Ajax: A New Approach to Web Applications. p. 22 (2005), http://www.adaptivepath.com/publications/essays/archives/000385.php
13. Krasner, G.E., Pope, S.T.: A Description of the Model-View-Controller User Interface Paradigm in the Smalltalk-80 System. system (1998)
14. Mesbah, A., van Deursen, A.: An Architectural Style for Ajax. Arxiv preprint cs.SE/0608111 (2006)
15. Paulson, L.D.: Building rich web applications with Ajax. Computer 38(10), 14–17 (2005)
16. Smith, K.: Simplifying Ajax-style Web development. Computer 39(5), 98–101 (2006)

Continuous Adaptive Mining the Thin Skylines over Evolving Data Stream

Guangmin Liang[1] and Liang Su[2]

[1] Computer Engineering Department Shenzhen Polytechnic Shenzhen 518055, China
gmliang@oa.szpt.net
[2] School of Computer Science National University of Defense Technology Changsha
410073, China

Abstract. Skyline queries, which return the objects that are better than or equal in all dimensions and better in at least one dimension, are useful in many decision making and real-time monitor applications. With the number of dimensions increasing and continuous large volume data arriving, mining the thin skylines over data stream under control of losing quality is a more meaningful problem. In this paper, firstly, we propose a novel concept, called *thin skyline*, which uses a skyline object that represents its nearby skyline neighbors within ε-distance (acceptable difference). Then, two algorithms are developed which prunes the skyline objects within the acceptable difference and adopts correlation coefficient to adjust adaptively thin skyline query quality. Furthermore, our experimental performance study shows that the proposed methods are both efficient and effective.

1 Introduction

For two objects $X = (x_1, x_2, \cdots, x_d)$ and $Y = (y_1, y_2, \cdots, y_d)$ in the d-dimensional space, X dominates Y if $x_i \leq y_i$ for $1 \leq i \leq d$. Skyline computing aims to find all objects that are not been dominated by other objects and roots in many decision making and monitor applications. For example, a data stream scene: a stock record with two attributes: risk and commission cost. Buyers may want to know the stocks which risk is minimized and commission cost is maximized, before making trade decisions. For simplicity, we assume that skylines are computed with respect to *min* conditions on all the dimensions, though it can be a combination with other condition such as *max* [1].

However, in [2], J.L.Bentley et al. proved that the average number of skyline objects is $O((\ln N)^{d-1})$, where N is the number of total objects. This is the cardinality bound most often cited and employed in skyline work. From this bound, we can see clearly that the number of skyline queries will increase exponentially along with the size of the original objects and the number of dimensions. Figure 1 and Figure 2 have proved above bound. Buyers in a stock market hardly make decisions if they see these plentiful results, even though the results are fast and efficient. Hence, accurate skyline query is lack of manageability and less uselessness for decision making. If another query returned over a half size of the skyline

T. Janowski and H. Mohanty (Eds.): ICDCIT 2007, LNCS 4882, pp. 254–264, 2007.
© Springer-Verlag Berlin Heidelberg 2007

dim	corr	indep	anti
2	1	13	51
3	3	74	641
4	12	286	4252
5	18	1106	12624
6	23	1997	26840
7	40	5560	41514
8	128	9664	55705
9	239	16857	67103
10	383	26062	75109

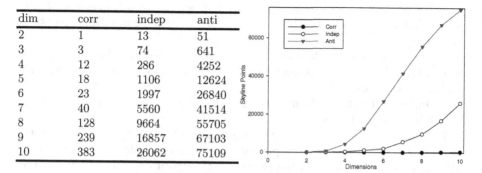

Fig. 1. The relation of skyline points and dimensions. All experiments data are three most popular synthetic benchmark data: correlated, independent, and anti-correlated [1]. The number of original points is $1000,000$. The range of each dimension is $[0, 1000]$.

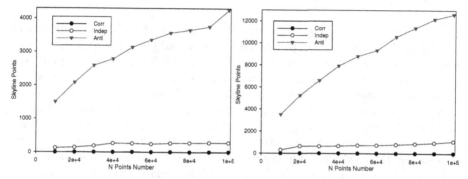

Fig. 2. The relation of skyline points and original data points. The dimension of left picture is 4 and dimension of right picture is 5. The range of each dimension is $[0, 1000]$.

points and the quality of result had no or less loss, this technique would be more important and meaningful for decision making applications.

On the other hand, there are numerous data stream applications that involve continuous processing: Network monitoring applications [3,4], financial applications track stock ticker data in real time to identify interesting trends [5], telecom fraud detection and so on. Data stream generally has characters: large volume and rapidly, potentially unbounded, continuously arriving and unpredictable and change over time. All these make the problem — mining thin skylines over data stream, becoming more challengeable.

These are the motivations of our research in the paper. To the best of our knowledge, there is no similar work existing in the literature in the context of adaptive thin skyline computation over data streams. Our contributions in this paper are as follows:

1. We propose a novel concept, called *thin skyline*, which uses one skyline object that represents its nearby skyline neighbors within ε-distance (acceptable difference).

2. Two algorithms are developed which prunes the skyline objects within the acceptable difference and adopts correlation coefficient to adjust adaptively thin skyline query quality.

3. Our experimental performance study shows that the proposed methods are both efficient and effective.

The rest of the paper is organized as follows. In Section 2, we present related work in skyline and stream computation. Section 3 provide our techniques for processing adaptive thin skyline problem and algorithms. Results of comprehensive performance studies are discussed in Section 4. Section 5 concludes the paper.

2 Related Work

Börzsönyi et al. [1] proposed first two algorithms for the skyline computation: the **BNL** (Block Nested Loop) and **DC** (Divide and Conquer) algorithm. Subsequently, skyline problem and its variants [6,7,8,9,10] have been extensively studied, and a lot of algorithms have been developed. Kian-Lee Tan et al. [6] proposed an alternate method — Bitmap, which maps each object to a bit string, and uses efficient bit operations to compute the skylines. **BBS** (Branch-and-Bound Skyline) [11] compute the skyline using nearest neighbor search indexed by an R-Tree with guaranteed minimum I/O cost, and prune the search space using the newly found nearest neighbor object. Algorithms in main memory may be found in [1,8,9], and the techniques related to database may be found in [7,8,12]. Recently, research on the skyline query has shifted to the subspace skyline computation [13,14,15] and skyline in the sliding window over data stream [10].

None of the algorithms referenced above was originally designed to support thin skyline computation over data stream. In paper [10], Xuemin Lin et al. consider the problem of efficiently computing the skyline against the most recent N elements in a data stream, specifically, the n-of-N skyline queries. Because of the inherent properties in skyline computing, authors had realized that the algorism scalability and proposed thin skyline problem. Following their study, we propose the concept of thin skyline and two effective algorithms.

3 Thin Skyline Problem and Algorithms

From Figure 1 and Figure 2, we know that the number of skyline queries increase exponentially along with the size of the original objects and the number of dimensions. In addition, data stream applications typically run in an environment where memory is limited (relative to the size of the stream) so that it is not feasible to work with the entire original objects in memory. Thus, intuitively, observing from Figure 3, we can process the skyline objects set directly,

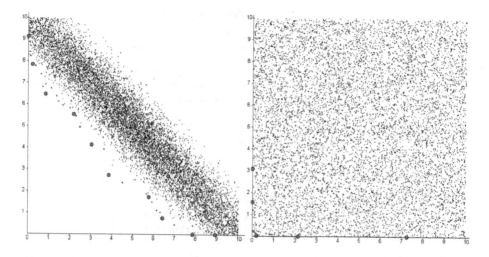

Fig. 3. 10000 points and 2 dimensions. Left picture is anti-correlation original points which has 30 skyline points and selected 10 skyline points. Right picture is independent original points which has 14 skyline points and selected 5 skyline points. The range of each dimension is $[0, 10]$.

and eliminate those objects which are close to the blue points.(Red points are skyline points, blue points are leaved subset of skyline set which is near to the other skyline points.)

In order to depict accurately how close degree of two points, we are naturedly aware of the geometry distance, that is, a d-dimensional metric space $\mathbb{R}^d$, which is a set of points with an associated distance function $dist$. Common used distance functions have Euclidian distance and Manhattan distance. Table 1 summarizes the notations used throughout the paper. The distance function $dist$ has the following properties:

1.$dist(X_1, X_2) = dist(X_2, X_1)$;

2.$dist(X_1, X_2) \geq 0$, and iff $X_1 = X_2$, $dist(X_1, X_2) = 0$;

3.$dist(X_1, X_3) \leq dist(X_1, X_2) + dist(X_2, X_3)$.

Behind of the paper we only use the Euclidian distance as the $dist$ function. That is:

$$dist(X_i, X_j) = \sqrt{\sum_{k=1}^{d}(x_i^k - x_j^k)^2} \tag{1}$$

Definition 1 (Thin Skyline Set). *Let Ω be the set of d-dimensional objects, and $\Omega_{Skyline}$ be the skyline set on Ω. The acceptable difference distance is ε and obviously satisfies $\varepsilon \geq 0$. $\Omega_{ASkyline}$ represents the thin skyline set that satisfies:*

1.$\forall X_i, X_j \in \Omega_{ASkyline}$, $X_i \neq X_j$, then $dist(X_i, X_j) \geq 2\varepsilon$;

2.$\forall X_i \in \Omega_{Skyline}$, then $\exists X_j \in \Omega_{ASkyline}$, s.t. $dist(X_i, X_j) \leq \varepsilon$.

Table 1. Notations

Notation	Definition
X_i	Point
$x_i^1, x_i^2, \cdots, x_i^d$	Concrete representation of X_i , d is the dimension of X_i
$dist(X_i, X_j)$	Distance between point X_i and X_j
W	Sliding window over data stream
N	Length of sliding window
$\rho(X_i, X_j)$	Correlation coefficient of vector X_i and X_j
ε	Acceptable difference distance
$\Omega_{Skyline}$	Skyline set
$\Omega_{ASkyline}$	thin skyline set
$|\Omega_{Skyline}|$	Number of skyline set
$|\Omega_{ASkyline}|$	Number of thin skyline set
$AvgDist_{Skyline}$	Average distance of points in skyline set
$AvgDist_{ASkyline}$	Average distance of points in thin skyline set

Definition 2 (Strongly Dominating Relationship). *An object $X_i \in \Omega$ strongly dominates another object $X_j \in \Omega$, noted as $X_i \rhd X_j$, if $X_i + \varepsilon \succ X_j$ ($X \succ Y$ means X dominates Y). That is to say: $\forall 1 \leq k \leq d$, $x_i^k + \varepsilon \leq x_j^k$, and $\exists 1 \leq t \leq d$, $x_i^t + \varepsilon < x_j^t$, reversely, X_j is a strongly dominated object by X_i.*

Definition 3 (Correlation Coefficient). *Given n d-dimensional objects, which $X_i = (x_i^1, x_i^2, \cdots, x_i^d)$, $1 \leq i \leq n$. Set matrix $\boldsymbol{A} = (X_1, X_2, \cdots, X_n)^T$ and vector $Y_j = (x_1^j, x_2^j, \cdots, x_n^j)^T$, then $\boldsymbol{A} = \begin{pmatrix} x_1^1 & \cdots & x_1^d \\ \vdots & \ddots & \vdots \\ x_n^1 & \cdots & x_n^d \end{pmatrix} = (Y_1, \cdots, Y_d)$, the correlation coefficient is defined as: $\rho(Y_i, Y_j) = \frac{E((Y_i - EY_i)(Y_j - EY_j))}{\sqrt{DY_i} \cdot \sqrt{DY_j}} = \frac{E(Y_i Y_j) - EY_i EY_j}{\sqrt{DY_i} \cdot \sqrt{DY_j}}$, and $EY_i = \frac{1}{n} \sum_{k=1}^n x_k^i$, which is the expectation of vector Y_i; $DY_i = E(Y_i - EY_i)^2 = EY_i^2 - (EY_i)^2$, which is the variance of vector Y_i.*

Definition 4 (Translation Function). *The value of correlation coefficient is between -1 and $+1$. When $\rho = -1$, Y_i is negative linear correlation of Y_j; When $\rho = 0$, Y_i is not correlation of Y_j; When $\rho = +1$, Y_i is positive correlation of Y_j. These three values are corresponding to anti-correlation, independent and correlation data distribution[1]. From Figures 1 and 2, we can observe that the correlation of every two dimensions has strong affect to the thin skyline result, and anti-correlation distribution has more and more skyline points than other distributions. So we construct a translation function which reflects the data distribution. The translation function is: $\Phi(\rho) = \frac{a+b}{2} - \rho \frac{b-a}{2}, 1 \leq a \leq b$.*

In common $a = 1$ and $b = 2$ or others. If b larger than 2, that is to say, we consider the influence of correlation coefficient more than ε. So we choose $\varepsilon \Phi(\rho)$ as the bound of difference distance to adaptively mining the thin skyline in data stream.

Theorem 1. *Given a dataset $\Omega_{Skyline}$, if $X_i, X_j \in \Omega_{ASkyline}$ and $dist(X_i, X_j) \leq \varepsilon$, then $\sum_{k=1}^d |x_i^k - x_j^k| \leq \varepsilon \sqrt{d}$.*

Proof. Because $(dist(X_i, X_j))^2 = \sum_{k=1}^{d} (x_i^k - x_j^k)^2 \leq \varepsilon^2$, Set $\left| x_i^k - x_j^k \right| = P_k$, then

$$(d-1) \sum_{k=1}^{d} (P_k)^2 = \sum_{1 \leq i < j \leq d} \left[(P_i)^2 + (P_j)^2 \right] \geq 2 \sum_{1 \leq i < j \leq d} (P_i \cdot P_j), \text{ so } \sum_{k=1}^{d} \left| x_i^k - x_j^k \right| =$$

$$\sum_{k=1}^{d} P_k = \sqrt{\left(\sum_{k=1}^{d} P_k \right)^2} = \sqrt{\sum_{k=1}^{d} (P_k)^2 + 2 \sum_{1 \leq i < j \leq d} (P_i \cdot P_j)} \leq \sqrt{\varepsilon^2 + (d-1)\varepsilon^2} =$$

$$\varepsilon \sqrt{d}. \qquad \qquad \qquad \qquad \square$$

3.1   Naïve Thin Skyline Algorithm

Generally, we only have the original data set in the beginning from data stream system. Intuitively, thin skyline set is a subset of skyline set, so a naïve method is: firstly, computing the basic skyline set, and secondly filtering some similar objects to obtain the thin skyline set. In the first step, we implement the stabling skyline algorithm over sliding window in paper [10] and save the basic skyline set in **SkylineList** data structure. At first, we sort the **SkylineList** by $\sum_{i=1}^{d} x_i$ (in code line 1), then we can break the iteration with the guarantee of Theorem 1 (code line 8) as soon as possible. The pseudo code of *NAS* algorithm is showed below.

Algorithm 1. $NAS(\varepsilon, \Omega_{Skyline})$
***

Input: ε is the distance, **SkylineList** is the basic skyline objects. **SortList** function uses a Monotonous $\sum_{i=1}^{d} x_i$ compare function and sorts all skyline objects descending.

Output: $\Omega_{ASkyline}$ is the thin skyline set;

```
1: SkylineList := SortList(Ω_Skyline);
2: var current := 0; var second := 0;
3: for (current := 0; current < SkylineList.count; current++) do
4:    for (second:=current+1; second < SkylineList.count; second++) do
5:       if (dist(SkylineList[second],SkylineList[current]) ≤ εΦ(ρ)) then
6:          SkylineList.delete(second);
7:       end if
8:       if (dist(SkylineList[second],SkylineList[current]) > ε√d) then
9:          break;
10:      end if
11:   end for
12: end for
```

3.2   Extended CF-Based Thin Skyline Algorithm

Although the *NAS* algorithm is effective and universal, it has two main problems: One, it must save the basic skyline set in memory which is wasted; the other, when a new data is coming, it must rerun the *NAS* algorithm to get the thin skyline set which can not be suitable for the data stream environment and can not be scalable to high performance mining. To solve these problems, a

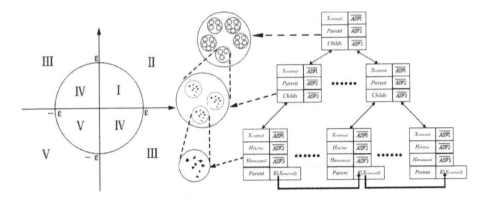

Fig. 4. Cluster regions   **Fig. 5.** Extended Micro-Cluster Feather Tree

general strategy is to apply data compression or summarization which can save the memory and run time. So we can partition the sliding window data into extended micro-cluster feature tree based on CF-tree [16] which only save the thin skyline set and the information of their close neighbors (two or more micro-clusters can build a larger micro-cluster and then all objects in sliding window form a micro-cluster tree).

Definition 5 (Extended Micro-Cluster Feature Tree, EMCF-Tree). *A extended micro-cluster feature tree for a set of d-dimensional objects* $X_1, \cdots, X_n$ $(X_i = (x_i^1, \cdots, x_i^d))$, *is defined as a* $(3d + 3 + L(H_{Skyline}) + L(H_{dominated}))$-*tuple* $(\overline{ASF1}, \overline{ASF2}, \overline{ASF3}, K(X_{centriod}), X_{centriod}, Parent, H_{Skyline}, H_{dominated})$. *The definition of each of these entries is as follows, Figure 5 is the whole data structure:*

1. The p-th entry of $\overline{ASF1}$ *is equal to* $\sum_{j=1}^{n} x_j^p$; *The p-th entry of* $\overline{ASF2}$ *is equal to* $\sum_{j=1}^{n} (x_j^p)^2$; *The p-th entry of* $\overline{ASF3}$ *is equal to* $\min_{j=1}^{n}(x_j^p)$; $K(X_{centriod})$ *is the ordinal of* $X_{centriod}$;

2. $X_{centriod}$ is belong to $\Omega_{ASkyline}$, which represents the centroid of its micro-cluster; Parent is pointer to its parent node, which is to trace back to modify its ancestors;

3. $H_{Skyline}$ is a heap to save the skyline objects within its micro-cluster; $H_{dominated}$ is a heap to save the dominated objects by $X_{centriod}$; n is the length of sliding window.

Main ideal of EMCFTA algorithm is as follows: (1) along with the data coming, algorithm constructs the extend-micro cluster-feather tree, and at the same time, from root node beginning, find the closest micro-cluster which is a leaf node following with the new incoming object(in line code 1). (2) when comparing the $X_{centriod}$ and X_{new}, from Figure 1, we can see clearly that the new incoming object only has five possible results, and EMCFTA algorithm deals with them respectively.(line code 2-12).

Algorithm 2. $EMCFTA(\varepsilon, \Omega_{Skyline})$

Input: ε is the distance, input the original data objects in Ω. The X_{new} represents a new object from the data stream.

Output: $\Omega_{ASkyline}$ is the thin skyline set;

1: find the closest micro-cluster from the EMCF-Tree, that is MC_d which also is the leaf node;
2: **if** $(X_{new} \succ X_{centriod})$ **then**
3:    X_{new} is located in region(V) of Figure 4, so $X_{centriod} := X_{new}$;
4: **else if** $(X_{centriod} \succ X_{new})$ **then**
5:    begin
6:     **if** $(K(X_{new}) - K(X_{centriod}) \leq n - K(X_{centriod}) mod n)$ **then**
7:      no action;
8:     **else**
9:      X_{new} is located in region(I) of Figure 4, so add X_{new} to $H_{dominated}$;
10:    **end if**
11:    end;
       /*X_{new} and $X_{centriod}$ are skyline objects*/
12: **else if** $(dist(X_{new}, X_{centriod}) \leq \varepsilon)$ **then**
13:    X_{new} is located in region(IV) of Figure 4, and add X_{new} to $H_{Skyline}$;
14: **else**
15:    X_{new} is located in region (III) of Figure 4, create a new micro-cluster leaf node to MC_d's parent, and X_{new} is the centroid object.
16: **end if**

---

4 Experiments

As mentioned earlier, there is no existing technique designed to support efficient computation of mining the thin skyline over data stream. In our performance study, we implemented a simulation system in C++ of Visual Studio 2003, the prediction veracities and the effects on reducing runtime cost of all our proposed models were tested. Experiments were performed on an Intel Pentium 4, CPU 2 GHZ, and RAM 512 MB, with Windows XP. Because the real data can be viewed as the composition of three data distributions, so we evaluate our techniques against the three most popular synthetic benchmark data, correlated, independent, and anti-correlated [1,7,8,9,10,6,12,15,13,14,11]. Details of the data generator can be found in [1]. All generated data value is between 0 and 1, the difference distance $\varepsilon \in [0,1]$ and dimension d is from 2 to 10.

Firstly, we compare $\Omega_{ASkyline}$ with $\Omega_{Skyline}$ in size at three data distributions. We already find that the size of the Skyline set will increase with the increasing of the size of the original data set and the number of dimensions. From Figure 6(a), we observe that the result set produced by our two algorithms is between 30% and 55% of the basic skyline set with $d = 5$ and $\varepsilon = 0.1$. If we increase the difference distance, the thin skyline result set will become smaller than 40% of the basic skyline set. Especially, the anti-correlation data distribution reduced more objects because we have the adaptive parameter. Experiment proved our algorithms can decrease adaptively the skyline objects and well be fitted with the change of data distributions.

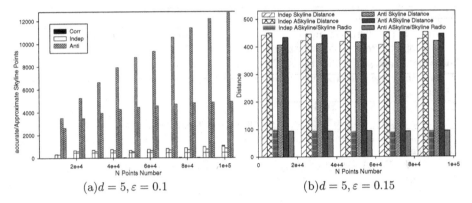

(a)$d = 5, \varepsilon = 0.1$ (b)$d = 5, \varepsilon = 0.15$

Fig. 6. Thin skyline set in left, average distance in right

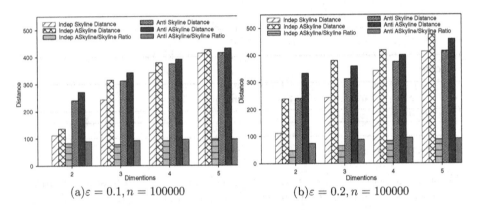

(a)$\varepsilon = 0.1, n = 100000$ (b)$\varepsilon = 0.2, n = 100000$

Fig. 7. Average distance

Secondly, we would examine the quality of thin skyline set. The data set and the parameters used in this experiment are as same as the first experiment. Because the number of basic skyline objects in the correlation distribution is fewer than other two distributions sharply, we only use the anti-correlation and independent distributions as next experiments. To measure the quality of thin skyline set, We use the average distance in $\Omega_{Skyline}$ and $\Omega_{ASkyline}$ which is the average distance among the arbitrary two objects. These two formulas are as follows:

$$AvgDist_{Skyline} = \frac{\sum_{i=1}^{|\Omega_{Skyline}|}(\sum_{j=2 \wedge j \neq i}^{|\Omega_{Skyline}|} dist(X_i, X_j))}{|\Omega_{Skyline}| \cdot (|\Omega_{Skyline}| - 1)/2} \qquad (2)$$

$$AvgDist_{ASkyline} = \frac{\sum_{i=1}^{|\Omega_{ASkyline}|}(\sum_{j=2 \wedge j \neq i}^{|\Omega_{ASkyline}|} dist(X_i, X_j))}{|\Omega_{ASkyline}| \cdot (|\Omega_{ASkyline}| - 1)/2} \qquad (3)$$

In Figure 6(b), the average distance ratio (equals: $\frac{100 \times AvgDist_{Skyline}}{AvgDist_{ASkyline}}$) is between 90 and 99 and the skyline objects have been reduced to almost 55% of

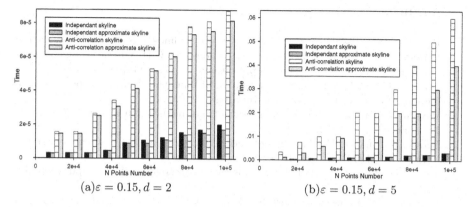

(a)$\varepsilon = 0.15, d = 2$　　　　　　　　(b)$\varepsilon = 0.15, d = 5$

Fig. 8. Runtime comparison

basic skyline objects. That is to say, in five dimensions we cut down almost a half skylines objects, but only decrease less than 10% skyline quality. Then we fix the object number to exam the quality with the change of dimension and difference distance. In Figure 7(a) and (b), we fix the object number to 100000 and observe that the average distance ratio are between 61 and 96, above 85 has 12 tests in total 16 tests, less than 75 only has 2 tests. The average ratio in 16 tests is 89.6. From this experiment, we observe that our algorithms are efficient and practicable which are meaningful for data stream mining applications.

Thirdly, we check the two algorithms efficiency. Similarly, the database and the parameters which are used in this experiment are as same as the previous. And in this experiment, we examine the total amount of time needed by each algorithm under different cases. Figure 8(a) shows different run time in $\varepsilon = 0.15$ and $d = 2$. Because of only two dimensions, the computation of distance is very fast in the **NAS** and **EMCFTA** algorithms. So **EMCFTA** only has $1 \sim 8\%$ improvement comparing to **NAS**. In Figure 8(b), due to the dimension up to five, we observe that **EMCFTA** algorithm is obviously faster than **NAS** about $10 \sim 18\%$, especially in anti-correlation distribution. So we conclude that **EMCFTA** algorithm is more suitable to large amount and changeable data stream environment.

5   Conclusions and Future Work

In this paper, a novel concept (called *thin skyline*) is proposed, and then two algorithms are developed which prunes adaptively the objects to guarantee thin skyline quality. Furthermore, our experimental performance study shows that the proposed methods are both efficient and effective. In future, we plan to develop a parallel and distributed algorithm to meet more scalable and changeable data stream environment.

References

1. Börzsönyi, S., Kossmann, D., Stocker, K.: The skyline operator. In: ICDE (2001)
2. Bentley, J.L., Kung, H.T., Schkolnick, M., Thompson, C.D.: On the average number of maxima in a set of vectors and applications. J. ACM (1978)
3. Cranor, C.D., Johnson, T., Spatscheck, O., Shkapenyuk, V.: Gigascope: A stream database for network applications. In: SIGMOD (2003)
4. Paxson, V.: Bro: a system for detecting network intruders in real-time. Computer Networks 31, 23–24 (1999)
5. Lerner, A., Shasha, D.: The virtues and challenges of ad hoc + streams querying in finance. IEEE Data Eng. Bull. 26(1), 49–56 (2003)
6. Tan, K.L., Eng, P.K., Ooi, B.C.: Efficient progressive skyline computation. In: VLDB (2001)
7. Kossmann, D., Ramsak, F., Rost, S.: Shooting stars in the sky: An online algorithm for skyline queries. In: Bressan, S., Chaudhri, A.B., Lee, M.L., Yu, J.X., Lacroix, Z. (eds.) VLDB 2002. LNCS, vol. 2590, Springer, Heidelberg (2003)
8. Papadias, D., Tao, Y., Fu, G., Seeger, B.: An optimal and progressive algorithm for skyline queries. In: SIGMOD (2003)
9. Luo, Y., Lu, H.X., Lin, X.: A scalable and i/o optimal skyline processing algorithm. In: Li, Q., Wang, G., Feng, L. (eds.) WAIM 2004. LNCS, vol. 3129, Springer, Heidelberg (2004)
10. Lin, X., Yuan, Y., Wang, W., Lu, H.: Stabbing the sky: Efficient skyline computation over sliding windows. In: ICDE (2005)
11. Papadias, D., Tao, Y., Fu, G., Seeger, B.: Progressive skyline computation in database systems. ACM Trans. Database Syst. 30(1) (2005)
12. Chomicki, J., Godfrey, P., Gryz, J., Liang, D.: Skyline with presorting. In: ICDE (2003)
13. Yuan, Y., Lin, X., Liu, Q., Wang, W., Yu, J.X., Zhang, Q.: Efficient computation of the skyline cube. In: VLDB (2005)
14. Tao, Y., Xiao, X., Pei, J.: Subsky: Efficient computation of skylines in subspaces. In: ICDE (2006)
15. Xia, T., Zhang, D.: Refreshing the sky: the compressed skycube with efficient support for frequent updates. In: SIGMOD (2006)
16. Zhang, T., Ramakrishnan, R., Livny, M.: Birch: An efficient data clustering method for very large databases. In: SIGMOD (1996)

Service Recommendation with Adaptive User Interests Modeling*

Cheng Zhang and Yanbo Han

Research Centre for Grid and Service Computing
Institute of Computing Technology, Chinese Academy of Sciences
P.O. Box 2704, 100080, Beijing, China
zhch@software.ict.ac.cn, yhan@ict.ac.cn

Abstract. In composing and using services, user's requirements are subject to uncertainty and changes. It can be difficult for users to maintain an overview of all available services and to make good choices among them. This paper proposes an approach to proactively recommending suitable services to users. Our major contribution is to have devised a novel user-interest model to describe user's interests adaptively. A reasonable way is put forward for picking up suitable services timely and its key problem is defined formally. Important properties of the model are theoretically proved, and the effectiveness of recommendations is verified with prototypical implementation and tryouts in public service area.

1 Introduction

Service composition has become an important means to build integrated applications. Users may develop such an application by repeating the interactive step of selecting suitable services and then gluing them to the target application. In this process, user's service requirements are subject to uncertainty and changes. While SOA promotes some nice features such as loosely-coupling, it may bring user's difficulty in maintaining a good knowledge of all available services and to pick up the right ones. There exist some efforts in service retrieval and service representation, e.g. [1], [2]. Some deficiencies can be identified as follows:

- Existing methods for service representations usually organize services in a certain manner. However, such previous arrangements may not suit best to user's individual requirements.
- Service retrieval techniques ask users to provide query requests explicitly and exactly. Thus the user has to frequently adjust requirements and inquire again. The complexity is augmented as a result.

To deal with the above problems, one feasible approach is to proactively recommend suitable services to users in an interactive manner for each step during

* This work is supported by the National Natural Science Foundation of China (Grant No. 90412010 and No. 70673098) and China Ministry of Science and Technology 863 Program (Grant No. 2006AA12Z202).

T. Janowski and H. Mohanty (Eds.): ICDCIT 2007, LNCS 4882, pp. 265–270, 2007.

a service composition process. In this paper we propose such an approach, which is named Proactive Service Recommendation (PSR). PSR tries to deliver "suitable" services, i.e. the services that are likely to be used in the current step. Major contributions of the paper include: A user-interest model is proposed. Some specific characters of this model make it good at adjusting user interests adaptively when composing services. Next, a reasonable way is proposed to select suitable services according to the user interests in each interactive step.

The rest of this paper is structured as follows: Section 2 describes the major idea of PSR. Section 3 proposes the user-interest model. Section 4 designs an algorithm to select suitable services. Section 5 evaluates our work with a discussion on related works. The paper concludes in Section 6.

2   User-Interest-Based PSR

In using and composing services, the user can get some useful information from the outputs of the previously-chosen services. If we look the outputs of all the usable services as a full set, the outputs of the chosen services exhibit the user's interests. Further, if a service can accept part of these interests as inputs, it possibly outputs more information about user's interests. Thereby, the existed interests could form the reference points for selecting services in later step. In terms of the above opinion, we proposed an approach to the user-interest-based PSR. The Fig.1 depicts the principle of this approach.

In each interactive step of the service composition the output parameters of the previously-chosen services form user's interest nodes, each of which has a weight calculated based on a user-interest model. All such nodes make up of the user interests. Then we rank the service candidates by a weighted value, which is calculated for each service by matching its inputs with the user interests. The services with higher rank will be recommended to the user.

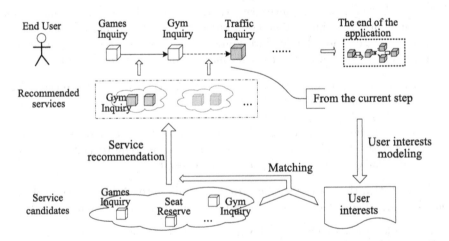

Fig. 1. The principle of the user-interest based proactive service recommendation

It's worth to emphasize that we regard the basic functional units of services as the recommended elements in this paper. Let's take the web service as an example, its operations will be recommended instead of the web service itself.

3   User Interest Model

Several characteristics about user interests can be inferred according to the discussion in Section 2. Firstly, the more an output parameter appears, the more the user is interested in it. Secondly, the previous user interests may be satisfied to a certain extent. Hence, we define the user-interest model as follows.

The output parameters of the previously-chosen services constitute a set denoted by $P=\{p_1,...,p_n\}$, where iterative parameters appear only once. The last interactive step in present is called the current step. A 2-tuple $(t, weight)$ is denoted by $INode(t)$, where $t \in P$ is called *interest node*, and weight indicates its importance. Further, $UserInterest=INode(t_i)$ is called *user interest* if $t_i \in P$ and $\forall(x)((x \in P) \rightarrow x \in \{t_i\})$.

Aiming for the specific character of the user interest mentioned above, we propose an approach to computing the weight of the interest node as follow:

$$weight_t = \frac{N_t}{N_{total}} + f(h) \tag{1}$$

t is an interest node whose weight is denoted by $weight_t$, and N_t is the total numbers it appeared until the current step. N_{total} records the total numbers of appearances of all interest nodes at that time. $f(h)$ is a function defined by:

$$f(h) = \frac{nh}{k} \tag{2}$$

n is the total number of interactive steps up to the current step, and h is the last step that t appears, briefly denoted by *position* later. k denotes the distance from the *position* of t to the current step. We define that $k = n + 1 - h$.

Clearly, $f(h)$ is a monotonic increasing function of q, and $weight_t$ is not only monotonic increasing with N_t when q is fixed but also monotonic increasing with q when N_t is fixed. Consequently, we can easily prove that $weight_t$ holds the closer-priority property. Namely, let t_1 and t_2 be interest nodes, h_1 and h_2 denote the position of t_1 and t_2 respectively. If h_1 is more than h_2, then $weight_{t1}$ is more than $weight_{t2}$. The proof is omitted in this paper because of the page limit.

4   Service Selection

As mentioned above we will discover the suitable services by parameter matching between the services' inputs and the user interests. Let p be an input parameter of a service and q be an interest node, if q can be assigned to p as its input, we say q is able to match with p. In order to improve the matching accuracy we reference some related works, e.g. [1], [3], to describe services with the ontology-based methods. As well known, the IsA relation demonstrates the inheritance between two concepts in the ontology. And the polymorphism principle tells us that the super-class concept can receive values from its sub-concepts. So we can compute the matching degree of two parameters according to their relationships in the ontology.

Let $Match$ denote the matching degree of two parameters p and q, the semantics of which are respectively mapping to the concept c_1 and c_2 in the ontology. Match can be defined as follows:

$$Match(p, q) = \begin{cases} 1/(d+1) & <c_1, c_2> \in IsA \\ 0 & <c_1, c_2> \notin IsA \end{cases} \tag{3}$$

Where d is the path length between c_1 and c_2 in the ontology. The above definition may potentially produce the many-to-many relations between the interest nodes and the service's input parameters. That is, the value of one interest node could be assigned to many input parameters and one input parameter can receive the value from different interest nodes. This paper only considers the one-to-one element matching between the interests set and the inputs set.

In order to precisely define this problem, we introduce the matching matrix which is denoted by C. Assume that the number of current interest nodes and the inputs of service S are respectively m and n, and then C_s is a nm matrix. Each row of C_s indicates one input of S and each column indicates one interest node. We also set $C_s[i,j] = match(p_i, q_j) * weight(q_j)$, where p_i is the input parameter which corresponds with the ith row, and q_j is the interest node which corresponds with the jth column. We use the matching matrix as a tool to formally define the matching problem mentioned above as follows:

$$Max \quad z = \sum_{i=1}^{n} \sum_{j=1}^{m} c_{ij} x_{ij}$$

$$S.t. \quad \sum_{i=1}^{n} x_{ij} \quad j = 1, 2, ..., m \tag{4}$$

$$\sum_{j=1}^{m} x_{ij} \quad i = 1, 2, ..., n$$

$$x_{ij} = 1 \quad or \quad 0$$

When selecting suitable services in a certain interactive step, the maximal value of z will be calculated for each service candidate and the services with a bigger outcome will take priority of recommendation. Well, how to calculate the maximal value of z becomes the key problem. The above definition tells us that it is a kind of assignment problems, so we can effectively solve it by the Hungarian method [4].

5   Discussion

The benefit of service recommendation consists in reducing the number of times for service retrieving from the whole service directory. In this section we will evaluate its effect based on the applied instances in the public service domain. Let RS_i be the set of recommended services in the ith interactive step, and ES_i be the set of services which are actually used in the ith step, and $|S|$ express the number of the element of the set S. Then, we define benchmarks for quantifying the effect of the recommendation as follows:

$$St f_{app} = \frac{\sum_{i=1}^{N} St f_{stepi}}{N}, \quad \text{where} \quad St f_{stepi} = \frac{|RS_i \cap ES_i|}{|ES_i|} \qquad (5)$$

Clearly, $|RS_i \cap ES_i|$ is the number of the recommended services which is contained in the set ES_i. Thereby, $St f_{step}$ is the proportion of recommended services to the actual used services in one step, and it states the satisfying degree of one recommendation. Similarly, $St f_{app}$ depicts the user's satisfactory degree for the whole composition.

Currently, VINCA tool is only applied in a small scope, it is hardly to collect test datum from a mass of samples. So we randomly choose forty applications from the system logs of five users, and then calculate the satisfactory degree of each application. In the end we compute the average of all satisfactory degrees. The result is 40.39%. This value explains that about 40 percent of the used services can be obtained from the set of recommended services. Namely, the times for looking up services from the whole service directory is reduced by 40%. It is convenient for users to discover suitable services.

6   Related Works

There are some related works on service recommendation. For example, the paper [5] adopts recommender system to dynamically selecting services, but it asks users to rate the executed services. The paper [6] uses both the user's requests and users' experiments to discover fitter services. These existed works are universally to retrieving services according to the requirements offered by the user. In order to discover suitable services timely and present them to users actively, some efforts, e.g. [7], [8], make use of the context information to arrange services and reduce the complexity of service discoveries. These works are well done but do not care about user's business requirements in the services composition.

A lot of research works have been done about the service matching. In the paper [9] the authors assume that there have been one-to-one mapping relations between the inputs of one service and the outputs of another, yet do not consider how to produce this mapping. Similarly, the paper [10] adopts the same assumption. Some other works, e.g. [11], allow the many-to-many relation between the parameters of services. Other works are similar with them such as [12] and more. We mainly concern about the one-to-one matching under many-to-many mapping relations, and formally define the problem of how to produce such matching.

7   Conclusion

This paper proposed an approach to proactively recommending suitable services to users. A user model adaptively depicting user's interests was proposed and a sound way for timely selecting suitable services was proposed. The paper discussed the properties of the user model in detail and the key problem of selecting services had been formally defined. Furthermore, experiments were carried out and evaluation was done on the basis of some practical cases.

Our further work will focus on two aspects: Firstly, we will concern about various approaches to service recommendation in a systematical way and consider how to use and combine them comprehensively. Secondly, we will further clarify the benchmark of the service recommendation.

References

1. Paolucci, M., Kawamura, T., et al.: Semantic Matching of Web Services Capabilities. In: Proceedings of the 1st International Semantic Web Conference, Sardinia, pp. 318–332 (2002)
2. Klein, M., Bernstein, A.: Searching Services on the Semantic Web Using Process Ontologies. In: Proceedings of the Int'l. Semantic Web Working Symp., Amsterdam, pp. 159–172 (2001)
3. Li, L., Horrocks, I.: A Software Framework for Matchmaking Based on Semantic Web Technology. In: Proceedings of the WWW 2003 Conference, Budapest, pp. 331–339 (2003)
4. Pazzani, M., Billsus, D.: Learning and Revising User Profiles: The Identification of Interesting Web Sites. Machine Learning 27, 313–331 (1997)
5. Umardand, S.M., Prabhakar, T.V.: Dynamic Selection of Web Services with Recommendation System. In: Proceedings of the International Conference on Next Generation Web Services Practices, Seoul, pp. 117–121 (2005)
6. Natallia, K., Aliaksandr, B., Vincenzo, D.A.: Web Service Discovery Based on Past User Experience. In: Proceedings of the International Conference on Business Information Systems, Poznan, pp. 95–107 (2007)
7. Maamar, Z., Mosterfaoui, S.K., et al.: Toward an Agent-Based and Context-Oriented Approach for Web Services Composition. IEEE Transactions on Knowledge and Data Engineering 17(5), 686–697 (2005)
8. Dey, A., Slaber, D., et al.: The Conference Assistant: Combining Context-Awareness with Wearable Computing. In: Proceedings of the 3rd International Symposium on Wearable Computers, San Francisco, pp. 21–28 (1999)
9. Medjahed, B., Bouguettaya, A., et al.: Composing Web Services on the Semantic Web. The VLDB Journal 12(4), 333–351 (2003)
10. Fang, J., Hu, S., et al.: A Service Interoperability Assessment Model for Service Composition. In: Proceeding of the IEEE International Conference on Services Computing, pp. 153–158 (2004)
11. Arpinar, I.B., Zhang, R., et al.: Ontology-driven Web Services Composition Platform. Information Systems and E-Business Management 3(2), 175–199 (2005)
12. Casati, F., Ilnicki, S., et al.: Dynamic and Adaptive Composition of E-Services. Information Systems 26(3), 143–162 (2001)

An Approach to Aggregating Web Services for End-User-Doable Construction of GridDoc Application*

Binge Cui

College of Information Science and Engineering, Shandong University of Science and
Technology, Qingdao, Shandong, China
cuibinge@yahoo.com.cn

Abstract. GridDoc is a Web-based application, which aims to support
the instant data integration by end users. This paper presents a service
virtualization approach to aggregating Web services into virtual data
services, and constructing user-customized data services to support the
GridDoc application. Some key mechanisms of the service virtualization,
namely the semantics annotation, service aggregation and virtualization
operations are discussed. The service virtualization approach has been
implemented and its application is illustrated. The paper concludes with
a comparative study with other related works.

1 Introduction

Many commercial software, such as Microsoft Office Excel and Infopath, can
import Web services as their data sources. However, current Web services are
designed for IT professionals, which don't fit for end users. As a matter of fact,
to facilitate the usage of Web services, we have to stride a number of hurdles,
e.g. how to define user-understandable data services, how to associate virtual
data services to underlying Web services, how to enable end users to customize
their own data services, etc.

In order to meet the above challenges, we propose a new service virtualization approach, and build a GridDoc application based on virtual data services
and their composition. A virtual data service is a business-user-understandable,
large-granularity service abstraction with business-level semantics. Web service
virtualization is the process of abstracting away Web service's technical details,
describing it with business-related semantics, aggregating semantically substitu-
tive Web services into one virtual data service, combining multiple virtual data
services into one customized data service with virtualization operators.

2 Basic Principle of the Service Virtualization Approach

Fig.1 illustrates a basic reference model of the virtualization approach. In Fig.1,
Virtual data services are defined by domain experts, and the definitions are

---

* Supported by Project of "Mountain Tai Scholar" Funded by the Government of
Shandong Province.

T. Janowski and H. Mohanty (Eds.): ICDCIT 2007, LNCS 4882, pp. 271–276, 2007.

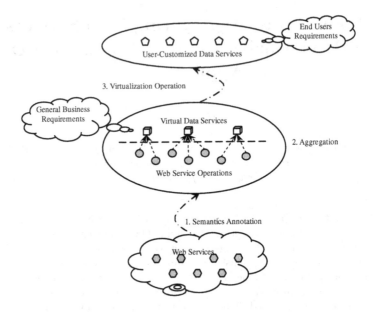

Fig. 1. Basic Principle of the Virtualization Approach

based on domain-specific norms of concepts and functionalities. Each virtual data service corresponds to an aggregation of Web service operations. A virtual data service is formulated based on meaningful combinations of activities (verbs) and concepts (nouns) as defined in domain standards.

User-customized data services are end-user-oriented service abstractions defined by transforming/combining virtual data services with virtualization operators. The structure of a user-customized data service includes 7 parts: identification, functionality, inputs, outputs, nonfunctional properties (NFP), virtual data services links and virtualization operations (SO). For example, if both virtual data service VDS_1 and VDS_2 can not satisfy the end users' requirements alone for mismatch of outputs, but the combined outputs of VDS_1 and VDS_2 can satisfy the end users' requirements. Then we can use the virtualization operator "Union" or "Join" on these two virtual data service to create a user-customized data service to achieve the service matching.

3   Process of Virtualization

3.1   Semantics Annotation

Semantics annotation is critical to reach unanimous understanding among syntax-diverse but functionality-similar Web services. In this paper, virtual data services, Web service operations and user-customized data services are all annotated with functional classification, inputs, outputs, and nonfunctional properties (NFP). Such annotation is saved in OWL format[1].

3.2   Web Services Aggregation

Virtual data services aggregate Web service operations with the same functional classification, inputs and outputs. Web services often operate in a dynamic environment as service providers remove, modify or relocate their services frequently. Aggregation of services is an effective mechanism to cope with the dynamism of Web services. When service operations are aggregated into one virtual data service, they can be selected dynamically and application-level fault tolerance is yielded[2]. Every virtual data service has its corresponding NFP-based service selection policy. When executing a virtual data service, it can avoid selecting an unavailable Web service operation and select the appropriate Web service operation to run according to its nonfunctional properties.

3.3   Virtualization Operation

It isn't always possible for end users to find the right virtual data services that satisfy their requirements. At this time, virtualization operators can be used to transform/combine virtual data services into a customized data service to meet end users' requirements. We design our virtualization operators from two perspectives, one is on the selection of services and the other is on the filtering/uniting/joining of the outputs of services. The fundamental virtualization operators include select, project, union, join and power.

Selection. The selection operator, denoted as σ, is used both in filtering the service outputs and filtering the involved Web service operations based on their functional classifications and nonfunctional properties (NFP). For example, as for filtering service outputs, we want the virtual data service "queryHotels" only present to the users the 3-star hotel information while the default query produces all hotel information. Following virtualization operation creates a customized data service "queryHotels_3star" by filtering the outputs of virtual data service "queryHotels" with condition "star=3".

$$queryHotels\_3star = \sigma_{out.star=3}(queryHotels) \qquad (1)$$

As for selecting involved Web service operations, following virtualization operation creates a customized data service "queryHotels _fs" by selecting the Web service operations of "queryHotels" virtual data service with response time less than 3 seconds.

$$queryHotels\_fs = \sigma_{responseTime<3s}(queryHotels) \qquad (2)$$

Projection. The projection operator, denoted as π, is used to select one or more attributes of the outputs. Following virtualization operation creates a customized data service "queryHotels_pr" by only rendering the name, star and address information of the virtual data service cqueryHotels".

$$queryHotels\_pr = \pi_{out.name,out.star,out.address}(queryHotels) \qquad (3)$$

Join. The join operator, denoted as $\bowtie$, is used for joining outputs of two virtual data services. Suppose that the information of teachers and their current incomes is needed. But there are only two virtual data services, one can provide the basic information of teachers, and the other can provide the information of their incomes. Following virtualization operation creates a customized data service "query_j" by joining the outputs of both "queryTeachers" and "queryIncomes".

$$queryHotels\_j = queryTeachers \bowtie queryIncomes \qquad (4)$$

Union. The union operator, denoted as $\cup$, is used for combining outputs of two virtual data services. Suppose that the information of students is needed. But there are only two virtual data services, one can provide the information of undergraduates and the other can provide the information of graduates. Following virtualization operation creates a customized data service "queryStudents" by uniting the outputs of both "queryUndergraduates" and "queryGraduates".

$$queryStudents = queryUndergraduates \cup queryGraduates \qquad (5)$$

Power. The power operator is denoted as ψ. This operator is used when end users need to combine all the outputs of the service operations that aggregate to one virtual data service. The following equation creates a customized data service "queryHotels_full" whose outputs will contain all the outputs of the Web service operations that aggregate to virtual data service "queryHotels"..

$$queryHotels\_full = \psi(queryHotels) \qquad (6)$$

4   Implementation

The architecture of GridDoc consists of three parts: Basic Service Layer, Virtual Data Service Layer, and GridDoc Design Environment[3]. At the Basic Service Layer, various available resources are wrapped into Web services and registered into Web service repository. This layer provides a service registering and annotating tool for service providers to submit their services.

The Virtual Data Service Layer is responsible to create, manage and execute virtual data services. A newly registered Web service operation will be aggregated into an already-existing virtual data service according to its semantic description. Each virtual data service should be attached with a service selection policy, which defines which Web service operation should be selected.

At the top layer, end users can insert a virtual data service into the GridDoc, or define a customized data service with virtualization operation first, and then insert it into the GridDoc. When the user- customized data service is executed, it will be processed by the Customized Data Service Interpreting component, which can decompose it into fundamental virtual data services. Then, the Service Routing/Selection component will select the right Web service operations for the virtual data service to execute according to the QoS of Web services and its service selection policy.

5   Application

In this section we demonstrate the application of the service virtualization approach by a real-world example. Suppose that one person is employed by two organizations, thus he can earn two incomes. When calculating the personal income tax, we should sum all of his incomes and then calculate the total income tax. The two incomes are provided by two Web service operations respectively, namely "QueryIncome_sdust" and "QueryIncome_ict".

Suppose that one of the end users wants to create a data service named "QueryIncomeTax" whose function is to query the personal income taxes of teachers. The customized data service can be built from two existing virtual data services, namely "queryTeacher" and "queryIncome". Virtual data service "queryIncome" has aggregated two Web service operations "QueryIncome_sdust" and "QueryIncome_ict", and their outputs should be combined. End users produce the customized data service by the following virtualization operation:

$$queryIncomeTax = \pi_{Name}(queryTeacher) \bowtie \pi_{Income}(\psi(queryIncome)) \quad (7)$$

This virtualization process is shown in Fig. 2.

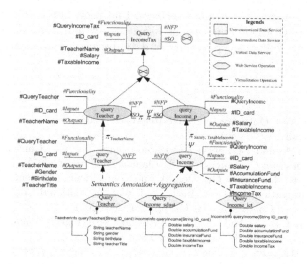

Fig. 2. An Example of Service Virtualization

6   Discussion

IBM proposed the Service Domain technology[4]. A Service Domain is an abstraction to a cluster of functional interchangeable Web services. It applies autonomic computing principles for aggregating Web services and Grid services. The Service Domain technology provides a service proxy layer - so called service

Grid that can create, filter, discover, cluster, organize, select, route, recover, and switch Web services and Grid services automatically.

VINCA_Virtualization[5] is a main module of VINCA integrated business-end development and execution environment. VINCA_Virtualization has the core mechanisms of services annotation, services aggregation, virtualization operation, and services convergence that provide key support to the binding and execution of business services.

All the above-mentioned approaches aim at making the service oriented applications more reliable. The service virtualization approach proposed in this paper focuses on how to support the user-customized data services based on virtual data services. The virtualization operators are our main contribution which is used to transform and combine virtual data services.

7   Conclusion

We have presented an approach for Web services aggregation and virtualization, which is a main component for end-user-oriented data integration. We discuss some key mechanisms, including services annotation, services aggregation and virtualization operations that provide important support to the binding and execution of user-customized data services. End users can define a customized data service for GridDoc applications using the virtualization approach, which improves the flexibility and reliability of data integration applications.

References

1. OWL: OWL Web Ontology Language Reference (2004),
   http://www.w3.org/TR/owl-ref/
2. Michael, N., Muninda, P.: Service-Oriented Computing: Key Concepts and Principles. IEEE Internet Computing, 75–81 (January/February 2005)
3. Cui, B., Qi, K., Ding, W.: GridDoc: A End-User-Oriented Presentation Model for Resource Integration. In: Proc. Int'l. Conf. 6nd International Conference on Grid and Cooperative Computing (GCC), pp. 261–266 (2007)
4. Tan, Y., Topol, B., Vellanki, V., et al.: Business service grid: Manage Web services and Grid services with Service Domain Technology (2003),
   http://www-106.ibm.com/developerworks/grid/library/gr-servicegrid
5. Yu, J., Fang, J., Han, Y., Wang, J., Zhang, C.: An Approach to Abstracting and Transforming Web Services for End-user-doable Construction of Service-Oriented Applications. In: Proc. Int'l. Conf. 2nd International Conference on Grid Service Engineering and Management (GSEM), pp. 248–258. Springer, Heidelberg (2005)

An Adaptive Metadata Model for Domain-Specific Service Registry[*]

Kun Chen[1,2], Yanbo Han[1], Dongju Yang[1], Yongshan Wei[1,2], and Wubin Li[1]

[1] Research Center for Grid and Service Computing Institute of Computing Technology, Chinese Academy of Sciences, Beijing, China
[2] Department of Computer Science and Technology, Shandong University of Science and Technology, Qingdao, China
{chenkun,yhan,yangdongju,weiyongshan,liwubin}@software.ict.ac.cn

Abstract. A domain-specific service registry should satisfy two requirements at least: coping with diverse service description requirements from different services; supporting semantic description on service interfaces for interoperation in a specific domain. This paper proposes an adaptive metadata model that supports flexible semantic description of service interfaces. It uses a simple inheritance mechanism to provide multiple metadata models on a light-weight generic metadata model and semantic annotation templates to facilitate interface semantic description for domain-specific services. The implementation and application of this metadata model in a real-world domain-specific service registry promises that a user can customize a metadata model and add interface semantic metadata in an easy-to-use way.

1 Introduction

As the basic function unit of SOA, services have a most commonly agreed-upon aspect that they are encapsulated reusable business functions defined by interfaces [4]. Consequentially, how service consumers discover appropriate services turns to be a key problem in SOA. Service registry acts as information mediation between service providers and service consumers. Since service description information is usually stored as service metadata, service registry puts metadata model a basic position. As a result, requirements on metadata model should be well considered when designing a service registry.

In fact, we are just facing some fair and reasonable requirements in a real-word project. The project is called Agriculture Technology Information Integration System (ATIIS), which uses Web services to integrate distributed agriculture technology information stored in different locations and provides a uniform access point for ender users. Agriculture Technology Information Service Registry (ATISR) is a part of it, which could register various services provided by different organizations and map their interface schema into an integrated view with domain ontology.

---

[*] This work is supported by the National Natural Science Foundation of China (Grant No. 70673098) and the Project of "Taishan Scholar" which is Funded by Government of Shandong Province.

T. Janowski and H. Mohanty (Eds.): ICDCIT 2007, LNCS 4882, pp. 277–282, 2007.

—**Multiple Metadata models can be defined.** Different services have different requirements on service description. In order to be adapted to the diversity of requirements, the definition of multiple metadata models should be supported.

—**Interface semantic annotation should be supported.** WSDL is a type of syntactic description. However, service discovery and interoperation need to know the meaning of service interface parameters. Domain ontology is used to add semantic annotations on WSDL interface parameters to tackle this problem.

The project is a representative in the applications of using Web services to integrate distributed and heterogeneous data. The same requirements are also existed in a wide spectrum of other scenarios such as e-government system and healthy care management, in which Web services are used for providing information and domain ontology is introduced to add interface semantic metadata.

A large amount of service registries have been proposed by academic world as well as some IT vendors [1,4]. However, most metadata models in them try to describe all aspects of a service, which makes them complex and not easy to use. In this paper, motivated by the above-stated requirements, we propose an adaptive metadata model which uses a simple inheritance mechanism to provide multiple metadata models for various services. Moreover, annotation template is used to facilitate interface semantic annotation for domain-specific services.

2   Related Works

As an industrial standard, UDDI [3] aims at providing a universal registry data model. It uses TModels to provide additional data to the UDDI core entities for different service descriptions. However, the taxonomic structure of TModel is complex and using it for extension requires extending the discovery interface, which is almost impossible for ender users. Moreover, UDDI core entities do not support semantic metadata. OWL-S [6] and WSMO [5] are two major initial and most popular semantic Web service description models. Although they both have extension mechanisms, we can not get a special extended model for the description of a particular group of services. WebSphere Service Registry and Repository (WSRR) developed by IBM [4] uses templates to model sets of metadata, allowing many different metadata models to be represented. However, for template definition, WSRR currently exploits only the subTypeOf relationship in OWL, which provides no better ability than the taxonomy used in TModel.

Much work has been done on semantic annotation. MWSAF [2] uses a media structure called SchemaGraph to facilitate the matching between XML schema and ontology to find the relevant ontology. Unfortunately, the matching results are not good if the WSDL file does not have a good structure or the ontology becomes much comprehensive. [8] proposes a template-based markup tool for web contents semantic annotation. But because web contents are various, structure and reusability of templates are main problems.

3   The Adaptive Metadata Model

3.1   Multiple Metadata Models

Two kinds of metadata models are related by the inheritance mechanism:

Generic metadata model: Generic metadata model is used to organize the common metadata items among all services.

Extended metadata model: Extended metadata model can be either inherited from the generic metadata model or another extended metadata model. It is used by a particular type of services for description.

General metadata model should benefit four activities for a service: discovery, substitution, composition and management [10]. Here, four types of general metadata in it are summed up. We think they can describe a service throughout its entire lifecycle, and provide necessary information for service application and service management.

Technical metadata, including service URL address, operations, input/output information and so forth, give the information of where the service is and how to use it.

Semantic metadata, such as operation semantic metadata, input/output semantic metadata, enable exact service discovery and service composition.

Profile metadata, which can be unstructured text including service description, organization name and so on. These metadata can be used by service consumers as well as the administrator of a registry for service browsing.

Management metadata, including service using times, publishing status and other records throughout a service's lifecycle. These metadata facilitate the administrator to manage registered services and service consumers to discover appropriate services.

All the profile metadata are put in a ServiceProfile property, management metadata in a ManagementInfo property, and technical metadata and semantic metadata in a ServiceGrounding property. The generic metadata model includes the three properties for describing common properties of all services.

Extended metadata are used to define special metadata items for a particular type of services. They can be referred by an extended metadata model. We define an extended metadata item as an ontology class in OWL, so it can describe various concepts a user needs and support semantic discovery.

In order to make the definition of extended metadata models easy, we consult to the inheritance mechanism in object-oriented filed, which allows for the definition of a subclass that inherits the features of a specific superclass [9]. Inheritance mechanism is a good method for reuse and specialization. Here, we only permit the simplest single inheritance. That means a sub metadata model can inherit only one super metadata model with its own extended metadata items.

This saves work, because users only need concentrate on new features. For example, a metadata model F for describing acquiring information services has been defined, and this metadata model has two extended metadata items:

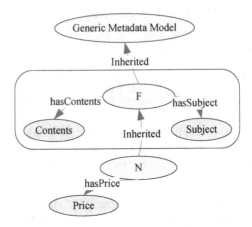

Fig. 1. Defining a new metadata model N by inheriting F

Subject and Contents. Now, if a user wants to describe payment acquiring information services, he can just define a new metadata model N by inheriting F and adding a new extended metadata item: Price. The user needs not care metadata in F, for N has inherited all of them automatically (Fig.1).

3.2 Semantic Annotation Templates

Services are encapsulated reusable business functions defined by interfaces. Business functions represent certain activities in a domain, and domain activity knowledge has commonness and is reusable [7]. Based on such a fact, we use an interface semantic annotation template to describe a business function. An interface semantic annotation template consists of four parts:

Template Name: describing business function of a Web service operation.
Operation: describing the operation with domain ontology.
Inputs: describing input parameters of the operation with domain ontology.
Outputs: describing output parameters of the operation with domain ontology.

Semantic annotation templates can be established by domain experts beforehand. A service may have several operations. However, in order to facilitate business function description, a semantic annotation template describes exactly one operation. So a service has to be split into several function units when using interface semantic annotation templates.

A template describes service interface schema with domain concepts and can be reused. On the one hand, semantic annotation templates hide ontological complexity from users, which liberates them from the burden of manual relating concepts in Web services to a domain specific ontology. On the other hand, as semantic annotation templates encapsulate and expose the domain knowledge and service interface schema to a service provider for configuration, the semantic annotation accuracy is higher than that of automatic semantic annotation methods which try to relate ontology with no meaning WSDL interface names.

4 Implementation and Application

ATISR is a part of ATIIS. It builts on the metadata model proposed in this paper. ATISR is implemented by three major components: Metadata model manager is used for managing multiple metadata models for diverse requirements on service description; Interface semantic annotation templates manager is used for mapping service interface schema into an integrated view; Service metadata manager provides CRUD operations on service metadata for the application layer in ATIIS such as task analyzer and results integrator, service monitor and service execution and interoperation engine.

To better explain how the registry works, a real application scenario is described as follows: A user uses the registry to publish a payment Web service that searches the expert information stored in Beijing Agriculture Bureau. He can use ATISR to achieve his goals with the following major steps:

Choosing or defining a metadata model: This user can browse all the metadata models have been established in the registry. He finds his service can be described by the searching information service metadata model, but he wants to declare the cost of his service. So he defines Price as an extended metadata item, and created a payment searching information service metadata model which inherited the searching information service metadata model with the extended metadata item: Price.

Filling in metadata items in the metadata model: After choosing the payment searching information service metadata model, ATISR will initial some metadata in this metadata model automatically, such as management metadata. The user should fill in or choose other metadata through a GUI.

Choosing and configuring interface semantic annotation templates: Then he chooses the searching expert information template and configures the sequence of the input and output parameters in the template according to his service WSDL file.

Finally, if the user submits, ATISR will check if these metadata consist with the payment searching information service metadata model, and stores them into a semantic database.

5 Conclusion

In order to satisfy the diversity of requirements on service description and support service interface semantic annotation in an easy-to-use way, we present an adaptive metadata model. The registry metadata model is implemented in ATISR. A real scenario described in 4 validates that a user can customize a metadata model he needs, and add interface semantic metadata easily and accurately. The metadata model only support simple singe inheritance now, however, we believe that more complex inheritance such as multiple inheritances will enhance its extensibility. Moreover, semantic annotation templates have strict restrictions on service interfaces now, how to make templates flexible is also among our future research goals.

References

1. Liu, J., Gu, N.: Service registration and discovery in a domain-oriented UDDI registry. In: CIT 2005. Proceedings of the 2005 The Fifth International Conference on Computer and Information Technology, pp. 276–282 (2005)
2. Patil, A., Oundhakar, S., Sheth, A., Verma, K.: METEOR-S Web service annotation framework. In: Proc. of the 13th Int'l. World Wide Web Conf., pp. 553–562. ACM Press, New York (2004)
3. [UDDI, 2003] UDDI: available at:
   http://uddi.org/pubs/uddi-v3.0.2-20041019.htm
4. IBM, IBM WebSphere Service Registry and Repository Frequently Asked Questions (February 2007), available at
   http://www-304.ibm.com/software/integration/wsrr/library/faqs.html
5. D2v1.0 Web Service Modeling Ontology (WSMO) available at:
   http://www.wsmo.org/2004/d2/v1.0/20040920/
6. OWL-S: Semantic Markup for Web Services, available at:
   http://www.w3.org/Submission/2004/SUBM-OWL-S-20041122/
7. Jianwu, W.: Research on a Domain and Business User Oriented Service Model Beijing, China, ICT, CAS (2007)
8. Kettler, B., Starz, J., et al.: A Template-Based Markup Tool for Semantic Web Content. In: Gil, Y., Motta, E., Benjamins, V.R., Musen, M.A. (eds.) ISWC 2005. LNCS, vol. 3729, Springer, Heidelberg (2005)
9. Berard, E.V.: Basic Object-Oriented Concepts, The Object Agency, Inc., available at http://www.toa.com/pub/oobasics/oobasics.htm
10. O'Sullivan, J., Edmond, D., Ter Hofstede, A.: What's in a Service? Towards Accurate Description of Non-Functional Service Properties. Distributed and Parallel Databases 12(2-3), 117–133 (2002)

Globalization from the Information and Communication Perspective

Wojciech Cellary

Poznan University of Economics
Department of Information Technology
60-854 Poznan, Poland
cellary@kti.ae.poznan.pl

Abstract. In this paper globalization is analyzed from the electronic information and communication perspective. Two kinds of communities are distinguished: traditional territorial communities and new kind of content communities. Content communities are the results of human communication via Internet. Content communities group people round a particular information content that is of interest to them. Features of both kinds of communities are analyzed, showing their fundamental differences. Basing on those differences, a conclusion is that global society is a myth, while information society is a reality.

1 Introduction

Globalization is a very hot topic investigated from very different perspectives. Recently, an extensive research results on globalization has been presented in a monograph *Globalization: A Critical Introduction* by Jan Aart Scholte [2]. In this monograph, the author presents how the ambiguous term "globalization" is understood on the basis of many different social and economic doctrines and theories. The author presents also how globalization applies to diverse categories of different nature: production, governance, identity, and knowledge.

This paper complements the monograph of J. A. Scholte by an analysis of globalization from a more engineering point of view. A question asked in this paper is the following: What social changes will follow from the fact that Internet permits people living across the globe to mutually inform and communicate? Internet as an information and communication medium is characterized by new features unavailable before. Will Internet be sufficient to emerge global society? If so, what this global society will be like?

A starting point for the analysis presented in this paper is a relationship between human communities and human communication, both personal and mass communication. This relationship is presented in Section 2. In Section 3, phone is briefly presented as the first personal medium enabling people distant communication. In Section 4, traditional mass media are analyzed, both electronic and non-electronic. Their contribution to community building is presented. Section 5 is devoted to the novelty the Internet brought to the personal and mass media. In Sections 6 and 7 two kinds of communities are analyzed: territorial and content ones. The first ones are traditional. The second ones arose as a result of the

T. Janowski and H. Mohanty (Eds.): ICDCIT 2007, LNCS 4882, pp. 283–292, 2007.
© Springer-Verlag Berlin Heidelberg 2007

Internet communication. In Sections 8 and 9, those two kinds of communities are compared, which leads to conclusions with regards to the global society and the information society. Section 10 concludes the whole paper showing social challenges people have to face in near future.

2   Communication and Communities

The essence of communities and societies is what is common within a group of people, i.e., bonds and relationships among people. People are related by common system of values, i.e., conviction what is good and what is bad; system of moral and social norms; history, tradition, common memory of the past, culture, symbolism, aesthetic, i.e., some common conviction what is beautiful and what is ugly; social identity; and finally, state as a form of organization of common life. Bonds and relationships among people are the result of communication of two kinds: first, personal communication, and second, social communication. Personal communication creates bonds among family members, close relationships with friends, looser relationships with collaborators, neighbors, more or less permanent customers and suppliers, and finally some volatile relationships with casual listeners. Social communication makes people feeling citizens of a country, city, region, and a continent, as well as members of some religious, political, professional, ecological, cultural or many other groups. From the social point of view, usually, a person strongly identifies with the nation, next with a city, where he/she lives, especially if he/she was born in this city, or spent most of his/her life in it. Next, a person identifies with the region, next – with the continent. Looser relationships with a continent, e.g. Europe, follows from the fact that a person is confronted with a need to identification with a continent rarely, mainly during international debates where a common position of the whole continent is presented. Such an experience is limited to a small number of people.

Up to recently, human communication was strictly related with a territory. Communication was dependent on transportation of people and material information media, i.e., paper. Bigger territory means longer distances, longer time and bigger costs of transportation. Thus, borders of organized territories determined the borders of communication and as a consequence – borders of interpersonal relationships.

Summarizing, smaller territory results in easier, more frequent, and more complex multi-aspect interpersonal communication. More frequent communication, stronger relationships. If strong relationships were created due to intensive communication, then those relationships are permanent though they may be weakened, because communication parties moved away territorially. Common home creates very strong, multi-aspect, and permanent familial bonds. Common quarter, or village creates strong neighborhood relationships. Common school, or work – friendship relationships. And so on. If such relationships are created, even longer absence of communication does not destroy them. They may be easily re-established after re-establishing communication.

3   Telephone – The First Personal Communication Medium

Telephony provided personal communication with a new quality, namely, telephony freed personal communication from dependence on transportation and, as a consequence, from dependence on territory. Due to telephones people who are arbitrarily distributed may personally communicate. Telephones became more available and more affordable when mobile phones were massively deployed. Today 2,4 billion people of 6 billion have mobile phones. However, voice communication provided by a telephone is a narrow communication channel as compared with personal meetings. More important, to call somebody by phone, it is necessary to know first his/her telephone number. Therefore, very frequently, first a relationship between some people is created basing on personal meetings, and next communication is continued by telephones. Big part of telephone communication is devoted either to make an appointment to meet, or to complement direct communication that took place at a personal meeting. In such case, narrow communication channel (voice only) is not a major constraint, if communicating persons know each other and already remain in some relationships.

4   Mass Communication and Territory

Up to date, mass communication was realized by non-electronic and electronic ways. Non-electronic ways comprise the press, books, official announcements, etc. Electronic ways comprise radio (FM – Frequency Modulation) and analog television. Such communication is restricted territorially. Restrictions follow partially from technology, partially from economy, and partially from respecting territorial identity for legal reason. FM technology of radio broadcasting is such that the range of FM radio is restricted. Moreover, basing on international agreements, antennas of FM radio are so oriented, and power of radio transmitters is so calculated that the range of a FM radio ends shortly beyond the state border.

More important feature of traditional mass communication is its broadcasting character. Traditional mass communication is characterized by a very limited number of information sources. In a country there are usually a few television and radio programs, as well as newspapers and journals that are massively watched, listened to and read. Views and evaluations are presented mostly by professionals supported by experts in different fields. Mass media professionals decide who, from among politicians, artists, scientists, etc., is invited to present his/her views to mass audience. Particular TV and radio stations, as well as newspapers and journals are characterized by well distinctive programs.

Due to its broadcasting character, traditional mass communication makes favorable conditions for creating social relationships on a given territory, because it contributes to unification of information, knowledge and views. Individuals feeling related with a given community or society may have an access to particular mass media on an individual basis, even if they stay out of the territory of that mass media impact. For example Poles living abroad may subscribe to

Polish press. However, real impact of mass media from one territory on people living on another territory is very small. Direct impact of German or Belorussian press on Polish society is marginal, even if German and Polish societies, as well as Belorussian and Polish societies are territorial neighbors, in both cases just separated by a river. Polish society learns about views of German society mostly indirectly, informed by Polish journalists analyzing mostly foreign articles written by foreign journalists.

A new quality to mass media communication has been provided by television. Double communication channel comprising voice and video increased significantly influence on society. Television penetrated with its message up to people who do not have habit to read printed texts, in particular to children and less educated people. However, television, as a side effect of its broadcasting character, cause passivity of viewers. Images ready to view reduce reflectiveness and thoughtfulness of viewers, while increasing inclination to imitate what they see and hear, i.e., what is conveyed to them.

A conclusion drawn from the above analysis is the following: up to recently, it was in fact a territory that decided about communication and thus interpersonal relationships among people, despite electronic communication media: telephone, radio and television.

5   The Internet as a Communication Medium

Internet is a communication medium of the global range. It is simultaneously available on every territory on the whole globe. Internet is a medium available for both people and enterprises. Internet is characterized by low technical and economical barriers. Those barriers are lowered due to rapid development of mobile telephony. Mobile telephony is able to access difficult areas (mountains, islands) and under-populated areas without a necessity of installation of expensive, wired infrastructure. The Internet is easy to use. Regardless of age, gender and education, all people may use the Internet after short training. Today Internet is multimedia. Internet is able to transmit information in the form of text, voice, image and video, both registered and on line. In near future virtual reality, i.e., three dimensional, animated, interactive images, will be a popular form of information transmission. An important distinctive feature of the Internet is that it is a medium with memory. If an author of information available in the Internet does not delete it, this information is available for ever.

Summary of the Internet characteristics as a communication medium is the following:

- Internet removes geographical constraints, because the Internet reaches everywhere on the globe, beyond all territorial barriers;
- Internet removes temporal constraints, because information is available on the Internet anytime;
- Internet removes constraints on information presentation, because information may be presented on the Internet in any form.

Important consequences to personal and mass communication follow from the above features of the Internet.

First, the Internet abolishes division on personal and mass communication. Internet is both personal and mass medium. Every Internet user may smoothly pass from personal to mass communication and vice versa.

Second, the Internet removes constraints on content publication. Every Internet user, without asking for authorization, may put any information on the Internet and publicize it world-wide. Of course, putting illegal content may and should be punished.

Third, the Internet removes constraints on content access. Every Internet user may read any information available on the Internet which is decided by its author (owner) to be public. Strictly taken, some countries censor Internet content. In longer time it will be, however, ineffective.

Fourth, the Internet abolishes fixed schedule of presenting information, which is a case of radio and television. Every Internet user, autonomously surfing among web pages, decides which content and in which order he/she likes to access it. In other words, due to interactivity, every Internet user spontaneously creates his/her own schedule of his/her own individual Internet session.

Fifth, information available on the Internet is searchable. Using search engines, it is possible to search information resources from all over the world to look for required information.

Of course, Internet is not above the law. Big part of information technically available on the Internet is not public, so it is available only for authorized persons. An example is information about bank account balance. It is available on the Internet, however, only to the owner of the account. Internal information of an enterprise is available only to its authorized employees. In general, every information owner (author) may restrict access to his/her information to selected people. He/she may also determine conditions under which his/her information is accessible, e.g., registration on the website, agreement to receive marketing information, payment, etc. Law concerning information as such has to be observed also in case of electronic information published on the Internet. For example, intellectual property rights cannot be violated, harmful content cannot be published, etc. The enforcement of the law on the Internet is difficult, because law is territorially constrained, while Internet is not.

Internet revolution in media is not limited to its global access. Revolutionary is the following:

- everybody may publish his/her own information, including comments to information published by others;
- information content may appear in any form: text, voice, image or video;
- published information is available forever (or almost) – Internet as a medium with a memory permits to asynchronous communication;
- published information is available everywhere, i.e., globally;
- information may be individually searched;
- information leads to other people interested in a given kind of information.

As follows from the analysis presented above, Internet as a new information and communication medium invalidates rules governing up to date mass communication. Invalidation of rules of mass communication leads to changes within communities that follow from mass communication. To prove the above statement, in two next sections we compare traditional communities, called *territorial communities*, with a new kind of communities originating from the Internet, called *content communities*. Territorial communities follow from traditional mass communication, both electronic and non-electronic ones, whose range is, as we have mentioned, territorially constrained. A territorial community follows from the fact that people settle the same territory. Content communities are a result of Internet communication unconstraint in time and space. Content communities group together people interested in the same content. Content communities are quite different from territorial communities.

6   Territorial Communities

The features of territorial communities are the following:

Multi-Aspect relationships – people who belong to a territorial community are naturally interconnected in different ways. Different aspects of their common life on the same territory cause a variety of relationships. Those relationships can be differently evaluated by particular members of a territorial community. But even if some relationships between territorial community members are perceived as dissatisfactory, other ones can be highly appreciated, so the bonds between persons last.

Transitivity – members of the same territorial community transfer bonds one to another. If children attend the same school, in a natural way their parents become interrelated too. Similar with acquaintances spreading from colleagues of a person to colleagues of colleagues, and so on.

Identity – members of a territorial community know each other by name or can easily find out the name of any member.

Known past – the past of territorial community members is known to the community. Members of a territorial community know or can easily find out what any person did in the past, where he/she has been living, where he/she has been working, what his/her views and opinions are.

Emerging authorities – in the territorial communities, a process of emerging authorities arises either in a formal way, i.e., by elections, or in an informal way by social recognition of someone's age, wisdom, experience, professional career, wealth, etc.

Following leader's views – due to emerging authorities, members of a territorial community share views of theirs leaders recognizing their knowledge or just trusting them.

Hierarchical structure – territorial communities incline towards hierarchical structure, in particular if they cover bigger territories. To a large extend, hierarchical structure is a result of high cost of communication on a big territory (cf. Section 2).

Difficulty in leaving a community – it is quite difficult to leave a territorial community. Leaving means, for example, selling the house and purchasing a new one somewhere else that is a very expensive operation, cut or reduce relationships with family and friends. In general, willingness to leave the place of residence decreases with age.

Common interests and common threats – territorial communities share feeling of common interests and necessity to face common threats. Both interests and threats have a long-term character.

Aiming at compromise – members of a territorial community are conscious that they are "condemned" to live together on the same territory, so that they are strongly motivated to reach a compromise to make their common life easier.

View unification – territorial communities favor unification of basic views. Opinions of the members of the community may differ in details, but in the matters important for the community their position is unified.

Summarizing, basing on the above analysis of community features, we can conclude that territorial communities strengthen and deepen the relationships among their members. Members of territorial communities are in favor to compromise and to unify views on fundamental matters. A territorial community is not a static unit – it evolves and causes many conflicts inside the community, but even evolving it conserves the relationships among community members.

7 Content Communities

Content communities are the result of possibilities provided by human communication via Internet. A content community is a group of people gathered round some information content which is a reason why content community members communicate with one another. This information content can be of various nature: professional (e.g., users of some complex software requiring advanced knowledge and experience to effectively use it), political (e.g., people reacting to some political events), social (e.g., people trying to protect unique ecosystem of a particular region), hobby (e.g., fans of old cars), psychological (e.g., people having the same dramatic life experience or the same problems). In general, each information about which views and opinions are exchanged among a group of its receivers, may be the beginning of a content community. Content communities may last for short time – e.g., in case of a sudden political event, or they may have a permanent character – e.g., community of open source software.

The features of the content communities are significantly different from the territorial communities ones.

Single aspect relationships – one content community is focused on only one aspect of the reality. For instance, for members of the content community devoted to Volkswagen Beetle, any other values, opinions or aspects do not matter, just those concerning this unique car brand. A member of the community is perceived by other community members only on the basis of his/her opinions and knowledge on this car brand.

Intransitivity – the fact that a son in a family is interested in old cars, e.g., Volkswagen Beetle, and that he belongs to a content community devoted to this car, does not create any kind of relationships between his parents and parents of other members of this content community.

Anonymity – members of the content communities are usually anonymous one to another. They frequently use nicknames hiding their true identity.

Hidden past – a member of a content community acts and is perceived by other members of this community, as if he/she has no history, not only outside the community, but also inside the community. It is enough for a member of a content community to change his/her nickname, in order not to be identified with his/her former actions and presented opinions.

Everyone is authority for himself/herself – authorities emerge with difficulties in content communities. Everyone perceives himself/herself as an authority. Content community members are mostly willing to express his/her point of view.

Manifestation of distinctness – first of all content communities group people who disagree with something. Such people are also the most active in communication within a content community.

Equality all members of a content community feel equal. Content communities do not emerge leaders. Every member believes he/she is authorized to express his/her own opinions, first of all negative, as we mention above.

Easy leaving a community – it is very easy to leave a content community. Leaving does not requires any procedures, and is done at no costs. It is just enough to never visit again the content community webpage.

Common interests – the content communities gather people sharing common interests which often, though not always, have a short-term character.

Keeping proper opinions – the content communities do not lead towards consensus and compromise among its members, because there are no drivers of compromise.

Keeping view diversity – the content communities do not lead towards unification of views and opinions. Their role is rather to manifest diversity of views related to a particular information content.

8   Internet and the Global Society

As follows from the comparison of characteristics of the territorial and content communities, presented in Section 6 and 7, they are radically different. The content communities on the Internet allow their members to acquit with various views and opinions presented by people from very different perspectives. Content communities serve rather to present people's own opinions acquired elsewhere than to accept opinions of others, i.e., unifying opinions, which is necessary to ensure sustainability of the community. Single-aspect relationships conduct to the radicalization of opinions on a given subject, because it absolves people from responsibility to take into consideration contexts and other aspects of the problem. Anonymity of the content communities members leads to the lack of consequence and responsibility for one's words. As a result, in the content communities there is no reason to achieve a consensus due to the lack of social pressure. There is no hierarchy, so a word of a fool is equal to a word of a sage. It leads to a confusion of those members of the community, who have not enough knowledge coming from the outside of the content community, and who cannot correctly evaluate value of others' opinions.

A conclusion from the above analysis is the following: the content communities do not contribute to creation of a society understood as a community of common values, and in particular to a global society. A uniform global society is a myth. Humanity is too complex to form a uniform society. There are too many differences in important factors, such as history, tradition, culture, religion, etc. To realize that consider so different societies as Eskimo and Pigmy. Finally, there is still too much mutual hostility between nations.

9   Internet and the Information Society

On the contrary to the global society, information society is not a myth [1]. The values of the information society are:

- information,
- knowledge, and
- wisdom.

Information society deals with an intensive information exchange. Information is understood broadly as every intangible products and services based on information, e.g., documents, financial products, software, and authorship works as scientific, professional, journal and artistic texts, recordings, interviews, music, movies, performances, etc. There is a strong need in the information society to share knowledge, in particular, to share payable knowledge, as a part of an economical activity. Knowledge sharing is necessary to interpret coming information correctly in order to benefit fully from it. Finally, in the information society, as never before, it is necessary to impart and posses wisdom to be able to benefit from knowledge. Wisdom is so important because in the information society changes are very frequent and rapid, so big parts of knowledge downgrade and become obsolete.

Information, knowledge and wisdom has been a value in every society. They were not discovered in the information society. However, in the information society they are simultaneously humanistic and economic values. Information society is immanently related with knowledge-based economy. Majority of people comprising a society living from creating, selling and buying information, knowledge and wisdom is a new social and economic phenomenon.

10   Conclusions

Nowadays, two qualitatively new challenges are faced. First, co-existence of traditional territorial communities with new content communities. Second, co-existence of the triple: information, knowledge, wisdom as both humanistic and economic values. We can expect rather a multitude of communities and local societies communicating one with another at the global scale than one global society. We should not expect unification of the society, but rather communication of social diversity. Globalization has to be understood as a multi-localization at the global scale. On the basis of such concept there is a conviction that conservation of social and cultural diversity is a necessary condition of the humanity to survive, as biological diversity is a necessary condition of the nature to survive. Globalization makes sense only if it will enrich humankind, not impoverish. As follows from the above, a key for human development is ability of local communities to communicate. Due to the Internet, information has a global range, however, communication does not. Communication arises only if transmitted information is acquired. Information acquirement depends on possessed knowledge, while knowledge is dependent on local culture. Contemporary challenge is not unification of views, but mutual understanding of local societies.

At the end of this paper, it is worth to mention that influence of the Internet on societies is very different from the influence of the Internet on economy. The same features of the Internet have different consequences in societies and economy. Contrary to unrealistic global society, global economy is a real option. This issue requires, however, a separate analysis.

References

1. Cellary, W. (ed.): Poland and the Global Information Society: Logging on. Human Development Report, United Nations Development Programme, Warsaw (2002), http://www.kti.ae.poznan.pl/specials/nhdr2002/start_1_en.htm
2. Scholte, J.A.: Globalization: A Critical Introduction, 2nd edn. Palgrave Macmillan, Basingstoke/New York (2005)

WAND: A Robust P2P File System Tree Interface

Saikat Mukherjee, Srinath Srinivasa, and Saugat Mitra

International Institute of Information Technology
Bangalore, India
{saikat.mukherjee,sri,saugat.mitra}@iiitb.ac.in

Abstract. WAND is a P2P meta-data management system providing a file-system tree interface. Users are able to share files on the global file-system tree. The file system tree is robust and maintains its structure even when nodes enter and leave the network. The key ideas that make the file-system tree robust are a concept of *virtual folders* and a novel algorithm to handle network partitioning.

1 Introduction

A significant challenge in a P2P system is to locate data elements in the network. Several efforts based around distributed hash tables (DHTs) and data-centric networking have been proposed to address this problem [1,7,13,11,4]. However, while hashing is suitable for keyword based searches, it is often desirable to evolve and maintain a global meta-data schema that allows users to browse through the network. Meta-data have taken various forms like ontologies, description logics, etc [3,10,6,9].

In our work, we consider a simple form for meta-data: a file system tree. The objective of this work is to evolve and maintain a global file system structure over a wide-area P2P network. The file system tree should be resilient to changes happening in the system and retain its structure as much as possible whenever peers leave without warning. The proposed model is called WAND (Wide-Area Network Directory).

A file system interface for a P2P network is advantageous because, (1) file systems are widely used with a number of support tools being available, (2) a file system for a P2P network can be mounted onto a user's local file system and accessed using available file system tools and (3) data creation, access, authentication, etc. can be seamlessly integrated into the user's local operating system functions. Intuitively, working with a tree abstraction directly is also advantageous because browsing a file system becomes easier and more efficient if the underlying abstraction is also in the form of a tree.

In a WAND network, peers share one or more directories from their local file system. WAND provides a file system tree where peers can mount their shared directories. The global file system structure is implemented in a way that each peer is in charge of one or more mounted directories. This enables

T. Janowski and H. Mohanty (Eds.): ICDCIT 2007, LNCS 4882, pp. 293–305, 2007.

distribution of meta-data handling load and robustness of the system as no peer has to maintain the entire directory structure and there is no single point of failure. The robustness of the directory structure depends upon two novel ideas: *virtual directories* and a distributed algorithm for detecting and handling network partitions.

In WAND, data files are not replicated and are managed solely by the peer hosting the file. The node id coupled with the local user id establishes a unique identity for each user in the network. Peers can write to one another's shared directories based on the directory permissions. Directory ownerships are also handled accordingly. A node/user is the *owner* of all the directories mounted by the user. If other users should be able to access a mounted directory, then the directory should have appropriate world read/write/execute permissions. WAND is not a full file-system in that it does not bother about managing data blocks and relies instead on the native file system on the peer hosting WAND.

2   Related Literature

There are a few other approaches towards building file systems over P2P networks. CFS [5] implements a *read-only* file system over a P2P network based on the Chord [1] DHT. Here, data blocks are distributed over the P2P system and are managed using the Chord protocol. Ivy [8] implements a *read-write* file system also over an underlying Chord layer. Ivy manages both data and meta-data using Chord. A log-based recovery mechanism is provided for recovery in the face of node failures. Meta-data consistency is maintained by reading logs from all nodes, while writing is done only to the local log. Farsite [2] implements a *serverless* file system where a centralized server is replaced by a set of loosely coupled untrusted workstations. The design of farsite can be seen more as a generalization of other client-server distributed file systems like NFS [12] and Coda. Farsite is suitable for large-scale read-only storage and small-scale read-write storage.The present day P2P networks like Gnutella [16], Bit Torrent [17] and Aires lack any form of data organization and hence cannot provide a file system tree interface. Most of the widely used DFS's like Network File Systems (NFS), Andrew File System (AFS) [15] etc. aim to provide a seamless sharing of resources amongst users and are more concerened about maintaining data coherence. But, a large P2P network is subjected to frequent updates by peers joining and leaving the network. In such scenarios maintaining the directory structure becomes more important. A system like WAND uses the concepts of Virtual directories and network partitioning detection algorithm, to provide robustness to the directory structure.

3   Overview of WAND

A WAND P2P network consists of a number of **nodes** or **peers** sharing one or more directories from their local file system. The network appears as a file system with a virtual root directory. Even though WAND provides only a file system tree, we shall be calling it a file system for the purposes of this paper. Applications using WAND regard the WAND file system tree as any other file system.

A node can mount a shared directory under a **mount point** in the WAND file system. A peer can enter a WAND network by either performing a `connect()` operation to a peer in an existing file system; or by invoking the `buildroot()` function. The former enables the peer to mount its local directories into an existing WAND directory tree, while the latter enables the peer to start a new WAND directory tree to which other peers can connect.

A peer shares a directory by `mount()`ing it under some existing directory in the WAND file system. The name by which a shared directory appears in the WAND tree is called its "mount point." The mount point may or may not have the same name as the local directory. Names of mount points need not be unique across the network; however, they have to be unique within a directory.

Native subdirectories of a shared directory will **not** be shared by default. They have to be explicitly shared and mounted in order to make their contents visible in the WAND system.

Files shared by a directory can be listed using the `listfiles()` command and can be copied using the `get()` and `put()` commands. A mechanism for mounting a WAND directory tree under the local directory tree of a peer is being implemented. Once this is complete, the operating system commands for listing files and copying them (for example `ls` and `cp` on Unix) will map to the above WAND functions underneath. A typical WAND directory structure is shown in Figure 1.

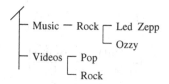

Fig. 1. A typical file system tree

The directories Music and Videos are called "root-level directories" (directories mounted below the root directory) and the other directories are called "sub directories."

A detailed description of the WAND architecture and the algorithms used to build, connect, leave and handle network failures in a WAND network can be found in [14].

4   Virtual Folders

One of the key features which make WAND robust is the concept of *virtual folders*. The root directory and all root-level directories (in the above example Music and Videos) are virtual folders. Virtual directories[1] are mount points

---

[1] We shall be using the terms "folders" and "directories" interchangeably.

that do not correspond to any native directory. As a result, a virtual folder will not have any shared files under them. They may only have other mount points corresponding to virtual folders or shared directories.

Using virtual folders provide two important advantages:

1. In any file system, the root directory is of prime importance. For instance, a Unix kernel would panic if the root directory has problems and cannot be mounted. This is addressed by making all the root level folders virtual.
2. When a node in the network leaves, the folders which it had mounted are automatically made virtual and ownership is transferred to another node present in the network, thus enabling the directory structure to remain consistent.

Root level consistency is maintained by distributing root directory information across the network in an asynchronous, need-to-know basis. In addition, all root-level directories are maintained in a closely coupled fashion where nodes at the root level jointly handle any updates or failures occurring at the root level. To achieve this, all the nodes in the network maintain the following information:

– For each shared directory, its path from the root in the WAND directory tree along with the corresponding owners (called the **parentlog**)
– For each mount point owned by it, a **vertical cache** containing its knowledge of the file system tree until a given depth. The depth of a vertical cache should be at least 2.
– A **horizontal** or a **root** cache, containing its latest knowledge about the state of the root directory

For instance, the vertical cache of "Rock" (under Music) would contain the following information:

Path	Owner
/Led Zepp	Q
/Ozzy	B

The paths in this table are constrained by a maximum depth k (which should be at least 2). This is a configurable parameter and can be configured independently by each peer based on how much information it can hold. The larger the average value of k the more resilient is the directory tree. However, this comes with size and communication overheads.

The horizontal or root cache of node P contains the latest information it has about the root directory and its contents. The horizontal cache maintains the following information:

– List of all mount points defined at the root level
– List of addresses of all nodes hosting mount-points at the root-level
– CLU (explained later) and the corresponding node

Each copy of the horizontal cache anywhere in the network is associated with a number called "count at last update" (CLU). The CLU is 0 when the root cache is created following a buildroot() command. The CLU is increased by one whenever the state of the root directory is updated. A CLU number indicates a unique state of the horizontal cache.

4.1   Cache Updates

A set of cache update policies determine how vertical and horizontal caches are updated. These policies are governed by configurable parameters that trade between higher levels of consistency and messaging overheads. Cache updates are of two forms: horizontal cache updates and vertical cache updates.

Horizontal Cache Updates: Horizontal cache containing root-directory information represents *common knowledge* of the root-level nodes. Any updates to the horizontal cache by a root-level node is sent to the rest of root-level nodes.

Each update of the horizontal cache causes the CLU to be incremented. The update message consists of the latest CLU count and the change in the horizontal cache since the last update. Inconsistencies, if any, are addressed by using the CLU number to decide the most recent cache version.

Vertical Cache Updates: Vertical Cache updates are sent from every child directory to its parent directory. The *Vertical Refresh Rate (VRR)* is a configurable parameter, which determines the percentage of change in the vertical cache that triggers the vertical cache update. The update message sent by a child node comprises only the change in the vertical cache since its last sent update.

Vertical cache updates at the root level are handled by first contacting any root-level node. The node then hashes the mount point name and determines the owner of the mount point whose vertical cache has to be updated.

4.2   Concretizing Virtual Folders

Virtual folders at any sub-directory level can be "concretized" by any node. Concretizing means that the node concretizing it would map a folder on its local machine to the virtual folder and thus it becomes the new owner of the concretized folder. Root-level virtual folders cannot be concretized.

After concretizing a virtual folder the new owner inherits the horizontal and vertical cache from the virtual folder's earlier owner and thereafter maintains them. The previous owner maintains a pointer to the new owner and associates it with the name of the folder. The information of the new owner is send to all the nodes in the virtual folder's associated vertical cache. These nodes then update their parent logs. Any other node who tries to contact the previous owner to access the folder is redirected to the new owner.

5   Handling Network Failures

Node failures can occur at two different levels in the WAND file system.

– A sub-directory node goes down: A sub directory node going down would result in the sub directories being inaccessible.
– A root level node goes down: Root level nodes are primarily responsible for maintaining the root level directory structure. Root level nodes are also the starting point of the parentlog of every directory.

5.1 A Sub-directory Node Goes Down

A sub-directory node going down is identified by either its children when sending an update to it; or by an outside node which asks for the Vertical Cache from that node during browsing the file system.

In either case the child node or the outside node informs the node's parent that it is down. The child node has its grand-parent information from its **parentlog** while in the other case, the visiting node derives the required information from the *pwd* variable stored in it. The *pwd* variable stores the path from the root directory to the current directory that is being browsed by a given node.

The parent node then creates a "virtual folder" for every mount point of the crashed node for which it hosted the parent folders. It then places itself as the owner of the virtual folder. This information is then sent to all nodes in its own vertical cache. The children on receiving this information update their parent log.

If the parent node is also down, then the child or visiting node that detected this crash traverses up the *pwd* or **parentlog** until it finds a reachable node. If none of these nodes also reachable then a network partition is suspected and the `network-partitioned()` routine is run.

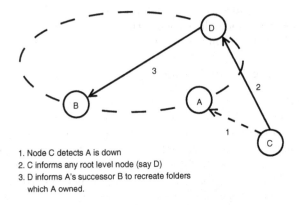

1. Node C detects A is down
2. C informs any root level node (say D)
3. D informs A's successor B to recreate folders
   which A owned.

Fig. 2. Root-level node goes down

5.2 A Root-Level Node Goes Down

Two types of events can identify a root-level node going down:

1. A child trying to send an update to its parent at the root level,
2. A node trying to create a new virtual folder at the root level, and

In a Chord ring, when a node leaves the ring, all its hash table information is handled by the logical successor node in the ring. In a WAND file system, the successor of the failed root-level node becomes the owner of all the virtual folders which were being held by the failed node.

Vertical cache information in all the mount points of the failed node are lost temporarily, till they are updated by their child nodes.

5.3   Handling Network Partitions

Network partitions are handled by splitting the file system tree into two or more subtrees. The splitting algorithm is such that a node tries its best to remain in its file system tree. But even after trying its best, if it still cannot contact any node, it decides to "walk away" and form its own network containing the same subtree to which it belongs. It does not matter whether the network is really partitioned; the objective is to maintain consistent subtrees when the tree splits.[2]

The entire process starts by probing the network for a partition. A probe is started by the following events:

- A parameter *Inactivity Period* is defined for each node, which keeps an account of the last time any activity took place in respect of that node. "Activity" denotes events like receiving a vertical cache update from a child; sending a vertical cache update to parent; horizontal cache updates; parentlog updates following a node crash; and any node asking for its vertical cache.

  The inactivity period counter is reset whenever any of the above event occurs. If the inactivity period elapses then the node suspects a network partition and starts a probe operation.

- A probe also begins when some other node calls the `network-partitioned()` function on a given node.

On beginning a probe, the node tries to contact other nodes in the following order:

1. *Nodes in its parentlog*: If any node X in the parentlog is reachable, then all mount points between X and the probing node become virtual folders and are owned by X.

2. *Nodes in its horizontal cache*: If none of the nodes in the parentlog are reachable; but some node in the horizontal cache is reachable, then the owner of the root-level directory of the parentlog is contacted. This then becomes the owner of virtual folders all the way to the probing node.

3. *The node corresponding to the maxCLU variable*: If none of the nodes in the horizontal cache are also reachable, the node with the maxCLU count is contacted to get its version of the horizontal cache.

When the probing node is unable to connect to any node in the above mentioned lists, it decides to "walk away". The walk away algorithm initiates the following actions:

- It sends a message called `walking-away()` to its immediate children.
- It then performs a `buildroot()` and creates virtual folders corresponding to all mount points in its parentlog.

---

[2] Presently network partitions are supported over the simulator and are tested for simulated networks.

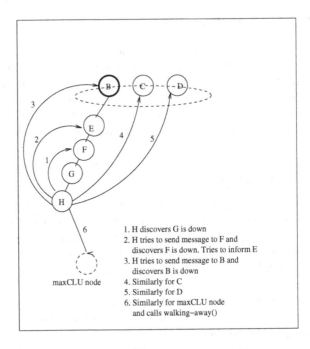

Fig. 3. Network Partition

When a node receives a `walking-away()` message from its parent, it also starts a probe operation, with some minor differences. The sequence of operations are listed below:

1. The child starts probing its parentlog starting from the grand parent
2. If none of the nodes are reachable, it tries its horizontal cache and the max-CLU node
3. If even does not work, then the node sends a `walking-away()` message to all its children, and performs a `connect()` on its parent and mounts its folders under them accordingly. If at this time, even the parent node is also not reachable, the node performs a `buildroot()` and creates virtual folders according to its parentlogs.

Figure 3 schematically depicts the "walking away" algorithm. It should be noted that once a node decides to walk away assuming the network to be partitioned, it is not called back even if a node in its subtree finds out that the network is not partitioned. There is also no mechanism to recombine the trees formed due to network partitioning.

6   Performance Statistics

A prototype of WAND has been implemented over Java and RMI. The implementation supports a subset of the features presented here. In addition, a simulator has also been implemented to simulate large WAND networks and network partitioning.

Performance of the WAND network is measured with respect to the number of messages being passed between nodes, latency in the system due to geographic distribution of nodes and consistency in the network view that each node has with respect to the actual network topology.

6.1 Messaging Complexity

Messages are passed in the network to update either the horizontal or vertical cache which change due to various events occurring in the network. A WAND network was simulated using randomized event occurrences. By varying VRR rate, different simulation runs were performed simulating a given number of events. The graph in Figure 4 shows that the number of messages being passed varies almost linearly with the number of events.

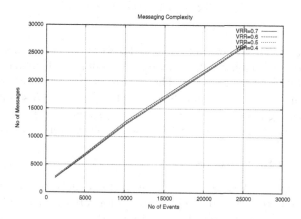

Fig. 4. Number of messages plotted against different values of VRR for a given number of events

6.2 Network Latency

Latency in the network is indicative of propagation delays involved while sending cache updates. It is a function of network topology and geographical distribution of the nodes involved in the cache update. The worst case scenario occurs when an update at one level triggers cascading updates as shown in Figure 5(a).

Figure 5(a) shows cascading updates for different tree heights. In the first case an update at child node F triggers an update at parent node E which in turn triggers an update at node D and so on.

The PlanetLab overlay network was used to set up a WAND network using PlanetLab nodes from all over the world (http://www.planet-lab.org/). To simulate the worst case behaviour, vertical caches of mount points in the tree were configured to trigger cascading updates. In addition, the tree was built such that

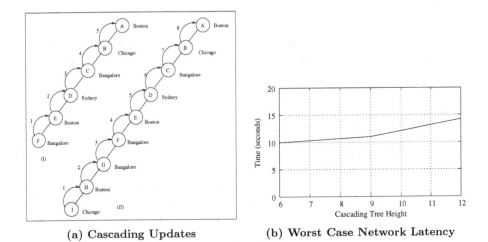

(a) Cascading Updates   (b) Worst Case Network Latency

Fig. 5. Network Latency

the distance between parent and child nodes were as high as possible. For instance, directory F is mounted by a node in Bangalore while its parent, directory E, is mounted by a node in Boston. The test results for different tree heights are shown in Figure 5(b). The graph shows a delay of about 15 seconds for a tree of height 12 configured in the worst possible fashion. The graph also shows a roughly linear growth in the delays as the height of the worst-case tree increased.

6.3   Fresh and Stale Reads

While traversing the WAND network, the vertical cache is used extensively to browse the file system tree. Too high a value for VRR may result in too low a frequency of cache updates resulting in stale reads.

The event associated with fetching vertical caches is a *Read* event. Reads can be classified as:

- Fresh Read: A read resulting in an accurate cache being fetched
- Stale Read: A read resulting in an inaccurate cache being fetched

A WAND network was simulated using randomized event occurrences and the number of fresh and stale reads occurring with changing VRR were tabulated. Figure 6 shows a graph depicting the fraction of fresh reads in a set of reads for two different simulation runs. As shown in the figure, the percentage of stale reads remain very low even when vertical caches were updated only after 70% change.

6.4   Network Partitioning

The network partitioning algorithm attempts to use the parentlog, root level nodes and the maxCLU node to check for network partitioning. The worst case

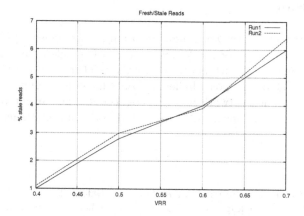

Fig. 6. Fresh and Stale Reads

messaging complexity involved in each network partition check is therefore the sum of;

1. The depth (indicative in the parentlog) of the node executing the network partitioning check
2. The number of nodes present at the root level
3. The maxCLU node

Figure 7 indicates the worst case messaging complexity in case of a network partition using the simulator. It is assumed that all the nodes in the parentlog and at the root level are separate nodes.

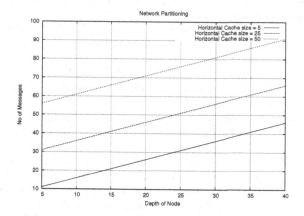

Fig. 7. Network Partitioning Performance

7   Conclusion

This paper presented WAND as a new meta-data management system for large P2P networks. Resiliency of the WAND network depends upon virtual folders and its algorithm to deal with network partitions. There are however, a number of open issues. One of the most challenging ones include merging a split WAND tree after a partitioned network becomes connected. The current version of the WAND software can be downloaded from http://planetlab.iiitb.ac.in/

References

1. Stoica, I., Morris, R., Karger, D., Kaashoek, F., Balakrishnan, H.: Chord: A Scalable Peer-To-Peer Lookup Service for Internet Applications. In: Proceedings of the 2001 ACM SIGCOMM Conference, pp. 149–160 (2001)
2. Adya, A., Bolosky, W.J., Castro, M., Cermak, G., Chaiken, R., Douceur, J.R., Howell, J., Lorch, J.R., Theimer, M., Enhofer, R.P.W.: Farsite: Federated, available, and reliable storage for an incompletely trusted environment. In: Proceedings of the 5th Symposium on Open Systems Design and Implementation (OSDI), Boston, MA, USA (2002)
3. Cannataro, M.: Architecture, metadata and ontologies in the knowledge grid. In: Proceedings of the IST Workshop on Metadata Management in Grid and P2P systems (MMGPS) - Models, Services and Architectures (2003)
4. Crespo, A., Garcia-Molina, H.: Routing indices for peer-to-peer systems. In: Proceedings of the 28th International Conference on Distributed Computing Systems (2002)
5. Dabek, F., Kaashoek, M.F., Karger, D., Morris, R., Stoica, I.: Wide-area cooperative storage with cfs. In: SOSP 2001. Proceedings of the 18th ACM Symposium on Operating Systems Principles, Chateau Lake Louise, Banff, Canada (2001)
6. Handschuh, S., Staab, S., Maedche, A.: Cream - creating relational metadata with a component-based. In: Proceedings of the First International Semantic Web Working Symposium (SWWS) (2001)
7. Huebsch, R., Hellerstein, J.M., Boon, N.L., Loo, T., Shenker, S., Stoica, I.: Querying the internet with pier. In: Proceedings of 19th International Conference on Very Large Databases (VLDB) (September 2003)
8. Muthitacharoen, A., Morris, R., Gil, T.M., Chen, B.: Ivy: A read/write peer-to-peer file system. In: Proceedings of the Fifth Symposium on Operating Systems Design and Implementation (OSDI), Boston, MA, USA (December 2002)
9. Nejdl, W.: Semantic web and peer-to-peer technologies for distributed learning repositories. In: IIP 2002. Proceedings of 17th IFIP World Computer Congress, Intelligent Information Processing (2002)
10. Nejdl, W., Wolf, B., Qu, C., Decker, S., Sintek, M., Naeve, A., Nilsson, M., Palmér, M., Risch, T.: Edutella: A p2p networking infrastructure based on rdf. In: Proceedings of the 11th International World Wide Web Conference (May 2002)
11. Ratnasamy, S., Francis, P., Handley, M., Karp, R., Shenker, S.: A scalable content addressable network. Technical Report TR-00-010, Berkeley, CA (2000)
12. Sandberg, R., Goldberg, D., Kleiman, S., Walsh, D., Lyon, B.: Design and implementation of the sun network file system. In: Summer USENIX Proceedings (1985)

13. Zhao, B.Y., Kubiatowicz, J.D., Joseph, A.D.: Tapestry: An infrastructure for fault-tolerant wide-area location and routing. Technical Report UCB/CSD-01-1141, UC Berkeley (April 2001)
14. Algorithms in WAND- Technical Report. Book title OSL-IIITB-05101, IIIT Bangalore
15. http://en.wikipedia.org/wiki/Andrew_File_System
16. http://en.wikipedia.org/wiki/Gnutella
17. http://en.wikipedia.org/wiki/BitTorrent

A Tsunami Warning System Employing Level Controlled Gossiping in Wireless Sensor Networks

Santosh Bhima, Anil Gogada, and Rammurthy Garimella

International Institute of Information Technology, Hyderabad, India
{bhima,anil_gogada}@students.iiit.ac.in, rammurthy@iiit.ac.in

Abstract. This paper deals with a Tsunami warning system based on distributed sensor networks employing level controlled gossip. Level controlled gossip is a technique that is being proposed which employs leveling and gossiping together. The technique reduces the number of messages by transmitting messages in direction of base station only and there by increases the life-time of wireless sensor network. By using various power levels at base station the sensor field is hierarchically partitioned into levels of increasing radius (containing various sensor nodes). The algorithm divides the entire sensor network into logical con-centric zones based on proximity from the base station, whereby the packet is transmitted from a node of higher depth to nodes in the next zone with lesser depth. The transmission probability increases with the proximity of the Tsunami wave to the base station. The primary advantage of the protocol is transmitting a critical event with higher probability and at the same time conserving lifetime of the network for future monitoring

1 Introduction

One of the major advances in the field of surveillance technology is the deployment of distributed sensor networks. This has provided a means to monitor areas which are either unreachable or hostile to human existence. For this reason, sensor networks have to be left unattended for long periods of time which makes replacement and recharging of batteries a difficult task. It is therefore crucial to take measures for utilizing available resources in an efficient manner. Hence to prolong the life-time of sensor networks we need to minimize the wastage of energy [1].

Tsunami is one such critical event which has to be monitored and the system (Tsu-nami Warning System) that monitors it should have a longer life time. The speed of the Tsunami wave is given by

$$speed = \sqrt{depth\ of\ the\ sea\ *\ g} \tag{1}$$

As the tsunami wave approaches shallow water, its speed decreases as the depth of the sea decreases. As the constant energy flux is dependent on both wave speed and wave height, the height of the wave increases as it approaches shallow

T. Janowski and H. Mohanty (Eds.): ICDCIT 2007, LNCS 4882, pp. 306–313, 2007.

water. Tsuna-mi wave length is of order 100km and time period is of order hours. So the monitoring application should cover vast area for extended period of time without malfunction.

Flooding is the basic way of transmitting a message in a network that does not de-pend on location information from external sources like GPS. [5] Pro-poses 'Flooding' as a way to route data. It also uses some techniques to avoid unrestricted flooding and reduce wastage of resources. There have been many improvements to the basic flooding. Despite those improvements, flooding pro-duces many messages un-necessarily.

Leveling is a technique that drives the information packets in the direction of the base station. This directionality property restricts the packets to be trans-mitted only from an outer layer to inner layer, thereby reducing the number of messages broad-cast [6]. We also use hierarchical partitioning to ensure this. In this paper, a progres-sive analysis of the available options for the system is made and the best ones among them are incorporated in the final model of Tsunami warning system.

The rest of this paper is organized as follows: Section II contains related work. Section III discusses about level controlled gossip, pure gossip methodologies and other implementation issues. Section IV concludes our paper. Section V presents future work.

2   Related Work

Gossiping, as of now has been used with or without using location informa-tion. Using location information the protocols such Regional gossiping [4] exist. But with the assumption of knowing location information, there exists a better protocol called GPSR [3].

Gossip based ad-hoc routing [2] is by far the efficient form of gossip that doesn't need location information.

We propose to use both leveling and gossiping (as in [2]) together as level controlled gossip routing algorithm.

To the extent of our knowledge level controlled gossip is a novel improvement over pure gossip. We have analyzed both pure gossip and level controlled gossip in the context of Tsunami warning system.

3   Description

3.1   Leveling

We have assumed that the base station has the capability of transmitting at various power levels. During the initial deployment the base station sends a signal for level 1 with minimum power level, all the nodes that receive the signal will set their level as 1. Next the base station increases its signal power to reach the next level and sends a level-2 signal. All the nodes that receive the signal that do not have a level assigned previously set their level to 2.

This process goes on until the base station sends signals corresponding to all the levels. The number of levels is equal to the number of different transmission levels at which the base station can transmit. Apart from this level information, there is no need of any local information. Leveling is done internally with out the help of any external facilities such as GPS and in this manner it differs from other protocols that assume local information [3] [4].

This process goes on until the base station sends signals corresponding to all the levels. The number of levels is equal to the number of different transmission levels at which the base station can transmit. Apart from this level information, there is no need of any local information. Leveling is done internally with out the help of any external facilities such as GPS and in this manner it differs from other protocols that assume local information [3] [4].

The probabilities associated with each level can be set during leveling phase. The probabilities decrease as we move from inner levels to outer levels as shown by the relation. $P1 > P2 > P3 > ... > Pn - 1 > Pn$. These probabilities can be varied any time by the base station to suite the monitoring requirements.

For proper communication between the levels, a node should have a coverage ra-dius R, which is at least 2L, where L is the distance between any two adjacent levels. The coverage radius

$$R = 2L + \epsilon, where\ \epsilon \tag{2}$$

should be minimal so as to decrease the energy wastage due to signal propagation beyond the intended levels.

3.2 Pure Gossiping

After the initial leveling, in pure gossip the transmission probability of a message is set according to the level in which Tsunami is first detected. Assuming that base station is in the direction of the coastal area, the criticality of the Tsunami increases with the proximity of the level in which it is initially encountered.

So, in the outer layers the gossip probability will be less and in the inner layers that are closer to the base station the gossip probability will be more. Once a message is received by a node, it checks to see if it is from a higher level. If it is from a lower or same level the message is discarded. If the packet is from a higher level, depending upon the gossip probability, the node either sends or discards the message that has to be transmitted.

Gossip based approach saves 35 % messages compared to pure flooding. These re-sults are extensively studied in [2]. From [2] the gossip probability ranges from 0.6 to 0.8 assuming the node degree as 8 in random networks. In pure gossip, nodes in all the levels transmit messages with equal probability, which is same as the probability of the level in which the event was detected. This is not the case in level controlled gossip where gossip probability increases during the transmission along the levels.

3.3 Level Controlled Gossip Approach

In Level controlled gossip, when an event is detected the message is broadcast with the probability of that level. When a node in the lower level receives this

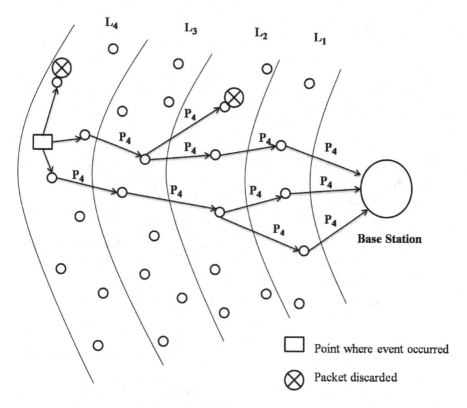

Fig. 1. Pure gossip approach: a node in level 4 starts broadcasting with its level probability. The nodes that chose to transmit the message will transmit it with same probability as that of the initial level probability (L4 probability).

mes-sage, it transmits the message with probability of its corresponding level. So, the same event is being transmitted at lower probabilities in outer layers and higher probabilities in inner layers.

The advantage of level controlled gossip is, it balances the gossip (probabilistic flooding) happening in the levels according to the proximity of the level to the base station. In the outer levels, the criticality of the event is less and hence it is broadcast with less probability. But as the Tsunami wave approaches the inner levels, the criti-cality of the even has increased. So the gossip probability of the event is also in-creased as we move inwards, level wise. This approach balances the network life time and monitoring reliability.

3.4   Combination of Pure and Level Controlled Gossip Approach

Let the critical region be defined as the region within a threshold distance from the base station, where the occurrence of Tsunami is highly possible and devas-tating. For Tsunami monitoring system, we found that combination of pure and level controlled gossip is more efficient than any of the individual approaches. As the monitoring area is huge, so events in the areas which lie under critical

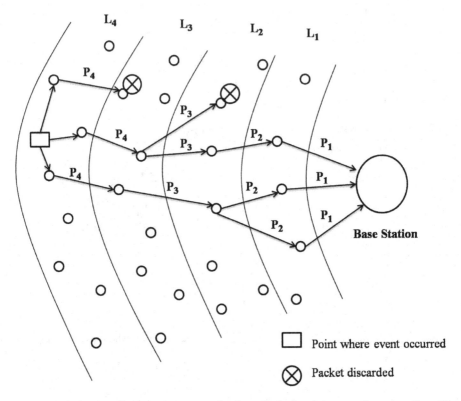

Fig. 2. Level controlled gossip approach: A node in level 4 starts broadcasting. The nodes that chose to transmit the message will transmit it with their own level probabilities. Some nodes discard the message.

region need to be reported with more prominence than the events in the areas which lie beyond the critical region. This should be done in a way that prolongs the network life time.

If level controlled gossip is used in the critical region and pure gossip in the regions beyond critical region, then there will be maximum improvement of the network life time with out risking the warning system. This is due to following reasons:

1) Messages from the non critical region are transmitted with the same minimal probability as that of the initial source level in which they are initiated, which saves number of messages in the inner levels (as the outer levels have less prob ability).
2) Messages from the critical region are transmitted with probabilities increasing inwards to base station. This approach optimizes the number of messages and at same time reports the event with safe probability.

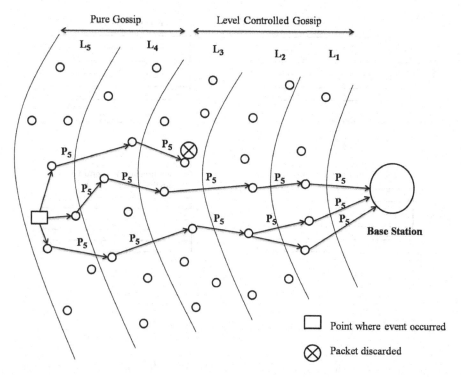

Fig. 3. Combined approach: First 3 levels are set to work in level controlled gossip mode and further levels in pure gossip mode. Here an event occurred in pure gossip region, so all the further gossiping happens as if the whole network is in pure gossip mode If the event had occurred in the level controlled gossip area, then the further communication would have happened as if the whole network is in level controlled gossip.

4 Simulation Results

Extensive simulation work has been done and the results prove that the approaches we proposed will increase the network life time by a huge time when compared to Gossiping. A network model of up to 700 nodes has been used for the simulation.

Fig. 5 below depicts that with a 700 node network model a Pure gossip approach has a larger network life time and efficient than Gossiping. With 700 node network the Gossiping protocol network dies down at around 60 events where as the Pure gossip protocol network can withstand up to 80 events.

Fig. 6 compares the network life time of Level controlled gossip with Gossiping. Initially with a 100 node network both the protocols last until 80-100 events are gen-erated but as the size of the network increases there is a drastic change in the perfor-mances. With a 700 node network model, a Level controlled gossip model lasts longer and is quite efficient than Gossiping.

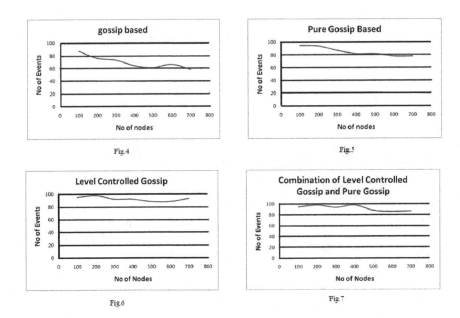

Fig. 4. Pure gossip Vs. Gossiping

Fig. 7 compares the network life time of a network model that employees a Combi-nation of Level controlled gossip and pure gossip with Gossiping. The graph shows that the Combination of Level controlled gossip and pure gossip is quite efficient than Gossiping. The results shows that both Level controlled gossip and the Combination of Level controlled gossip and Pure gossip yields almost same results and the network lasts for the same period.

5   Conclusion

We proposed a novel idea of level controlled gossip which applies the concept of leveling and level controlled probabilities to pure gossip. Initial studies have shown that level-controlled-gossip, with appropriate variation of probabilities with levels, depending on the factors like node density, proximity from the base station, is a worthwhile improvement over pure gossip and other improvements of flooding which do not use GPS.

In the context of Tsunami warning system it is shown that level controlled gossip fits aptly. Choice between uniform and non-uniform density of nodes is studied in the lines of cost of implementation and network life time. Uniform density is found to be the better approach.

Finally the order in which clustering and leveling has to be carried out for efficient network performance is analyzed. It is found that the order does not affect the per-formance of the network.

References

1. Younis, O., Fahmy, S.: HEED: A Hybrid, Energy-Efficient, Distributed Clustering Approach for Ad Hoc Sensor Networks. IEEE Transactions on Mobile Computing 3(4) (October- December 2004)
2. Haas, Z.J., Halpern, J.Y., Erran, L.: Gossip-Based Ad Hoc Routing. IEEE/ACM Transactions on Networking 14(3) (June 2006)
3. Karp, B., Kung, H.T.: Greedy Perimeter Stateless Routing (GPSR)for Wire less Networks. In: Proc. ACM MobiCom, pp. 243–254 (2000)
4. Li, X.-Y., Moaveninejad, K., Frieder, O.: Regional Gossip Routingfor Wire less Ad hoc Networks. Mobile Networks and Applications(MONET) 10(1-2), 61–77 (2005)
5. Cheng, Z., Heinzelman, W.B.: Flooding Strategy for Target Discovery in Wireless-Networks. Proc. ACM MSWiM 11(5), 607–618 (2005)
6. Arora, S., Srninvas, M.B., Ramamurthy, G.: Power Aware, Probabilistic and Adaptable Routing Algorithm for Wireless Sensor Networks. In: NCC 2004. National conference on Communications, IISc, Bangalore, pp. 60–64 (2004)
7. Bandyopadhyay, S., Coyle, E.: An Energy-Efficient Hierarchical Clustering Algorithm for Wireless Sensor Networks. In: Proc. IEEE INFOCOM, pp. 1713–1723 (April 2003), http://citeseer.ist.psu.edu/bandyopadhayay03energy.html
8. Kawadia, V., Kumar, P.R.: Power Control and Proc. IEEE Clustering in Networks. In: INFOCOM (April 2003), available:
http://citeseer.ist.psu.edu/kawadia03power.html

Relation Extraction and Validation Algorithm

Lobna Karoui[1] and Nabil El Kadhi[2]

[1] École Supérieure d'Électricité, France
Lobna.Karoui@suepelc.fr
[2] L.E.R.I.A. Lab, France

Abstract. Ontological concept Relation extraction is a difficult research problem. In this paper, we aim to extract multi-type relations from the text analyses and the existent relations (in the concept hierarchy). Our approach combines a verb centered method, lexical analyses, syntactic and statistic ones. It is based on a rich contextual modeling that strengthens the term co-occurrence selection, a lexical analysis, a use of the existent relations in the concept hierarchy and a stepping between the extracted relations to validate them and facilitate the evaluation made by the domain experts.

1 Introduction

The relation extraction is a difficult open research problem. Till now, relation extraction is realized either by applying a statistic approach [3], a linguistic one [1,2] or a hybrid one [4]. Generally, also, the searches extract only one or two types of relations. In contrast, our objective is to extract multi-type relations by combining several text analyses and considering the word features.

In this paper, we propose our relation discovery approach which is based on three analyses: the lexical one, the syntactic one with a verb centered step and a globally syntactic one and the statistic one. When we apply only one or two analyses, there are obligatory some missing relations. To avoid this case, we combine various analyses to define complementary processes that insure the extraction of the relevant and varied relations among words. So, we define a method that extracts several relation types, exceeds the sentences limits in order to clearly represent the reality of the word in its contexts and combine a verb centered approach with other ones in order to extract more domain relations and evaluate them at the same time. Actually, our contribution is firstly extracting relations by using several analyses and particularly the structural aspects of the HTML documents and secondly evaluating them by considering either a crossing between different analyses or some statistic elements.

2 The Fundamental Ideas of Our Approach

We begin by defining our objective which is extracting different relation types by studying the several existent text analyses and by taking into account the

T. Janowski and H. Mohanty (Eds.): ICDCIT 2007, LNCS 4882, pp. 314–320, 2007.
© Springer-Verlag Berlin Heidelberg 2007

features and roles of the words. Also, we hope using, firstly, the same contextual approach (used in the concept extraction) in order to look if this source permits us to discover other relations or the same previous ones modeled in the concept hierarchy produced by the COCE algorithm [5]. Our approach, which is directed towards ontology extension, concerns three main lines: a lexical analysis, a syntactic one and a statistic one.

The **lexical analysis** exploits some lexical patterns which can generate relevant words associations able to be deducted from the globally syntactic analysis. It allows us to discover at the same time implicit and explicit semantic relations. For example, by using the relation of coordination with "and", we discover an explicit relation which can exist in the syntactic analysis. On the other hand, by using the effect of the punctuation, we are able to discover implicit relations as in the example "accommodation: hotel and shelter.", we remark that hotel and shelter have a relation between them and also with the term accommodation. In our work, we have defined some lexical patterns such as "NP, NP" or "NP: NP, NP" or "NP of NP", etc (NP: nominal phrase).

The **verb centered analysis** which is a syntactic one consists of selecting verbs and their arguments in the verb phrases. Then, we extract two relation types: the explicit relations by looking for the allies of the verbal phrases (VP) in the nominal phrases (NP); and the implicit relations by looking for the allies of the VP in contexts wider than the sentence. This syntaxico-contextual analysis allows us to find other relations. By looking for relations around the verb after selecting it, we insure a progressive evaluation of the produced results. In other words by focusing on the verbs which can be interesting for an expert, we limit the number of word associations and facilitate the evaluation of the final results by him. For example; if we have the following sentences: "There are several means of transport. Among them, the tourism office offers some special cars". By using the first analysis, we extract a relation between the words "office" and "car" which is not interesting in this case. But, when we use the second analysis that uses a bigger context than a simple sentence, we extract a relation between "transport" and "car". So, in some cases the first analysis which is the most used one, does not give the right word associations because the verb does not really put the connected words in an association able to generate a semantic relation. Also, by avoiding some useless associations, our approach facilitates the understanding and the evaluation of the other generated relations.

An important point related to this analysis is the choice of the verb. It is necessary to know how selecting the good verb in a sentence and which one gives the relevant relations. In some sentences, in French language, we find two or three verbs in the same structure such as "Invite to come to sample cheese" or "Invite to observe fragment of rocks". For the first example, the problem is which verb should be related to "cheese" is it "invite", "come" or "sample". Another possible problem with verbs is their role and not only their number in the sentence. We remark in some structures that sometimes verbs does not return relations between words but rather some properties such as in the following example: "pets are forbidden in park" or "waters surround the park".

The **globally syntactic analysis** allows us to exploit all the relation types existing between the textual units without limiting them on those centered on the verb. Therefore, we are going to find relations of coordination, object and subject, etc. This analysis permits to extract the explicit relations e.g. within the following sentence: "There exists different types of accommodation such as hostsćhambers, hotels, shelters.", the syntactic analyser discovers the relation between "accommodations" and "chambers" thanks to the grammatical word "such as".

For the **statistic analysis**, we apply a distributional analysis. This analysis applied to a unique speech expresses the tracks of some external laws involved in the speech production. It studies the contextual properties of words in the corpus. In our case, we exploit the treatments which have been used for the concept extraction by benefiting of the contextual analysis represented by our contextual hierarchy and the position of a word in this model. Consequently, we use the word distribution in their contexts as well as relation between these last ones to calculate a statistic index that expresses the degree of association between words. The stylistic analysis is included into the contextual analysis explained in our previous work [5] since we take into account the document structure and the word position in it. This analysis insures an implicit semantic relation discovery. It also permits us to use the concept hierarchy, its existent relations and the word pairs weighting in order to either enhance the existent relations or evaluate them.

Our previous context definition is an appropriate one for the concept extraction since it gives the semantic associated words. Our objective is different in the relation extraction since we hope find the related words and not just the more semantic ones. Thats why; we take into account other types of contexts such as the window context (small) and the paragraph. The window context is used with a proximity degree in order to well define the related words. Defining a context as a paragraph considers all the words inside a paragraph as neighbors and computes their cooccurrences. This context definition is important too since it permits to give some complementary information with the structured and proximity window contexts. The structured context depends on a "contextual hierarchy" (C.H) based on HTML elements and "link co-occurrence" (L.C). A contextual hierarchy is a tag hierarchy. It illustrates possible relations existing within HTML documents and between them. The structural context definition represents the terms adaptability in its corpus. The associated contextual model respects the word location in order to take a multitude of term situations into account when computing its weight [5].

3   The Relation Extraction/Validation Algorithm

The relation extraction is based on the notion of context. In this research, we search the contexts that contain the related words. By using the different presented contexts, we categorize four types of contexts which are: the structured context, the linguistic context (verb centered, globally syntactic and lexical analyses), the documentary context (paragraph) and the proximity window context (proximity window). Our relation extraction approach uses all of these analyses and consequently context definitions to extract new relations (not those existent in the clustering results and revealed by the previous works) and try to validate them automatically. More details about these ideas are explicitly presented in the following steps.

Our relation extraction/validation algorithm applies different type of analyses. It categorizes two types of relations which are the valid one (that can be validate par the different crossing steps) and the non valid one. It is composed by five steps:

Step 0 permits to apply the different analyses to extract relations.

Step 1 applies an internal filtering to eliminate the relations that represent the links between the terms inside the formed clusters. Those relations are not interesting because they exist in the build concept hierarchy. At the end of this task, we obtain a new set of relations (see example after Table1)

Step 2 permits a filtering by crossing the relations resulting from the different analyses. We propose two types of crossing for the first validation step: between the statistical results and between the statistical and linguistic ones. The statistic crossing is done between the structured relations and the paragraph relations because we thought that we can find an interesting intersection between them. The hybrid crossing is reserved for the proximity window relations and the other linguistic and lexical relations. This type of crossing is more refined than the first one. We can do other ones but in the first experiments we consider only these choices. At the end of this step, we obtain a first set of valid relations and a second one of non valid relations.

Step 3 takes into account the set of non valid relations and applies a statistic filtering. This latter is done by defining the value of two parameters either by the domain expert, the system or by default. NO is the percentage of word occurrence in the corpus. FN is the normalized frequency of a word in the corpus. The set that respects those parameters contains the selected relations that will be valid only if the DC (degree of confidence that is defined by the user at the beginning of the application) is bigger than 50%.

Step 4 takes into account the case when the DC is less than 50%. In this case, we apply a strong statistic filtering by multiplying the value of each parameter NO and FN by two. The relations that respect these new values are valid.

Step 5 permits to deduce from the valid relations some new relations and tries to label all the valid relations either extracted or deduced at the end of this process.

Our algorithm depends on some parameters like the Degree of confidence, the number of occurrence (NO) and the frequency number (FN). The DC must be defined by the user because it explains its confidence in our application. However, the NO and FN can be defined either by the domain expert, the system by deducing them from the DC value or by default (by the system maker). If the system computes these values, if the DC is bigger than 50% then the NO and the FN maintain their default values but if the DC is less than 50% then the NO and the FN are multiplied by two.

Our algorithm permits not only to extract relations but also to validate them, deduce from them some new relations and label some of them. All these tasks are realizable by five analyses and our algorithm instructions.

4 An Illustrative Example

To summarize the impact of our approach, we can say that it is a "verb-centered approach" and tries, at the same time, discovering the probably missing conceptual relations which are not mediated by verbs. So, since our approach is not limited to the linguistic or the syntactic level, we are able to extract more relations than the conventional SVO type. Also, our relation extraction method is based on the use of "Context" since we believe that the correct word relation needs to be chosen on the basis of contextual evidence. Thanks to the contextual analysis which is used in our approach, we can detect different types. Let us take the following HTML code as an example to show the importance of combining several analyses with different context definitions and their impact on the automatic validation task.

Example 1. <h1> *California lodging, luxurious accommodation* </h1> <p> *The California country offers hotels and camping to the tourists. These accommodations are only in the north east but shelters are placed in the south. There exist also castles that are renewed for the same purpose and considered as luxurious accommodation like the 5 stars hotels. Castles and shelters are lodging that are the least chosen. Some tourists are more interested by an accommodation that was closer the nature: camping, shelter, caravan, etc.* </p>

In our approach, we propose to extract relations by using several analyses in order to obtain the relevant possible associations between the concepts. At each step, we extract the possible relations from the previous example.

The extracted Relations. The Table 1 represents the extracted relations. For instance, the stylistic relations are generated thanks to the relation between the contexts which are modeled in our contextual hierarchy (in this case between <h1> and <p>). The pragmatic ones are due to the context analysis without any relation with the stylistic characters. It depends on the contexts limits that could be varied from a section of a sentence to two associated documents (related by a hyperlink). In our case, by considering two sentences which are "The California country offers hotels and camping to the tourists." and "These accommodations are only in the north east but shelters are placed in the south.", we can deduce that accommodation refers to hotel and camping. Only a set of globally syntactic relations can be found by the lexical patterns. Other relations that could be found in two different analyses imply directly their validity such as the relation number 5 which is induced from a lexical analysis (two strings related by ",") and the relation number 13 which is produced thanks to a stylistic element (two strings

Table 1. Some extracted relations

Lexical Relations

1- camping -> shelter
2- shelter -> caravan
3- caravan -> camping
4- accommodation closer to nature -> camping + shelter + caravan
5- lodging -> luxurious accommodation

Syntactic Relations

Verb-cent

6- lodging (are)-> castles + shelter
7- castles (are considered) -> luxurious accommodation

Globally syntactic

8- Hotel (and) -> camping
9- Accommodation (but) -> shelter
10- Castles (and) -> shelter
11- Luxurious accommodation (like) -> 5 stars hotel

Statistic Relations

Pragmatic

12- accommodation (refers to) -> hotel + camping
13- castles + shelter (least chosen) -> lodging

Stylistic

14- lodging -> luxurious accommodation
15- lodging -> hotel + castles + shelter + camping + caravan + 5 stars hotel

---

existing in the same HTML tag <h1>). An example of a valid relation is the relation number 6 that is repeated thanks to the relation number 13. In this case, we deduce that the relation 6/13 is valid. However, the relation 3 exists only as a lexical relation thats why we can not confirm the validity of this relation. In such case, only the statistic values of the correlation between the two words camping and caravan can validate their relation or the domain expert at the end. This is another manner to validate the extracted relations. So to evaluate them, we apply the analyses crossing, then the statistic values and at the end the domain experts for the rest. We present some types of relations which are labeled: the relation number 11 "belong to the category", The relation number 16 "is", the relation number 18 "synonym", the relation number 19 which is a comparative relation "least chosen", the relation number 20 "is a category of", etc. We present a deduced relation example which is (luxurious accommodation castles + 5 stars hotel) produced by the relations 11 and 7.

By using a concept hierarchy and the extracted relations, we do the internal filtering. For this, we eliminate from the whole set of relations those that exist in the word clusters. For instance, if we have the word cluster: hotel, camping, lodging and as extracted relations: R1 hotel, camping, R2 camping, lodging and R3 camping, accommodation, we delete the R1 and R2 because they relate the words existing in the cluster but we maintain the R3.

5   Conclusion

The relation extraction steel remains a difficult task. Our method combines several analyses in order to extract different relation types and avoid missing some relevant relations (which is the case when we use only one approach as statistic, syntactic, etc.). Our approach is based on an exclusive interest to the document style during the statistic process, a rich contextual modelling that strengthens the term co-occurrence selection, a lexical analysis, a use of the existent relations in the concept hierarchy and a stepping between the various extracted relations to facilitate the evaluation made by the domain expert of domain.

References

1. Nazarenko, A.: Compréhension du langage naturel: le problème de la causalité. Thèse de doctorat (1994)
2. Hearst, M.A.: Automatic acquisition of hyponyms from large text corpora. In: Proceedings of the fourteenth international conference on computational linguistics, Nantes, France, pp. 539–545 (1992)
3. Grefenstette, G.: Use of syntatic context to produce terms association list for text retrieval. In: SIGIR 1992. Conference in Research and Developement in Information Retrieval, Copenhagen, Denmarke, pp. 89–97 (juin 1992)
4. Bruandet, M.F.: Domain Knowledge Acquisition for an Intelligent Information Retrieval System: Strategies and Tools. Expert systems applications, 231–235 (1990)
5. Karoui, L., Aufaure, M.-A., Bennacer, N.: Context-based Hierachical Clustering for the Ontology Learning. In: IEEE Proceedings of the 2006 IEEE/WIC/ACM International Conference on Web Intelligence 2006, Hong-Kong, pp. 420–427 (2006)

A Fair-Exchange and Customer-Anonymity Electronic Commerce Protocol for Digital Content Transactions

Shi-Jen Lin and Ding-Chyu Liu

Department of Information Management, National Central University
No. 300, Jhongda Rd., Jhongli City, Taoyuan County 320, Taiwan
sjlin@mgt.ncu.edu.tw, dingchyu@ms23.hinet.net

Abstract. This paper devises a new e-commerce protocol that can ensure fair exchange and customer's anonymity for digital content transactions. The proposed protocol considers the complete transaction process: negotiating, withdrawing, purchasing, and arbitrating phases. The offline arbitrator reduces the possibility of becoming a bottleneck. By scrupulous analysis, the proposed protocol achieves fair exchange, customer's anonymity, and good efficiency.

1 Introduction

Fair exchange and customer's anonymity are two important properties in e-commerce protocols [2, 3]. Fair exchange ensures that either both or neither a customer or a merchant obtain the other's item. Customer's anonymity ensures that the real identity of any customer is not revealed. Many protocols can achieve fair exchange in the meantime, but few protocols can ensure customer's anonymity. To our knowledge, two protocols [2, 3] that have both properties have been proposed. Unfortunately, these protocols are flawed. However, we think that Zhang et al.'s protocol (ZSM) [3] is relatively good. Because its TTP does not keep encrypted products and it uses symmetric key to protect products, its performance will be better than Ray et al.'s protocol (RRN) [2].

The objective of this paper is to propose a new e-commerce protocol that can ensure fair exchange and customer's anonymity with the assistance of an offline arbitrator. The proposed protocol is based on ZSM. However, ZSM only focuses on purchase and arbitration. Therefore, it will be modified and extended. The main contributions of this paper are threefold. Firstly, the proposed protocol considers the complete transaction process and ensures fair exchange and customer's anonymity. Secondly, customers use symmetric keys to communicate with other participants and the proposed protocol uses symmetric keys on encrypting/decrypting digital contents to alleviate computational overheads. Thirdly, the partially blind signature electronic cash [1] is introduced into the proposed protocol to improve the efficiency of payment.

The remainder of this paper is organized as follows. Section 2 details the proposed protocol. Section 3 provides the protocol evaluation and comparison. Finally, Section 4 outlines our conclusion and future work.

T. Janowski and H. Mohanty (Eds.): ICDCIT 2007, LNCS 4882, pp. 321–326, 2007.

2   The Proposed E-Commerce Protocol

The principal participants of the proposed protocol are customer (P_C), merchant (P_M), bank (P_B), arbitrator (P_A), and producer (P_P) of digital contents. The notations used in the protocol description are summarized in Table 1.

Table 1. Natations used in proposed protocol

Item	Interpretation
$h()$	$h()$ is a one-way hash function. The length of hash value is l bits.
pk_i, sk_i	$pk_i = \{e_i, n_i\}$ and $sk_i = \{d_i, n_i\}$ denote RSA-based public key and private key respectively where $i \in \{M, B, A, P\}$, $e_B > 2^{l+1}$, and $e_i d_i \equiv 1 \mod \phi(n_i)$.
sek_{ij}	sek_{ij} denotes a session key between two participants generated by the SSL.
$E_k(X)$	$E_k(X)$ is the ciphertext of a data item X encrypted with a key k.
(X, Y)	(X, Y) denotes the concatenation of data items X and Y.
DC_{pid}	DC_{pid} denotes a digital content. pid is a unique product number.
k_{pid}	k_{pid} is P_M's symmetric key for encrypting/decrypting DC_{pid}.
k_C	k_C is P_C's symmetric key for encrypting/decrypting electronic cash.
Z_n^*	Z_n^* is the set of all positive integers which are less than and relatively prime to n.
$f()$	$f(x) = x^2 \mod n_A$ is a one-way function, and its domain and range is $Z_{n_A}^*$.
$Cert_{pid}$	$Cert_{pid} = (desc_{pid}, hdc_{pid}, f(k_{pid}), Sign_{pid})$ is a certificate. $desc_{pid}$ is the description of DC_{pid}, $Sign_{pid} = E_{sk_P}(h(desc_{pid}, hdc_{pid}, f(k_{pid})))$ is P_P's signature, and $hdc_{pid} = h(E_{k_{pid}}(DC_{pid}))$.
tn	tn is a unique transaction number.
r_C, r_M	r_C, r_M are random number chosen by P_C and P_M respectively during the purchasing phase, where $r_C, r_M \in Z_{n_A}^*$.
t	t is a reasonable time to finish a transaction.
DB_1, DB_2	They are P_B's databases. DB_1 temporarily keeps electronic cash with a time period $2t$. This electronic cash is submitted to P_M by P_C for purchasing digital contents, but it has not been redeemed yet. DB_2 keeps spent electronic cash until the expiration date of electronic cash for double-spending check.

The proposed protocol has following assumptions. (1) Participants (besides P_C) have their own asymmetric key pair. All participants can look others' public key up in CA's directory server. (2) P_M contracted with P_P for selling DC_{pid}. P_P only needs to certify DC_{pid} for P_M once, i.e. P_A issues $Cert_{pid}$. Here, P_M could determine k_{pid}. Then, P_M can sell DC_{pid} for as many times as P_M can without any involvement of P_P. (3) P_A is an offline arbitrator, and it is trusted by other participants. (4) P_C and P_M have their own account in P_B. The proposed protocol consists of four phases: negotiating, withdrawing, purchasing, and arbitrating phases.

● **Negotiating phase (NP).** P_C determines to purchase a digital content DC_{pid}.
N1: P_C searches digital contents and determines to purchase DC_{pid} from P_M.
N2: P_C establishes a secure channel with P_M.

N3: P_C sends $E_{sek_{CM}}(pid)$ to P_M.

N4: P_M replies $E_{sek_{CM}}(tn, pid, price)$ to P_C where $price$ is the price of DC_{pid}. P_C checks the accuracy of pid and $price$.

- **Withdrawing Phase (WP).** P_C withdraws electronic cash from P_B.

W1: P_C establishes a secure channel with P_B.

W2: P_C login P_B's banking system. At this moment, P_B knows P_C's account.

W3, W4, and W5 are the same as the blinding stage of Cao et al.'s electronic cash [1]. However, $\alpha = r^{e_B}uh(m, (((u^{e_B}\bmod n_B)y)\bmod n_B))\bmod n_B$ has replaced the blinding message $\alpha = r^{e_B}uh(m, u^{e_B}y)\bmod n_B$ in Cao et al.'s electronic cash.

W6 is the same as the signing stage of Cao et al.'s electronic cash.

W7 is the same as the unblinding stage of Cao et al.'s electronic cash. Finally, (s, m, v, c) denotes the electronic cash. s is P_B's signature. m represents the serial number of electronic cash. v is the common information of electronic cash containing denomination and expiration date.

- **Purchasing phase (PP).** P_C uses (s, m, v, c) to purchase DC_{pid} from P_M.

P1: P_C sends $E_{sek_{CM}}(tn, pid, E_{k_C}(s, m, v, c), kr_C, E_{pk_B}(tn, r_C))$ to P_M where $kr_C = k_C r_C^{-1}\bmod n_A$, and r_C^{-1} is the multiplicative reverse of r_C modulo n_A.

P2: P_M sends $E_{pk_B}(tn, M, Veri, E_{k_C}(s, m, v, c), kr_C, E_{pk_B}(tn, r_C), Sign_{M1})$ to P_B. The $Veri$ means that P_M requests P_B to verify $E_{k_C}(s, m, v, c)$, and $Sign_{M1} = E_{sk_M}(h(tn, M, Veri, E_{k_C}(s, m, v, c), kr_C, E_{pk_B}(tn, r_C)))$ is P_M's signature. P_B computes $k'_C = kr_C r_C \bmod n_A$, decrypts $E_{k_C}(s, m, v, c)$ with k'_C to get (s, m, v, c), and performs the verification of (s, m, v, c) by the equation $s^{e_B}(h(m, (c^{e_B}\bmod n_B))c)^{\tau(v)} \equiv 1\bmod n_B$ where $\tau(v) = 2^l + h(v)$. P_B also performs the double-spending check via comparing (s, m, v, c) with the records in DB_1 and DB_2.

P3: P_B replies $E_{pk_M}(tn, M, v, f(k'_C), Sign_{B1})$ to P_M if (s, m, v, c) is a legal and unspent where $Sign_{B1} = E_{sk_B}(h(tn, M, v, f(k'_C)))$ is P_B's signature. In the meantime, P_B keep $(tn, M, (s, m, v, c))$ in DB_1 for a time period $2t$. Namely, the transaction must be finished within a reasonable time t. Otherwise, P_B will release (s, m, v, c) after the time $2t$, and P_C must restart a new transaction.

P4: P_M sends $E_{sek_{CM}}(tn, E_{k_{pid}}(DC_{pid}), kr_M, co_{tn}, Cert_{pid})$ to P_C if the verification of $E_{k_C}(s, m, v, c)$ in step P3 is positive and the denomination in v is equal to the price of DC_{pid}. $kr_M = k_{pid}r_M^{-1}\bmod n_A$, r_M^{-1} is the multiplicative reverse of r_M module n_A, and co_{tn} is P_M's commitment for transaction tn. For computing co_{tn}, P_M defines $p(x) = (r_M + r_M^{-1}x)\bmod n_A$, computes $f(r_C) = f(k'_C)f(kr_C)^{-1}\bmod n_A$, $hv_{tn} = h(tn, f(r_C), f(r_M))$, $ep_1 = E_{pk_A}(p(hv_{tn}))$, and $ep_2 = E_{pk_A}(p(h(hv_{tn} + 1)))$. P_M's commitment is $co_{tn} = (ep_1, ep_2)$.

P5: P_C sends $E_{sek_{CM}}(tn, r_C)$ to P_M if following verifications are positive. (1) P_C uses pk_P to verify $cert_{pid}$ and confirms that $E_{k_{pid}}(DC_{pid})$ is the product she/he would like to buy through the equation $h(E_{k_{pid}}(DC_{pid})) = hdc_{pid}$. (2) P_C computes $hv'_{tn} = h(tn, f(r_C), f(r_M))$ and $f(r_M) = f(k_{pid})f(kr_M)^{-1}\bmod n_A$, and then verifies co_{tn} through $E_{pk_A}(f(r_M) + 2hv'_{tn} + f(r_M)^{-1}hv'^2_{tn}) = f(ep_1)$ and $E_{pk_A}(f(r_M) + 2h(hv'_{tn} + 1) + f(r_M)^{-1}h(hv'_{tn} + 1)^2) = f(ep_2)$. If co_{tn} is correct, it indicates that P_A can use co_{tn} to help P_C to recover P_M's r_M.

P6: P_M sends $E_{pk_B}(tn, M, Depo, (s, m, v, c), Sign_{M2})$ to P_B after P_M gets the plaintext of (s, m, v, c). P_M computes $k_C'' = kr_C r_C \bmod n_A$. If $f(k_C'') = f(k_C')$, P_M can decrypt $E_{k_C}(s, m, v, c)$ with k_C'' to get (s, m, v, c). The $Depo$ means that P_M requests P_B to credit the denomination in v to P_M's account, and $Sign_{M2} = E_{sk_M}(h(tn, M, Depo, (s, m, v, c)))$ is P_M's signature.

P7: P_B replies $E_{pk_M}(tn, ack, Sign_{B2})$ to P_M if $(tn, M, (s, m, v, c))$ exists in DB_1. P_B credits the denomination in v to P_M's account, removes $(tn, M, (s, m, v, c))$ from DB_1, and keeps $(tn, M, Depo, (s, m, v, c), Sign_{M2})$ in DB_2 until the expiration date of (s, m, v, c). $Sign_{B2} = E_{sk_B}(h(tn, ack))$ is P_B's signature, and ack represents an acknowledgement.

P8: P_M sends $E_{sek_{CM}}(tn, r_M)$ to P_C after receiving $E_{pk_M}(tn, ack, Sign_{B2})$.

P9: P_C computes $k_{pid}' = kr_M r_M \bmod n_A$. If $f(k_{pid}') = f(k_{pid})$, P_C decrypts $E_{k_{pid}}(DC_{pid})$ with k_{pid}' to get DC_{pid}.

Above-mentioned processes are a normal transaction. When any step mistakes, participants can abort the transaction or request P_A to arbitrate.

• **Arbitrating phase (AP).** After P_C sends r_C to P_M, if P_M does not reply r_M within a reasonable time t or replies $r_M'(\neq r_M)$, P_C initiates the arbitrating phase within the time period $2t$.

A1: P_C establishes a secure channel with P_A.

A2: P_C sends $E_{sek_{CA}}(tn, r_C, f(r_M), co_{tn})$ to P_A and requests P_A to recover r_M.

A3: P_A sends $E_{pk_B}(tn, Sign_{A1})$ to P_B. $Sign_{A1} = E_{sk_P}(h(tn))$ is P_A's signature.

A4: P_B replies $E_{pk_A}(tn, status, Sign_{B3})$ to P_A after it searches DB_1 and DB_2 according to tn. $Sign_{B3} = E_{sk_B}(h(tn, status))$ is P_B's signature and $status$ is the status of transaction tn. The possible values of $status$ are 0 (none of record about tn in DB_1 and DB_2), 1 (transaction record about tn kept in DB_1), or 2 (transaction record about tn kept in DB_2).

A5: (1) P_A replies $E_{sek_{CA}}(tn, failure)$ to P_C if the value of $status$ is 0 or 1 which means that P_A cannot carry out arbitration because the arbitrational time has exceeded the time period $2t$ or the expiration date of (s, m, v, c), or P_M has not redeemed (s, m, v, c) yet, otherwise (2) P_A helps P_C to recover r_M. P_A computes $hv_{tn}'' = h(tn, f(r_C), f(r_M))$, and solves the following equations for r_M'.

$$\begin{cases} (r_M' + w h v_{tn}'') \bmod n_A = (ep_1)^{d_A} \bmod n_A \\ (r_M' + w h(h v_{tn}'' + 1)) \bmod n_A = (ep_2)^{d_A} \bmod n_A \end{cases}$$

If $f(r_M') = f(r_M)$ and $(r_M' w) \bmod n_A = 1$, P_A convinces that the request from P_C is valid. P_A replies $E_{sek_{CA}}(tn, r_M')$ to P_C. P_A also keeps (tn, r_C, r_M') for future inquiries from P_C or P_M.

A6: After receiving $E_{sek_{CA}}(tn, r_M')$, P_C computes $k_{pid}'' = kr_M r_M' \bmod n_A$ and decrypts $E_{k_{pid}}(DC_{pid})$ with k_{pid}'' to get DC_{pid}.

3   Evaluation and Comparison

The proposed protocol is evaluated by three viewpoints: fair exchange, customer's anonymity, and operational efficiency. About fair exchange, the explanations of possible misbehaviors of destroying fairness are as follows.

Case 1. P_C sends P_M incorrect kr_C and/or r_C in step P1. P_B will detect an error because it is unable to compute the correct k'_C in step P2.

Case 2. P_C sends inadequate denomination in v to P_M in step P1. P_M will detect the inconsistency between the denomination and the price of DC_{pid} in step P4.

Case 3. P_M sends P_C incorrect DC_{pid} and/or $Cert_{pid}$ in step P4. P_C will detects P_M's misbehavior in step P5 because $h(E_{k_{pid}}(DC_{pid}))$ is unequal to hdc_{pid}.

Case 4. P_M sends P_C incorrect kr_M and/or co_{tn} in step P4. P_C will detect P_M's misbehavior in step P5 because the verification of co_{tn} with kr_M is negative.

Case 5. P_C sends $r'_C(\neq r_C)$ to P_M in step P5. P_M computes k''_C in step P6 and will detect an error because $f(k''_C) \neq f(k'_C)$, i.e. k''_C cannot decrypt $E_{k_C}(s, m, v, c)$.

Case 6. P_M sends $r'_M(\neq r_M)$ to P_C in step P8. P_C computes k_{pid} in step P9 and will detect an error because $f(k'_{pid}) \neq f(k_{pid})$. If this situation occurs, P_C will request P_A to recover P_M's r_M by the arbitrating phase.

Based on above analyses, the proposed protocol shows good quality of fairness.

About customer's anonymity, none of the participants (besides P_C) know P_C carriying out transaction tn and P_C's real identity during the negotiating, purchasing, and arbitrating phases (Table 2). Therefore, the proposed protocol guarantees that P_C can maintain her/his anonymity.

About operational efficiency, this paper makes efficiency comparisons between the proposed protocol and RRN, because the latter contains the complete transaction process. Table 3 shows that the proposed protocol is superior to RRN on the following items: arbitrator's operation, the number of electronic cash, the protection of digital content, extra storage for digital content, key management, communication round, and total time cost. Furthermore, because electronic cash in the proposed protocol includes its expiration date, P_B purges the spent electronic cash in DB_2 which is beyond its expiration date. Therefore, the number of spent electronic cash kept in P_B will be finite.

Table 2. The customer's information possessed by each participant

Information	P_C	P_M	P_B	P_A	P_P
P_C's identity (in WP)	Yes	No	Yes	No	No
P_C's identity (in NP, PP,and AP)	Yes	No	No	No	No
P_C carries out transacion tn, purchases DC_{pid}, and spends (s, m, v, c).	Yes	No	No	No	No

Table 3. The comparisons between the proposed protocol and RRN

Item	The proposed protocol	RRN
Arbitrator (TTP)	Entirely offline	Offline**
The number of Ecash	Single	Multiple
Protection of DC	Symmetric encryption	Asymmetric encryption
Extra storage for DC	Nil	TTP
Key Managememt	Simple	Complex
Communication round	NP: 4*; WP: 6*; PP: 8; AP: 5*	NP: 3; WP: 2n; PP: 6; AP: 4
The time cost of NP	$4T_{sym}$	0
The time cost of WP	$5T_{exp} + 2T_{mul} + 8T_{sym} + 1T_h$	$4nT_{pub} + 2nT_{exp} + nT_{mul} + 2nT_h$
The time cost of PP	$22T_{pub} + 2T_{exp} + 7T_{mul} + 12T_{sym} + 15T_h$	$(9n + 18)T_{pub} + nT_{exp} + 1T_{mul} + 2nT_{sym} + (2n + 7)T_h$
The total time cost from NP to PP	$22T_{pub} + 7T_{exp} + 9T_{mul} + 24T_{sym} + 16T_h$	$(13n + 18)T_{pub} + 3nT_{exp} + (n + 1)T_{mul} + 2nT_{sym} + (4n + 7)T_h$
The time cost of AP	$10T_{pub} + 2T_{exp} + 5T_{sym} + 4T_h$	$7nT_{pub} + nT_{exp}$

DC: digital content; T_{pub}: the time to execute public key encryption or decryption; T_{exp}: the time to execute modulus exponent; T_{mul}: the time to execute modulus multiplication; T_{sym}: the time to execute symmetric encryption or decryption; T_h: the time to execute one-way hash function; n: the number of electronic cash. * The number of rounds includes establishing a secure channel. ** Customers download an encrypted product from the TTP at the beginning of RRN.

4   Conclusion and Future Work

Fair exchange and customer's anonymity are two important properties that e-commerce protocols need to address. This paper proposed a new e-commerce protocol that can ensure both properties for digital content transactions. By scrupulous analysis, the proposed protocol can achieve fair exchange, customer's anonymity, and good efficiency. Furthermore, the comparison shows that the proposed protocol is superior to RRN. Therefore, the proposed protocol is well-designed and has significant potential to increase e-commence transactions.

The proposed protocol at this time is in its early stage of development. In the future, we intend to implement the proposed protocol in a web-based platform to demonstrate its efficiency and applicability on e-commerce transactions.

References

1. Cao, T., Lin, D., Xue, R.: A Randomized RSA-based Partially Blind Signature Scheme for Electronic Cash. Computers & Security 24(1), 44–49 (2005)
2. Ray, I., Ray, I., Natarajan, N.: An Anonymous and Failure Resilient Fair-exchange E-commerce Protocol. Decision Support Systems 39, 267–292 (2005)
3. Zhang, N., Shi, Q., Merabti, M.: An Efficient Protocol for Anonymous and Fair Document Exchange. Computer Networks 41, 19–28 (2003)

A Practical Way to Provide Perfect Forward Secrecy for Secure E-Mail Protocols*

Sangjin Kim[1], Changyong Lee[2], Daeyoung Kim[3], and Heekuck Oh[2]

[1] Korea University of Technology and Education,
School of Information and Media Engineering, Republic of Korea
`sangjin@kut.ac.kr`
[2] Hanyang University, Department of Computer Science and Engineering,
Republic of Korea
`chylee@cse.hanyang.ac.kr, hkoh@hanyang.ac.kr`
[3] Empas Corporation, Republic of Korea
`kdy1029@empascorp.com`

Abstract. People are concerned with spam mails and viruses or worms contained in e-mails. However, people often neglect the security issues concerning the content of e-mails. In this paper, we propose practical and secure e-mail protocols that provide perfect forward secrecy. Unlike previous proposals, our protocols can be deployed without any change to the current infrastructure. Moreover, we provide a way for the sender to securely send an identical e-mail to multiple receivers.

1 Introduction

1.1 Overview of Secure E-Mail Service

Currently e-mail is one of the most widely used Internet service. Various kinds of contents are exchanged using e-mails and if they are not protected properly user privacy may be violated and important data may be exposed. However, security issues concerning e-mails are often neglected. Currently, we can use PGP (Pretty Good Privacy), or S/MIME (Secure/Multipurpose Internet Mail) to securely exchange e-mails. However, they do not provide perfect forward secrecy. As a result, if the long-term private key of a user is exposed, all e-mails protected using the corresponding public key will also be exposed. There are various key agreement protocols that provide perfect forward secrecy. However, these protocols cannot be directly applied to e-mail service. Since e-mail is a stateless protocol, the sender does not directly communicate with the receiver when sending e-mails.

---

* This research was also supported by the MIC (Ministry of Information and Communication), Korea, under the HNRC (Home Network Research Center) - ITRC (Information Technology Research Center) support program supervised by the IITA (Institute of Information Technology Assessment).

T. Janowski and H. Mohanty (Eds.): ICDCIT 2007, LNCS 4882, pp. 327–335, 2007.

1.2 Related Work

Sun et al. proposed two secure e-mail protocols that provide perfect forward secrecy [1]. The basic idea of the first protocol is to use the basic DH (Diffie-Hellman) protocol with a help from a server. To this end, the receiver must send its ephemeral DH public key to the server beforehand to receive a secure e-mail. Since receivers cannot forecast when and how many secure e-mails will be sent to him/her, receivers must deposit many ephemeral DH public keys in advance. Moreover, the receiver must maintain the private keys corresponding to the ephemeral public keys he/she has sent to the server. Furthermore, to receive e-mails from multiple devices, receivers have to portably carry the private keys safely. Therefore, receivers require a cryptographic hardware such as smart card to receive secure e-mails. The second protocol of Sun et al. tried to remove this disadvantage. This protocol uses a cryptographic primitive called CEMBS (Certificate of Encrypted Message Being a Signature) proposed by Deng and Mao [2]. However, as suggested by Dent [3], this protocol does not provide forward secrecy.

Kim et al. proposed two secure e-mail protocols that provide perfect forward secrecy [4]. However, like Sun et al.'s work, the second protocol does not provide perfect forward secrecy. In the first protocol, Kim et al. tried to solve the problem in Sun et al.'s protocol by performing a key agreement protocol between the receiver and the server. They used the resulting session key to encrypt the ephemeral private key chosen by the server. Therefore, compromises of long-term private keys do not reveal any ephemeral private keys. Thus, providing perfect forward secrecy. In the second protocol, Kim et al. tried to improve the efficiency of the protocol by using a signcryption primitive. However, they did not consider the effect of the signcryption scheme on perfect forward secrecy. To fix this problem, one of the values of the signcryption must also be sent to the receiver encrypted using a key that preserves perfect forward secrecy.

Both Sun et al. and Kim et al. work have another critical problem. They both assume that the sender and the receiver share the same server. Moreover, they assume that this server is an existing mail server such as SMTP server. However, these assumptions do not fit into current e-mail infrastructure and require changes to existing mail servers. Normally, the sender contacts its SMTP server to forward its e-mail to the destination SMTP server. During this transfer, intermediate SMTP servers may be involved. Finally, the receiver contacts its POP (Post Office Protocol) or IMAP (Internet Message Access Protocol) server. Moreover, senders and receivers may be using web-based e-mail services. In this case, the integration of services cannot be controlled by the users. Furthermore, the sender and the receiver generally do not share the same SMTP servers.

2 Backgrounds

2.1 Mathematical Background

Definition 1 (Forward Secrecy). *We say that a key establishment protocol provides the forward secrecy if the advantage of an attacker compromising past*

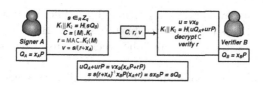

Fig. 1. Signcryption Scheme of Zheng and Imai

session keys is negligible, even though he/she has compromised the long-term keys of one or more participants.

Definition 2 (Perfect Forward Secrecy). *We say that a protocol provides the perfect forward secrecy, if the forward secrecy is preserved even if the adversary has compromised the long-term keys of all the participants.*

Our system uses an elliptic curve based signcryption scheme proposed by Zheng and Imai [5]. Signcryption provides both functions of public key and digital signature with a cost significantly lower than that required by signature-then-encryption. The protocol of Zheng and Imai is given in Fig. 1. Here, the triple $\langle C, r, v \rangle$ is the resulting signcryption on message M using the private key x_A of A and the public key Q_B of B. We assume that signcryption scheme of Zheng and Imai is secure.

3   Our Protocol

3.1   System Setup

The server T does the followings to setup the system.

- T generates an elliptic curve group $\mathbb{G}$ which order is a prime q. q must be large enough for EC-DLP and EC-CDHP to be computationally infeasible in $\mathbb{G}$.
- It selects a generator P of $\mathbb{G}$ and publishes $\mathbb{G}$ and P.

Users who wants to send a secure e-mail must register with the trusted server T. In our system, we assume the followings.

- A registered user A shares a symmetric key K_{AT} and a counter C_A with T.
- The senders and receivers know and have each others' authenticated public keys.
- In case of protocol for single recipient, the sender and the receiver must have a public key pair generated from the same elliptic curve group $\mathbb{G}$.
- In case of protocol for multiple recipients, the sender must register all the receivers' public key in the server database.

It is obvious and inevitable that senders and receivers must have public key pairs to send and receive secure e-mails. Moreover, they must have each other's authenticated public key. However, they may have different types of public keys. Therefore, the third assumption may be too strong. However, in order to use signcryption schemes, the sender and the receiver must have public keys of the same type.

When a user wants to sends an identical e-mail to n receivers, it would be impractical and inefficient if the user has to run the same protocol n times. Moreover, the message size of the e-mail should not increase proportional to n. To solve this problem, we use a one-time public key pair generated by the server. The sender uses this public key to signcrypt the content of the e-mail. To unsigncrypt this e-mail, each receiver contacts the server to acquire the corresponding private key. In this process, the server should be able to authenticate the receivers. To this end, users register authenticated public keys of potential receivers at T. T uses the registered public keys to authenticate receivers. This assumption is not a strong one, since the sender must know all the public keys of the receivers to send a secure e-mail to multiple receivers.

3.2   Our Protocol for Single Recipient

Our protocol consists of the following three sub-protocols: the protocol between the sender A and the server T, the protocol between the sender A and the receiver B, and the protocol between the receiver B and the server T. The sender A's and the receiver B's private keys are x_A and x_B, respectively. The corresponding public keys are $Q_A = x_A P$ and $Q_B = x_B P$, respectively.

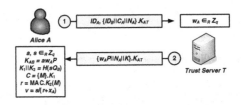

Fig. 2. The Sub-protocol between the Sender and the Server for Single Recipient

The protocol between A and T is depicted in Fig. 2 and it runs as follows.

- **Step 1.** A generates a nonce N_A and sends the receiver identifier ID_B, the current counter value C_A, and N_A encrypted using the symmetric key K_{AT} to T. Here, identifiers denote the e-mail address of users. We use a counter to check the freshness of message 1. The use of K_{AT} allows the server to authenticate the sender.
- **Step 2.** T decrypts the ciphertext and checks whether the value C_A is greater than C_A it maintains. T updates its counter to loosely synchronize with A. It then selects $w_A \in_R \mathbb{Z}_q^*$ and generates a random symmetric key K. After that, it stores N_A, ID_B, K, w_A in its database and these data can be searched using N_A. Finally, T encrypts $w_A P$, N_A, and K using K_{AT} and sends the ciphertext to A.

- **Step 3.** A decrypts the ciphertext and verifies N_A for freshness. If it confirms, A selects $a, s \in_R \mathbb{Z}_q^*$ and computes $K_{AB} = aw_AP$, it then signcrypts the e-mail message M which results in triple $\langle C, r, v \rangle$. Finally, A updates the counter C_A.

The protocol between A and B runs as follows. Actually, the sender attaches the message in a normal e-mail to the receiver.

- **Step 1.** A encrypts v using K_{AB} and encrypts ID_A, aP, N_A, and K using the public key of B. A then sends C, r, $\{v\}.K_{AB}$, and $\{\text{ID}_A\|aP\|N_A\|K\}.+K_B$ attached in an e-mail to B.

In this sub-protocol, v must be encrypted with a key that provides perfect forward secrecy. If v is sent without any protection, an adversary who has obtained A's private key can compute s which allows the adversary to compute K_1 and K_2 shown in Fig 3. Thus, violating forward secrecy. As one can see from this sub-protocol, our protocol does not require any changes to the existing SMTP servers or POP servers. Since the message is attached to a normal e-mail, the service can be used in any e-mail environment.

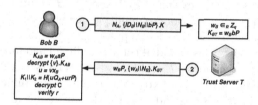

Fig. 3. The Protocol between the Receiver and the Server

When B receives a secure e-mail, it uses the hyperlink in the e-mail to contact the server. The protocol between B and T is depicted in Fig. 3 and it runs as follows.

- **Step 1.** B selects $b \in_R \mathbb{Z}_q$ and generates a nonce N_B. It then computes bP and sends N_A, $\{\text{ID}_B\|N_B\|bP\}.K$ to T.
- **Step 2.** T uses N_A to search its database. It then retrieves K associated with N_A and decrypts the ciphertext to authenticate the requester. We must note that K is known to only A, B, and T. If it confirms, it selects $w_B \in_R \mathbb{Z}_q$ and computes w_BP and $K_{BT} = w_BbP$. Finally, it sends w_BP and $\{w_A\|N_B\}.K_{BT}$ to B.
- **Step 3.** B computes $K_{BT} = bw_BP$ and decrypts the received ciphertext. He then verifies his nonce for freshness and correctness of K_{BT}. After that, B computes $K_{AB} = w_AaP$ and uses it to obtain v. Finally, B unsigncrypts the triple $\langle C, r, v \rangle$ to obtain M and to authenticate A.

One may think that K can be used instead of K_{BT} in message 2. However, this approach does not provide perfect forward secrecy. This is because K is sent to B encrypted using B's public key. Therefore, an adversary who has obtained B's private key can obtain K and aP. Moreover, this allows the adversary to obtain w_A which results in K_{AB}. We must note that $w_B P$ is not protected. Since basic DH protocol suffers from the man-in-the-middle attack, it would be safer if T signs this value. However, the other DH public key bP is exchanged encrypted. Moreover, even if an attacker swaps bP with some other value, B can detect this by computing K_{BT} and decrypting the ciphertext. Therefore, the man-in-the-middle attack is not possible.

B cannot directly authenticate the senders of the messages it received. However, we must note that only A can generate the correct triple $\langle C, r, v \rangle$ on message M. Therefore, once B can verify the signcryption included in the e-mail from A, he can be sure that this message is for him, A has sent it, and T is the correct trusted server used by A. This is because B has assurance in the public key of A and the signcryption used in this protocol is secure.

3.3 Protocol for Multiple Recipients

Our protocol for multiple recipients is very similar to protocol for single recipient. In the protocol for single recipient, the sender encrypts a key received from T using the recipient's public key. This key is used by T to authenticate receivers. If we directly apply this method to multiple recipients case, we would have to encrypt the key with each recipient's public key. Moreover, the sender has to send n different e-mails. This would affect scalability. Therefore, in our proposed protocol for multiple recipients, T authenticates receivers by verifying signatures sent by the receivers. We must note that T may have difficulty in verifying certificates of receivers. To this end, this role has been given to the sender. The sender registers authenticated receivers' certificates in T and T uses these to verify signatures of receivers. This confirms to our second assumption.

The protocol between A and T runs as follows.

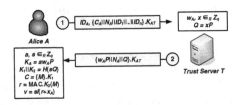

Fig. 4. The Sub-protocol between the Sender and the Server for Multiple Recipients

- **Step 1.** A generates a nonce N_A and sends the current counter value C_A, N_A, list of IDs of multiple receivers encrypted using the symmetric key K_{AT} to T.
- **Step 2.** T decrypts the ciphertext and checks whether the value C_A is greater than C_A it maintains. T updates its counter to loosely synchronize with A. It then selects $w_A, x \in_R \mathbb{Z}_q^*$ and generates a random public key $Q = xP$. After that, it stores N_A, x, w_A and the list of IDs in its database and these

data can be searched using N_A. Finally, T encrypts $w_A P$, N_A, and Q using K_{AT} and sends the ciphertext to A.

- **Step 3.** A decrypts the ciphertext and verifies N_A for freshness. If it confirms, A selects $a, s \in_R \mathbb{Z}_q^*$ and computes $K_A = aw_A P$, it then signcrypts the e-mail message M using Q which results in triple $\langle C, r, v \rangle$. Finally, A updates the counter C_A.

Unlike our protocol for single recipient, the public key used in signcryption is generated by T. This is because single signcryption must be verified and decrypted by multiple users. The merit of this approach is that receivers do not have to posses public keys suitable for signcryption. On the other hand, the demerit of this approach is that the content of the e-mail is also exposed to the server. We must note that this approach used in the protocol for multiple recipients can be applied to the protocol for single recipient. In this case, the merit and demerit given above will also applied to that protocol.

The protocol between A and multiple receivers runs as follows. As with protocol for single recipient, the sender attaches the message in a normal e-mail to the receivers.

- **Step 1.** A encrypts v using K_A and sends C, r, $\{v\}.K_A$, aP, and N_A attached in a e-mail message to multiple receivers.

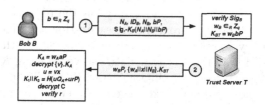

Fig. 5. The Protocol between the Receiver and the Server

The protocol between one of the receiver B and T is depicted in Fig. 5 and it runs as follows.

- **Step 1.** B selects $b \in_R \mathbb{Z}_q$ and generates a nonce N_B. It then computes bP and signs $\{N_A \| N_B \| bP\}$ and sends the signature to T.
- **Step 2.** T uses N_A to search its database. It first verifies that ID_B is one of the recipients related to N_A. It then retrieves certificate of ID_B registered by the sender of the e-mail A. It uses this public key to verify the signature. If it confirms, it selects $w_B \in_R \mathbb{Z}_q$ and computes $w_B P$ and $K_{BT} = w_B bP$. Finally, it sends $w_B P$ and $\{w_A \| x \| N_B\}.K_{BT}$ to B.
- **Step 3.** B computes $K_{BT} = bw_B P$ and decrypts the received ciphertext. He then verifies his nonce for freshness. After that, B computes $K_A = w_A aP$ and uses it to obtain v. Finally, B verifies the signcryption of M using the triple $\langle C, r, v \rangle$.

As was the case in protocol for single recipient, B cannot directly authenticate the senders of the messages it received. The only difference between two protocols is that one uses the public key of the receiver to signcrypt the e-mail message and the other uses a one-time public key generated by T. However, in both cases, if the signcryption is valid, it is clear that A is the signer of the signcryption. Moreover, only T can present the value needed to compute the key K_A which is needed to obtain v. Therefore, Bob can be sure that this e-mail was from A.

4   Analysis

4.1   Security Analysis

In this section, we argue that our protocols provide perfect forward secrecy. In the protocol for single recipient, the long-term keys are x_A, x_B, and K_{AT}. Therefore, a forward-secure adversary is assumed to have these long-term keys. In addition, the adversary also has messages exchanged. Since we assume that the signcryption used is secure, he/she must be able to unsigncrypt the triple $\langle C, r, v \rangle$ to obtain the content of the e-mail included in the signcryption. However, v is exchanged encrypted using K_{AB}. As a result, if our defined adversary can compute or obtain $K_{AB} = aw_AP$, he/she can obtain the content of given e-mail. Since K_{AB} is established using an elliptic curve Diffie-Hellman protocol, one requires either a or w_A. Since our adversary has the receiver's long-term keys, he/she can obtain aP or w_AP from the messages. However, due to the ECDLP, it is computationally infeasible for an adversary to obtain the required value from these values. However, w_A is exchanged encrypted using K_{BT}. Nonetheless K_{BT} is also established using an elliptic curve Diffie-Hellman protocol and the ephemeral private keys are never exchanged. Therefore, the protocol for single recipient provides perfect forward secrecy. The protocol for multiple recipients can be similarly argued. The only difference is that x instead of x_B is needed to obtain the content of the e-mail. This x is exchange using K_{BT} which is a key that provides perfect forward secrecy. Therefore, the protocol for multiple recipients also provides perfect forward secrecy.

5   Conclusion

In this paper, we have proposed two new secure e-mail protocols that provide perfect forward secrecy. Our proposed protocols have the following novel aspects. First, our protocols are practical in that they do not require changes to existing infrastructure and can also be used in web-based e-mail services. Second, we also consider the case when a sender wants to securely send an identical e-mail to multiple receivers. To our knowledge, there has been no proposal which considers multiple receivers. Both our protocols provide perfect forward secrecy.

References

1. Sun, H., Hsieh, B., Hwang, H.: Secure E-mail Protocols Providing Perfect Forward Secrecy. IEEE Comm. Letters 9(1), 58–60 (2005)
2. Bao, F., Deng, H., Mao, W.: Identity-based Encryption from Weil pairing. In: Proc. of the IEEE Symp. on Security and Privacy, pp. 77–85. IEEE, Los Alamitos (1998)
3. Dent, A.W.: Flaws in an E-Mail Protocol of Sun, Hsieh, and Hwang. IEEE Comm. Letters 9(8), 718–719 (2005)
4. Kim, B.H., Koo, J.H., Lee, D.H.: REP: A Robust E-Mail Protocol Providing Perfect Forward Secrecy. In: Proc. of the KIISC Chungcheong Regional Conf. KIISC, pp. 37–48 (2005)
5. Zheng, Y., Imai, H.: How to Construct Efficient Signcryption Scheme on Elliptic Curves. Information Processing Letters 68, 227–233 (1998)

Augmentation to GT4 Framework for B2B Collaboration over Grid

Jitendra Kumar Singh, K.N. Praveen, and R.K. Ghosh

Department of Computer Science and Engineering, Indian Institute of Technology,
Kanpur, India
jksingh26jun@gmail.com, {praveenk,rkg}@cse.iitk.ac.in

Abstract. We propose a framework for secure and trusted business to business (B2B) collaborations over grid. The core of the proposal consists of a centralised rating system for assignment and maintenance of trust and reputation scores of enterprises.We also propose augmentations to the Globus Toolkit 4 (GT4) [8] for implementing the proposed rating system. It involves integration of three functionalities, namely, (i) building a suitable token structure according to the model of a security token, (ii) building and deploying a trust service which keeps track of the ratings of the collaborating business entities, and (iii) building an information aggregator source which provides these ratings and related information from the trust service to the GT4 default index service.

1 Introduction

Grid provides a scalable, secure and high performance platform for discovery and access negotiation of remote resources. Grid computing is no longer confined to scientific computations. In corporate world, many companies have started using grid to scale up a system that can support many users. Grids provide a convenient alternative to scale web applications, such as distributed online gaming gambling, specially when they become popular. On-demand computing where companies can buy time from an outsourcer's computing facilities is also catching up. Grid computing, thus, has now become indispensable in corporate computing and business processing.

Business enterprises can use grid for discovery and negotiation of accesses to the remote services in order to outsource the incompetent process involved in their products/services and concentrate on their core competencies. Outsourcing improves cost effectiveness, at same time allows meeting deadlines more aggressively. Our idea is to develop a model for large collaborative business processes mediated over the Internet. Trust and security are major concerns that are likely to hinder large business processes to be successfully conducted in a global scale. Also discovering the right partner for collaboration is an issue when an enterprise enters an increasingly competitive market.

Let us abstract out the four major functional requirements for a scalable business to business collaboration over a computer network. These are: (i) secure and

T. Janowski and H. Mohanty (Eds.): ICDCIT 2007, LNCS 4882, pp. 336–344, 2007.

hierarchical collaboration, (ii) discovering services and resources, (ii) monitoring of services and resources (after service allocation), and (iv) cross-platform collaboration. Grid Security Infrastructure (GSI), which tackles the problem of securing business transaction details through its robust authentication, authorisation and encryption mechanisms, takes care . the requirement (i). The Index Service provides necessary information that helps in discovering various services and resources, thus taking care of the requirement (ii). Monitoring and Discovery Service (MDS) can be used for requirement (iii). Since grid is web service based architecture the problem of cross-platform collaboration is handled by its built-in standards. The only problem that remains to be dealt with is the *trust* related to business deals. Other web technologies addresses parts of the above requirements and have to be suitably integrated for a non-trivial business to business collaboration.

Although e-commerce has been in existence for quite a while now and there exist many business models with different trading practices [1], not much work has been done on BPO automation. The reference [2] talks about business process management automation categorizing the challenges in successful automation of business process into exception handling, unavailable functionality, deployment limitations, and IT resource constraints. Web services [3] are developed to wrap legacy software or a software written without the intention to be used remotely and to provide access to software remotely. The web services use SOAP messages for communication. These two technologies are the bases for B2B commerce. The reference [4] states various B2B frameworks based on XML. The reference [5] deals with structuring and standardizing product data in B2B e-commerce.

Business and trust go hand in hand. There can be no fruitful business without proper trust among participating enterprises. So with e-commerce various model for quantifying trust has developed. An extensive survey of how the trust model has developed and what are the challenges in defining a trust model can be found in paper [6].

To represent trust management adequately in the context of outsourcing, we propose a rating system in the form of a centralised trust management model. In the proposed rating system, for each business entity in the system, we maintain a *rating reputation, normalisation factor*, and a *trust value*. When a business transaction is initiated between two parties, they exchange signed *trust tokens* each having *once use property*. These tokens are used for mutual rating of the partners after the transaction is completed. The rating score can be viewed as the rater's perception of trust about the rated party on a fixed scale. We also propose necessary augmentations to the GT4 to implement this model.

2   Trust Model

The notion of 'Trust' is subjective, may not be exactly quantifiable and its measure is largely based on inter-personal relationships (physical form of communication) among business partners and evolves over time. Apart from time, trustworthiness is also based on a number of clues derived from person-to-person interactions. In summary trust is a subjective probability through which one individual expects another individual to deliver some thing or perform some actions on which the former's welfare depends [6].

Let us investigate how a trust and reputation model be evolved for business deals mediated over the Internet. Our proposal is for a central trust server based architecture, in the line of certification authority, which can be easily extended to a distributed architecture. A centralised trust server maintains three values for each business entity, namely, (i) a trust value t, (ii) a rating reputation r, and (iii) a normalisation value n. The values of t ranges in the interval [-5, +5], where -5 represents the least trust-worthy entity and +5 represents the most trust-worthy entity. However, it is possible for t to range in any continuous real interval $[-a, a]$ without any loss generality. This value essentially signifies the general perception of trust-worthiness of an entity as a business partner. The value of r ranges in the interval $[0, 1]$. The rating reputation of a business entity represents how well it has rated its partners in the past. A value $r = 0$ means that that the past ratings of this business enterprise has largely deviated from the trust value of the rated business enterprises, while $r = 1$ means that the ratings done by the business enterprise are in agreement with those provided by other business enterprises. The normalization value n used to neutralize over-rating (or under-rating) nature of the business enterprise and varies in the range $[0.5, 2]$. The normalization value $n > 1$ indicates that the concerned enterprise usually over-rates, while the value $n < 1$ indicates under-rating. There is another constant w (window size) which allows assignment of appropriate weight to new rating against the old ones. The window constant is an integral value which is much larger than t, r and n. The initial values of these three values for the newly added enterprise are $t = -5$, $r = 0.1$, and $n = 1$.

After each business transaction, an enterprise submits a rating to the centralised server which updates
1. the trust value t of the rated, and
2. the rating reputation r and normalisation value n of the rater

using the rating given g by the rater, the current rating reputation and the normalisation value of the rater.

The trust framework should be able to overcome a number of challenges and maintain trust values in a central server. We visualise the trust model in the form of a peer-to-peer trust network. Some of the major challenges in maintaining trust values have been discussed below. Certain important properties which help to maintain trust values have been quoted in Lemmas 1-3. The proofs of these lemmas are easy and have been omitted due to lack of space.

2.1   Low Incentive for Rating

Trust parameters updates are performed as follows:

$$t_{new} = t + \frac{r\langle g/n \rangle}{w}, \quad r_{new} = r - \frac{|\langle g/n \rangle - t|}{10w} + \frac{1}{w^2}, \text{ and } n_{new} = n + \frac{\langle g/n \rangle - t}{5w}, \quad (1)$$

where $\langle g/n \rangle$ represent a quantity belonging to the same range as g. More precisely, if $(g/n) > 5$, then $\langle g/n \rangle = 5$. Similarly, if $(g/n) < -5$, then $\langle g/n \rangle = -5$.

With each honest rating, a rater gets an increase in rating reputation due to the presence of factor $1/w^2 > 0$ in computation of new rating reputation. This factor is expected to increase the business of the enterprise because other enterprises interested to increase their reputations would like to enter into business deals with enterprises with high rating reputations. They will all expectedly get good business deals. This implies that our model is able to meet the challenge arising out of lack of incentives for not rating.

Lemma 1 (Reward for honest rating). *If the difference in normalized value of the rating given and the current rating is within [0, 10/w] then it is an honest rating and the rater is awarded points equal to* $(1/w^2) - |\langle g/n \rangle - t|/10w$.   □

There is bound on maximum value of rating reputation which is 1. If new rating reputation becomes greater than this maximum value then it is set to the maximum value. Similarly for the minimum value which is 0, if the rating reputation becomes less than the minimum value then it is set to the minimum value.

2.2   Unfair Rating

Enterprise giving unfair rating will degrade its rating reputation and after many unfair ratings due to its very low rating reputation its rating will not affect trust value of a rated enterprise. We carried out some simulation experiments to validate the above fact. Figure 1 provides a plot of these experimental results for negative unfair ratings, all with varying window constants between 10 to 90. The results for positive unfair rating are similar.

Lemma 2 (Unfair Rating degrades rating reputation). *Lower bound on the number of unfair rating after which its rating reputation becomes zero is* rw.   □

2.3   Quality Variations over Time

Window constant w takes care of quality variations over time and gives higher weight to last w ratings. The window constant basically assumes that the number of ratings provided so far is w (the window size). If an enterprise performs well during last w transactions its reputation is increased.

$$\frac{tw + \langle g/n \rangle r}{1 + w} = \frac{tw}{1 + w} + \frac{\langle \frac{g}{n} \rangle r}{1 + w}$$

If w is very large, $1 + w \approx w$ and $\frac{w}{1+w} \approx 1$ Therefore, new trust t_{new} becomes equal to $t_{new} = t + \frac{\langle g/n \rangle r}{w}$.

Lemma 3 (Role of Window Constant). *Trust value calculation give high weightage to last ratings.*   □

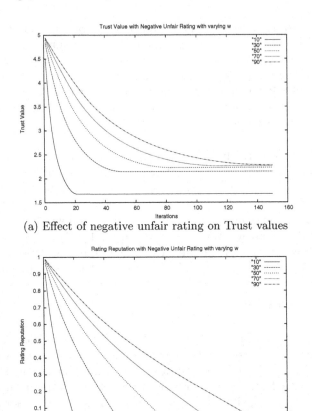

(a) Effect of negative unfair rating on Trust values

(b) Effect of negative unfair rating on Rating Reputation

Fig. 1. TV and RR with negative unfair rating for different window constants

2.4 Discrimination

If the victim has a high rating reputation then it can surely make a difference.

Lemma 4 (Punitive Reaction). *The maximum change in trust value of rated enterprise without doing any change to rating reputation of the rater is* $10/w(1+w)$. $\qquad \square$

For victims having low rating reputation we propose two approaches:

- the first approach assumes that enterprise knows that it is being discriminated, and
- the second approach consists of centralized server taking responsibility of finding the discrimination.

Both of these gives the victims a high temporary rating reputation for that rating.

One important concept here is that in the case of discrimination, very few enterprises are given bad service (discriminated) as compared to the number of enterprises who are served well. This percentage would be called Maximum Discrimination Ratio (MDR) dr, whose value will be around 0.1. So if the percentage number of victims is below maximum discrimination ratio then it means that discrimination indeed is being made. This value is chosen to be around 0.1 because the higher number of victims (lets say above 0.4) would be essentially due to the enterprise performing badly.

Complain Token: When an enterprise suspects a rating discrimination by one of its business partners, it can send a complain token with rating to the trust server. The server, after receiving a complain token against an enterprise, starts monitoring of ratings given to the enterprise to check if the complaint is genuine. It also checks that the rating given is negative for each complain token. After a number of ratings (let it be called monitoring constant m which may be equal to window constant w) have been received for this enterprise, the server checks whether it has received $dr * m$ or less number of complain tokens in respect to the enterprise. If so, then it updates the trust value of enterprise with the rating given along with the complain tokens with full rating reputations of the raters. No change made to the rating reputation and normalization value of the rater. Figure 2 shows the simulation results with varying window constant. The graph shows the variations in trust values of an enterprise using complaint token model with different monitoring constants. The places, where sharp decreases in the values are observed, correspond the places where the complaint tokens have been used to update the trust values. Until this time, the trust service stores the complaint tokens with their ratings and after the completion of mc iterations, checks whether the number of tokens is less than or equal to $mc * dr$. Following this it updates the trust value of the discriminator with the rating given with full rating reputation ($r = 1$) on behalf of the rater.

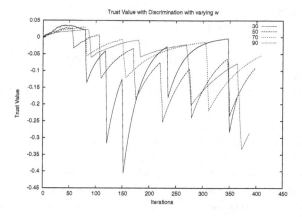

Fig. 2. Effect of processing complain tokens on trust values

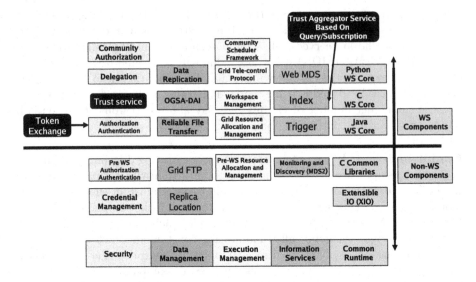

Fig. 3. Integration of trust service to GT4 architecture

3   Trust Architecture in GT4

Key to trust architecture is a mechanism whereby a business enterprise can rate its partner after a transaction is over. We visualise the rating to be mutual between the partners, as in B2B collaboration every service provider is a client and vice versa. After appropriate negotiations, and before starting the business process, the enterprises sign trust tokens and exchange them with each other. When the transaction is complete, each of the participating enterprises submits the token it has along with a rating values to the central trust service. The trust service checks the authenticity of the rater and updates the trust parameters of the participating enterprises appropriately in its database. Additionally, at the time of negotiation, the trust service provides current trust values to the enterprises so that they would be able to identify competent business partners. Figure 3 depicts the proposed addition (the white text on pure black portions) in the GT 4 architecture.

Thus the major requirements for implementation of the trust model are as follows:

Building a suitable token structure on the model of a security token: The trust tokens form a part of the authentication and authorisation layer in the sense that they are used for authenticating the rater by the trust service. The idea of the trust token is similar to that of a security token which is used in the authentication process of GT4. But, it is a *once to be used* resource issued to the business entities participating in a transaction. A token has four important attributes, namely, (i) sender, (ii) receiver, (iii) time of issue, and (iv) signature.The entity which signs the token is referred to as the sender, and the entity with whom the token to be exchanged is referred to as the receiver.

Building and deploying a Trust service which keeps track of the ratings of the involved business entities: The trust service is a web service deployed within the Globus service container which implements WSRF (Web Service Resource Framework) specified classes. A normal interaction between an enterprise and the trust service happens in the following way.

1. First a mutual authentication takes place.
2. Then the enterprise submits its rating to the trust service along with the Trust token.
3. Next, the trust service checks whether the token is valid or not. A valid token is something that is not used, not expired and is not a self rating (`sender==receiver`).
4. Then the service does the appropriate operations on the trust parameters (trust value, rating reputation, normalisation value) of the enterprises.

Building an information aggregator source: As mentioned earlier, the information services (MDS) are web services used for monitoring and discovery of resource and services on grid. One of these services is the Index Service which collects data from various sources and provides a query/subscription interface to that data [9]. These sources (also called aggregator sources) and the Index Service (also called aggregator sink) are connected by the aggregator framework. The index service has the data about the web services visible to the users. So, the trust model can be completely defined by developing an aggregator source to provide the trust attributes from the trust service to Index Service.

4 Conclusion

In this paper, we have seen how to meet the challenges of secure collaboration and discovery of services by utilizing the power of grid. The focus of our attempt has been to solve the problem of finding the trust-worthy service providers by developing a centralized trust model that caters to the requirements of a reliable trust system. We have proved that the proposed model tackles all kind of problems from low incentives of providing ratings to unfairness and discrimination. We also provided an outline of the augmentations to be made to the Globus Middleware Toolkit so that B2B transactions can be enabled/automated with minimum human intervention. Unfortunately, the implementation details could not be provided due to lack of space. The proposed centralised trust model can be scaled easily to a distributed trust model, and can be implemented on some number of (virtual) communities. We just need to evolve a suitable way for updating the trust parameters when a rating involves business partners from different virtual communities with possibly different normalization constants. However, for fullfledged business collaboration over grid, apart from trust model, there is a need to provide other mechanism. For example, business outsourcing should not reveal trade secrets of an entity to others, and the collusion among a group of enterprises against the business interests of other enterprises is also prevented.

Acknowledgments

The implementation of the proposal for augmentation of GT4 was possible due to computing resources brought with a grant from MHRD, Government of India under project No. MHRD/CS/20050062.

References

1. Mahadevan, B.: Business models for internet based e-commerce an anatomy. California Management Review 42, 55–69 (2000)
2. Business process automation... without software (2003), http://www.bitpipe.com/detail/RES/1091729984_521.html
3. Web services activity (2002), http://www.w3.org/,/ws/
4. Shim, S.S.Y., Pendyala, V.S., Sundaram, M., Gao, J.Z.: Business-to-business e-commerce frameworks. Computer 33, 40–47 (2000)
5. Fensel, D., Omelayenko, B.Y.D., Schulten, E.: Product data integration b2b e-commerce. IEEE Intelligent Systems 16, 54–59 (2001)
6. Josang, A., Ismail, R., Boyd, C.: A Survey of Trust and Reputation Systems for Online Service Provision. Decision support system 43(2), 618–644 (2007)
7. Sotomayor, B., Childers, L.: Globus Toolkit 4: Programming Java Services. Morgan Kaufmann Publishers, San Francisco (2005)
8. Globus Toolkit Official Documentation. http://www.globus.org/toolkit/docs/
9. GT4 Documentation on Index Service. http://www.globus.org/toolkit/docs/4.0/index
10. GT4 Documentation on Aggregator Source. http://www.globus.org/toolkit/docs/4.0/aggregator

Author Index

Agarwal, Anjali   197
Alouneh, Sahel   197
Anandavelu, N.   110
Anbalagan, N.   110

Badrinath, G.S.   158
Baynat, Bruno   184
Bhatnagar, Shalabh   19, 135
Bhatt, Anuj   203
Bhima, Santosh   306

Cabani, Adnane   240
Cellary, Wojciech   283
Chatterjee, Nevadita   73
Chaturvedi, Vijay Prakash   19
Chen, Kun   277
Cheng, Weifang   31
Cheung, David W.L.   248
Cui, Binge   271

Das, Ashok Kumar   79
Das, Sajal K.   158
Dhar, Sagnik   203
Dong, Dezun   31
Dziong, Zbigniew   146

Eddon, Guy   209
El Kadhi, Nabil   314
En-Nouaary, Abdeslam   197

Garimella, Rammurthy   306
Geetha, T.V.   110
Ghosh, R.K.   336
Gogada, Anil   306
Gore, M.M.   116
Gupta, Phalguni   158

Han, Yanbo   265, 277
Harish, M.   110
He, Jifeng   225
Hemachandra, N.   135
Herlihy, Maurice   209

Itmi, Mhamed   240

Janakiram, D.   166
Jhumka, Arshad   42

Kanchanasut, Kanchana   67
Karoui, Lobna   314
Khalil, Ibrahim   172
Khot, Rohit   54
Kim, Daeyoung   327
Kim, Sangjin   327
Konduri, Sastry   89
Kothapalli, Kishore   54
Kulkarni, Sandeep   42

Lee, Changyong   327
Lee, Thomas Y.T.   248
Li, Jing   225
Li, Wing-Ning   89
Li, Wubin   277
Liang, Guangmin   254
Liao, Xiangke   31
Lin, Shi-Jen   321
Liu, Ding-Chyu   321

Mahalakshmi, G.S.   110
Mitra, Saugat   293
Mukherjee, Saikat   293
Mulerikkal, Jaison Paul   172

Negi, Atul   73

Oh, Heekuck   327

Panda, Brajendra   89
Patnaik, L.M.   203
Pécuchet, Jean-Pierre   240
Peleg, David   1
Picconi, Fabio   184
Ponnavaikko, Kovendhan   166
Poola, Ravikant   54
Potluri, Anupama   73
Praveen, K.N.   336

Rakesh, V.   19
Ramaswamy, Srinivasan   240

Sarker, Jahangir   146
Sen, Jaydip   97
Sengupta, Indranil   79
Sens, Pierre   184
Shen, Changxiang   31

Singh, Jitendra Kumar   336
Srinathan, Kannan   54
Srinivasa, K.G.   203
Srinivasa, Srinath   293
Su, Liang   254
Subramanyam, Harihara   97

Tran, Con   146
Tripathi, Ashish   116
Tripathy, Somanath   129

Vemu, Koteswara Rao   135
Venugopal, K.R.   203

Wei, Yongshan   277
Wongsaardsakul, Thirapon   67

Yang, Dongju   277
Yee, Patrick K.C.   248

Zhang, Cheng   265
Zhu, Huibiao   225

Lecture Notes in Computer Science

Sublibrary 3: Information Systems and Application, incl. Internet/Web and HCI

For information about Vols. 1– 4518
please contact your bookseller or Springer

Vol. 4882: T. Janowski, H. Mohanty (Eds.), Distributed Computing and Internet Technology. XIII, 346 pages. 2007.

Vol. 4877: C. Thanos, F. Borri, L. Candela (Eds.), Digital Libraries: Research and Development. XII, 350 pages. 2007.

Vol. 4872: D. Mery, L. Rueda (Eds.), Advances in Image and Video Technology. XXI, 961 pages. 2007.

Vol. 4871: M. Cavazza, S. Donikian (Eds.), Virtual Storytelling. XIII, 219 pages. 2007.

Vol. 4858: X. Deng, F.C. Graham (Eds.), Internet and Network Economics. XVI, 598 pages. 2007.

Vol. 4857: J.M. Ware, G.E. Taylor (Eds.), Web and Wireless Geographical Information Systems. XI, 293 pages. 2007.

Vol. 4853: F. Fonseca, M.A. Rodríguez, S. Levashkin (Eds.), GeoSpatial Semantics. X, 289 pages. 2007.

Vol. 4836: H. Ichikawa, W.-D. Cho, I. Satoh, H.Y. Youn (Eds.), Ubiquitous Computing Systems. XIII, 307 pages. 2007.

Vol. 4832: M. Weske, M.-S. Hacid, C. Godart (Eds.), Web Information Systems Engineering – WISE 2007 Workshops. XV, 518 pages. 2007.

Vol. 4831: B. Benatallah, F. Casati, D. Georgakopoulos, C. Bartolini, W. Sadiq, C. Godart (Eds.), Web Information Systems Engineering – WISE 2007. XVI, 675 pages. 2007.

Vol. 4825: K. Aberer, K.-S. Choi, N. Noy, D. Allemang, K.-I. Lee, L. Nixon, J. Golbeck, P. Mika, D. Maynard, R. Mizoguchi, G. Schreiber, P. Cudré-Mauroux (Eds.), The Semantic Web. XXVII, 973 pages. 2007.

Vol. 4822: D.H.-L. Goh, T.H. Cao, I.T. Sølvberg, E. Rasmussen (Eds.), Asian Digital Libraries. XVII, 519 pages. 2007.

Vol. 4816: B. Falcidieno, M. Spagnuolo, Y. Avrithis, I. Kompatsiaris, P. Buitelaar (Eds.), Semantic Multimedia. XII, 306 pages. 2007.

Vol. 4813: I. Oakley, S. Brewster (Eds.), Haptic and Audio Interaction Design. XIV, 145 pages. 2007.

Vol. 4810: H.H.-S. Ip, O.C. Au, H. Leung, M.-T. Sun, W.-Y. Ma, S.-M. Hu (Eds.), Advances in Multimedia Information Processing – PCM 2007. XXI, 834 pages. 2007.

Vol. 4809: M.K. Denko, C.-s. Shih, K.-C. Li, S.-L. Tsao, Q.-A. Zeng, S.H. Park, Y.-B. Ko, S.-H. Hung, J.H. Park (Eds.), Emerging Directions in Embedded and Ubiquitous Computing. XXXV, 823 pages. 2007.

Vol. 4808: T.-W. Kuo, E. Sha, M. Guo, L.T. Yang, Z. Shao (Eds.), Embedded and Ubiquitous Computing. XXI, 769 pages. 2007.

Vol. 4806: R. Meersman, Z. Tari, P. Herrero (Eds.), On the Move to Meaningful Internet Systems 2007: OTM 2007 Workshops, Part II. XXXIV, 611 pages. 2007.

Vol. 4805: R. Meersman, Z. Tari, P. Herrero (Eds.), On the Move to Meaningful Internet Systems 2007: OTM 2007 Workshops, Part I. XXXIV, 757 pages. 2007.

Vol. 4804: R. Meersman, Z. Tari (Eds.), On the Move to Meaningful Internet Systems 2007: CoopIS, DOA, ODBASE, GADA, and IS, Part II. XXIX, 683 pages. 2007.

Vol. 4803: R. Meersman, Z. Tari (Eds.), On the Move to Meaningful Internet Systems 2007: CoopIS, DOA, ODBASE, GADA, and IS, Part I. XXIX, 1173 pages. 2007.

Vol. 4802: J.-L. Hainaut, E.A. Rundensteiner, M. Kirchberg, M. Bertolotto, M. Brochhausen, Y.-P.P. Chen, S.S.-S. Cherfi, M. Doerr, H. Han, S. Hartmann, J. Parsons, G. Poels, C. Rolland, J. Trujillo, E. Yu, E. Zimányie (Eds.), Advances in Conceptual Modeling – Foundations and Applications. XIX, 420 pages. 2007.

Vol. 4801: C. Parent, K.-D. Schewe, V.C. Storey, B. Thalheim (Eds.), Conceptual Modeling - ER 2007. XVI, 616 pages. 2007.

Vol. 4797: M. Arenas, M.I. Schwartzbach (Eds.), Database Programming Languages. VIII, 261 pages. 2007.

Vol. 4796: M. Lew, N. Sebe, T.S. Huang, E.M. Bakker (Eds.), Human–Computer Interaction. X, 157 pages. 2007.

Vol. 4794: B. Schiele, A.K. Dey, H. Gellersen, B. de Ruyter, M. Tscheligi, R. Wichert, E. Aarts, A. Buchmann (Eds.), Ambient Intelligence. XV, 375 pages. 2007.

Vol. 4777: S. Bhalla (Ed.), Databases in Networked Information Systems. X, 329 pages. 2007.

Vol. 4761: R. Obermaisser, Y. Nah, P. Puschner, F.J. Rammig (Eds.), Software Technologies for Embedded and Ubiquitous Systems. XIV, 563 pages. 2007.

Vol. 4747: S. Džeroski, J. Struyf (Eds.), Knowledge Discovery in Inductive Databases. X, 301 pages. 2007.

Vol. 4744: Y. de Kort, W. IJsselsteijn, C. Midden, B. Eggen, B.J. Fogg (Eds.), Persuasive Technology. XIV, 316 pages. 2007.

Vol. 4740: L. Ma, M. Rauterberg, R. Nakatsu (Eds.), Entertainment Computing – ICEC 2007. XXX, 480 pages. 2007.

Vol. 4730: C. Peters, P. Clough, F.C. Gey, J. Karlgren, B. Magnini, D.W. Oard, M. de Rijke, M. Stempfhuber (Eds.), Evaluation of Multilingual and Multi-modal Information Retrieval. XXIV, 998 pages. 2007.

Vol. 4723: M. R. Berthold, J. Shawe-Taylor, N. Lavrač (Eds.), Advances in Intelligent Data Analysis VII. XIV, 380 pages. 2007.

Vol. 4721: W. Jonker, M. Petković (Eds.), Secure Data Management. X, 213 pages. 2007.

Vol. 4718: J. Hightower, B. Schiele, T. Strang (Eds.), Location- and Context-Awareness. X, 297 pages. 2007.

Vol. 4717: J. Krumm, G.D. Abowd, A. Seneviratne, T. Strang (Eds.), UbiComp 2007: Ubiquitous Computing. XIX, 520 pages. 2007.

Vol. 4715: J.M. Haake, S.F. Ochoa, A. Cechich (Eds.), Groupware: Design, Implementation, and Use. XIII, 355 pages. 2007.

Vol. 4714: G. Alonso, P. Dadam, M. Rosemann (Eds.), Business Process Management. XIII, 418 pages. 2007.

Vol. 4704: D. Barbosa, A. Bonifati, Z. Bellahsène, E. Hunt, R. Unland (Eds.), Database and XML Technologies. X, 141 pages. 2007.

Vol. 4690: Y. Ioannidis, B. Novikov, B. Rachev (Eds.), Advances in Databases and Information Systems. XIII, 377 pages. 2007.

Vol. 4675: L. Kovács, N. Fuhr, C. Meghini (Eds.), Research and Advanced Technology for Digital Libraries. XVII, 585 pages. 2007.

Vol. 4674: Y. Luo (Ed.), Cooperative Design, Visualization, and Engineering. XIII, 431 pages. 2007.

Vol. 4663: C. Baranauskas, P. Palanque, J. Abascal, S.D.J. Barbosa (Eds.), Human-Computer Interaction – INTERACT 2007, Part II. XXXIII, 735 pages. 2007.

Vol. 4662: C. Baranauskas, P. Palanque, J. Abascal, S.D.J. Barbosa (Eds.), Human-Computer Interaction – INTERACT 2007, Part I. XXXIII, 637 pages. 2007.

Vol. 4658: T. Enokido, L. Barolli, M. Takizawa (Eds.), Network-Based Information Systems. XIII, 544 pages. 2007.

Vol. 4656: M.A. Wimmer, J. Scholl, Å. Grönlund (Eds.), Electronic Government. XIV, 450 pages. 2007.

Vol. 4655: G. Psaila, R. Wagner (Eds.), E-Commerce and Web Technologies. VII, 229 pages. 2007.

Vol. 4654: I.-Y. Song, J. Eder, T.M. Nguyen (Eds.), Data Warehousing and Knowledge Discovery. XVI, 482 pages. 2007.

Vol. 4653: R. Wagner, N. Revell, G. Pernul (Eds.), Database and Expert Systems Applications. XXII, 907 pages. 2007.

Vol. 4636: G. Antoniou, U. Aßmann, C. Baroglio, S. Decker, N. Henze, P.-L. Patranjan, R. Tolksdorf (Eds.), Reasoning Web. IX, 345 pages. 2007.

Vol. 4611: J. Indulska, J. Ma, L.T. Yang, T. Ungerer, J. Cao (Eds.), Ubiquitous Intelligence and Computing. XXIII, 1257 pages. 2007.

Vol. 4607: L. Baresi, P. Fraternali, G.-J. Houben (Eds.), Web Engineering. XVI, 576 pages. 2007.

Vol. 4606: A. Pras, M. van Sinderen (Eds.), Dependable and Adaptable Networks and Services. XIV, 149 pages. 2007.

Vol. 4605: D. Papadias, D. Zhang, G. Kollios (Eds.), Advances in Spatial and Temporal Databases. X, 479 pages. 2007.

Vol. 4602: S. Barker, G.-J. Ahn (Eds.), Data and Applications Security XXI. X, 291 pages. 2007.

Vol. 4601: S. Spaccapietra, P. Atzeni, F. Fages, M.-S. Hacid, M. Kifer, J. Mylopoulos, B. Pernici, P. Shvaiko, J. Trujillo, I. Zaihrayeu (Eds.), Journal on Data Semantics IX. XV, 197 pages. 2007.

Vol. 4592: Z. Kedad, N. Lammari, E. Métais, F. Meziane, Y. Rezgui (Eds.), Natural Language Processing and Information Systems. XIV, 442 pages. 2007.

Vol. 4587: R. Cooper, J. Kennedy (Eds.), Data Management. XIII, 259 pages. 2007.

Vol. 4577: N. Sebe, Y. Liu, Y.-t. Zhuang, T.S. Huang (Eds.), Multimedia Content Analysis and Mining. XIII, 513 pages. 2007.

Vol. 4568: T. Ishida, S. R. Fussell, P. T. J. M. Vossen (Eds.), Intercultural Collaboration. XIII, 395 pages. 2007.

Vol. 4566: M.J. Dainoff (Ed.), Ergonomics and Health Aspects of Work with Computers. XVIII, 390 pages. 2007.

Vol. 4564: D. Schuler (Ed.), Online Communities and Social Computing. XVII, 520 pages. 2007.

Vol. 4563: R. Shumaker (Ed.), Virtual Reality. XXII, 762 pages. 2007.

Vol. 4561: V.G. Duffy (Ed.), Digital Human Modeling. XXIII, 1068 pages. 2007.

Vol. 4560: N. Aykin (Ed.), Usability and Internationalization, Part II. XVIII, 576 pages. 2007.

Vol. 4559: N. Aykin (Ed.), Usability and Internationalization, Part I. XVIII, 661 pages. 2007.

Vol. 4558: M.J. Smith, G. Salvendy (Eds.), Human Interface and the Management of Information, Part II. XXIII, 1162 pages. 2007.

Vol. 4557: M.J. Smith, G. Salvendy (Eds.), Human Interface and the Management of Information, Part I. XXII, 1030 pages. 2007.

Vol. 4541: T. Okadome, T. Yamazaki, M. Makhtari (Eds.), Pervasive Computing for Quality of Life Enhancement. IX, 248 pages. 2007.

Vol. 4537: K.C.-C. Chang, W. Wang, L. Chen, C.A. Ellis, C.-H. Hsu, A.C. Tsoi, H. Wang (Eds.), Advances in Web and Network Technologies, and Information Management. XXIII, 707 pages. 2007.

Vol. 4531: J. Indulska, K. Raymond (Eds.), Distributed Applications and Interoperable Systems. XI, 337 pages. 2007.

Vol. 4526: M. Malek, M. Reitenspieß, A. van Moorsel (Eds.), Service Availability. X, 155 pages. 2007.

Vol. 4524: M. Marchiori, J.Z. Pan, C.d.S. Marie (Eds.), Web Reasoning and Rule Systems. XI, 382 pages. 2007.

Vol. 4519: E. Franconi, M. Kifer, W. May (Eds.), The Semantic Web: Research and Applications. XVIII, 830 pages. 2007.